In Search of the Self

EATING THE "I"

An Account of The Fourth Way—
The Way of Transformation in Ordinary Life

William Patrick Patterson

Edited by Barbara C. Allen

Arete Communications, Publishers
Fairfax, California

Eating The "I" is a true story without invention. However, the names of most of the characters, with the exception of Lord John Pentland and Sunyata, as well as some personal descriptions, have been changed to protect privacy.

Paintings on the cover and back cover, Constantine Dies and The Petitioner, are by the author. Photographs of paintings by Lloyd Francis.

Design by Wordplay Consulting

Library of Congress Catalog Number is 91-72941.
Patterson, William Patrick
Eating The "I": An Account of The Fourth Way—The Way of Transformation in Ordinary Life
Bibliography: Includes index
1. Esoteric Psychology
2. Life Story
3. Fourth Way
4. Self-Transformation
5. Father Mythos
6. Sunyata

Third softcover printing 1997
Second softcover printing 1993
First softcover printing 1992
Softcover ISBN: 1-879514-77-X

First casebound printing 1992
Casebound ISBN: 1-879514-76-1

Printed on Acid-Free Paper. ∞
The paper used in this publication meets the minimum requirements of the American National Standard for Information Sciences—Permanence of Paper for Printed Library Materials, ANSI Z39.48-1984.

Printed in Canada

Arete Communications, Box 58, 773 Center Boulevard, Fairfax, CA 94978–0058

For my sons, John and Matthew,
and for sons and daughters everywhere
embarking on the great and mysterious
adventure of Self Remembrance

In life never do as others do.
Gurdjieff's Grandmother

You know, brother, how we breathe:
we breathe the air in and out. On this
is based the life of the body and on this
depends its warmth.
So, sitting down in your cell, collect
your mind, lead it into the path of the
breath along which the air enters
in, constrain it to enter the heart
together with the inhaled air,
and keep it there.
Keep it there but do not leave it

silent and idle:

instead give it the following
prayer:

*Lord Jesus Christ, Son of God,
have mercy on me.*

*On Prayer From The Heart
Philokalia*

We do not do it, but without us
it cannot be done.

Jeanne de Salzmann

CONTENTS

PROLOGUE

I HAD BEEN IN THE WORK ONLY A SHORT TIME WHEN JOHN PENTLAND, MY teacher, told me, "Perhaps someday you'll write a book about The Fourth Way—the way of transformation in life." His words went in like a sword. Now, some twenty years after receiving this task, that sword is coming out of the stone.

With the recent passing of Madame Jeanne de Salzmann, Gurdjieff's personal secretary and, since his death in 1949, the leader of the worldwide Work, most of Gurdjieff's direct students are gone. A few have left accounts of their experiences with Gurdjieff and their understanding of the teaching he brought at so great a cost. The book you hold now comes from a different place in the octave of the teaching. For my generation, like all succeeding, can commonly encounter Gurdjieff only through his books. Yet his spirit lives on in the powerful ideas and practices of the Work. But, effectively, what matters is not how close or remote one is to Gurdjieff in terms of ordinary time, but how sincere and persistent is the search.

The intent here is to give a direct and unvarnished account of my years in an esoteric school of The Fourth Way. My interest is in the collision that occurs between the teaching and the "I," the conditioned self-identity. This meeting is ancient and archetypal, an evoked alchemy between the impersonal and personal; the objective and subjective. My aim is to portray the wonder and misunderstanding, the discovery and resistance, that marks the seed of this potentiality for a new life.

Eating The "I" is a story of my struggle with ignorance and arrogance, the friction between the desires and the non-desires, that led to many suffered truths and some hard-won understanding, all coming under the masterful teaching and example of the remarkable man who Gurdjieff chose to lead the Work in America, Lord John Pentland.

In writing of my search, I made a compact with myself: I would invent nothing—I would tell the story exactly as I experienced it. The reason is both simple and beautiful. Life needs no invention. So-called ordinary life is extraordinary when I pay attention. Free attention frees the moment. Impressions once static are now dynamic, multidimensional. The moment expands. The physical "becomes" the metaphysical. The symbolic and mythological come into play. The dance begins. Do I identify? Through hard experience I learn that, though rarified, the symbolic, the mythological, are still content, still things. Beyond them lie emptiness, silence, real I. Awakening to the elegance of this truth, I see the work is not to change myself, but my vibration. In certain places, then, to reflect this change in fluidity and inclusiveness, tenses are changed.

This book is not, nor is it intended to be—a "pure" reflection of the Work. The aim instead is to give an intimate report of how I worked and did not work with the ideas. And how, too, they influenced and inspired me and, yes, how they tore me, the "I," apart. I have not painted any sparrows yellow, nor otherwise gilded my idiocy. It should be noted, however, that there is a "mixing" of ideas here. This is because of my attraction to not only the ideas of Gurdjieff, but also those of Jung, Heidegger and certain others. So read with a critical eye.

There is, of course, concern about publishing an intimate work on the esoteric. Gurdjieff's teaching is not for everyone. Nor should it be. The Esoteric Tradition is just that: esoteric. Without the material necessary to understand in Gurdjieff's sense the relativity of the scale of vibration, recognition of this fact is not commonly possible. Gurdjieff took great pains to "bury the bones," to guard against the teaching falling into unprepared or profane hands. As is well-known: when the esoteric is made exoteric, when real knowledge is bought too cheaply—a lawful deflection and distortion must result. Once again then we witness the spectre, too common to our time, of a once sacred channel giving only ordinary tap water. Let us keep in mind, as well, what Rene´ Guénon wrote in his masterwork *The Reign of Quantity*:

> *Every truth of a transcendent order necessarily partakes*
> *of the inexpressible; it is essentially in this fact that the*
> *profound significance of the initiatic secret really lies; no*
> *kind of exterior secret can ever have any value except as an*
> *image or symbol of the initiatic secret… But it must be*
> *understood that these are things of which the meaning and*
> *the range are completely lost to the modern mentality, and*
> *incomprehension of them quite naturally engenders hostility;*
> *besides the ordinary man always has an instinctive fear of what*
> *he does not understand and fear engenders hatred only too easily.*

Perhaps a warning is also in order. Namely, that to practice any of the ideas mentioned herein, independent of the inner knowledge and objective pressure that only an authentic teacher and school can apply, will only cement the person further into his or her most cherished "I"; and so produce yet another instance of the ego burying the essence alive, the true "living death."

My wish and intent here is to walk the razor's edge between the exoteric and esoteric, casting a little sacrificial human flesh into the public fires as payment. In striving to fulfill the task given to me over twenty years ago, I must of necessity put my "I" on display. It might just as well be anyone's fixed idea of themselves. Idiots are idiots. The heart of the matter lies in the essential collision of worlds, that of the timeless with the temporal, and That which remains ever the same. This account describes, then, what it is like to voluntarily undergo the unorthodox and uncompromising spiritual discipline of the mainstream school, yet ever honors its hidden core and tradition.

Lastly, I only add that I have been much aided in this remembrance by my diaries and my "Irish memory," inherited from my Mother, the greatest natural storyteller I have ever known, save Sonny Lacey of the Aran Isles, the storykeeper of the Tuatha da Danaan. To Barbara, my wife, who has borne with so much, and for whose sensibility, loyalty and love, as well as painstaking editing, I offer a thankful namaste. To Chögyam Trungpa, Rinpoche, the great creative guru of Crazy Wisdom, I fly a kite from the heart. To Sunyata, the rare born mystic, now in what he called the "Invisible Real," I give a big smile and wink. To Jean Klein, the karuna sage, who gave the needed encouragement to finish this task, I offer heartfelt gratitude. And to Henry John Sinclair, Lord Pentland, the great teacher and warrior of the Gurdjieff Work, I say—I carry you with me always.

A SON'S SEARCH

I HAD DIED AND DIDN'T KNOW IT. I was still in the body, talking, acting like everyone else, but inside...nothing. There was no one there. The past was too painful, the future I couldn't imagine. All my dreams exploded right in my face. All I had believed in, worked for, lived for—*my whole world*—all gone now. Just another story. A slab of memory. I was one of the living dead, and too dead to know it.

I stayed in the apartment most of the day lying on the old mattress on the living room floor, propped up on a pillow, burying my head in books on hermetic wisdom and now and then, peering out the frosted windows into the dull gray winter haze, maybe finally I'd get up and brew some tea, open the mail, take a walk down to the East River. But mostly I'd stay inside, napping, observing the cats, staring at the texture on the ceiling, my mind blank, the body just lying there. I'd wait for Barbara to get home to make dinner, eat, and then play backgammon for quarters. It was my way of making pocket money. She thought too much with a quarter on the line.

Thinking hurt. I couldn't think any more. Too much thought and the forehead froze up like a rock. Made me really tired. I was always exhausted. Though I'd get nine, maybe ten hours sleep. I never dreamt. Just went right out. Before going to work Barbara would cajole and shout me awake...finally getting my eyelids to open.

Even with the blinds drawn the daylight cut the eyeballs. My mouth tasted like rubber cement. I'd promise her I'd get up. Even sit up, talk to her, promise to take the garbage down, do the dishes, make the bed, *do something* today. *Yes, today I'd do something.* But once the front door closed, once I heard her going down the stairwell, I'd set the alarm for an hour later then hit the sack again. She always called when she got to work. About an hour ten to fifteen minutes later. I'd sound good, not groggy. She'd remind me about the garbage, the dishes. At the end she'd always say brightly, "Stay up now." "Sure," I'd tell her. But as soon as she hung up I'd dive under the covers again. Off I'd float for a few more hours. But I had to be up before noon. That was a must. Otherwise I'd miss *The New York Times* and *Daily News.* No matter how bummed out, I'd force myself out of bed, put my feet down on the cold wooden floor. Take a long hot shower, pull on an old pair of jeans, yesterday's shirt and hurry down to the cigar store on York and 83rd. This was the time of day I felt the best, felt like the old "me." Being around people didn't hurt so much. Still, it was a relief to get back home. I'd toss the papers on the mattress and make breakfast in the tiny walk-through kitchen between the living room and bedroom. It had a small skylight. I'd watch the clouds passing or just stare up into the ghostly gray vastness, waiting for two eggs-sunny-side-up to cook, the two slices of raisin bread to toast, the jasmine tea to steep. Then I'd fill half an eight-ounce glass with V-8 juice, throw in a heaping teaspoon of wheat germ, and open the bottles of vitamins, taking two 250 mg. of vitamin C, 400 mg. of vitamin E, a super high potency B complex. I wasn't a health nut. I just felt I needed all this to keep awake. I'd schlep it all out to the mattress where I'd eat and read the morning papers, always turning to the sports section first, and working my way through the book review, chess column, entertainment, women's page. Never read the business section. The front page I put off as long as possible. Too much horror. Absurdity. Lies.

After the papers I'd throw the coins, asking the *I Ching* what kind of day it would be. I got a lot of "Crossing the great water." I'd open *Fragments of an Unknown Teaching* or some other book on early gnosticism. Maybe dip into *The Tibetan Book of The Dead.* Usually, I'd fall asleep or I'd watch Thea and Ayesha for a while. Thea was a furry calico, beautiful and loving, totally trusting. She would always jump on my chest, make a spot for herself and purr away. Ayesha was an alley cat, scrawny and neurotic, never coming near anyone. We'd gotten her free from the Cat Lady, an old woman in the West Village whose whole apartment, except for a small bedroom, was full of mangy, beat-up, abandoned cats and kittens. Apparently, Ayesha had starved on the streets and had never gotten over it. No matter how much we fed her or how often, Ayesha attacked her food as if it was her last meal. She ate frantically, her little paranoid head darting back and forth, terrified of her food being stolen. She'd eat so fast she'd vomit it all up, then gorge again. We had to feed her in the bathroom. Gradually, she stopped the throwing up but she always ate like a hungry ghost. Thea and Ayesha were my only constant companions. I'd spend a lot of time looking into those cat eyes, seeing if I could get inside their heads, see if they had thoughts or feelings. But they'd just stare back. Or ignore me. Afterward, I'd usually water the two dracaena canes in the corner. I'd get into the books then. I had about five going at once. Sometimes I'd sit like a stone, staring aimlessly at the record player. This was a quiet, uneventful life. No excitement but no anger either. I didn't name it. It was like I'd been washed up on some smooth, soothing island beach, a timeless stretch of space, an in between world. Kind of flat, empty, opaque. Why think about it? I didn't have the energy.

Months went by. All the time this thought kept going around: *How much longer can this go on?* One day it came and wouldn't leave. It finally forced me to think about things. I was still young, only thirty-three. *The Times* had had a piece on the life expectancy for U.S. males being seventy-two years. That meant thirty-nine more years on this "island." Which I didn't mind. But could I expect Barbara to support me that long? Which was why, I suppose, I finally did something: I wrote a letter to a young guy I'd read about named Murphy who had just inherited twenty-five million dollars. The papers said he'd ridden down Park Avenue in a white stretch limo at the height of the lunch hour tossing fistfuls of hundred dollar bills at pedestrians. Murphy wanted to give all his money way—"I want to give it," declared Murphy, "to people who have ambition, some worthy cause or aim in life they want to fulfill." My aim was simple: to keep eating. I sensed Murphy wanted something less prosaic so I dreamed up the idea of going to India to do research. I'd read a story about Hindus in Benares dumping burnt corpses in the Ganges, and millions of them drinking and washing in that same river water, and no one got sick. No typhoid. Not even a good case of the runs. That was strange enough, but the image of standing there waist high in the Holy Ganges washing armpits and suddenly the feet of a corpse float into sight! Well, Kali and sons had death and life flowing side by side there. Not like here where death is ignored as an impolite fart.

So, I wrote Mr. Murphy a letter, making a case for his giving me $7,500 to research "Death in Life in The Ganges." That would buy some time. I could see it vividly: me just hanging out on the banks of the Ganges, acting the crazy white sadhu in loin cloth, smoking some good Shiva ganja, doing some tantric lovemaking, and catching a lot of Morpheus before taking the big float down the Ganges. That felt good. Writing Murphy his letter was the first thing I could remember doing besides taking down the freaking garbage. Weeks went by. Nothing. Day after day only bills and junk mail in the mailbox. Then one miserable afternoon I turned on the TV and who do I see on the boob tube but Murphy! Murphy, my savior, eyes all agleam, waving hilariously to the world, his hands now in handcuffs. Murphy had escaped from the sanatorium. He was rich, it was true, but also crazy.

After that, things weren't quite the same. Never watched the tube. Cats and flies no longer mattered. A lot of dead space, that's what the apartment felt like. I don't know…maybe I'd become bored. Remembered some critic saying, "Boredom is rage spread thin." No, I wasn't so much bored as I was concerned. Afraid, I guess. Felt like "the future"—the idea of it—had poisoned me. Barbara, she was even winning in backgammon now.

After a while though life in the apartment returned to normal. I don't know when but one morning my Mom called. She and my Father were down in Florida again. "This time," she said, "for good." They had bought a two-bedroom, ranch-style home in Vanguard Village, she said. It was an adults-only development near Fort Lauderdale. Since my Father retired, four times they had been back and forth between Pittsburgh and Florida.

"Now we're sinking our roots," she declared. There was a long pause. "How 'bout you?" she asked.

"Oh, I'm fine," I said.

"Your Father, he wants to know"—she said it delicately—"how 'the work situation' is?"

"Oh, well…you know, I've sent out some letters." These things, they take time." She didn't respond. I tried to be upbeat. "I just read an article that says it takes an average nine months to find a new job."

"Oh yes, yes, that's true," she agreed. Another pregnant pause. "Your Father, he says to tell you there's always a spare bedroom for you down here."

"Thanks, Mom."

"Keep your chin up, McGee," she said.

A few days later a box arrived parcel post. In it was my Mother's Bible and a small idealized picture of Jesus; the one she always kept on her vanity. The same day I found a letter in the mailbox. Stamped across it in big red letters was the word, "Undeliverable." I opened the letter. It was a long entangled argument that never seemed to get to the point. Reading it, I got strange feelings. It was as if I had tuned into two channels at once. I was reading the words but I was also aware of the assumptions behind the words. The words made sense, but the premises—they were unreal! This writer was off in some dream world. But the words, they all sounded strangely familiar. I skipped to the last page. What I saw lifted me bolt upright on the mattress. There at the bottom of the page was my signature: *William Patterson.* I wrote this letter! Standing there, stock still, in gaping silence, letter in hand, the shock and the question zinging all through me: *Who was this "I"?*

"New Gods in America—have you heard of it?" inquired the Englishman.

At the cigar store one morning not long after I'd received the Bible, I met a writer, Peter Rowley. He had written a book about what he called, "the new spiritual teaching coming to America."

"Have you ever heard of Gurdjieff?" I asked.

I expected a negative answer but instead Rowley smiled, knowingly. Only a few evenings before, he had interviewed a man who had studied with Gurdjieff. "He's head of the Gurdjieff Work in America," Rowley confided.

"Can I meet him?"

Rowley seemed unsure. "They don't make a show of things," he said. "They're rather secretive."

"I know, I know," I said thinking of all the years I had looked for someone who knew of Gurdjieff and found no one.

Rowley eyed me a moment. "Let me telephone him. If he agrees, I'll get back to you."

I could hardly believe it. Some seven years before I had read a book by Gurdjieff. I'd come upon it in a strange way. I had noticed a small white wood-frame bookstore had opened up near my apartment. One evening I walked in, not looking for anything in particular, but suddenly I became aware of this odd feeling. Every book I looked at—either from its cover or title—I *knew* what it was about. I browsed from row to row, examining one book jacket after another, having the same odd experience of knowing. Finally, the bookseller approached me.

"Looking for something special?" he asked.

I shrugged. I didn't know what I was looking for. Finally I heard myself tell him: "I'm looking for a book I've never read before."

He looked at me as if I was a bit daft. There were maybe ten thousand titles on the shelves. But then somehow he understood. "Ohh," he said, "you're looking for something 'seminal'?"

Seminal—that was the word. The feeling I had was so faint and new I could never have found a word for it. "Yes, something original," I said.

He thought a moment. "Why, yes, I think I have just what you're looking for." He went to the back of the counter, reached into a bottom drawer and put a blue hard bound book into my hand. "Just arrived last week," he said.

Meetings With Remarkable Men was the book's title. I stared at the author's photo. The face was like none I had ever seen. The head was completely shaved, egg-like, with an immense domelike cranium, like someone from outer space. The eyes were sly, direct, yet dark and soulful. The right eye wandered a bit. The mouth was hidden by a thick dark mustache. An unusual feeling swept through me. I had no words to name it.

I read the book straight through. It was a travel-adventure book but not of the usual kind. Gurdjieff belonged to a small group of people who called themselves "Seekers of Truth." They had traveled to remote and dangerous locations in Persia, Egypt and the Hindu Kush in search, not of excitement or gold, but real knowledge. Gurdjieff was interesting but exasperating. I couldn't quite make out what he was getting at. He seemed to be taking great pains to conceal what he was trying to communicate. But why? Why write about something you don't want known?

Perhaps the bookseller could explain something about this "Gurdjieff." But when I returned the bookstore had vanished. Only an empty white store front remained. I peered in the window. Nothing but rows and rows of shelves stripped bare of books. Could this bookstore have appeared just to give me this book? That was absurd. But the feeling persisted.

While I waited for Rowley's call I remembered another book I had read six months before. It was Ouspensky's *In Search of The Miraculous*. Ouspensky, a noted mathematician and journalist, had been a close student of Gurdjieff's. Unlike Meetings, it seemed a practical, straightforward manual on changing one's level of being. It was a lucid, scientific explanation of how the three foods man eats—physical food, air, and impressions—can be transformed by sustained conscious self-atten- tion. The scale and strength of the ideas overwhelmed me. They were unlike anything I had ever come across. They seemed to come from an entirely different or- der of being. I was fascinated and wanted to know more. But that had to wait. For just then, I was within a few steps of becoming a millionaire.

Four years before I had left a good job at IBM to start a magazine for young sin- gle New Yorkers called *In New York*. It was the first of its kind and an instant success. I found having a voice—any voice in New York—opened a lot of doors. As publisher and editor of this young, hip magazine I had entree to many levels of so- ciety. A whole new world opened up to me. I was invited to parties on Park Avenue, the Upper West Side, the Village. Suddenly, I found myself talking to people like Marshal McLuhan, Andy Warhol and Nico, the satirist Paul Krassner, the under- ground writers Ray Bremser and Charles Bukowski, and a bevy of pop society types. I appeared on TV and radio shows promoting *In New York*. It was exciting at first but, after awhile, the glamour faded. The people and the parties, the endless chit- chat and self-promotion, grew tiresome.

The pressure of writing, designing, publishing and mailing and distributing In New York was relentless. It never let up. The constant wheeling 'n dealing, the cash flow hassles, the deadbeat advertisers and writers and illustrators who never met deadlines wore me down. I could never keep ahead of the magazine's debts. I kept owing the printer more and more money. I was about to chuck it all. Then the Dav- id Susskind Show called. They wanted to interview me for a show on the "The Young Single Society." I decided I'd do the Susskind Show and pack it in.

The morning after the show two young fast buck entrepreneurs from California called. They were in town to do a deal with a big travel agency. They told me they managed a slew of singles-only apartment buildings, the newest fad in rentals. A sto- ry about them and their company, Energy Dynamics, had appeared in *Business Week*. Now they were expanding, building "an empire dedicated to the single life style."

That afternoon we met for lunch at Maxwell's Plum, a new upscale bistro, for lunch. Amid the hanging ferns, mirrors, murals and pink tablecloths, the Californians told me they saw *In New York* as the centerpiece of their singles empire. Their idea was to start similar magazines in other cities that would cover the local singles scene and then tie this all together with a national magazine, *Single America*. It sounded good but where would they get the cash? They handed me a letter from a Wall Street underwriter. "We're going to float a stock issue," they said. They showed me letters of credit and letters from all their big time business connections. Told me of the companies they'd already acquired. The fast buck boys believed in what they called, "electricity and motion." They were well on their way to getting rich. Did I want to team up with them? They wanted to buy my magazine. "We're going to offer you enough cash and stock to make you a millionaire," they told me. There was one little hitch. The cash part of the deal was only $3,000. But

I would get 100,000 shares of stock in Energy Dynamics. They expected to take the company public at $10 a share. When I balked they sweetened the deal by hiring me as a v.p. at $50,000 for the first year with a guaranteed $10,000 increase every year for five years. Seeing as how, after expenses, I was currently getting by on $25 a week, I didn't see how I could lose.

The plan was to create the national singles magazine first. They gave me a free hand. I convinced the designer, who'd designed Look magazine and *The New York Review of Books,* to do the design. Within months I showed my new bosses a four-color prototype of *Single America.* They loved it. Distributors loved it. Advertisers loved it. The champagne poured and we all toasted to the imminent success of *Single America.*

Unfortunately, two months before the company's initial public offering, the stock market began to fall. And as it kept falling the market for new stock issues dried up. The underwriter came one morning and told us he couldn't take us public. "But we have a letter from you," the Californians screamed. "So sue!" he cried. "Eight new issues I got hanging out there already. Two fell off the clothes line, schmucks. So sue me, fine. I just go belly-up."

So we ran around trying to find money. But everyone was running for cover. Finally, Energy Dynamics went Chapter Eleven and the fast buck boys ran off. Now everyone came to me. The writers, the artists and the designer—they all held me responsible and demanded to be paid. I had gotten them involved, they told me. I was to blame. I was a creditor just like them, I told them. Legally there was nothing they could do. Morally I felt like shit. The guilt was overwhelming, paralyzing.

The printer, an old friend, was especially angry. He had continued to print *In New York,* as well as the prototype of the new magazine. The Californians had paid off the magazine's initial bills of seven thousand dollars and then run up hefty debts. I had no money. I offered him what I had in my apartment. One morning he showed up with a van and hauled off my furniture, bed, TV, even the toaster. The stuff wasn't worth more than a few hundred dollars. He left me standing in my pajamas in an empty apartment without even a goodbye. The paper millionaire was now a pauper.

Soon after I lost the furniture I was evicted and moved in with Barbara. I'd been living in a weird floating world without contours ever since and now I sensed that somehow this chance meeting with Rowley was the way out for which I had been unconsciously waiting.

Within a few days Rowley called. He gave me a telephone number and a name, "Lord John Pentland."

The name struck me as odd—what kind of person calls himself a "Lord" in America? Nevertheless, I called immediately.

"HELLO, THIS IS LORD PENTLAND."

The voice is low, unforced, impersonal. I feel like I've called a morgue. My breathing clutches. I can't get the words out. I struggle. Somehow I manage to tell him:

"My name is Patrick Patterson. Peter Rowley gave me your number."

"Yes," the voice answers in that same disembodied monotone. "Why do you want to see me?"

The question hits like a spear. Why had I called? My mouth becomes pasty. I begin to perspire. I can hardly breathe. Finally I blurt out—

"I've been interested in Gurdjieff for a long time. Years ago I read his book *Meetings With Remarkable Men*. It really struck me but I could never find anyone who knew anything about him. Then, the other day, I met this fellow, Peter Rowley, and—"

"Yes. I understand all that. But—why do you want to see me?

Why? Isn't that obvious? Suddenly, I realize the absurdity: I had called the man and didn't know why. I feel foolish, angry.

"Well, in any case," he says after a long pause, "do you wish to see me today?" He sighs like he is very tired and adds, "Or...should we let it go till next week?"

The way he says "next week" I know what he expects me to say.

"Today!" I blurt out. I'd waited seven years.

"All right, then," he declares quickly in an altogether different tone, and proceeds to give me detailed directions to his office in Rockefeller Center. As if talking to a child who is sure to forget, he repeats the directions very slowly.

"See you at six o'clock this evening," he says.

"Yes," I agree, but hesitantly. "See you...then."

I expect a goodbye. But no, he says nothing. But he doesn't hang up either.

It is weird. Like a time shift or something. I am dimly aware that the whole conversation has been like that.

And now here I am, with him there, and neither of us speaking with this empty, irritating gap between us.

Finally, just as I am about to open my mouth to speak—"Goodbye," he says quickly and hangs up in my face...

I stood holding a dead phone. I felt like some kind of idiot. Who was this guy? What was I getting myself into? But I felt sort of quiet inside. I could hear myself thinking about what had happened.

Later, I remembered in Ouspensky's book, *In Search of the Miraculous*, Gurdjieff had said that in order to come to the teaching a person first had to be disappointed in themselves and the world. Disappointed? That was a laugh. I had died. I had always thought "death" meant physical death. I never suspected it came in so many flavors. I had been effectively erased, fog bound whereabouts forgotten, in the great wasteland of the psychological void. Now perhaps the fog was lifting.

I hurried to Rockefeller Center. I stood in front of the RCA Building. It seemed like a massive burial tomb. Inside it was cool, dark and silent, bereft of people, save for a few grizzled guards whiling away the time. I took the elevator to his floor and slowly made my way down the dimly lighted corridor, the only sound was that of my soles squeaking on the marble floor. Finally, I came to a door reading:

John Pentland
The American-British Electric Corporation
The Hunting Group of Companies

I knocked several times. I expected to meet a portly and dour English gentleman wearing a vest and a gold watch chain. He'd have jowls, wear glasses. Perhaps have a crop of white hair. No answer. I waited. The office was dark. Empty. I cursed. Had he forgotten? Was he playing a trick? I was about to leave when, on impulse, I tried the brass door knob. It clicked. The door opened. The light was faint, ghostly, the office painted in shadows and blackness. I felt like a burglar. An ordinary business office. On the walls were large geological and topographical maps. I glanced at some papers on a desk. This "Lord Pentland" was the company's president.

I was about to leave when I heard the sound of a door opening. I took a few furtive steps forward and peered down a long corridor. In the pale light I saw a tall silent figure, very erect, slender, moving through the shadows toward me. He seemed like some prehistoric bird. He was upon me almost before I knew it. The face was totally impassive. The eyes aware. Yet without expression. The neck was very long, reed-like. It seemed too slender for the head. The eyebrows were dark and bushy. The shoulders were broad. He was balding.

"Hello," I said feigning cheeriness.

No greeting, no response. It was as if I hadn't said anything.

Weird. The two of us, strangers, standing in a dark hallway, half our faces in shadow, and him just standing there. He regarded me impersonally and without the slightest embarrassment. I felt as if he was drinking me in, weighing me in some way. What an odd duck! I could see him as perhaps the abbot of some distant, time-forgotten monastery—but hardly a disciple of a man like Gurdjieff. No, he must be just a caretaker. The teaching must have died with Gurdjieff.

Finally, the eyes and face still without expression, his lips formed a smile. In a low voice, just above a whisper, he said:

"Would you follow me?" A long arm motioned me down the corridor.

We walked down the dusky hallway; the only sounds in my ears were the soft pad of his slippers and the squeak of my shoes. His office was large and ordinary, a little sparse. Without ornamentation. No exotic souvenirs of travels with the Seekers of Truth. No secret symbols of knowledge. Only a few framed family photos. The view was impressive. St. Patrick's Cathedral, Saks, the traffic and crowds along Fifth Avenue, the Manhattan skyline, the bridge to New Jersey. I turned from the bank of windows. He had brought a chair to the side of his desk.

"Sit wherever you like," he said, half-motioning me to a chair by his desk.

Deliberately, I took a chair in front of the windows. He noted that, then took a seat opposite me on a small couch against the wall. His look was as impassive as it had been in the hallway. I took him in now as well. I noticed his ears. They were large, without lobes, nearly coming to a point at the top. Rather elfin-like. This

"Lord" wasn't much of a dresser, even for a businessman. He wore charcoal trousers, baggy and beltless, an old dull pea green cardigan, white business shirt, a nondescript wool tie. The dress of a professor of archeology, a scientist maybe. Hardly the stuff of a sly, swashbuckling man like Gurdjieff.

We continued looking at one another. We hadn't sat long when the last rays of the day's sun streamed into my eyes forcing me to move my chair. I was glad for the excuse to move. I thought that might break this awful silence but he continued watching me. I felt like a bug under a microscope. There was something unnerving about him. I sensed he wasn't there in some way. At least not the way I was; the way normal people are. Was he playing some game? I vowed not to speak before he did. Just then he spoke:

"Why have you come?" His voice was soft, unhurried, almost indifferent.

The same question as on the telephone. Again, I felt the same doubt, same bewilderment. *Why* was I there? *What* did I want? *What* had brought me here? I had no answers. I began talking, rambling on, telling him of my early life, how my parents had spoiled me, treating me like a rich kid, buying me anything I ever wanted.

"Well, at least," I said, "it made me realize that material things couldn't make you happy and then, too, death took it all away, so what was the meaning of it all?"

He went on listening

I recounted how I'd studied psychology and philosophy and found no answer with either. Just mind games. Religion seemed too ordinary, played out, and you had to accept its answers on faith.

He made no comment.

"I don't know what life is about," I told him, "but something in me just can't accept that it is all meaningless—there has to be some reason for human life."

I thought he might respond, but he didn't. I waited. He motioned that I should continue.

I told him, too, how after college I'd gone to San Francisco to work in advertising, but was drafted into the Army. Afterward, I'd come to New York. Worked as a copywriter for Montgomery Wards. Later for J. Walter Thompson and BBD&O. Finally ended up at IBM. I told him about how I had started *In New York*, its success, then about the fast buck boys.

Like a broken water main, the whole story burst out of me. I must have talked for a good hour. But he listened, however long and convoluted. He had an amazing ability to listening. He gave no sign of how he felt. Perhaps he only appeared to follow. I couldn't tell. When I got to my theories of what life might be about, its purpose and meaning and all, well, I did notice he seemed to tire visibly. He was in his sixties. Probably had a long day.

I ended by telling him of my spiritual experiences, the light and the telepathy, the inner knowing. I was just getting to the good part when—unbelievably:

He yawned!

Right in my face. No attempt to cover his mouth. No, "excuse me." Not the least embarrassment. He acted as if nothing had happened. Perhaps the "Lord" was a bit senile? Was this another Murphy deal? A wild goose chase? Gurdjieff had died in 1949. This old gaffer—was he just a museum piece?

I hurried then to the end of the story. I was about to excuse myself and leave when—the bastard yawned again!

It was the most incredible yawn I had ever seen. The mouth opened wide, showing a huge cave of teeth and tongue. The neck muscles and tendons stretched full out. Then a loud sucking in of air and the mouth clapped shut, the nostrils exhaling a stream of spent air. The whole mechanical movement of the musculature happened in slow motion, like it was all under his control. He kept his eyes on mine the entire time. They showed nothing. Not the least guilt or apology. Was all this deliberate? If so, why?

I wanted to get the hell out of there, fast. But I didn't. I thought of moving, but couldn't. The thought wasn't strong enough. So we just sat, wrapped in all that heavy silence, all that empty space. It was withering.

"Tell me…" he inquired, feigning a curiosity, "can you experience all that now?"

There was a slight undertone of challenge in his voice. I saw immediately what he meant: I'd talked about my "spiritual experiences" as if they were a continuing part of my life. I felt like a fish with a hook in its mouth.

"No," I finally admitted, a bit reluctantly.

He nodded, acknowledging the truth of my admission.

"But I could then," I added tersely.

"Can you do this now?" He wasn't going to let me off the hook.

I looked out the window. The Manhattan skyline stood in sharp black silhouette against the graying twilight. The lights in the buildings, all yellow—they seemed like thousands of impenetrable cat eyes. What was his point? What was he trying to prove? That I was an idiot?

"No," I finally said somewhat sheepishly, "I can't do it now."

"That's true," he shot back quickly.

It was as if we had come to something now, something important. His voice was so direct, sharp, not whispery at all. And the way he pronounced the word "true"— the elongated tail he put on the 'rue'—flashed right through me. Was he suggesting everything I'd said up to that moment wasn't true? Or only half-true? That only my admission—that *I couldn't do it now*—was worth anything?

The chair felt uncomfortable, unforgiving. I shifted in it uneasily, crossing my legs, clasping my hands around my knee, leaning forward. He shifted as well. More hard silence. I had the most unusual feeling then. It was like a "double feeling." It was as if I was lying and telling the truth—and at the same time.

But everything I'd told him was true! It had happened. I wasn't making it up. So why this feeling of lying? Mentally, I kept seeing reruns of my actions, my words rebounding on me. It was as if I was in some kind of instant replay.

Then his original question—*Why have you come?*—bubbled up in me again.

Suddenly I understood. I hadn't answered his question. I hadn't admitted I didn't know why.

That unlocked something. For immediately I remembered what had brought me—what I wanted. Why had I forgotten?

"I want to become conscious," I told him, another tone in my voice.

Something happened in the room then. There was a shift of some type. Same room, same two people, yet it was all different. I felt the space growing, getting larger and larger, like an invisible balloon expanding. The sense of time changed. It was as if time "thinned out." The moment was electric. The whole atmosphere was more subtle, alive.

"Can you help me?" I asked softly.

He sat there, very still, not immediately answering. His hands were folded on his lap, palms up. For a long time he peered into them. It was as though he was reading tea leaves or studying a yantra. He seemed to weigh my question carefully, evaluating my strengths and weaknesses, pitting them against all the obstacles I would encounter. At last he looked up.

"Yes…I think we can."

I felt elated. But inside me the undertone in his voice echoed. I realized that he had said "yes" only by a hair's breath. That I was more a long shot than a calculated gamble.

Lord Pentland's face seemed ancient, timeless.

"Yes, you can be helped," he continued, a small measure of certainty in his voice. Then he added "…if you are *sincere.*"

Sincerity! The word exploded in me. I was telling him the truth. How had I been insincere? I hadn't lied. I was serious.

Again, the whole atmosphere and tempo changed.

Lord Pentland suddenly began speaking in a brisk, matter-of-fact manner. It seemed that he and some others met once a week to discuss some of Mr. Gurdjieff's ideas. "If you would care to attend, why I suppose that might be all right…and if you chose to do so, well, of course, your becoming part of this group would be of some trouble but, then again, not so much as to preclude your at least attending a meeting or two; provided, of course, that you actually want to do so…*do you?*"

This was an entirely different "Lord Pentland."

I nodded, thinking to myself that he pronounced the name "Mr. Gurdjieff" with so much feeling, respect; yes, even reverence. I'd pronounced the name.

Lord Pentland mentioned that since Christmas was so near there would be no meetings until January. He would be going to San Francisco for a time but when he returned he promised to be in touch.

We both got up then and went to the doorway. Instead of motioning me through it, he paused to glance at me. It was as if he was considering taking me into his confidence.

"Would you like to read another of Mr. Gurdjieff's books?" he asked, his voice a near whisper.

For some reason, I couldn't speak. I felt paralyzed. All I could do was nod.

He turned and reached into a bookcase behind his desk, taking from it a thick dark blue book the size of a travel guide. The binding was worn. It had obviously been read and reread many times. He looked at me directly and began to hand me the book. I put my hand out to receive it—but his hand stopped just inches from my outstretched fingers. It was as if we were caught in a freeze frame—him holding the book, me with my hand out. I felt stupid. Why didn't he just give me the book?

"You know," Lord Pentland mused, taking a long breath, "a man like Mr. Gurdjieff comes along only once in a million years."

What did that mean? Whatever, I nodded politely.

"That's *very hard* to appreciate…if you know what I mean?" he said softly, peering at me, as if he were trying to detect my level of understanding.

Was he saying Gurdjieff was a saint? An avatar? A messiah of some kind? What was he talking about?

"Would you like to read my copy of *All and Everything?*" Lord Pentland asked, his eyes pinning mine.

Again, all I could manage was nod.

"Mr. Gurdjieff gave it to me himself," he added, his voice exceedingly low as if he wanted no one else to hear.

"All right," I answered. "Sure."

"Would you like to borrow it?" he asked.

I couldn't speak. I felt like I was cut in two. One part standing there inert, one part watching. But watching what? It took an enormous effort of will, but I got it out—

"I would like to—yes!"

The corners of Lord Pentland's mouth turned up into something of a smile, a kind of small acknowledgment. But of what? That I had wanted to read the book? That I had asked for it?

He still made no motion to give me the book. Did he want me to reach for it? Was I dreaming this? I couldn't tell.

He actually smiled now. A kindly smile, soft and radiant. It was wonderful. I felt all this energy. My body was suddenly alive with all this energy. Then he turned to the bookshelf, carefully replacing the threadbare copy.

I stood there bewildered, with this ridiculous feeling of having been rejected. Like he had given me a test which I'd almost passed. But—but what was the test? And why?

Lord Pentland gestured me silently out into the pitch black hallway. I felt this was a goodbye. I walked slowly, awkwardly, past the empty row of desks, my soles squeaking in my ears, struck with this deep sense of rejection.

The shadowy office, the desks and chairs, business machines—who would ever suspect that such a conversation (if that was what it was) could happen here in ordinary life, in the RCA building? It felt unreal. Like everything was a prop in some movie set. It was as if I had auditioned for a role in some rare movie. I'd almost gotten it, but wasn't right for the part.

At the outer door, trying to put the best face on it, I turned to say goodbye.

Lord Pentland loomed tall in the darkness. He appeared quite fatherly now. I felt a strong feeling for him, like some connection had been made. He smiled. "I'll be getting back to you sometime after the holidays," he said.

I stared at him blankly.

He added, "You might look into what it means to remember oneself."

I nodded. I was accepted after all!

Lord Pentland extended his hand. His gesture released all the swirling energy inside me and I grabbed it. I shook his hand so strongly, that both our hands pumped madly up and down. I smiled from ear to ear but he just stood there impassively, looking on without expression. Weird. I felt embarrassed. Suddenly this sinking recognition washed over me—*only my hand was doing the shaking!*

A dead fish! The bastard had given me a dead fish handshake. Lord Pentland's hand was completely passive, limp. Mine was pumping both our hands up and down like a piston. My mind was thinking one thing, my body doing another. And this weirdo is just standing there. I felt like a fool. What was he doing to me! And *why?*

"Goodbye, Pat," Lord Pentland said warmly, as he ushered me out and gently, but quite deliberately, shut the door right in my face.

I SAILED HOME FULL OF ENERGY. I TRIED TO TELL BARBARA WHAT HAD HAPPENED, but it was all a jumble. How could I explain what had happened? I didn't know what happened.

"Well, it must have been good for you," Barbara said at last. "You look so alive."

Her remark stopped me. I felt my body. I went into the bathroom and looked in the mirror. My eyes were different. It was true. I felt really good.

But how could so much energy come from all that suffering?

During the next weeks I devoured every Gurdjieff book I could find. I'd never known ideas of this potency and practicality. The incredible sweep and scale of the concepts, their power and precision, exhilarated me. They were like nothing I had ever read or heard before. It was as if these ideas came from an entirely different world. I felt my mind opening, becoming active and alive, as the ideas formed in me a vision of human life and its purpose I'd never even dimly imagined.

The central idea seemed to be that man (the word standing for humanity) was not complete. He was a self-developing organism who as he was now was only a "man-machine" living a life of imitation. He lived an ant's life, devoid of any authenticity. Man was shallow, asleep, a counterfeit. Man was dead to his real self. Programmed, mechanical, lost in his head, his groin, his gut—man lived an idiot life of illusion, imagination. Man's greatest stone-hard belief was that he was free, awake, independent where in reality he was only a phantom in a dream world.

The actuality was that man existed as a many-headed, crazy quilt of hundreds of changing and conflicting thoughts, moods and desires. To each of these he said "I." To each thought, mood or desire—no matter how incongruous or opposite—he said "I."

What was this "I" that man called himself?

Man had no I at all. Man was many "I"s. And each was different, had different ambitions, or no ambition. Different world views, or no world view.

As unlike as they might be, each of these different "I"s was totally convinced that it, and it alone, was the one and only I.

Hypnotized by this imaginary notion of "I"—steeped as every "I" is in false personality, self-love and vanity—man's fundamental belief in himself as having a permanent, indivisible I was rock hard. Man spends his whole life polishing and defending what in actuality has no unified and independent existence: his so-called "I."

Whether he realizes it or not, man is under the control of many subtle forces. To actually do in life, to keep to a line of action—with all the shocks, changes in tempo, building or depleting energies—he must have the power to sustain and nourish himself. That took real will, not ego will predicated as it was on ego desire. Real will came only from real and indivisible I.

The work, or method, Gurdjieff gave for coming to real I was to *self-remember.* What this means is not easy to define. Self-remembering is a subtle and shifting experience; very fluid and spatial, having many levels of meaning. But to begin with it means, according to Ouspensky, to come to a direct feeling of oneself. Further, Ouspensky said that the attention should be divided. One part of the attention guards the mind, keeping it clear and free of identification with thoughts. Another part, at the same time, experiences the body. So, there's a kind of "double attention."

With the mind being relatively clear and rooted in the experiencing of the body, a person can observe himself or herself impartially, without judgment. He can see his reactions, defenses, the way he actually is in the world at that moment. To see in this way is the beginning of the practice of *self-observation.*

It was a lot to take in. I didn't understand it but still, inexplicably, I felt in these ideas a deep truth. I felt a resonance in me that I knew to be true. I read them over and over, thrilled at the breadth and practicality of the perspective. The only idea I really had trouble with was that each person was supposedly made up of many "I"s. Intellectually, I could understand it. But I couldn't feel a lot of different "I"s in me. In fact, I could only feel one "I." And "I" felt like "I." Like me. Now I couldn't exactly say what that "I" was but I knew it all the same. Sure, I had my different moods and desires and thoughts, and, yes, often they were quite contradictory. Did that mean "I" wasn't "I"? Was I asleep? I certainly didn't feel like I was asleep.

And this idea of self-remembering—it really didn't seem that hard. Was too much being made out of something very simple? One day I decided to experiment: I'd go to the cigar store, buy a candy bar and return, all the time dividing my attention between my body and the outer world.

I pulled on my Navy pea coat, feeling the arms go into the sleeves, slowly buttoning the large buttons, deliberately opening and closing the door and then walking slowly down the three flights of stairs, sensing the smoothness of the old handrail, sensing my weight shifting from one leg to another, hearing the steps creak under my weight, opening the door and stepping out onto 84th street. It was cold as hell and the snow was gusting and whirling between buildings and cars, building up huge snow banks. Long icicles hung from the gutters and roofs of the buildings. The scene was so vivid.

Then I noticed a bearded man in a blue turban coming down the street. He must be a Sikh, I thought. Would I ever go to India, I wondered. See the Ganges? Visit Benares? I remembered Larry, the character in Somerset Maugham's *The Razor's Edge*. He had gone to India in search of truth.

Back in the apartment, I slung the wet pea coat over a chair and plopped down on the mattress. The phone rang. Wrong number. Thea jumped onto my chest. We had had her declawed. Tomorrow we would take the bandages off her front paws. How would she feel when she discovered she had no claws? The dracaena cane was still sagging. I picked up the engraved Masonic sword and took it out of its sheath. I'd stuck it into the planter and tied the dracaena cane to it. The fucking metal had oxidized. I should have known better. What a fool! The sword was my grandfather's. I picked up the newspaper and opened it—

Suddenly it hit me!

I shot straight up on the mattress.

I had stopped remembering myself.

I'D BEEN TOTALLY ASLEEP AND DIDN'T KNOW IT! HOW COULD THAT HAVE happened? Mentally, I retraced my steps. I saw myself pulling on my coat, going down the steps, the scene outside, then I'd seen the Sikh and suddenly I was thinking about India…damn!

And all this "I" stuff. Had one "I" decided to experiment and another simply forgotten? I picked up Search and reread the material on man's different "I"s. Because of my experiment, the words were no longer so theoretical. The ideas had a ground.

…Man had no permanent and unchangeable I. All his thoughts, moods, desires, and every sensation he has of himself reinforces his feeling of being an indivisible entity., his notion of himself as "I." Every moment of his life he is saying, thinking, or feeling "I." It is an ongoing trance. In reality man's "I" is always changing and adapting to circumstances, real and imagined…His "I"s are in a continual struggle for supremacy. Man does not see this but, even if he did, there is nothing strong and permanent enough in him to take charge of his changing "I"s. Man is a slave to the "I" of the moment. In the name of this "I" he is living, paying tribute and suffering his whole life. Whatever the dominant "I," it is of the same origin— the result of external influences that have been unconsciously identified and reacted to in terms of "I."

Yes, just like my Sikh who called up the "I" in me that dreams of going to India.

I wrote a letter to Lord Pentland telling of my experiment and surprise at its outcome. Several days later Lord Pentland called. He seemed pleased. "Your making such an effort on your own initiative," he said, "showed the right spirit." A small group was meeting that evening at 6:30 P.M. "You might attend, if you still have a mind to," he said.

"Yes, I'd like to very much."

He gave the address very slowly, then repeated it; still not confident I would remember it.

"He might have given you more notice," Barbara said when she came home from work. She put the bags of groceries down in the kitchen. "What are we going to do about dinner?"

"Let's have it when I come home."

"It's warming up outside. Make sure you put on galoshes."

"Yeah, okay," I said, pulling on my Navy pea coat, and darting out the door.

I was already down the first flight of stairs when I heard the door open and Barbara shout after me—"Your galoshes!"

"I don't need 'em. I'm wearing boots," I yelled back.

"Why don't you ever listen to anyone?"

Outside, the night had the look of magic. The big bare elms lining the street, their limbs collared in white, looked like ancient sentries frozen in time. Melting ice everywhere. Sparkling like millions of watery diamonds under the street lights. The wind had died down. Barely a sound. A deep silence everywhere. As I walked, I heard the cars up on First Avenue, their tire chains crunching and click-click-clicking against the hard packed street snow. I hurried along, stepping across puddles of melted snow, filled with the expectation of embarking on a new adventure. At last my life was moving off dead center.

The soles of my boots were oozing with water by the time I got to the 86th Street subway stop. I didn't care. I didn't want to bother taking off galoshes at my first meeting. At the Bloomingdale's stop, I took the subway stairs two at a time to street level. The big Roman numeral street clock showed I was a good ten minutes early. The address turned out to be an expensive townhouse, just off Park Avenue. Lord Pentland had made a point of telling me the group (he had emphasized it was a "preparatory group") met in the basement. The townhouse was dark. An ornate circular symbol on the black basement door caught my eye. Was this the group's symbol? I quickly opened the wrought iron gate and hurried down the steps. In the center of the symbol was a figure of Mercury-Hermes, wings on his heels, holding bolts of lightning. Around the edge of the circle was lettering. It didn't read "Society of Hermes" or "Seekers of Truth" but—*Holmes Protection Agency*

The wind laughed in my ears. A solemn faced couple was slowly passing by. They craned their necks, observing me closely, but saying nothing. My heart pounding, I knocked at the door. No answer. I smiled and tried the door knob. Locked. Did I have the wrong address? I stuck a freezing hand deep into a pocket and pulled out a crumpled up piece of paper. No, this was it. I walked around the block a few times and then, my heart still pounding, knocked again at the door. Still, no answer. Was this another of his stupid games?

The wind had come up again, smacking my face and sending shivers through my body. I walked again. The streets and sidewalks were freezing up. The world was being forced back into hard shape. My boots soaked up to my ankles now. Water oozed out with every step. The thought came a few times to remember myself, but I was shaking with cold, every breath immediately condensing in the cold of the night. This was no time for that. Coming down the street on the opposite side, I saw that same couple, that same flat peculiar look on their faces. I walked up and back down the block. I kept gawking at the little crumpled piece of paper. Would Lord Pentland have deliberately given me the wrong address? I noticed now besides "the odd couple" there were others walking up and down the street. Some nodded to one another.

Perhaps the address was right but the time was wrong? No, he repeated it and I wrote it down immediately. I remembered in his office I'd seen a letter addressed to him at a Riverdale address. I hurried back to the corner coffee shop, got the number from the operator and phoned. A cultured woman's voice answered.

"Hello," she said, her voice remote and controlled.

I introduced myself and told her of my situation.

"The meeting," she informed me, pronouncing each word exactly, "is at 7:30 P.M."

"But he told me it was 6:30!"

"Perhaps you didn't hear rightly."

There was a pause. Then a click at the other end. I stood holding a dead receiver to my ear, cursing to myself. People in the coffee shop regarded me curiously.

I hurried back to the townhouse and knocked on the basement door. It opened now, and in the doorway stood a striking young woman, quite handsome and dressed completely in black. Her blonde hair, long, straight and combed to a sheen. Her skin was very white and her make-up extremely pale, except for the cheeks which were heavily blushed. The contrast of her dress—black cashmere sweater, black pleated wool skirt, black high top boots—set against the stark whiteness of her skin startled and unnerved me. I managed to stammer:

"Is this where—"

Without a word, I was motioned inside. She pointed out a coat rack and, at the end of a short hallway, a door. Then, taking no more notice of me, she sat down in a plain chair by the door. She cupped her hands in her lap, the left in the right, and fixed her gaze on the wall. Her manner was aristocratic, ethereal. But what was she doing? Trying to remember herself?

The basement was brightly lighted, low-ceilinged. The walls, painted an off-white. The floor, bare. The hardwood polished to a mirror-like gleam. Banquettes, rather uncomfortable looking, lined one wall. It all had a look of being carefully thought out, then crafted with great care. There was nothing distinctive or personal. No ornamentation. It reminded me of Lord Pentland's office.

Despite the basement's bright lighting, I felt as if I was in a cave. I had this dim intuition that I had happened onto the threshold of a strange new world. A world for which I had no reference. The feeling only intensified upon my opening the door in the rear. The room was square, plain and softly lighted; its walls a craggy red brick. At the far wall stood two ordinary, hard-backed wooden chairs. A small Persian rug separated the two chairs from two rows of facing chairs, perhaps twelve in all.

Many chairs were already occupied. I noticed "the odd couple" at once. The others were people mostly in their thirties and forties. They looked like lawyers, businessmen, bohemians, working class, several students. No one type. But all sat erect, motionless, not speaking, totally serious, their eyes either closed or gazing at the brick wall. The atmosphere gave off a weight and somberness such as I had felt only once before, and that was in a medieval Catholic church in Seville. Only here there was no altar, no bleeding Jesus, no prayerful saints or heavy incense. Gurdjieff, I recalled, told Ouspensky that "If you like," this teaching is "esoteric Christianity."

My impulse was to sit in the second row. I forced myself into a chair in the front row, though at the end. I closed my eyes. I was exhausted, my boots and pant legs soaked, my feet were cold as ice. The room was warm. I kept dozing off. At one point, though I'd heard no sound, I became aware someone had entered the room. I opened my eyes. There, facing the group, was Lord Pentland, stork-like, his body very still and angular, though quite broad across the chest and shoulders. His legs were spread apart, the feet squarely planted on the floor. Beside him sat an Armenian-looking woman. Her skin was pale and her hair, thick and black, was pulled tight into a bun. She, too, wore very little make-up. She was wearing a pink blouse, buttoned high at the neck, a black brocaded vest, black skirt and black boots. Probably in her late thirties. Intellectual-looking.

Lord Pentland sat for a time, then abruptly stood up. He took off his suit jacket and hung it on the back of his chair. I noticed he still wore no belt. His shirt had rumpled up in the back. He resumed sitting, hitching up the crease of his trousers and continuing silently to regard the group. I had the feeling that he was somehow all alone in the room. That we weren't there.

The silence continued, the only sound that of inhalation and exhalation of air. It sounded so odd, like animals feeding. My thoughts were so loud, distinct. My mind was jumping all over the place. My body began to ache. Why didn't he start the meeting, the lecture, or whatever this was! But, no, the silence continued, the intensity building. The atmosphere became almost palpable. I felt like screaming.

Presently, and very slowly, Lord Pentland looked off to his left. It was such a simple movement and, because of that, extraordinary. For it looked as if his neck and head were detached from the rest of his body. The neck and head didn't move separately but as one unit. The eyes never preceded the movement; the rest of his body remaining entirely motionless. The movement was effortless, yet completely controlled. The effect was eerie. Inhuman. Like the turning of the periscope on a submarine. I remembered the time in his office when he yawned. I felt a strange fear. What had I gotten myself into?

Lord Pentland's eyes fixed on the short, big bellied man at the end of the first row. There was no expression, no gesture of recognition, no welcoming. His face conveyed not the slightest personal interest. This "eye ceremony," or whatever it was, occurred in perfect stillness. He went from one person to another in the same way. Almost before I knew it, Lord Pentland's eyes were on mine. Unaccountably, my body shook. It was as if I had received a jolt of some type. I felt naked. Like I was being X-rayed. Perhaps I was being initiated, but there was nothing in his eyes. They were empty, indifferent. Thoughts whirled up like a tornado. Was I looking into the eyes of a dead man? Could he read my thoughts? Was he…his head and eyes moved to the person behind me.

This went on, no one moving, just breathing. Soon, it was over. I thought he'd begin the lecture now. Instead, he resumed his former posture. In reaction, a few people shifted in their chairs. Another cleared his throat. The silence had changed. It was forced now, brittle. The room, the space in it, grew very tense. Finally, from behind me, came this small female voice, hesitant and fearful. It was hard to make out what she was saying…something about making some inner effort. She had noticed that this effort was somehow not of the same quality as when she…and I couldn't make out the rest. Then she began to weep.

Why the weeping? What had she said? It had sounded like nothing at all.

After a time, Lord Pentland answered. "We are remembered," he said. "We don't remember ourselves."

His voice was low, dispassionate, yet it reverberated through the room.

"We can't remember ourselves," he added and paused. Now his voice was soft, kind. The woman's weeping stopped. "And yet…yet there is this wish to make ourselves available."

He looked from person to person. "This wish to awaken—that is our birthright."

Silence filled the room again.

Lord Pentland regarded the fat man again at the end of the first row.

"You woke up for a second, did you not?"

Lord Pentland looked at me, or in my direction. "But then personality took over," he said. "You fell in with it."

He sighed as if this were all rather hopeless.

Who was he talking to? The fat man? Me? The weeping woman?

Lord Pentland looked at the ethereal blonde in black who had greeted me at the door. She was sitting a seat away. She had cupped her hands in her lap just like the Armenian woman. Her blue eyes shined. Her lips pursed together in an adoring Cheshire cat smile.

"You should watch that," remarked Lord Pentland soberly.

She seemed to glow but her face froze. Her cheeks seemed to redden.

Lord Pentland craned his neck looking beyond the blonde to the weeping woman.

"Your observation—it shows you are working," he declared, nodding approvingly. "Before we can observe ourselves, simply record what is going on, we must remember ourselves. I hope that is clear to everyone."

"Lord Pentland, I—" began the fat man.

"The Work of The Fourth Way does not come cheaply," interrupted Lord Pentland continuing to speak to the woman behind me.

There was a long pause then before he went on to say something about "the scale of impressions," but I couldn't follow it.

The tension of speaking broken, everyone rushed to ask a question now. One person had noticed that self-remembering made his mind still. She had a new sense of the body. Another that when he was present impressions seemed more vivid, powerful. Another that it made him feel isolated.

Some gave reports, others asked questions. Few were simple or clear. They were very much like the people themselves: either elaborate or convoluted; cryptic, guarded or anemic. I could follow none of them for very long. After a while, the questions reminded me of birds. That is, one would flit nervously from branch to branch; another skitters back and forth making a great fuss; still another takes a few halting steps and no more; a few even try to fly, flapping their wings proudly, yet never leave their perch.

Whatever the question, Lord Pentland listened attentively. His answers were always spare, precise, right to the point. His answers surprised me. They always seemed to come from a different place than the question. He always gave a perspective I'd never considered. Many times he seemed to be answering not the question the person had brought, but the question behind the question; the question the person was unconsciously hiding.

"The conditions here," he mentioned at one point, "are of course artificial. They are to allow us to see and hear ourselves. It's a waste if we are merely asking a question and expecting an answer." He paused, glanced at the Armenian woman, then at each of us. "What is important here, I dare say, is happening quite beyond the level of words."

The room crackled. Yet not a person spoke.

"Well…let us go on then," he sighed, exhaling a long stream of air.

A male voice coughed and then spoke. It was the fat man again. His voice was heavy with seriousness, a sense of piety. He related something about getting onto a bus, seeing that it was nothing more than a steel box, noticing how identified, how asleep, all the passengers were, and then having "the flash of the terror of the situation, the absurdity of life," as he put it.

"You got a great deal of satisfaction from that, did you not?" retorted Lord Pentland.

The fat man swallowed.

Lord Pentland added dryly. "You use big words. You should watch that."

A long, horrible pause. The fat man sat frozen to the seat, his face looking as if he was trying to spit out a stone too big for his throat. Finally:

"Yes, sorry," the fat man said contritely. "That's a department I should watch."

Lord Pentland let the words hang in space, acting as though he didn't fully understand. Finally, he challenged the fat man tersely:

"What do you mean…*de-part-ment?*"

The fat man looked skewered like a stuck pig.

His initial question was asked with all the self-important righteousness of a judge passing sentence. He had categorized each of the passengers on the bus, sticking each in tight mental compartments.

The fat man finally answered, his voice smaller, very careful. He built an intricate web of definition and defense, but continued to circle around the word "department." He saw something but kept himself blind.

Lord Pentland, disgusted, or feigning disgust (I couldn't tell), finally broke him off: "You received a great deal of satisfaction from seeing everyone—how do you say it?—asleep? Isn't that right?"

The fat man's head heaved forward. He let out a great gust of air. But his tone remained very "religious." "Self-love, yes, yes. I can see that now," he admitted. "I always fall into that trap. It's one department...ahh, area that—"

Lord Pentland looked tired; as though he was doing all he could to fight off sleep.

"Yes, I see. It's clear to me now," the fat man said, nodding his head.

"Clee-ear?" said a puzzled Lord Pentland, suddenly awake and fully engaged. "What is clee-ear?"

It was as if a cleaver had hit the fat man right between the eyes. I felt like his mind came to a complete stop.

Seconds passed. Another voice suddenly jumped in. It was definite, big and hard. Very macho.

"Clear is seeing the contradictions!"

Lord Pentland sat looking through us, as if somehow we had disappeared from his world.

I stretched to see who had spoken...two seats from the blonde-in-black sat a glaring man with a short angular forehead, long jutting nose, sharp chin. In profile he reminded me of a crocodile.

"Well! What do you think of that?" the crocodile man demanded.

"Is that two questions? Or one?" inquired Lord Pentland softly.

"Whatever you like."

"Liking or not liking...they have no place here," Lord Pentland pointed out. He glanced at the Armenian woman. She nodded.

Lord Pentland's eyes slowly returned to the crocodile man who continued to glare, his whole upper body arched forward in his seat, intent and unrelenting. He wanted his answer.

Lord Pentland smiled politely and, looking somewhat world-weary, breathed deeply. Then he chuckled good-naturedly.

"Well, if we could see the contradictions," replied Lord Pentland at last to the crocodile man, "between what we say and what we feel...well, I suppose we wouldn't be here, would we?"

The crocodile man grumbled and nodded his head. "Lord Pentland," he inquired sharply, "you are saying we would not be studying how to awake, if we were already awake. Is that what you are saying?"

Lord Pentland told a story:

"One day," he began, his voice very flat, without emotion, "I wormed my way into having lunch with Mr. Gurdjieff and some others, though I had not been invited. Mr. Gurdjieff said nothing at the time, but the following day he took me to a Turkish bathhouse on the outskirts of Paris. The sense was that this was a reward for something I had done that had been in his eyes especially praiseworthy. I was, of course, elated."

Lord Pentland spoke plain-faced and in a monotone, making no effort to capture our attention. Somehow, that made the story even more riveting.

"While I undressed," he said, "Mr. Gurdjieff took the owner of the bathhouse aside, to whisper something but, in fact, he spoke quite loudly, telling the man that "his special friend" was to be given "the best of treatment." Thereupon a masseur was summoned, a huge man, who proceeded to beat me to a pulp while of course Mr. Gurdjieff looked on, not being above showing a certain sly satisfaction. Afterward…"

As he got to the end, his voice had moved to lower and lower registers…until it dropped to only a hair's breadth from the inaudible.

We had all craned forward striving to hear.

He then—our attention totally taken—abruptly stopped.

The moment didn't move—it stuck in space like a freeze frame.

Everyone reacted differently.

The blonde continued smiling, her lips firmly pursed. The fat man looked as if he had gotten back on his bus. The crocodile man just sat. The antsy, stringy fellow next to me with blond hippie-style hair tied in a pony tail, tattered jeans, and well-worn cowboy boots, sat slouched in his chair, his legs crossed, arms folded, head cocked to the side, smirking.

Lord Pentland looked first impassively at the stringy fellow, then at the fat man, then at others in the group. He obviously was waiting for a question about the Turkish bath story. But no one spoke. Why was it so hard to speak?

At last the crocodile man spoke up: "You mentioned before that—and I quote—'If we could see the contradictions we wouldn't be here.' You mean to say we wouldn't be here in this room listening to you? Or what?"

Lord Pentland's eyes searched the ceiling and walls as if he were looking for something. He whispered to the Armenian woman who began to scan the room's horizon as well.

"Lord Pentland, let me ask you," broke in the stringy fellow in a shrill voice—

"No, I think not," answered Lord Pentland swiftly but softly.

"But I just wanted to—"

"You see, It is like this" uttered Lord Pentland, nodding to the crocodile man, and completely ignoring the stringy fellow. His manner was now somewhat academic: "To hear means simply that I cannot be, I'm afraid, thinking of anything else. I must be empty. Do you see?"

"No!" thundered the crocodile man, his head shaking, his eyes riveted into the floor.

Lord Pentland gazed about the room, seeing if anyone else might have a question.

Lord Pentland's words danced in me. I seemed to be hearing in a way I'd never heard before. I felt this impulse to talk. Should I? It was only my first meeting. The question grew inside me. Finally: I took the leap:

I told a long rambling story about having hitchhiked out West and being picked up by a dog handler in a pickup truck, its bay filled with dogs in cages. He had talked for miles and miles about dogs, their good points and bad, how you had to handle one this way and another that way. Out in the desert near Las Vegas, he had stopped to check his tires. To illustrate what he meant, the trainer took a toy bulldog out of its cage, pointing out to me where it was strong and weak, what was particularly fine about it, and so forth. He knew dogs. You could see it in the way he handled the dog, moving it this way and that, opening its jaws, lifting its paws, straightening its legs, shaping its tail.

"Now it seems to me," I reasoned, "that he was very clear about what he was doing. He knew dogs inside out. He had no illusions. Would this be an example of having gone beyond contradiction?"

Lord Pentland had turned to me when I began to speak, placing his full attention on me. As I told the story, I suddenly found it harder and harder to speak; like there was some force pressing in on me. The words kept coming out of my mouth, but suddenly…I feel as though I have expanded into space…That recognition immediately brought me right back into the body. But then again…I find my sense of "I" not located in the body, but in a vast, quiet space. Again, once realized…I came right back into my body.

As I alternated going in and out of the room I noticed only a few words had gone by. The shifting back and forth quickened. It became such a struggle to speak. By the end of the story, my forehead was beaded with sweat and I was exhausted.

For a long time I felt Lord Pentland gazing at me.

I felt myself coming together again, my body filling up with energy.

He continued to peer into me. I felt completely open, exposed, like I was on an operating table having surgery.

Finally, with a faint nod of his head, Lord Pentland acknowledged that I had been heard. He craned forward in his chair, as if to get a better look at this peculiar human specimen. Having satisfied his curiosity, he withdrew his attention, abruptly rose and disappeared from the room, the Armenian woman dutifully following.

"Hmmmn," whispered the stringy fellow next to me with a big grin, "feel like you farted, but can't smell it, huh?"

"What?"

"Heh, hard of hearing, too," he grinned, gave me a quick elbow in the ribs and chortled—"well, that's not saying any of these other pig fuckers are in any better condition."

Outside, the stringy fellow was waiting for me, hopping up and down, from foot to foot, his frozen breath blowing long ribbons of smoke into the cold night air. He introduced himself as Soren. He said he'd been in the Work for fourteen years, mostly in San Francisco. He'd just moved to New York and lived in a walk-up in the Village on Thirteenth Street off Ninth.

As we walked, Soren talked in a rapid-fire rhythm, gesturing and commenting, charging wildly through the slush. He was extremely thin, a classic ectomorph, with a long nose and angular face. The eyes were narrow, sly and challenging. He had this nervous, jumpy energy. He wanted to know when I had first met Lord Pentland. It surprised him that it was only a month ago.

"Hah! You must be on the 'fast track,'" he declared. "Usually takes months or years before you're asked to come to a meeting."

"Really?"

Immediately, he picked up on the undertone, my attitude.

"Judas priest!" he cried, shaking his head in mock outrage. "Talks too much, listens too little, thinks his shit doesn't stink. Oh boy, is this going to be a major excavation job!"

At the subway we parted, Soren calling out: "Well, my boy, see you next week. The liars' club meets every week, you know."

"Lion's club?"

He came running back. He gave my ear lobe a pull. "Liars' club. Got that? L-i-a-r-s. Heh-heh."

THE GARDEN OF EARTHLY DELIGHTS, BOSCH'S WEIRD PAINTING, WAS IN TINY irregular pieces on the dining room table. Barbara sat in robe and slippers, *Tosca* blaring, eating pistachio ice cream and ruminating about where to put the next piece in the jigsaw puzzle.

"Don't track that in here. Leave your boots outside," she said pointedly without looking up.

"But—"

"Your boots are soaked."

"How do you know?" I made a face.

"What did you tell me just last night? "

"What?"

"How when people asked Gurdjieff why he had come to America he told them, 'To tell people that when it rains the sidewalks get wet.' Same goes for boots, Patricio."

I stuck out my tongue, pulled off the boots and tossed them into the hall.

"Not so much noise." Barbara cried without looking up. "The landlord."

I gave her a kiss. She softened a bit and handed me a towel from her lap.

"Dry off. You're soaking. Getting the floor all wet. And, please, don't ask 'how do I know?' All right?" She pulled the robe tight around her.

It was always such fun to tease her. She was so completely serious.

I dried off. "Sorry, Barb," I said. "Still love me now?"

"Put the towel back in the bathroom."

"You had it out here all the time. How did you know I'd come home—"

"Patterson, don't push me!" She jammed an eye into one of Bosch's weird creatures.

"Okay. Okay. You Latvians are something else." I went to the bathroom and tossed a towel across the end of the tub.

She had followed me. "Not there. On the towel rack."

I bowed dutifully. Gave her a namaste and embraced her. "Do you still love, Mr. Poogle?" I purred in her ear.

She didn't reply. I persisted.

"Poogle's a pain but, yes," she admitted at last, the thorns shorn from her voice. "I'm stupid but I do."

"Tell me," I asked "—what do you mean when you say, 'love'?"

She pushed me away and gave me a rap on the chest. "Not that again," she fumed. "I don't want to go through that ever again!"

"What again?" I asked innocently.

She stalked off.

"Well, Barb," I deadpanned, "if you're just tossing words around…"

She whirled around and stamped her slipper into the floor. "Christ! You make me so angry! Now get your socks off, too. They're soaked, in case you haven't noticed. And not on the floor. In the hamper."

"*Achtung, bitte.*" I gave her a Nazi salute.

She shook her head, her hazel eyes flashing, and went back to her Bosch.

I sat down on the mattress and picked up a book. But I was too tired to read. No, it wasn't that. My mind was clear and my body quiet. I was still in a way I'd never been before. I watched Barbara working the puzzle. *Tosca* was over thank God and now the room was filled with a piano piece by Satie. I found the pauses in the music so alive. They reminded me of Barbara. She was very still, silent. That was her natural way. That had attracted me at once. I could never name it before. We had met in a small church on Park Avenue at the wedding of a mutual friend. I remembered I was sitting in a pew, thinking of nothing, when suddenly I see coming down the aisle this incredibly beautiful young woman. My attention was immediately captured. Tall, slender and erect, she moved so gracefully and without the least conceit. She seemed very silent, contained, remote in some way. I felt a certain mystery to her. As she passed my pew, I felt an extraordinary quality of sensitivity. There was something very deer-like to her. Her face was very long and angular, with full wide lips and hazel eyes. The neck was thin and very long like a swan's. Her hair was long and brown. I had never seen a woman like this. The image struck something so deep in me. I was totally transfixed, and she had not even said a word. I knew I had seen her before. But where? Where? Modigliani! Yes, she was like one of his women. I'd kept a poster of one of his reclining nudes taped to a wall in college. Just then a thought shot through my head like a bullet— *That's the girl you're going to marry!*

I wanted to get out of that church—immediately.

But the ceremony had started. I was trapped. I resolved to leave at once but the bride called to me after the ceremony. She said the reception had to be cancelled and asked if I would take some of her friends to dinner. So there I was hosting five women at the Brown Jug over on First Avenue. Among my dinner companions was, of course, my Modigliani woman. She hardly said a word and took no particular notice of me. I remained captivated. There was something so serene about her, so fine and measured, so feminine. Her name was Barbara Allen and she was from California, some place called "Topanga Canyon."

A few evenings later, I took Barbara to dinner at Pete's, a small Italian restaurant by Gramercy Square. She was polite, attentive, but said very little. I told her story after story. I couldn't get her to open up. Later, we went to see an avant-garde French movie, *Ground Zero,* at St. Marks Place. As we walked back to the Sage House, her boarding house in the Village, I talked about the film. She listened but made no comment. My heart sank. I just couldn't get her interest. When we arrived at the boarding house, I asked—in desperation—"Well, what do you think?"

She smiled softly and very gently corrected the French pronunciation I'd used in talking about the film.

I was shattered...Jesus!

But then that long swan neck extended and she kissed me on the lips. Very soft and very moist and alive. The kiss was so delicate, so beautiful. Ah! The beautiful Barbara Allen and Sweet William! My heart sang the whole way home.

That weekend I took her up the Hudson to the outdoor pool of the New York Athletic Club. I hurriedly undressed and got into my bathing suit, and waited outside the women's' changing room. I didn't think about it, but I guess I expected she'd wear a full-piece bathing suit as she seemed rather reserved—but there stood my Modigliani woman in a golden bikini.

It was the first time I'd seen the full line of her figure. The perfect proportions of her shape, especially the smallness of her waist which only emphasized the hourglass roundness of her hips—the sight thrilled me. I felt, as well, such a sense of the feminine with her. Yet blended with this was an interesting masculine quality, like a subtle wash in a quiet watercolor.

My ardor must have embarrassed her, for when she saw me she did a little dip to the side, her long slender arms opening out like a ballerina, her smile a question to me as much as a greeting. It was more then either of us could contain, and we set off immediately for the pool. On mad or divine impulse, I dared to audaciously put my hand on her bare waist. An electric shock shot through us both. On her skin I felt the goosebumps rise and beneath it her hip bone shifting back and forth as we walked. Stunned, barely breathing, neither of us speaking, as soon as we got to the pool we both quickly dove in.

We dated for a long time then. After *In New York* went bankrupt, I moved in with her. I was there about two months when one evening at dinner she asked:

"Are you serious about us?"

"Of course, I'm serious," I said, wondering what she meant.

"No, I mean serious…serious about a real relationship."

It was a weekend and we were having dinner. I'd lit candles and opened a bottle of red wine. The apartment was dark except for the candlelight and the moonlight coming through the windows.

"But isn't this 'real' enough?" I asked. "I mean…we're living together, aren't we? Isn't that enough?"

She said nothing. I felt her sadness.

"You mean…what you're talking about is 'marriage'?" I couldn't believe it. We had never once discussed it. She had never even hinted at it.

She nodded.

"But…but I hardly know you."

"We've been dating now for five years," she said softly.

"I know. But, Barb, you keep changing."

She smiled and cleared the dishes.

A month or so later we got engaged. Engagements back in my hometown lasted two or three years. I was figuring on something like that. I was buying time. I hadn't figured on Barbara's mother. Like all mothers, every time she called she wanted to know: "Have you set the date?" Barbara kept putting her off. But the pressure built.

Marriage made no sense to me. I had no money. I was out of work. I was burned out. I didn't even know if I could ever work again. Barbara worked at Rockefeller Center editing a newsletter for the Agricultural Development Council. Her future looked bright. Mine, except for the Work, was all black. Finally, I gave in. We set the date: October third.

During the next days I tried to self-remember. The thought would remind me and I'd try to "feel the body," dividing my attention between the mind and the body, but in a flash I'd forget. It seemed so easy, at least intellectually. But self-remembering wasn't intellectual. I tried to explain it to a friend. He thought it was no big deal. He already did remember himself. When I told him he was asleep, it was just like Ouspensky said. He woke up for a moment, then fell right back asleep. His whole world was happening in his head. He had no experience of his body. But, of course, he didn't see it. In him, I could see it all so plainly—why couldn't I see it in myself? With a philosophical friend I talked about the different "I"s.

"What is it that knows it's sitting here?" he asked. "I *know* I am sitting here, of course. How can that be questioned?"

"But who is this I?" I asked.

He thought about that a moment. "The I that knows, that's aware of itself."

"But what is this self you're talking about?"

"Hey, I just know that I know and that's it, right? Questioning my own sense of existence is a nice parlor game but it doesn't lead anywhere. Caterpillar or butterfly, I still exist, still have to pay the rent. The either/or problem still comes back to me. You know, me, the knower of me."

I was amazed. He was angry. Discussing his notion of himself was somehow forbidden territory. He was so open on so many subjects. I had the impression there was this wall around him. That he couldn't hear and (this seemed odd but was a fact nevertheless) he was not supposed to hear.

I went on experimenting with self-remembering. Nothing earthshaking happened. But little by little I came to realize it took energy to self-remember. It was like sticking your finger into a fast-moving river. The unceasing pressure to "go down stream" was so great. I got distracted so easily. I'd even find myself thinking about self-remembering, *thinking* I was doing it, but it was all thought. As the days went on, I suddenly saw something else: my attention was all up in my head. Particularly the forehead.

Despite the failure—and I came to wonder what I meant by that word—the idea of self-remembering began to dominate me. I'd read about it, think about it, talk about it. I'd get up in the morning and all I would wish was to remember myself! The intensity might make me relatively awake for a split-second or so, but then life as usual. The waking dream state. Then I realized that wasn't being awake. That, in fact, I didn't know what the word meant. If I didn't know what it meant to be "awake"—did I know what it was to be "asleep"?

It was depressing. And funny, too. When I was really down about it all I thought I was being serious, that in some way I was remembering. But this was just a form of what I came to call "Work sleep."

The next week going to the meeting I ran into Soren. We were early so he suggested we go to the Ex-cel, a coffee shop on Lexington. "It's where a lot of 'workees' hang out," explained Soren. "Run by Greeks. Workees pretend they're in Alexandropol. You know, that's where the big G. was born."

Soren slurped his coffee, talking a mile a minute, taking in the whole scene. Soren told me he was into symbols, magic and chemistry.

"You into symbols?" he asked.

"I don't know."

"Well, you're not."

"How can you say that."

"If you were, you'd know.

"How would I know?"

"How would you fucking 'know'?" Soren stuck his kisser right in my face. 'Where'd LP get you from anyway?"

"Why do you call him 'LP'?"

"Why don't *you* call him 'LP'?"

"It sounds, I don't know, disrespectful."

"Ouspensky calls Gurdjieff 'G,' doesn't he? Pig-fucker! The Work must be really getting hard up to take in someone as illiterate as you."

"Look! What makes you—"

"Now-now-now. Let's not identify. Feel the energy in you now, the raw anger. You're a mesomorph, a warrior type. Probably want to hit me now, huh? That's a lot of mechanical shit. Right?"

He was right. I was angry, there was an impulse to smash him. It felt right. But that "rightness" was maybe part of the sleep, the identification.

"Look!" Soren said.

He took a napkin and drew a complicated design on it. It was a triangle enclosed in a circle. Then he drew a strange angular line through the circle and triangle. I'd seen it somewhere before, but I couldn't quite remember. Soren said it was the key symbol of the Work. If you could read it, it showed how the three foods, physical food, air and impressions, interacted to produce the substance to make a Kesdjan body, or soul.

"What's that?" I asked.

"Gawd! They really turned down your lights this time, didn't they?"

I felt the anger surge in me, but this time it didn't reach my head. It was odd. I was watching my anger.

Soren gave me a mincing little smile. "Hey, you're learning! Good. Well, look"—he held up the napkin—"know this, my boy, and you know everything."

I stared at the crude design. I suddenly realized what it was.

"Right," Soren whispered, giving me a big smirk. "The enneagram."

I pressed him for more information, but instead he talked about this Jungian painter he knew in the Village. He thought I should meet him. "You were breast-fed, right! Well, Casey has all these college girls he gets to pose for his classes. You'd go ape. Hey, well, it's about that time. Can't be late for the Big Banana, can we?"

"The who—?"

"Why do you pretend you don't hear when you don't like what I say?" Soren's eyes glared at me.

He had caught me.

"Well, I don't know—"

"Yes, you do."

"Why do you demean him like that?"

"Judas priest! What a goody-goody we have here. Self-righteous son-of-a-bitch, aren't you?"

Soren shot out of his seat. He leaned over the table and, first checking that no one was listening, whispered: "The Work is gnostic, impersonal, buddy boy. The faster you get that through that thick head, the better. Now let's get outta here."

The basement seemed a little less forbidding now, the people not so odd. The meeting began as before. Silence, the "eye ceremony," then more silence. This time I was the first to speak. I told Lord Pentland of my experience of shifting back and forth—being in the room, then out of it. I had heard myself speaking, too. I had never heard myself before. And when I had finished the story of the dog handler and he hadn't replied—well, it really shocked me.

"The experience kept coming back to me all week," I said. "Then one night I woke bolt upright, and I suddenly knew why…"

I had been looking at Lord Pentland all the while, but now I suddenly felt embarrassed. I wasn't sure why—I didn't know what I was going to say next. But my heart began thumping, my breath choked. I felt like there was this big hand pushing against me, warning me to stop. I struggled to speak. Finally, I got it out—

"…why I really spoke up last week was that I wanted…I wanted…your attention. My question wasn't real. I just wanted your attention."

The room went totally dead.

Lord Pentland sat smiling at me.

It was as if I had crossed some hurdle. He seemed pleased. I felt his energy coming to me. It filled me. I had this odd sense that we were alone in the room.

"But why is it," I asked after a time, "that we have to suffer to understand? Why can't we learn without suffering?"

"We have no real and permanent I," he answered. "Rather, we are composed of many different 'I's. Each of these 'I's is like a total person, a complete belief system. One 'I' takes us over completely. Very often this 'I' knows nothing about all the other 'I's. One 'I' may do something then and the others know nothing about it. Realizing this truth—that what you call 'Patterson' isn't real—demands a very large payment."

That week I read and reread Ouspensky's *Search*. I compared passages, underlining key ideas. After a bit, the architecture of the book became more apparent. I saw how an idea was introduced, then in succeeding chapters developed and connected with other ideas. In a way, each idea was a circle, one that continued to widen and interconnect with ideas on its level, as well as with those above and below it. Everything was connected. The scale of ideas was enormous. There was such a deep feeling that resonated throughout the book, but it was buried beneath the ideas. People I showed the book to felt it was "too intellectual, not enough feeling." They seemed to mistake sentimentality for true feeling. I was amazed that they couldn't see it.

I kept wondering why I couldn't see myself as clearly as I saw other people. One night, propped up in bed with *Search*, I had the feeling that the book was speaking directly to me. The answer jumped off the page. I couldn't see myself because I still took myself to be a unity, a real individual. I couldn't stand the shock and suffering of seeing how contradictory I was. I didn't want to see how I continually said one thing and did another, and papered over this inconsistency with some facile rationalization. My life was being lived in the service of all my "I"s. I couldn't see the "I"s because of what Gurdjieff called "buffers" between the "I"s. These buffers were like psychological partitions, or screens, that separated the "I"s and kept them ignorant of one another. My whole psychological structure had divided and partitioned itself.

In reading and rereading Gurdjieff's mind-twister, *All and Everything*, a new perspective began to be established. Slowly, bit by bit, I began to see that a payment was demanded. Nothing was free. I had to volunteer to consciously work and consciously suffer. I must stop identifying so much, stop giving in to my negativity, my self-pity. I must work so that the non-desires dominated my desires. I must struggle to see my many "I"s—see them impartially, without blame. Then one day, in the heat produced by our long and relentless struggle with my "I"s, the fine inner substances that this friction has produced in me will be coated and crystallized. New and more intelligent bodies will be formed. New vibrations will be established. Then "I" will be I. I will actually be what I have only imagined myself to be: a real man, free, impartial and independent. I will be I, without quotation marks.

Every meeting now became more and more riveting. Lord Pentland's answers were like a food for which I'd long craved but was too starved to know it. At one meeting the fat man, Paul, asked about his life, its meaning. His voice and manner were serious, earnest. I began to see I had judged him and I didn't even know him. Lord Pentland answered him with such feeling. I realized I had judged him as well. This judging was going on all the time.

"Each life is a unique life," said Lord Pentland softly. "Each moment is unique. All we can know is the life we have and that one day it will end. We can know nothing beyond that. We can theorize. We cannot know. We are like a dying leaf falling from a branch. It is a waste of time to speculate about what we will find when we land, and it prevents us from knowing that we are falling."

Helen, the ethereal blonde (who continued to dress in black) asked: "Very well, Lord Pentland, but what about good and evil? Aren't they a part of everyone's life? And if they are, can't I know more than just my life?"

"There is no good or evil," he answered. "Only lying."

At another meeting Lord Pentland was speaking about the scale of things, visible and invisible, and how normally we have such a small idea of their real function and purpose. Soren asked about remembering yourself when you eat.

"Do you know that physical food is first being food?" asked Lord Pentland.

"Yeah," answered Soren. "Of course."

"I don't think so," observed Lord Pentland. "To know the scale of something…to be able to remember when you are actually eating, for example, would be a very big movement."

Philippe asked about the relationship between real will and self-will.

"Real will," said Lord Pentland, "can only come from unity. Otherwise, it is simply the will of one of our 'I's. Not yet being whole our actions, regardless of aim, can never be pure. We must give up self-will again and again. Self-will can only be given up when it is active. Mr. Gurdjieff said that the non-desires should predominate over the desires."

I related an observation about trying to fix a record player. "I collected myself before trying to fix it," I said. "But when I couldn't, I tried to force it."

Lord Pentland scrutinized me. "You have interesting and important experiences," he said at last, "but you ask such small questions."

His answer was like a slap in the face. I didn't get angry. He had "hit me" with absolutely no emotion.

"The question is rarely the one we think it is," he explained, his voice softer. "It is never the well thought out, intelligent construction. It is the one we are almost afraid to ask, the one we would never ask, because we don't think it's worthy of being a question." He paused, "I think Mr. Gurdjieff would agree with that."

The way he said "Gurdjieff" I had the impression that he still talked to him; it was as though for him Gurdjieff had never died. That he lived on in some way. Perhaps Gurdjieff lived on in Lord Pentland.

There was another quality, too. It had to do with hearing. I recognized I had never heard anyone speak like Lord Pentland. He had such a strange way of communicating. He would speak in long spirals, taking something ordinary like walking into a room full of people or eating a heavy meal or taking a first sip of tea on a cold afternoon—and going up and down with it, exploring every nuance. It was as if he was playing scales. I would think I was following him, but then realize that he had lost me long ago. Then he would come right to the point, and everything he had said, like a giant kaleidoscope, would suddenly interconnect and emerge.

It also had to do with his uncommon use of ordinary words. He would sometimes use words, usually quite common words, with a particular or peculiar pronunciation or intonation that gave them new meaning. He used words artfully but without affectation. At just the place where an "I" would defend itself, his words would corkscrew through the jamming mechanism, coming as they did in overtones or undertones, their pitch ascending or descending, the tempo changing, even his voice dropping to a barely audible whisper, so that to hear, you were forced to give all your attention. He used his voice like a paint brush. It was now moist or wet, now dry, hard or feathery. It nourished and enriched the words, giving them a life beyond themselves. For long after their original utterance, sometimes days, weeks and even years later, they still "echoed" in you. And sometimes, like little time bombs, his words suddenly exploded in you with all their intended meaning. He spoke, then, in dimension, easily moving from one level of vibration and meaning to another, always knowing where he was, never getting lost. There were no dead, mechanical spaces. And as with *Meetings with Remarkable Men*, Lord Pentland chose to communicate by intentionally trying not to communicate. He played the group as if we were an instrument, arousing our attention, then deliberately making it difficult to hear him or follow his train of thought. The result was that we all strained to hear, our attention totally galvanized, captured by his every word. Just then he would say something that bewildered or befuddled us, shocking our attention back into ourselves. In this way, he showed us that we had identified, fallen completely asleep, had forgotten to remember ourselves.

After one meeting, Lord Pentland motioned to me. He said if I was interested, I could begin an exercise. I was to sit quietly with my eyes closed, wait until I had come to a certain stillness and then direct my attention on the body. I was to do that for ten minutes a day. "Perhaps you can report on what you discover at the next meeting," he said.

I began the next morning sitting cross-legged on the edge of the mattress in the living room. I closed my eyes but they kept blinking. I heard sounds of cars passing on the street below, a bus grinding gears along York Avenue, the radiator moaning. There was a long period of quiet. Then I heard this strange noise. Finally, I realized it was Ayesha playing on the floor with a dry lima bean. Her paws were sending it skidding across the floor. Then she would pounce on it, sending the bean skittering again. I had watched her do that a thousand times. But I had never heard it. The wind lashed the window panes, the skylight rattled. A buzzing noise came close and a fly landed on my forehead. "This" was what I was going to report on?

As I continued to sit each day, focusing my attention on the body again and again as time and again I found myself in a web of thoughts, I suddenly became aware of how sounds distracted my attention. I went deeper into myself, paying no attention to outside sounds. As I relaxed more and more, the sensation of the body changed. It felt less hard, more fluid. But my attention would still distract me. I would lose myself in a thought and not even know it. I only knew I was lost after I was lost. I would get angry with myself. Then I recalled Lord Pentland saying the anger was a judgment, another thought. Identifying with it meant going to sleep again. The mind seemed to be always moving. It would be still for a few seconds and I would clearly have the impression of the body. But then off it went again. What would still the mind?

One day I dozed off while sitting. I awakened with this sound in my ears. It wasn't an ordinary sound but a sound below that of everyday sounds. It was like a streaming vapor, a running brook, or steam from an old locomotive a long way off. I listened intently, trying to come to an exact formulation. The current of "sound" went on and on. It was always there, but on a frequency lower than that of everyday sound. I wanted to talk about "the sound" at the next meeting, but what to say? It would sound so peculiar, foolish. I thought the sound might go away, but it didn't. In fact, I began to hear very high electronic sounds that would come in and over it, and then disappear.

I said nothing about this at the meeting, though several times Lord Pentland looked at me pointedly, silently urging me to speak. I kept telling myself I would at the next meeting. But something in me kept resisting. Maybe I was just hearing my blood, I told myself, or had an early case of tinnitus.

I AM IN A CAVE. IT IS PITCH BLACK. I HAVE TO FEEL MY WAY ALONG. MY HANDS come to a corner and guide me around. Ahead, light pours through an opening. Crawling closer, I see Lord Pentland sitting on a brocaded pillow atop a big slab of stone. A few others from the group sit around him. The cave is lit by torches. I sit down on the big stone next to Lord Pentland. No one speaks. We listen to the sound of the cave, the stillness. After a long while, Lord Pentland puts books of matches on both my knees. Without his speaking, I understand I am not to let the matchbooks fall.

"Would you like to hear about yourself?" he asks.

He speaks very softly but I hear him perfectly. He begins to tell me who I am—or rather, those things that keep me from being who I am. But the words are like water. I can't hold them. They pass right through my fingers. I concentrate all my attention.

"…and you are petty," I hear him say.

Others from the group crawl through the opening.

"I can't hear you," I say. "They're making too much noise. Speak louder."

Lord Pentland sighs. He seems riled. "Of course you can hear," he declares.

I realize then: I didn't want to hear. A sense of shame comes over me. I hear one word about myself and it seals my ears. Being half-deaf is a defense, a lie.

Lord Pentland looks at me sternly—"You can hear, if you really want to."

I woke up. The dream had been more vivid and intense than the ordinary world. It also conveyed a message. *Petty.* I'd never thought of myself like that. What did he mean? The word was a surprise. I recalled Lord Pentland once telling me in a meeting, "See doubt in yourself." It'd surprised me then, too. What kept me from seeing myself? Why couldn't I see myself like I saw others? Were we really all blind? I remembered asking Lord Pentland at a recent meeting, "How can I distinguish between imagination and truth? I feel like certain things are true."

"Feelings have nothing to do with it," Lord Pentland replied sharply. "Feelings can tell us nothing. All we really know of our feelings are the results of injured feelings. The way to know is to first experience wholeness." He paused. "We cannot be whole as long as imagination takes us from ourselves. It is difficult to talk about imagination for the more we talk, the more we imagine. Instead of using imagination to see the future, we should use it to return to the past, to inspect those times when we have not lived up to ourselves. We have passed these moments by. They will never return. They're lost and not repeatable. We should not expend crocodile tears over this, but rather see where and why we lost ourselves. Only by using imagination in this way can we, perhaps, come to a point where we will know something about it."

Imagination had become a question for me because I had begun dreaming a lot. Not the usual chase and run dreams. But what I call "teaching dreams." Lord Pentland was in one dream. He was talking to me about hypnosis when I suddenly awoke. There was a spot of bright light on the wall coming through the window. I stared at it. Suddenly, inside me, a voice began talking. Not in individual words but whole paragraphs of feeling, of intuition. My brain acted as a relay, stepping down the vibration, rendering it in human words.

Lie still, said the voice. *Do not forget your body.*

I put my attention on my body sprawled out in the bed next to Barbara.

Just as you want to get up to the astral plane, it said, *there are spirits that want to return to earth and are looking for bodies to inhabit.*

I wondered if I was going crazy. That was nothing like the inner chatter, the dialogue, that went on in me. This was on another level entirely.

You realize now that you can't do anything yourself—that you aren't conscious and can't really know. You should surrender and act as a vehicle. If you just sit quietly, you will be told what to do, what to say.

For a long time there was only silence, a waiting. A great flow of energy coursed through my body. Finally, I asked:

"Who are you? Where do you come from?"

You're not mature enough.

"How do I know that yours is a good voice?"

This can only be established over a long period of time. It takes trust. There was a pause, then the voice added, *You screwed up the last time, you know. It was over power.*

"What!?"

You thought you were doing it, instead of God.

"What are you talking about?"

Do you remember reading that magazine, Inner Space?

"That was months ago."

It had an article on a medium who communed with a spirit called Seth.

I remembered now: After having read the article I felt this subtle force, an inner urging, directing me to take a walk. I didn't want to go on any walk. It was silly. Finally, I relented. Nothing happened, but from then on I would be awakened in the middle of the night and this voice would tell me to go to the East River or somewhere. The energy at those moments was enormous. And that sound below sound would be loud in my ears. Reluctantly, I would be out on the streets at three or four in the morning. Barbara thought I was finally going bonkers. During one early morning "visitation," I woke her up. I felt this light coming from my forehead and my throat. Barbara opened her eyes and screamed. Then the next morning, taking down a bag of garbage, I lifted the garbage lid and saw—placed neatly on the heap of refuse, face up—a copy of a Hari Krishna magazine. I felt it had been placed there purposely. I thumbed through the magazine. The artwork was very gushy, idealistic, naive. It disgusted me.

That magazine in the garbage can—it was a test.

"A test?"

Seekers fall into two categories. Either power or love. You have chosen power.

It was true. I didn't want to love. I wanted to know. I wanted knowledge, real knowledge. And, yes, knowledge was power, though I had never thought of it that way. But I hadn't made any choice. It hadn't even been a question for me. But I realized now that given the choice, I would choose knowing before loving—I wanted to know what I loved, not love blindly.

I never heard the voice again but afterward the "tests" came in other ways; though, of course, I never perceived them that way.

One of the strongest and most unusual came when Barbara and I went to the New School to hear a concert of ragas by an Indian holy man, Pran Nath. We were going up the aisle at intermission when behind me I heard this infectious childlike voice ring out—"Hello there, luv!"

I turned. There was a small, beaming magical creature with long curly copper-red hair. She had large luminous eyes, green and cat-like, circled with black kohl.

"Hello, luv," the high child's voice sang out again in an Australian accent. "What's the matter? Don't you know me?"

I'd never seen her before and yet I knew her. She was such a bizarre sight. Long cascades of thick red hair. The green eyes set against the corpse-white skin. Necklaces, amulets, bracelets all jangling with her every move. Layers of colorful sequined clothes festooned with beads. But strangest of all—the tattoos. Around her lips was a black lyre-shaped design. Each cheek had three small full moons. And the back of each hand bore very intricate Celtic-like designs.

"Vali," I cried. "It's you! What are you doing here?"

She rushed into my arms, her body all warm and soft. She buried her head in my chest and squeezed. "Ohhh," she giggled, "I've come to sell some drawings from, you know, 'the weird time.'"

Vali hugged Barbara with just as much abandon and did a little dance of glee, her skirts swooshing back and forth, the ornaments jangling.

I felt a strange sense of reliving all this. I felt like I was awake and asleep at the same time.

Vali and I had never met, but we had exchanged several letters. That was a few years ago after a review I'd written of an underground film for *In New York*. She lived in the hills in southern Italy, far away from everyone. Her only companions were her husband, Rudi, a pet fox, Foxy, and a menagerie of goats, pigs, chickens, geese and dogs. She drew these colorful, dramatic portraits of herself, Rudi, her animals and dream figures—they were highly imaginative, somewhat sinister, and painstakingly rendered. The style was rich in fantasy, magic and powerful sexuality.

"Vali, how did you know it was me?" I asked. "I never sent you a photo."

"Oh, I didn't know, of course," she answered, her bracelets tinkling together. Her head cocked from side to side as she bounced back and forth on her bare feet. I noticed both her feet were tattooed as well. "It just happens, you know. You meet whoever you're supposed to meet. And you just know them, huh? That's all, luv."

Following the raga concert, Vali invited us back to an artist-friend's loft on 17th and Broadway. There was a party for her there that night. She wanted us to come. There was no resisting her.

As we walked up Fifth Avenue—Vali skipping and dancing along—she wanted to know if we had seen the solar eclipse the previous Sunday. It was the day she arrived, she said.

"Watching the sun slowly vanish," she recounted, "watching it shrink into a tiny crescent and then disappearing—ohh, it was such a sight!"

"She's so alive!" Barbara murmured.

We entered a big, heavy-looking building. The elevator was out so we had to walk six flights, Vali taking the steep steps like a mountain goat while we trudged behind. The loft was pitch black except for a single amber bulb hanging by a long cord from the skylight. The eyes soon adjusted to the darkness. The loft was filled with Village-types stretched out on the floor, leaning against the walls, arguing, taking tokes, necking. On the walls, like faint billboards, hung huge canvases. All depicted exotic female nudes, each fantastically rendered and dripping with sex. From the two big concert-size speakers came Led Zeppelin. Jimmy Page was doing one of his intricate guitar riffs on "Stairway to Heaven."

It was a vintage Village scene, the kind I'd always wanted to be part of.

Vali handed us papercups full of cheap red wine and darted off, greeting everyone in her laughing little Australian accent—"Hello, luv! How are you tonight?" She seemed to view everyone as either an old friend or a new playmate. She exuded a tremendous energy, blowing kisses, waving, dancing little toggling steps to and fro. She was like a goddess of delight. But beneath the sparkling surface, I dimly sensed another "Vali." This "Vali" was not to be taken lightly.

I remembered George Plimpton's piece about her in his *Paris Review*. Vali had been born in the Australian outback. Vali's parents were Irish; her father a sailor, her mother a violinist, her best friends, the aborigines. In her teens Vali had become the leading dancer with the Melbourne Modern Ballet Company. She left Australia for Paris in 1949. There, living on the Left Bank, she posed for Picasso and other artists, and spent her nights dancing till dawn. A favorite haunt was the Bal Negre on the Rue Blomet frequented by dancers from Senegal and the Camerouns. A lover of the mystical, darkness and the moon, Vali was devoted to the Irish poets, particularly Yeats (which she pronounced "Yeets"), and to Thomas Chatterton, the eighteenth century English poet; he a suicide at eighteen by arsenic. She took heroin and opium, got hooked, and became a street walker. She lived with Colette's housekeeper. She was wan and dying when she was found by an Austrian warlock of sorts, Rudi, who took her into the hills of the Almalfi coastline overlooking the Mediterranean.

"God! Look at her," whispered Barbara, "she has no fear."

Vali laughed and joked, treating everyone as friends, regardless of their reactions. Her vitality and openness overcame all resistance. Soon the sound of Led Zeppelin and the Stones died off and into the room came a thunderous African drum beat that shook the walls. Instantly, Vali sprang out onto the floor, dancing under the amber light bulb, her knees bent, her bottom stuck out and gyrating, her bare feet, jangling with ankle bracelets, stamping out a powerful beat on the wooden floor. Her arms undulated like snakes as her flaming mane of hair whipped from side to side—the room was all Vali.

"For chrissakes!" a voice in the darkness said. "Who's she?"

One French writer, having seen her dance, described Vali as "a cheetah on a leash." In this loft there was only cheetah. No leash.

Someone said he'd seen her dance at the Albert Hall in London, fronting a Rolling Stones concert." She's far out, man. Far out!" said an appreciative voice. "Yeah, Jagger really got off on her."

The drum beats trailed off and Vali came and sat with us on some old pillows and cushions. We lit a candle and sIpped the rotgut wine. In the candlelight, her face bathed in shadow, Vali looked like a white Maori. She told us of her early life in the outback and how she went on walk-abouts with her aborigine friends.

"What about your tattoos?" I asked.

"Me mum has one on her chin," she said. "All the tattoos I did myself." Vali preened, laughing at herself. "I've given the gift to many of my friends," she added.

I nodded but said nothing.

"It's a mark of kinship," Vali whispered.

I nodded and felt shivers.

"Would you like one, luv?" Vali's eyes danced with light and excitement.

"No. Thank you, but—"

"Luv, I'll just give you a little fox face or a half moon," she giggled, the green eyes begging and teasing. With her index finger, she drew a little half moon on the back of my right hand. "Why we could put it right here," she suggested. "Would look lovely, it would. Do you dare, luv?"

I felt a weakening. There was such a force to her. I almost agreed but something warned. I became aware then of this "yes" and "no" inside me. There was a big struggle.

"Oh, c'mon, luv. It would look so lovely!"

"No."

Vali looked so sad, like I had refused a very special gift.

"I'm sorry," I said, and touched her hand. It was so warm.

She brightened then took my hand and lifted it near the flickering candle. She poured over my palm, the candlelight dancing on her face. She minutely inspected each line, pinching the skin here and there, spreading the fingers, pulling them back, extending the thumb—this was serious divination.

"Well, luv, was the drink that did you in the last time. That's for sure."

"What?"

Vali laughed. "You were a seaman and drowned."

"What?"

"What else do you see?" Barbara asked.

Vali scrutinized my palm again, her eyes following the lines as if she was reading a road map. Occasionally, she made little knowing sounds. Finally, she closed my fingers and gave my hand back to me.

"Capable hands," Vali stated. She gave capable a special meaning and my hand a little squeeze. "Can do whatever you want in this lifetime, luv."

I nodded.

"Up to you."

She might return to New York sometime soon, she said, and would like to see us. I gave her our phone number.

The loft filled again with drum beats. Vali gave a big smile and then, like a great cat, she was up from the cushions in a leap and out onto the dance floor.

Several days later another powerful and exotic being entered my life.

His entrance was innocuous enough. One morning shortly after the meeting with Vali I opened the mailbox and there was this ornate and colorful flyer. It told of the arrival of Chogyam Trungpa, Rinpoche, the eleventh Trungpa Tulku, or divine incarnation. Discovered shortly after his birth in 1939, the flyer said the tulku had been enthroned by the Gyalwa Karmapa, the head of the Karma-ka-gyu school which dated back to the monastic tradition founded by Gampopa, a pupil of Milarepa, in 1079. Thereafter, monks rigorously trained the boy tulku in the secrets of Tibetan Buddhism. At nineteen he was appointed Supreme Abbot of Tibet's Surmang Monasteries. With the Chinese invasion in 1959 he and a large band of monks escaped, making their way on foot over the Himalayas. Sent to the West by Karmapa, he attended Oxford University, and founded a monastery in Scotland. The tulku, a Master of Crazy Wisdom, was now bringing the dharma to America. One statement in the flyer particularly struck me: *The East has answered questions that the West has yet to ask.*

How could that be? I wondered. How could there be questions that we hadn't even asked?

I reread the flyer. Suddenly I recalled the rumor that Gurdjieff was the Tibetan lama, "Lama Dorjieff." More interesting, Gurdjieff had received initiation and teaching at the mysterious Sarmoun Monastery. Surmang and Sarmoun? Could it be the same monastery? The idea tantalized.

I felt this urge to see the tulku. I knew Lord Pentland would be against it. "Mixing teachings and teachers," I had heard him say, "is like mixing drinks when you don't know yet how to drink." I knew that was true, yet the idea of meeting this young master of crazy wisdom—he was only thirty-one—fascinated me.

"Why do you always want more? Why are you never satisfied?" Barbara said, exasperated, when I told her about the tulku.

"Look, babe," I said, "I'm dedicated to the Work, but...well, I don't know. Don't you see? When was the last time you met a Tibetan tulku?"

Barbara shook her head. "You're incorrigible," she said.

"Ahh, Barb—you're just afraid I'm going to run off with the tulku," I said.

She gave me her patented "you're-hopeless" look, and went back to her crossword. Barbara didn't talk much, but when she did it was usually right to the point. With just a few words she cut through layers of bullshit. She rarely went to excess, rarely indulged. Lord Pentland had brought her into the group a few months after me. Though she feared him, she had a great respect for him and the Work.

I kept the pressure up about seeing the tulku. Finally, Barbara gave in. He was in Canada now. No one knew when he would cross into the United States. Memorial weekend was coming up. I had a hunch. And so that weekend Barbara and I hitchhiked to Barnet, Vermont, a tiny rural community, where the tulku's followers had bought a farm called Tail of the Tiger.

It was twilight when we arrived at a winding dirt road that led up the hill to the farm. Nobody around. Just land. All this space. It seemed strange to get out of Manhattan. And the sky seemed so still, so empty. It was a luminous grey that seemed to have no end. The sun was just going down and a new moon was already up. A roly-poly, jolly American girl with thick glasses and long black hair came down the road.

"Hi, there, my name is Kesang. You're very lucky. Rinpoche has just arrived," she called. "He wasn't expected until next week. How'd you know he was coming?

You must have good karma."

"We felt something and just took a chance," I said, elated.

Kesang nodded approvingly and led us to the large ramshackle farmhouse. We went in a side door to the kitchen. She went off to get Rinpoche. The farmhouse was on its last legs. The whole place had slipped and tilted to one side. The big plank floor, like the whole kitchen, was rather charmingly off center.

Presently, Kesang appeared in the doorway. She motioned and laughed and soon into the kitchen hobbled a small boyish figure. He wore a yellow pullover, much too big for him, and leaned unsteadily on a cane. He seemed painfully shy, ill at ease. This was the eleventh Trungpa, a tulku, a realized and reincarnated being, the Supreme Abbot of the Surmang Monasteries? We had come all the way from Manhattan for this?

He bowed to us. We sort of bowed to him. A strained silence followed. We all just stood there gawking at one another. Finally Kesang, embarrassed, explained that Rinpoche had had an auto accident in Scotland. He had been driving back late one evening to the monastery, she said, and his car had slid out of control on a curve. "And what do you think he crashed into?" asked Kesang, laughing. "A joke shop!"

We all laughed. Then the boy tulku bowed again and hobbled away.

I felt sad but relieved—there was no comparison between the Lord Pentland and this tulku. We thought of leaving, but it was too late. The next afternoon, as we were packing up, Kesang came by. She mentioned that in a month or so Rinpoche would be giving his first seminar in America. Rinpoche would lead meditations and lecture on Gampopa's *The Jewel Ornament of Liberation,* a sacred Buddhist text. Would we be coming? I hedged. Kesang said if we liked he could arrange a private interview with Rinpoche. I really had no interest in seeing him. "Oh, c'mon," cried Kesang. "You've come all this way. Don't stop now." We looked at each other; me, wary and him with an infectious twinkle in his eye. "What's 'Rinpoche' mean?" I asked. Kesang's face fell silent and she said simply but with so much feeling, "Precious One."

Not long after, Kesang was motioning me down a narrow, creaking hallway to a room at the back of the farmhouse. The foundation had apparently slipped even more at the rear of the house, and the floor was so tilted it was like walking in a fun house. And when I opened the door, just like in the old horror shows, it even creaked. The room was small and dark. The only light came from a small half-opened window. A light breeze blew the window's one tattered curtain. The room seemed empty. As if no one was there. Then, behind me, I felt a presence. I turned. There behind a small desk sat the boy tulku. But he was no longer the boy tulku. Instead, I was face-to-face with an imposing figure, perfectly still; an ancient, timeless look set on his Asian features. He was impassive, yet alert. There was this strange quality: it was like he was there, and not there.

I sat down on the dusty plank floor. I looked up at him. He took a long puff from a cigarette. Then he took a sip from a can of beer. Whatever I expected, I didn't expect this. We sat for a long time just looking at one another. Now and then, he took a puff or a swig of beer. But his dark Oriental eyes never left mine. Finally, I handed him the gift I had brought, an Indian fighter kite. I had read Tibetans were fond of flying kites. He accepted the kite silently, inspected it, nodded, and put it down next to the ashtray. Then took another swig of beer. His eyes stayed locked on mine. I didn't like looking up. It was making me angry. Why wasn't there a chair? But I wasn't going to look away. Suddenly, his hand made a quick motion, tamping out his cigarette in a small ashtray. It was already piled high with butts. Then he tossed the beer can in the metal waste basket, lit up another cigarette, and unceremoniously burped.

Somehow, I had thought it was protocol that he speak first. Where I'd gotten that idea I couldn't remember, but I stuck to it. My eyes weren't moving but my mind raced around, running out all sorts of scenarios. At one point, I noticed that the contours of his face began to move. It was like I was looking at him from underwater. It gave me a weird feeling. I remembered then my Father coming home from work, the *Pittsburgh Sun Telegraph* under his arm. He'd go up to bed, lie across it diagonally face down, his hands on either side of his face, and sleep before dinner. I'd look at the paper with its big red headlines, war pictures and stories. My Mother would read it to me. The stories were about how the Japanese were torturing and killing American soldiers. My Mother would mutter under her breath: "Those dirty rotten Japs, the yellow cowards. Torturing our poor boys like that!" Her voice was shouting in my head and, all of a sudden, I became aware that I was looking at this Tibetan character who reminded me of one of those Japs—inscrutable, heartless, cruel. I wondered: could this guy read thoughts?

"Do you have a question?" he asked finally, his voice high-pitched and squeaky.

I thought a moment. I had forgotten what brought me here. The image of "the Japs" still fresh in my mind, I found myself asking—"What's the difference between imagination and reality?"

He didn't answer at once. My impression was that he sort of ate the question. Finally, he said having imagination was something like buying a new suit. That we have a certain feeling, a certain expectation about the suit. But once we wear it, get to know it, then, "The suit becomes what it has always been—a suit."

Who was it was that had the imagination? Who was it that had the reality? Who did all this occur to? I asked.

"No one," replied Rinpoche, his squeaky voice very definite. After a long pause, he added: "There is only Mahi Ati—what is."

He exhaled then and long streams of smoke whirled from his nostrils. He reminded me of a Maha Kala, a horrific fire-breathing wrathful deity.

I persisted. "What is it that is? "

His face vibrated. He told me: "Only the wild space of nowness."

"Why don't I experience it, this Mahi Ati?"

Rinpoche polished off a second beer, tossed the can in the basket. The can pinged on the rim but fell in. He looked decidedly bored. He burped again, loud, and began to speak, talking in a disinterested monotone of the lack of discriminating awareness that gives birth to the person, and that this idea of the person gives birth to karma, and the whole wheel of birth and death. "All imagination, all samsara." And he added, "Americans have very fertile imaginations."

"What stops us from remaining in discriminating awareness once we've seen that the person isn't real—that he's just a grand bit of imagination?"

"Mistrust." The word went right through me. Mistrust.

Quickly, Rinpoche reached down, picked up his cane and, with some effort, stood up. I did as well. He put a hand, small and fragile, on my shoulder.

"I hope we can talk again," he said softly in that funny squeaky voice, his tone suggesting that he somehow needed to talk to me.

"Of course, of course," I heard myself say, full of nauseating 'person.' How was it that I was hearing the stupidity but couldn't stop it?

Rinpoche grinned, giving me a toothy smile and patted me on the shoulder. I felt as if he were telling me he understood everything I was experiencing, and that it was all right. I could be a conceited ass. It was okay.

For a few moments we stood together, saying nothing.

"Silence…" Rinpoche murmured, "is when the heart speaks."

Barbara saw him after me and came out all aglow. We decided to stay the night. The following morning we were saying goodbye to Kesang and some others in the vegetable garden. Just then the farmhouse door creaked open and a small figure limped quickly out onto the slanting porch. He was dressed in a silky purple shirt with long billowy sleeves. He wore jet black pants and around his neck was knotted a bright red scarf. The sudden image, his clothes and especially his manner and vitality, made Rinpoche seem like a magician-king. In his hand he held the red and gold Indian fighter kite.

But Rinpoche could hardly walk, much less run—how was he going to fly a kite?

The brilliantly colored figure stood on the porch, peering into the cloudless blue sky, still as a tiger waiting for prey. Soon, a gentle breeze appeared. He caught it perfectly, sailing the kite out into the air. The fighter kite was only a few feet from the ground, he had to work quickly and he did, his hand yanking the kite string in small, powerful, snapping motions. Little by little, the kite began to rise. Soon the red and gold kite was at roof level, flashing in the sunlight, darting and fluttering like a wild bird freed from its cage. Higher and higher it flew as the small powerful figure on the porch deftly snapped its string.

Rinpoche played with it a while. I felt he was reliving something. Such a vibrant sadness. Finally, he motioned me to him. He handed me the kite string.

"Don't fly too high now," the squeaky little voice laughed. Then the purple, black and red figure turned and limped off, disappearing through the doorway, the door creaking and banging shut.

On the bus back to the city, my mind still filled with darting images of a red and gold kite-bird. I slept most of the way back. When I awoke I saw on an adjacent seat a copy of *The New York Times*. I picked it up and began reading the sports section. The stories all read like a dream. Finally I came to the op-ed page. I never bothered with the editorials. But a headline jumped out at me:

"...and a Tennis-Ball Moon"

> It has recently been discovered that the earth and the moon do not make up an isolated, self-sufficient two-body system as men have believed for centuries. Rather, they are part of a three-body system whose third member is a tiny "quasi-moon" only a mile or two in diameter. Toro, as this third body has been named, wanders around the sun five times in the time that it takes earth to make eight circuits. When Toro comes too near earth—9.3 million miles at the closest point—earth's gravity tends to change Toro's curvilinear path so that on its next passage it is further away from earth; in turn, earth's gravity affects this revised path so that on its following pass it is closer to earth. Hannes Alfven, a Nobel Physics laureate, has compared Toro to a tennis ball being used by an earth playing tennis with itself. It is still uncertain whether Toro has always been a member of the earth-moon system or is a relative newcomer captured comparatively recently, say 400 million years ago. Dr. Alfven thinks Toro has been earth's unseen companion since the creation of the solar system; but, even if he is wrong on that point, the present evidence suggests that it will take at least 200 million years before Toro might conceivably crash into this planet.

Toro!—this moon was exactly what Gurdjieff wrote about in *All and Everything*. He claimed that in the early days, when the solar system was still being formed, a comet had crashed into the earth. The shock of collision had sent two large pieces of the planet flying off into space. The larger fragment is what we know as our moon and the smaller our scientists know nothing about. He called this smaller moon, Anulios.

It all had seemed so fantastic to me when I read it. I thought Gurdjieff was making it all up for some reason. But it was true. How had he discovered this? In the writings of pre-sand Egypt? At an Essene monastery? Among the Kashmir Shaivites of the Hindu Kush? In hidden schools of the Bon and Buddhist sects of Tibet? From inspired readings of ancient sources? Writings of the Pythagorean school? Plato's *Timaeus*? Nicomacus of Gerassa's *Theologomena Arithmetica*? Athanasius Kircher's *Arithmologia*?

When we arrived home, I quickly pulled out my books and began searching.

Nothing. I spoke to Soren who had compiled a massive library of very old books; his idea being that each would give fragments of the real knowledge and that, if he searched enough sources, meticulously cross-referencing, the whole hidden picture would begin to emerge. I thought the Toro-Anulios connection would really interest him. But all Soren wanted to hear about was our experiences with Rinpoche.

I COULDN'T LOOK AT LORD PENTLAND. I WAS FILLED WITH SHAME. I thought I understood what I was doing. But it was only now, here—sitting before him in the group meeting—that I realized my willfulness in seeing Rinpoche. He had talked so often about our not being who we thought we were. Our image of ourselves was a fiction, he said. We had never seriously investigated our notion of ourselves as an individual. Though we might say otherwise, in accordance with the teaching, we all still believed we had an independent will, that we could do. It took great courage and resolve to see the fact of the matter: that we were simply a bundle of "I"s.

This idea of the "I"s hit like a hurricane now. It was no longer just a concept. The "I" that had taken me to see Rinpoche was not the "I" that sat here in this chair. This was a different "I." This "I" screamed, pointed fingers, tore me apart. So who was I? The one that went to see Rinpoche? Or this one that wanted blood, my blood. Another "I" came up, trying to calm things, be reasonable. Another "I" shrank with guilt. The different "I"s came and went. They were so distinct now. Suddenly, I realized I didn't know who I was. But immediately I felt I must be the reasonable "I," the rational one, the peacemaker. This "I" could see that a mistake had been made but it was not so great that I should be sent to hell as this blaming "I" demanded. Was this real I? Was this the I that Lord Pentland spoke about?

When the time came for the "eye ceremony," I had to will my eyes open; the feeling of guilt was that heavy. Lord Pentland had such an uncanny ability to read thoughts. He would know at once where I had been. I expected a look of complete disgust, derision. Instead, his eyes were soft, sad even, when they came to me. And then I noticed his whole upper body and head were silhouetted with an electric blue light. The light hovered about him. Was this a halo? An aura? It was exactly what I'd seen in medieval paintings. But those were just representations. I closed both eyes. I opened them. The light remained. It shone about him like a mantle. A silent recognition came: *he is letting me see him.*

Helen asked the first question, her mouth set in that little pursed smile. Behind it I felt a smirk, not for anyone in particular but for life itself. She was a painter. Came from old wealth. Owned a townhouse in the mid-seventies. She spoke of going to Central Park over the weekend and seeing amid the beauty all the gambling, drugs, vulgarity.

"How can I see all this?" she asked in a plaintive voice. "See it without judging?"

"When there is complaint there is no seeing," answered Lord Pentland. "To see, the mind and body must first be quiet." He glanced impassively about the room, adding, "Those who aspire to be saints must look on many sinners."

Sinners. The word pulled tight in my stomach like a knot.

Ruth was smiling, nodding as if she understood perfectly. A tall willowy woman in her mid-forties, Ruth's disarming innocence hid her quite cunning and conspiratorial nature. An income tax expert, she had found the group through reasoning that if it existed, it would have to file tax returns. She had become the group's secretary, rising quickly, I was told, by volunteering whenever Lord Pentland needed something done. She looked on him adoringly, and brought him homemade candied apples like a school girl.

Ruth dabbled in astrology and offered to do everyone's chart in the group. At first I thought the offer was quite generous but then I realized she would know everyone in the group through their stars. I mentioned this to her. She giggled and pushed back her glasses and eyed me slyly. "Quite so," she whispered, intrigued that I had divined her secret agenda.

Before entering the Work, Ruth had lived for many years with a woman writer, an ardent feminist. Ruth and her writer friend had seen Lord Pentland together once a week for about a year. Lord Pentland stressed the need for "a payment." Finally, he told Ruth she could enter the Work, but not her friend. Further, that the relationship must end and Ruth must move out immediately.

"It was such a shock," Ruth told me over tea at a coffee shop one evening after a meeting. "Any other 'payment' I was prepared to make so, of course, wouldn't you know, he would pick that!" She grinned approvingly at Lord Pentland's insight. "But I really suffered," she added.

Others told me she was much softer now, "not so butch." Her clothes and manner changed and she was becoming a "Ruth" none of us, including her, had ever known before. I noticed that she was also developing a schoolgirl crush on Lord Pentland. At his instigation, she had begun dating men and had even had an affair.

Now she had come to the point of asking about getting along with her mother. "I come from a large family of Sephardic Jews and we're very close, in a way," Ruth said. "I try to get along with my mother but, well, we don't get along at all. Not really."

Lord Pentland smiled good-naturedly at Ruth. It was as if he were rewarding her. It was a big step she had taken.

"To achieve in the Work, we must come to an understanding of our mother," Lord Pentland began, his voice rumbling like an ocean wave. "After all, without our mothers we wouldn't be here. That's an obvious fact, but we often tramp right by it, if you see what I mean."

He asked her to think of some little thing that might please her mother, to give her that and, regardless of what her mother's reaction was, not to become identified with it. "Don't get caught up in guilt," he warned. "There is no payment in guilt."

"What's guilt?" put in Soren quickly. "Work books never mention the word."

"Guilt..." answered Lord Pentland, "is inner considering."

I was sitting in a stew of guilt. It was all over me. Inside, it was like a mad animal farm, the barn on fire and all the animals shrieking. All the blaming, explanations, justifications—it was all guilt, inner considering.

What was it that saw this? I wondered. What saw all the different "I"s?

Philippe, the crocodile man, a French engineer, spoke about remembering himself on a train. From the way he spoke I felt he had obviously rehearsed his question many times, played through the moves, move and counter move, like a chess master.

Lord Pentland acted as if no one had spoken.

Frustrated, Philippe expelled a blast of air. "Look, Lord Pentland. I see quite well that when I am asleep—"

"When I am asleep, I'm afraid I am just that—asleep. I do not see I am asleep until afterward. Isn't that true?" inquired Lord Pentland.

"Yes," admitted Philippe. "And that moment that I awaken I see how stupid I've been."

"Stupid is a judgement. It means I am still in reaction, still identified. I must be very quick otherwise I fall asleep and think I am awake. Do you see?"

"But—"

"What happens when we wake up, if only for a moment?" asked Lord Pentland.

"You wake up, of course! What is there to say?" shouted Philippe.

"There is nothing to say but a great deal to notice. Tell me, has anyone had this experience? Can someone tell us what it is like to wake up?" He looked about the group. His manner was challenging.

Not a single person spoke.

"Oh, come now," chided Lord Pentland good-naturedly. "Many of you have been attending these meetings for some time. We must have come to something, hmmn?"

Finally the weeping woman, her voice very low, tentative, ventured, "There is a kind of stop. It's like for a split second the dream stops. You see you have been in your head. You are suddenly 'there' in a way that makes you realize all else has been imagination."

"Yes, that's right. Thank you for that. There is a time to remain silent and a time to speak. It's important to know the difference. Now, tell me, please, if I get angry with myself for being such a dunderhead, well, where am I then?"

"You are back in your head. You are asleep again," said the weeping woman, now in a stronger, more certain voice. "You've identified."

"Quite so. Very good," nodded Lord Pentland. "Of course, if I see the thought and do not identify with it, I am observing. Isn't that true?" Lord Pentland looked straight at Philippe, who shook his head with a certain pride; like, yes, he had been right all the time. "But if I fall in love with the observation then, well, I am lost again. So you see this 'self remembering' and 'self observation' are by no means as easy as I might think, hmmm?"

As Lord Pentland spoke, I had come down into the body. I finally relaxed. It was subtle, so subtle I would ordinarily miss or dismiss it, but there was a new sense of myself sitting in the chair. Some areas of the body, I noticed, relaxed more easily than others. My breathing became longer, more settled, not as quick or shallow. At one point, I became aware of this tension in the forehead. Later, I felt a hard knot, almost painful, in the pit of the stomach. All this was interesting but, after all, what did it mean?

While I was thinking that over, I heard Paul ask: "Can we consciously—or unconsciously—affect another person?"

Paul taught ballroom dancing at a West Side studio at night and taught driving during the day. He worked long hours for little money. He kept his life so busy he had no time for himself.

Lord Pentland did not respond. Someone began to speak but suddenly stopped. It was as if Lord Pentland was demanding Paul to go deeper into his question, his feelings.

Paul was staring into the floor, fighting himself. "I'm thinking about my mother," he said somberly. "She's been, well, in an asylum. She's been getting better of late and I thought, well, that perhaps it might be because of my own improvement."

"We can give another person a spark," Lord Pentland told him.

Paul nodded but said nothing else.

A tense silence descended on the room.

My mind was still racing round and round about Rinpoche. I sat looking at Lord Pentland and the blue outline around his head and upper body. Finally, a feeling welled up in me and I just exploded:

"You said a few meetings ago that there is no such thing as "good" or "bad" in itself. And now you talk about saints and sinners and…and"—the words wouldn't come out! They were too big for my throat. I thought I would choke…

Lord Pentland waited patiently. He acted unconcerned; as if nothing were happening.

Finally, like a nasty glop of phlegm, the words finally shot out my mouth:

"If there's no good and bad, then how can there be saints, sinners and"—I took a long, deep breath— *"guilt?"*

The electric blue aura around Lord Pentland grew brighter. It was as if he had absorbed, eaten my emotion. The room crackled.

His face looked like that of a Chinese lohan sculpture.

He began to speak in that deep, familiar voice, just above a whisper. His mouth was moving, but I could not hear him. It didn't matter. I felt that he was stitching me back together. I'd had a psychic rupture.

Rick, a cabinet maker, asked a question. He seemed to be asking for an affirmation of some kind. His question, like most of ours, was only a means to a mind's end. It wasn't so much the words he used but the intonation that gave it away. Or was I imagining this?

I was getting tired. My mind wouldn't focus. One moment, the mind was here, listening; the next, eaten up with thoughts. Suddenly I saw Lord Pentland was right: I never knew when I was gone. I only knew that I wasn't here when I came back! Gone was gone. Dreaming was dreaming. Here was here. There wasn't any in between stage. Or was there?

In the midst of this I heard Lord Pentland use the word "idiosyncratic." Only he elongated it, pronouncing it as *idio-sin-cratic.* He had been answering Philippe's

question. He looked straight at me when saying the word, as if this was for me.
Idio-sin-cratic!

Like a pinball, the word caromed through my mind. Some part of me tried to block it. But he had put such a "spin" on the word it evaded all my defenses, lighting up one meaning after another: *I was an idiot. A sinner. Autocratic. Aristocratic.*

The moment went on. My mind had completely stopped. I was just sitting there.

Lord Pentland's eyes looked into me for a few moments, then he looked off into space. Then back again, but indifferently.

"Which 'I' is it," I asked, a bit uncertainly, "that is hearing all this?"

"I am here to investigate this question," Lord Pentland said.

"But how?"

"I must watch, observe. Not get caught up, trapped in the contents of my experience which are of no real interest. Our inquiry is into the experiencing itself. I can't go slow enough, if you know what I mean."

I nodded that I did and knew immediately that I didn't. Jesus!

"You understand?"

"Yes."

"Too bad," Lord Pentland declared and sighed.

On the way to the subway, Soren was going on about Jack Casey's art studio and all the nubile young models. Seeing I wasn't biting, he exclaimed—"Of course all that exposed pussy would probably scare your black Irish heart to death!"

"C'mon."

"Well, 'c'mon,' yourself. After all, you're into guilt, aren't you?" Soren deftly moved in and out, dodging a parking meter, a tree and a passing couple. "Big mammaries. A big threat to mommy love, heh?"

"Soren! What the hell you talking about?"

"Okay, so mother is on the back burner this week. Well, what about the 'Rimp'?"

"I shouldn't have told you."

"Look your 'Rimp' is only this week's guilt number, heh? You got plenty to choose from." Soren gave me a big shit-eating grin, smacked me on the shoulder and flew down into the subway station, two steps at a time. He was some weird bird all right. I liked him. He knew a lot, saw through a lot of crap. But there was something funny about him, too. I didn't understand his relationship with Lord Pentland. He always seemed to be fighting him, on guard, and concerned that he was having too much influence over his wife, Miriam.

I walked home, trying to stay in my body. But remembering oneself in movement out in the world made quite different demands than sitting alone in the apartment in the mornings.

Barbara had been sick and missed the group meeting. I told her about it. She laughed when I described how Lord Pentland pronounced "idio-sin-cratic."

"Your mother raised you just like Little Lord Fauntleroy," she said.

"What do you mean?"

Her brow frowned. She was surprised I didn't see it. "Well, you know, the little aristocratic lord…?"

"Ahhh, c'mon. You're making too much of this."

"Didn't you tell me that every time you went to someone's birthday party she bought her pride and joy a toy?"

"Okay. Yeah. But who isn't spoiled in some way?"

"Haven't you told me, too—god knows how often—about how your father's parents always thought of themselves as 'aristocrats' who had lost their wealth?"

"So…?"

"Look, your parents meant well," Barbara continued, "but they raised 'little Billy' in a black-and-white world that—"

Billy. Hearing the name my Mother called me had a strange effect on my body. I remembered my sister calling me that, unconsciously insisting I was still a child.

"What about you?" I shouted at Barbara. "Your mother had visions of the Junior League, right? She dressed you in white gloves and patent leather shoes. Is it any surprise that you end up winning that award. What was it? One of the ten best dressed college girls of the year."

"…and your world was all hammered together with those damn high principles and a holier-than-thou condescension. You drive everyone up the wall."

"You play the 'invisible' role. Act like you're not here," I said. "It's no better."

"You were given a picture of the world and you judge yourself and everybody with it. Why is it that nobody's ever good enough?"

"But look at the world—look at all the…"

And off we roared into another argument.

I had begun sitting for forty minutes each morning. Whether I was sitting or not, I continued to hear this sound-below-sound, or whatever it was. I wanted to ask Lord Pentland about it, but I didn't exactly know how to put it. He had given us a certain exercise of sensing the body when we sat. But we were only to begin it when we had come to ourselves, come to a relative stillness. Many images of my adolescent sexual escapades came up. I began to go back over my life. I sensed this strain of guilt running through many experiences. What was I guilty about?

One afternoon my Mother phoned.

"Are you all right, Pat?" she asked.

"Yeah, Mom. I'm fine."

"Well, is everything going all right. It's been a long time since we heard from you. Do you have a job yet?"

"No, no, a few bites. But, you know, nothing yet."

"It's been a long time, hasn't it?"

"Yeah, I suppose so. It depends how you look at it."

"Well, you know you can always come and live with us, get your feet on the ground, get a new start in life."

"Yeah, Mom, I know that. Thanks. I appreciate it. But, well, you know, a lot's happening here now. Things will turn around. Don't worry."

"Did you receive the Bible?" she asked.

"Yeah. Came a few weeks ago."

There was a long pause. "That's funny. We sent it—"

"Oh, yeah. Right. I remember now. I guess that was three months ago, huh?"

"Well…a little longer, I believe."

The conversation went flat then. We talked about how Aunt Ossie, my Father's elder sister, had come down and stayed six weeks and expected to be waited on and served, acted like some queen. Finally, my Mother began telling me what a good boy I had been, how my Father was so proud of me, talked to all their friends about his son up in New York and how I was always…she paused, "Well, you weren't like the others," she declared. "You always had a mind of your own. So serious. You were always, well, different."

"You mean like 'perfect,' Mom?"

"Well, I don't know about that. But close to it," she said. "You were the light of my life. Why do you remember when I would tell you all those Lone Ranger stories."

"Mom, you're a real natural born storyteller. You have a great imagination."

She didn't say anything for a moment. "Yes, but every side has two coins."

"What?"

"Just seeing if you're awake up there. You know what I mean. My imagination sometimes gets the better of me." She paused, adding in a lower tone, "I can imagine all sorts of things."

"You used to sing me songs, too, to bribe me into eating my lunch."

Over the phone came this wonderful voice from my young years.

> *You are my sunshine, my only sunshine*
> *You make me happy when skies are grey.*
> *You'll never know, dear, how much I love you.*
> *Please don't take that sunshine away.*

"Mom!" I laughed. "You're a real character! Do you know that?"

"You were always so serious, even as a child. I could never tell what you were thinking."

"Why was that do you think?"

"I don't know. Daddy and I never knew why. You asked so many questions. You just were, that's all."

"Say, tell me," I said, "I've been wondering about it—how did your dad treat you?

"What do you mean?"

"Well, I don't know, there was a lot of guilt going on, a lot of blaming, wasn't there?"

"Oh, no," she answered. "My father didn't talk all that much. But what he said—he meant. But there wasn't any guilt or blame."

"But what if one of you kids defied him?"

"No, no one ever did."

"No one? Ever?"

My Mother thought a moment. "Well, he just had to look at the kitchen wall and we'd all settle down."

"The wall? What was on the wall?"

"Oh, he kept a big horse whip coiled up there."

"So that was why no one ever acted up?"

"My brother, Bill, he was hard to control…My parents, you know, couldn't do anything with him. Bill never liked school. The teachers used to beat him. The truant officer was at our house so many times my mother and he became good friends."

"But when he'd stand up to your father—what would happen then?"

My Mother hesitated. "Why do you always make so much out of everything? This was years ago. What's all that matter now?"

"C'mon. I'm just interested, that's all."

"Well, now let's leave well enough alone. That's all water under the bridge."

"Mom—"

"Oh, for goodness sakes, he'd take him down to the barn and whip him. Now what do you suppose he'd do?"

"You mean the same whip your father used on the horses?"

"It was real and Dad knew how to use it. Bill found that out the hard way. Both were stubborn in the same way, but my Dad—he had the whip. After all, he was the Father."

lord pentland asleep! there he sat, eyes closed, even lightly snoring!

I had been asking him about the origin of this guilt feeling I had. I'd told him about going back over my life, and the conversation I had had with my Mother. He seemed interested at first, but as I went into more detail, trying to establish a psychological context in which to see better what I was feeling…well, inexplicably, Lord Pentland seemed to sag in his chair and, at one point, he even fought down several big yawns.

Finally, his head dropped to his shoulder—he'd fallen asleep!

I didn't know how to end my question. My mouth went on talking to this slumped figure who was just about to fall off his seat. I felt like killing the bastard. It was so hard for me to talk about this. I thought I should get some credit for being brave enough to bring it up. But he had brushed it off like it was nothing.

In the middle of a sentence I just gave up and stopped talking.

Lord Pentland jerked in his seat a few times, so much so that he shook himself awake. He looked around the room curiously. He didn't know where he was.

This whole meeting thing was really weird. Why the hell was I wasting my time with this oddball! In the middle of these thoughts I begin to feel this enormous radiation from Lord Pentland. My thoughts stopped. Finally, he spoke:

"It takes a great deal of work to see oneself. It does not come cheaply or quickly. You should understand that."

"I don't understand," I shot back. "The question I asked—"

"We are not engaged in a psychological exercise here," he sniffed. "The contents of one's life are of no interest to us. We don't realize how much we have been conditioned by ordinary psychology. Like many of these 'new movements' of so-called consciousness-raising, it's become part of the general societal sleep. A kind of inversion of values is going on in the name of the usual catch-alls of 'freedom,' 'justice' and the like."

He studied me a long time. I felt like he was weighing whether he should go further, whether I was up to it.

"You've heard of 'pearls and swine' I'm sure," he said at last, pronouncing each word as if dissecting it. "Well, one has to have the proper preparation, and this may be a bit too early, but let me hazard this much…" He glanced about the room, looking to see if there was anyone even somewhat awake. "The first step in self-remembering is to bring attention to the body. You see, I have the experience of the sensation of the body—of myself sitting in a chair, for example. I become aware of what is going on inside me as well as outside. Impressions become much sharper, more vivid…It gives an altogether different quality to the moment, if you see what I mean. What's important here is that we come to a certain 'inner separation.' We've got to be keen enough to separate what we take to be real from what is real, do you follow?"

"No," I admitted. "I'm confused."

"So you are," he agreed, smiling broadly. Everyone burst into laughter. "Try to remember this much: if I take everything I experience as myself—well, then where am I seeing from? Where is the struggle between the real and the imaginary?"

He had such a clear way of speaking. I felt like I was completely transparent to him. He arched his eyebrows and bent forward, wanting to know if there might be anything else that could be cleared up.

I told him I'd just read a book, *The Way of The Pilgrim*. It was about a peasant who had become enlightened through the constant repetition of the Jesus Prayer.

"I liked the first half a lot," I said, "but the second half I could hardly stomach—you know, where he goes into all this sin and guilt business."

Everyone roared again. I was angry. "I've never bought the idea," I declared, "that people were 'sinners' and had to ask for mercy, begging their father like little children."

Lord Pentland seemed to chew that over.

"I'm not looking for a father!" I announced.

Lord Pentland motioned to Vicki, the assistant group leader, that she should answer me. She smiled and shook her head. He nodded, appearing to understand. He gazed up at the ceiling for a time, as if he were calling on angels to help him with me.

"I am so mechanical," he said softly and with much feeling. "I have such a small area of free will, I know so little of what I am doing…how is it possible that I can have any genuine guilt?" He paused, his eyes searching us. "There is of course a difference between remorse and guilt. Remorse I rarely feel and almost immediately kill. Isn't that right? But guilt?…" He looked straight at me. "Well, in the end, it's not worth a penny of our time."

Soren began to say something—

Lord Pentland held up a hand. "The early Christians…" Lord Pentland stopped and reflected a moment. "Their practice was the 'Jesus Prayer.'"

He let that sit a long while. Then he repeated the words simply, without emphasis. Yet they rumbled off the brick walls—*Lord Jesus Christ, have mercy on me.*"

Initially, he explained, the prayer was given in this way. However, when a disciple had come to a certain level of understanding, an addition was given. He paused and said— "*Lord Jesus Christ, have mercy on me, a sinner.*"

The feeling in the room, the atmosphere, was so still. I could hear my heart beat.

"Are you implying we are not at that level yet?" Philippe said gruffly.

"We are not even on the map yet."

"Map? What map?"

"The Ray of Creation."

"Ohh!" exclaimed Philippe.

"The Jesus Prayer was a cry for enlightenment," Lord Pentland explained. "Of course, one not only had to wish for enlightenment and practice conscious action, but to achieve it one had to be lucky enough to have Heaven grant it. You see, there is a descent as well as an ascent. To know the difference when it is happening…that would be a very big thing." *

THE SECRET OF ASHA

PURE NONSENSE!" SNAPPED LORD PENTLAND.
I had spoken in the group meeting about hearing what I called "a sound-below-sound." I had been meditating and heard this sound. I had wondered about its origin, I said, and so one evening I had decided to concentrate all my attention on it. Soon, a mental picture came of this slimy green half-reptilian, half-human creature. I felt like it was in the room with me. I was afraid to open my eyes. Suddenly, I told him, the radiator gave a loud ping and my eyes popped open. The room was empty. "What is it that I was hearing?" I asked.

"There is nothing to what you've said," answered Lord Pentland. The words were terse, the feeling behind them severe. He paused, then issued a warning: "You're dealing with the profane."

The sharpness of his words rooted me to my chair. My breath froze. What did he mean? Why was he so angry? I felt like a pawn on a chess board.

"It was a sound below the normal range of sound," I explained. "It's a kind of humming sound in the background. Sometimes a high electronic-type sound shoots in over it. I think—"

"Now what book did you read that in?" Lord Pentland challenged. The words hit like a slap in the face. His upper body came forward, his eyes fixed on mine.

"But I didn't read it in any book. It just happened, that's all."

"You are not working on yourself. Instead, you are dabbling in stupidities and giving yourself up to your imagination."

"That's not true," I protested. "I read a lot, but I've never read anything that refers to that sound."

Lord Pentland slowly took me in, head-to-foot. He searched me in some way, looking for some weakness, but not finding it.

"But don't you think…" interrupted Helen.

A look from Lord Pentland stopped her cold.

"And I've never read a book on black magic!" I added angrily, the word "profane" still hot in my mind.

"So!" Lord Pentland cried. "You think you can do black magic, do you!"

A force from him shot into me. There was such derision in his voice. But I was angry and defended my ground. I refused to be cowed. He was wrong. Dead wrong. Why was he twisting my words? I was only reporting what I had observed.

The room crackled with tension. I wasn't backing down. Neither was he. Events had spiraled dangerously.

Vicki, the Armenian woman, spoke up. "Of course, nothing is 'nonsense,'" she said softly, "if looked at in a larger way. It is a report of what happened. Or, at least, what one believes has happened." She stopped and looked at Lord Pentland.

Lord Pentland nodded, acknowledging what she said. Vicki continued, carefully picking her words. "There's no way to tell if such a sound was actually heard, but from the way he spoke"—she nodded in my direction—"I think he has heard it. And this is a gift."

"A gift, yes," countered Lord Pentland quickly. "But, we all have our gifts. So what? How does that make us more conscious?"

"I've heard that sound, too," interjected Helen.

Lord Pentland agreed, his tone less sharp. "But still…what are we to do with it? How does it make us more conscious? Consciousness has many levels, many degrees."

"But how do I distinguish between imagination and truth?" I asked, utterly surprised at the turn of events and trying to understand. "I feel certain things are true but somehow…"

"Feelings have nothing to do with it," declared Lord Pentland sternly. "Feelings can tell us nothing. All we really know of our feelings are the results of 'injured' feelings. The way to know is to first experience wholeness."

Lord Pentland paused. His eyes slowly circled the room then came back to me. "We cannot be whole," he continued, "as long as imagination takes us from ourselves. It is difficult to talk about imagination for the more we talk, the more we imagine. Instead of using imagination to live in the future, we should use it to return to the past to inspect those times when we have not lived up to ourselves."

He glanced at Soren who sat sprawled in his chair, his arms folded across his chest, his long skinny legs stretched out, one cowboy boot crossed over another.

Soren snorted but sat up.

"And have we lived up to ourselves?" Lord Pentland asked, his voice gravelly, low. He turned the words in his mouth as if he were making pottery. "I think not," he said.

A long silence followed. The room pulsated with energy.

Lord Pentland again glanced at Soren. "The past will never return," he observed. "It is lost and not repeatable. We shouldn't expend crocodile tears over this but, rather, see where—and why—we lost ourselves. Is that clear?"

Soren sniffed and shook his head as if it was all a lot of rubbish. Slowly, Lord Pentland turned in his chair till he fully faced him. Soren kept staring into the red bricks, impervious and sulking.

In a deliberate, perfectly controlled set of movements, Lord Pentland's cheek muscles pulled upward, the skin at the corner of his eyes wrinkling, as the corners of the mouth turned up...and only then, when the movement had reached its full extension, did the lips part into a smile. A smile, but only so slightly. A smile for Soren who continued to glower.

"We can only remember ourselves for as long as we have the energy for it. But I'm afraid we are always spending our energy in the candy shop, indulging ourselves with sweets of the imagination. That, or leaking it away with negativity. It is a very big work not to express emotions that have turned sour, negative. It is only when we have a certain control over their expression that we can begin to study and struggle with them."

"What are negative emotions?" asked Ruth. "The Work says they're not real. That's hard to believe."

Lord Pentland drew back in his chair. "This is not a house of belief. Belief has no place here. Rather we are engaged in a scientific exploration of the world within worlds which we inhabit." He came forward now and slowly surveyed the group. "Our efforts turn negative so quickly—why is that? How is it that we can remain open only such a short time? The moments of coming to ourselves are so short. The liberated energy gives what might be called 'free attention.' And yet almost immediately it is eaten up by parasites whose psychological existence is fed by identification and negative imagination. Our attention is taken again...as it is at this moment if I have been merely listening with the head, captivated and seduced by imagination. Then there is no self-attention and I am, dare I say it...a-sleee-ep."

The word sliced and hissed through my body electrifying and momentarily freeing my attention. I had been completely caught up in the words. No sensation of the body. Completely dumb to myself.

Lord Pentland smiled slightly. He glanced at Vicki, then Helen. They both beamed. And with that the meeting ended.

I wanted to be alone. Barbara took the subway and I walked. I couldn't understand why Lord Pentland had answered me so vehemently. I was hearing the sound even as I spoke, so it wasn't memory and it wasn't imagination. And why the talk about "black magic"? I had never had any interest in black magic. I did have a taste for the peculiar and exotic, but certainly not the profane. What was he talking about? My head went round and round. I was going no where. I noticed I wasn't hearing the sound. It had left. Or perhaps I had left it.

I began sitting twice and sometimes three times a day. Each time I sat I felt as if I was unloading a lot of baggage. The mind more readily became still and I became aware of all these parts of me that were tense and hard. The sitting changed my tempo, balancing it, making it more compact and smooth. The body seemed to take on a certain "weight." After I sat I'd pick a time during the day to remember myself. Usually, I'd miss the moment. But the recognition of having been asleep was always a shock. When I didn't identify with the reaction, usually a judgment of myself, and kept my attention free, the sense of myself was so strong. I'd also attempt to remember myself for certain short periods during the day, say, when I went for a walk in Carl Schurz Park. But that, I found, was much too long a period with too many distractions. As I worked in this way, I chose actions that were smaller, shorter in duration.

Before going to sleep at night, I would close my eyes and recall the events of the day, beginning with when I first awakened. I would picture myself as I got out of bed, showered and shaved and sat. I saw myself going for a paper and coming back and fixing breakfast and feeding Thea and Ayesha. The mind always wanted to speed through things. I had to keep slowing it down. Thoughts would come up and reactions and I'd be lost. I'd start at the beginning again, running the reel of mind-film.

Lord Pentland had said that in self-remembering we had to get "the taste" of an observing I—one that would see "Patterson" and not get drawn into his world. For "Patterson" could never observe "Patterson." It was important, too, he said, that our observation differentiated four basic centers in ourselves: thinking, emotional, moving and instinctive. Each was a "mind" in itself and had its own thinking, associations, language, memory and so forth. The thinking center worked by means of comparison. The emotional center worked with feelings and emotions; feelings were always pleasant or unpleasant, never neutral. The moving center controlled all movement as well as dreams and day dreams. The instinctive center was made up of breathing, digestion, the five senses and, of course, the sex instinct. In observing ourselves we were to relate the phenomena to the proper center. It took a great deal of energy and discrimination to sustain self-observation and so, quite often, I found it was only "Patterson" observing "Patterson"; that is, one "I" was watching another "I." It was depressing. But, of course, that was a state as well. In making these feeble attempts, I came to the realization that I was asleep, virtually always identified with my thoughts and states. That galvanized in me a strong wish to wake up. At the same time, I noticed this feeling of hopelessness.

"No effort of this kind is ever lost," Lord Pentland counseled. "It makes a mark, something accumulates. There will come a time, when you would normally fall asleep, you'll find yourself present. Right now you are only remembering yourself by thought, by memory. Later, it will be different."

I noticed that, perhaps because of these efforts to be present, the quality of my dreams had changed. The dreams were speaking to me now. They had the quality of coming from a different dimension or level. I'd had a dream only recently in which I was awake yet asleep. An operation was being performed on the crown of my head. Connections were being changed and rerouted. The image I had was that of an old telephone switchboard where an operator transferred incoming and outgoing calls.

Soon, the summer recess was at hand. Lord Pentland began the last meeting rather quickly. "As this is the last meeting," he declared, "why don't we ask the question—Why am I here?"

No one volunteered an answer and so he continued: "I mean to say what is it that brings me here? Of course, there is a renewal of energy...but what else might there be?"

Helen said it was because of the "great sense of life" it gave her. "Most of my life is filled with dead spaces."

"Yes, that is all very well," Lord Pentland agreed. "But that's an explanation, isn't it? When I am faced with an unknown, what is the first thing I do? I give an explanation. If I don't have one, I find one. But we all had the chance to do other things, but we came here instead. Isn't that some clue? Do you follow?"

No one said a word. He had asked me that same question when we first met. Now, six months later, I still had no clear idea.

Lord Pentland continued, but now in an altogether different voice. "There will come a time when each of you will have to ask yourselves: 'Why am I here?' And the answer will have to fulfill not just the inner life but the external life as well. You will measure your answer against something in the external world."

The silence built. Still no one spoke. My mind was going like crazy, running out different scenarios. It was odd to be so aware of the mind as an organ; one among many.

"To find out why I do things," Lord Pentland declared, "I must begin not to do them. Suppose, for example, that I make up my mind that I will not buy a morning paper as I usually do. A struggle will ensue. I will find out then why I buy it."

He looked at Vicki. "Do you know why you are here?" She smiled, nodding, but remained silent.

"Many forces, many influences, are working upon us," Lord Pentland observed. "They change in power and position constantly. We must try to be aware of the process. You see, we have all volunteered to become conscious. Our aim is not to further our illusion of being awake with power, money or prestige but, rather, to see ourselves as we really are. This aim will call up many obstacles to our awakening. That is lawful. The recognition of certain situations or people and all that they call up in us as being, in fact, obstacles, is a necessary step in not identifying. The power of suggestion runs very deep, I'm afraid."

Ruth spoke about Gurdjieff not liking cut flowers in the house. Perhaps that was a national trait because Armenians do not like flowers in any place but the garden. On the other hand, perhaps he was trying to suggest something.

Lord Pentland laughed good-naturedly. He said we must not be too concerned with flowers. He looked at Miriam (who had recently come into the group) saying, "Flowers are nice to look at but we should not lose their scent in the process." He told a story about Mr. Gurdjieff and his students from the Prieuré giving movement demonstrations at Carnegie Hall. It seemed the men's room door and the door to the exit looked exactly the same. Any number of people had mistaken one for the other. At the end of one rehearsal, Mr. Gurdjieff had gone towards the men's room door, thinking it was the exit. "Mr. Gurdjieff later told us," recounted Lord Pentland, "that the momentum of his moving center was such that he had to summon every bit of himself to say—No!"

Lord Pentland paused, looking now to one, then another of us, craning his neck this way and that, searching for at least one person who understood. But no one! The corners of his lips pressed together. I felt his derision. It came right into me. I felt my anger— why did I always react with anger? And I felt, too, we were all hopeless, mechanical idiots. Even the faintest movement on his part caused enormous reverberations.

He suddenly smiled. "You see, I'm afraid we live under the power of suggestion. Most all of our thoughts and our so-called feelings are programmed. Mr. Gurdjieff always warned his students about suggestibility and yet...he would try to suggest." He looked at us slyly, adding—"Something interesting there."

Lord Pentland glanced at his watch. He smiled. "I expect this is as much work as we can assimilate for one semester," he said. "It is time for the summer break. We can begin again in the fall...or not. Whatever is the wish of the group."

"Yes," we all said.

THE GOTHIC CHURCH WAS IMMENSE AND MADE OF GRANITE. LORD PENTLAND had told me to be at the church by 7:15 P.M. I was to bring my passport. Halfway there I realized I'd left the passport at home. I figured it was better to be on time than go back for it. Entering the church, I find myself in the business end. There are many people working at desks, most of whom I know either from the Work or my past. I am motioned through an archway. I enter a vast, circular hall, like an ancient Roman arena, with tiered seating, horseshoe-shaped, mounting to the roof in a steep vertical ascent. Every seat is occupied. I stand on a small, brightly lit stage. There is a long line of people leading to a desk at which sits an older woman, hair in a bun, very businesslike, filling out registration cards. She is checking passports.

Instead of requesting my passport she asks—"What can you do?"

"I'm a writer," I reply.

"Where have you been published?" Her voice is no-nonsense.

I know but somehow can't remember. I go blank. I can feel her attention on me. I am embarrassed. I know I am a writer—what does it matter what I say?

"I wrote a four-column article once," I tell her.

She notes this, but in the margin of the card; as if she knows it isn't the whole truth.

"Where?" she asks flatly.

"New York Times," I answer emphatically.

She makes no notation. "I see—and did you get paid?"

She isn't letting me off the hook. Should I go on pretending? Or admit I can't remember?

Finally, the woman tells me another woman will be taking her place. "I will be in a room waiting for you," she says. "Please take your shirt off and I will wash your back."

The lighting has grown more intense. My eyes hurt. I look up. Hanging from the ceiling like a banner is a huge white sheet of paper. It is shimmering with light. There is handwriting on it. A very young hand. A report of some type, like a psychologist's assessment. As I read I realize it is all about me. A phrase leaps out: "He can do nothing until he learns what he can do."

What can I do actually? What can I take responsibility for? That woman wasn't joking. This is for real…A man appears in a white coat wearing a head mirror, the kind used for an eye exam. He motions me through another arched doorway. I look into the audience. There is Lord Pentland. He is looking on with some interest. The archway has Dutch doors. The top is closed, the bottom open. I can't open the upper door. Finally, I smash my way through. I realize then I could have just bent down and slipped underneath. I feel clumsy, stupid, foolish.

I was down at Soren's telling him about this. I called it my "Passport Dream." We were sitting in the kitchen. Small, cramped, painted a bright yellow, it was the only room with furniture. The only room, too, whose window wasn't covered with a large piece of black muslin. It was also the only room with electric light. In the rest, he burned candles. Most people in the Work were pretty normal but this Soren was one weird guy. But he knew a great many things. Sometimes, I got the feeling he was a modern day Merlin. Most people are either good with their heads and lame with their hands, or they can fix anything but their brain is shut down. Soren's hands were as good as his head. He could build or repair practically anything.

Soren sat leaning back on a beat-up chair, listening somewhat pensively. He was in his usual attire, ratty T-shirt, jeans and beat-up boots. The guy was so skinny and angular. He was a classic ectomorph. He reminded me of a giant centipede.

"That dream sure shows where your head is at," snorted Soren. "Always figured you for some covert religious freak."

"C'mon, cut the crap. What do you think?"

Soren rapped a beat on the table with a spoon. "Yeah? About which part, eh?"

"That sentence: *He can do nothing until he knows what he can do.* What's that mean?"

Soren sprang up, knocking over the chair, flung open the refrigerator door and took out a carton of orange juice. He poured himself a big glass, not offering me any. With the toe of his boot, he flipped the chair up, kicked it against the wall, plopped back into it, stretched out, and put his feet on the table, one leg crossed over the other.

"What do I look like? The Answer Man?" He took a big slurp of juice and wiped his mouth with his wrist. "I guess you think it makes you special, right?"

"C'mon, no games."

"Who do I look like?"

"Dr. Freud."

At that, Soren sat bolt upright in his chair, mimicking Lord Pentland, giving me the eye ceremony. Then yelling, his veins popping—

"It's a d-r-e-a-m! Got it? Just another fuckin' dream. Just like the one we're having now. Eh?"

"I'm talking about a 'sleeping dream'—not a 'waking dream.'"

"Who gives a rat's ass? All the same, isn't it?"

"Some dreams are 'teaching dreams.' They come from a higher place than the usual fear-desire type dream."

Soren jumped up and banged around in the fridge. "Miriam! You by any remote fuckin' chance know where the goddamn liverwurst is?"

"In the fridge, Soren," called a high sweet voice from the bedroom.

"Yeah? You find it then!" Soren leaned against the sink, arms folded.

"Look, I'm hungry. So stop the shit, huh? Make me a sandwich. I've gotta be at Casey's in five minutes."

"Miriam, he treats you like a slave," I told her.

"Hear that! You're my slave," chortled Soren.

Miriam stood by the fridge, holding up a package of liverwurst like a prize fish, peering pensively up at the ceiling, turning over my remark, as if she was in philosophy class. Finally, she said, looking at me—"Yes, I see what you mean. I suppose I am his slave."

"Well, why do you let this guy get away with it?" I asked.

"Butt out, buddy boy." Soren said, sticking out his chin. "Cut the white knight stuff, huh?"

"I think Pat is maybe right, Soren," mused Miriam. She was taking great care in the spreading of mayo on Soren's sandwich.

Soren shook his head in disbelief. "Next, you two will be on TV. God, what drivel," he spat.

"Soren always gets antsy, nasty 'I' up," Miriam told me, "especially when he gets hungry." She glanced appreciatively at Soren. "He's an old soul, you know."

Miriam worked diligently on the liverwurst sandwich, like it was to be her masterpiece.

"Miriam!" yelled Soren. "Put your mind to the mayo, huh? And I like rye, not white. Damn, you never listen, let alone remember."

Miriam nodded dutifully. She sneaked a glance at me, giving her patented much-put-upon smile.

Soren was still steaming. "My slave, that's a laugh," he said. "She's running the whole damn show here. She's just clever enough to hide it. You like playing 'Lady of Sorrows,' don't you?"

"Oh, Soren," sighed Miriam. "Skinnies need their food or they just go berserk."

On the way to Casey's studio, I pressed Soren about the dream. "Shit," he laughed, poking me hard in the ribs, "you're just a reincarnated Fundamentalist who somehow got washed up on the shores of the occult. You're just another empty soda bottle some fool stuck a ding-a-ling message inside. Why make something out of nothing?"

Casey's studio was just off Broadway. We pressed the buzzer and took a slow, rickety elevator to the sixth floor. Its heavy door banged open and suddenly there we were inside a large whitewashed loft packed with people and easels and tin cans filled with paint brushes. Soren pointed to a bespectacled, ruddy faced man with a shock of long white hair standing at a workbench. He was stretching a canvas. The man had a white mustache and wore a black and white checkered wool shirt. He chuckled when he saw Soren and me.

"Say," the man laughed, "look what the devil dragged in."

He put down the canvas, picked up a corn cob pipe, and came over to us, a big smile on his face. I liked him immediately. "Hello," he said to Soren. "Is your friend an artist?"

"Naw, he's no artist," answered Soren, elbowing me in the ribs. "Just another a closet sex maniac."

"Well-well-well," said Casey exuberantly. "You've come to the right place."

My face flushed. I smiled.

"We're all a bit like that, you know," confided Casey, winking. He motioned toward Soren. "Him in particular."

Soren was unzipping his leather portfolio and spreading his latest drawings across Casey's desk.

"That the best you can say?" sneered Soren.

Casey laughed, took a cursory glance at the drawings, made a few comments, and went back to the workbench. Despite his hearty greeting, Jack Casey seemed a little shy, introverted maybe; not altogether comfortable with people. It was like he was seeing you from a place deep inside himself, and not wanting you to know it.

A class was just beginning. The students, mostly women, scurried around, setting up easels, squeezing tubes of paint on to palettes, cleaning brushes. Then I saw on the other side of the room, by the door to the freight elevator, a very feminine young woman, willowy and naked, sitting in a chair on a small platform. Her eyes had a far off look, as if she were all alone, dreaming of some time long ago. Her breasts were large, her pubic hair full. She had hooked a long supple leg over one of the chair's arms, the other stretched out before her showing a long, lovely calf. One arm was cocked back on one of the chair's arms to support her, the other she draped along the other arm. I was fascinated. I'd never seen a woman pose naked before. It was so private, so personal. It was as if I was looking into her bedroom. In a way, it was the first time I had ever seen a woman, recognized the difference, the quality of "other." I felt Soren watching me. I looked over. He gawked and drooled. I was embarrassed. I had to laugh but I felt like punching him, too.

Casey quickly set up an easel and motioned to me. He pinned a large sheet of heavy paper to a board and clamped it onto the easel. He smiled, took my right hand, and put in it a stick of charcoal.

"Here, Pat" he said softly. "Now go to work."

I stared at the black stick.

"Don't think about what you're doing," Casey advised. "Just put down what you feel. Let it happen. Okay?"

He gave me a playful nudge, took a puff on his pipe, and walked off.

My easel was only some five or six feet from the model. I felt a fear in me—a fear of looking at the nude form reclining on the chair. I glanced at her, furtively, I made some pitiful little scratch marks on the paper. The high screeching sound of the charcoal rubbing on the paper gave me shivers. I looked at my fingers. They were black from the charcoal. It all felt so strange but soon, seeing that no one cared, I grew bolder and just stared at this incredible form before me. My eyes traveled all over her body, slowly taking in and savoring each part, the skin texture, the bones, the recesses and rises, the sloping softness of the bosom, the set of the pelvis. It was as if I was eating the impression of her. It was a rare food, a taboo food. I swallowed hard. Something deep down in me was stirring, coming to life. I remembered then a moment I had long ago forgotten…

I am standing on the porch and my Father is counting out fifty dollar bills to a fat, sweaty man who then hands my Father a piece of paper. My Father reads through it slowly, then tears it up. The man walks off and my Father, ignoring me, goes inside the house.

I had loved to draw. And when I was twelve or thirteen, I had seen an ad showing this drawing of a beautiful woman in the newspaper. "Draw me!" the headline commanded. The ad was for a national art contest. I drew her at once and sent my drawing into the Famous Artists School. Soon, I received a letter from the school telling me that while I did not win, I was "a diamond in the rough." I only needed an art education, the letter assured me, to succeed as an artist. One Saturday morning not long after, a salesman knocked on our door. My Father was asleep. The salesman told my Mother what a wonderful, raw talent I was. I needed only the proper instruction of the Famous Artists correspondence course. It was expensive but obviously really worth it. With me faithfully promising several times that I would complete all the lessons, my Mother signed the contract. When my Father awoke, we showed him the art materials for my first lesson. Instead of sharing our excitement, his neck got beet red and his face turned to stone. I had never before seen him angry like this. He made a telephone call. I didn't hear what he said, but in no time there was this salesman, back on our porch, breathless and sweaty, fearful, too, holding out a fat stubby hand while in angry silence my Father counted one-by-one a handful of fifties into his palm. I never drew after that. It wasn't that I had the urge to. I'd just never thought about drawing.

Twenty-three years had passed and now, standing in Casey's loft, I felt as if I'd come upon a long buried treasure—a treasure that all these years had silently awaited my discovery.

I knew I had to come back to the studio, but I had no money. Casey told me not to worry. I could pay him when I got a job. After that, I went to Casey's class every Tuesday afternoon and all day Saturday. I drew and drew and drew, spending hours, often whole afternoons, making drawing after charcoal drawing. One day, not saying a word, Casey handed me some old brushes and a few used tubes of paint. He took down the paper from the easel and put up a canvas.

"See what this feels like. Okay?" he said, squinting through his glasses.

Paint with a brush? Only painters did that. I was just hacking around. I was no painter. But Casey insisted, so I took the brush. He had gessoed over a used canvas. He clamped it onto the easel and handed me a palette. I began to paint the way I had first used the charcoal, furtively. Every time the brush touched the canvas, it gave a little, like it was alive. It seemed like a piece of skin. Something had transpired, a click. One that I could only dimly intuit. It was way beyond the level of the mind. Still, I painted as if my hand was crippled. The harder I tried, the worse it got. Weeks went by, me battling the canvas, getting nowhere, Casey standing behind me, smoking his corncob, saying nothing, finally walking off. Late one Saturday afternoon after everyone had gone and I was still doing battle, Casey said—

"Let's try this," Casey said and squeezed a whole tube of cadmium red onto my palate.

"What are you doing?"

Casey added little curly slurps of yellow ochre and ultramarine blue.

"Casey! What the hell you doing?"

"Give me your brush," he said. I handed it over, thinking he wanted to inspect the hairs. He gestured with my brush toward my painting, "Now go ahead and paint."

"Give me the brush."

Casey smiled and took the brush back to his desk and sat down. He folded his arms, and puffed on his pipe, paying no attention to me. I looked at the canvas. Then at my palette with all the colored nipples.

"You want me to paint with my fingers?!"

He nodded.

"But I'm almost through with the painting!" I told him.

"So?"

"So—I'll ruin it without a brush!"

"What do you want—a painting? Or do you want to paint?" he shouted.

I stood staring at the painting. I'd worked hard on it. Okay, it wasn't very good. But it was my first real painting.

Casey sighed and opened up an art book.

I looked down at all the colors. The thought of using my fingers to paint—a memory came up.

I was in the Army. I was on KP taking out the garbage. The redneck mess sergeant hollered, "What's wrong, Patterson? You 'fraid to get yore cotton pickin' hands dirty!" My Father was paranoid about germs. He had warned me about never sharing a soda with anyone. Before every meal, he always carefully inspected his plate, the knife, fork and spoon. A speck of what he called "foreign matter" and the plate had to go back to the kitchen.

The sergeant took my arm and led me outside to one of the big garbage cans. He stood on one side, me the other. "Roll up yore sleeves, boy!" he ordered. Then he grabbed my wrists and plunged my hands into the broken egg shells, the grease, the oil, everyone's leftovers. The smell was god-awful. Both our arms were buried up to the biceps in gook and garbage. Our faces were about an inch apart. He's got this crazy look in his eyes and garlic on his breath. He holds my wrists tight and moves my hands around in the slimy goop, laughing and roaring, "See, son. Jist good ole' red-blooded American garbage! Won't kill ya!"

I stuck an index finger into some cadmium red, whooshed it across the skin of the canvas. Put the other index finger into the blue. Made a jiggling line with that. Got some yellow with the thumb and worked that in. It looked rotten but it felt great. I broke out tubes of cadmium orange, sap green, Prussian blue, mixed them all together like colored mud with my hands and just splattered the paint onto the dripping canvas. It felt good!

As I worked, I became aware of a certain taste. My tongue was swirling around inside my mouth. Suddenly, I realized: I was tasting the colors! Red, blue, green: each color had its own taste. On the canvas itself—before it had all been just a mish-mash of color—now I saw hints of figures, faces, animals. The painting began "speaking" to me. I worked to bring out the invisible forms I was seeing. A whole silent world of form and shapes was waiting to come into existence. I brought the forms out of their world and into ours. Suddenly, I became aware that the canvas had depth. It had become three-dimensional. Alive. A world unto itself. The key to the world was perception. I was seeing. My vision, my creative imagination, had come alive. I had somehow stepped "inside the skin." I lived in that timeless world full of silent voices for I don't know how long. When I stepped back out, people looked at me funny. Like I had gone some place I shouldn't. Casey sat in his swivel chair in the corner behind his old oak desk, smoking his ratty yellow pipe, with a cat-like smile.

I looked in the mirror. My clothes, my face, my hands, my arms, even my hair—all covered with paint! I looked like a savage. Casey handed me a can of paint thinner. I went to the tub and cleaned my brushes and myself. I never did get the stuff all off me. And I didn't want to either. I knew that somehow I'd become a painter. Good or bad, didn't matter. I'd tasted the colors, saw the faces and forms, gone to the other world. A world of the psyche. A world of imagination.

TEN HOURS EACH DAY I MEDITATED IN A HOT, DUSTY OLD ATTIC. BARBARA and I had gone to Tail of the Tiger for Rinpoche's seminar on *The Jewel Ornament of Liberation.* We'd arrived a day early and put up a tent by a stream that zigzagged through the property. After dinner Kesang had asked if I wanted to see Rinpoche. In minutes I was again in the little narrow backroom. He drinking beer, smoking; me sitting uncomfortably on the floor. It was as if no time had passed.

I told him I was in the Work and about Gurdjieff. He had never heard of either. I described the practice of self-remembering. He didn't seem interested. I persisted. Finally, he told me:

"I don't give a damn about it."

"But what about—"

"Jealous gods. It makes jealous gods."

"But—"

His hand flew out like a sword, cutting the air in two. He didn't want to hear it. "Why did you come here?" he demanded.

I stared into the floorboards. I shrugged, smiled. It seemed so silly, but it was the truth. "I like you," I said.

He smiled.

"What you said last time," I told him, "really touched me. I could maybe repeat what you said but I really don't understand what you mean."

Rinpoche leaned forward, nodding his agreement.

"It seems to me from what I've read the heart of the Tibetan way is meditation."

He agreed.

"I want to learn how to meditate. That's why I've come."

Rinpoche took a long drag on his cigarette, tamped it out slowly in the ashtray. A sly little smile flashed across his face. "You *really* want to learn?" he asked in that high, squeaky little voice.

"Yes."

He took a swig of beer, considering my request. He looked as if he might burp but thought better of it. "All right," he told me finally. "Go up to the attic and sit. You sit every day for two weeks, ten hours a day. Okay?"

"Beginning when?" I was feeling unsure.

He checked his watch. "Tomorrow."

"But—"

"Tomorrow morning. Early."

I nodded agreement, but only faintly. I couldn't believe what I had done. I had just paid two hundred dollars for a seminar on *The Jewel Ornament*—and I was going to spend it sitting in some attic?

"You sure you want to do this?" asked Rinpoche, his voice squeaking with sweetness. Five hundred voices in me shouted "No!" I nodded my "Yes."

Rinpoche nodded, too, the movement of his head synched perfectly to mine. It was as if he was moving my head up and down for me. He proceeded to give instructions on meditation. I was to sit cross-legged, with the spine straight, the eyes closed, the hands resting on the knees. "Follow every out-breath," he told me. "Follow the breath all the way to the end of the exhalation. Then do nothing. Just let the inhalation happen naturally. Follow the out breath again. And so forth." He said if my attention wandered during the out breath, to bring it back to the breath. I was to follow the breath in this way for forty-five minutes. Then take a fifteen minute break. Then follow the breath again for forty-five minutes. I was to do this from seven o'clock in morning until five in the afternoon. Do that for two weeks. Then we would talk.

What the hell had I gotten myself into? For chrissakes!

Rinpoche gave me big toothy smile. As I left, he patted me on the back. It was as if he were a king sending an emissary off on a long, dangerous journey.

When I got back to the tent, Barbara was digging a rain trench. I told her about meditating in the attic. She was pissed. "That's my money!"

"I told you I'd pay you back."

"Good! And while you're at it up there—get a little common sense, too."

The next morning I was up at daybreak. It was a beautiful midsummer's morning. The air was so fresh that breathing seemed like eating air. The sky was vast. Off in the valley hung a single puffy white cloud. It looked like giant cotton candy. Down stream I heard someone rustling about. They turned on a radio. The Beatles sang, "Lucy in the Sky with Diamonds." Some crows and blue jays yacked. In the distance, a neighbor's big boxer barked. By the time I reached the farmhouse kitchen, my shoes were soaked with dew. I had a bowl of cereal, made a sandwich for lunch and filled a jug of water. I climbed up the narrow, slanting steps to the attic. I pushed open the door. It looked as if no one had been up there for years. Full of cobwebs, dust, dirt and debris. Piled up in one corner an old rusted bicycle with no wheels, a broken high chair. In another corner stacks of *Life*, *Look* and *Time* magazines, old newspapers. There were spiders everywhere. Here and there the remains of flies, mosquitoes, moths, rat droppings. Only two windows in the attic. Not much ventilation. I cleaned a space and sat down. I noticed the rafters were exposed. They looked like the rib cage of some huge animal.

By the rafters beneath one window I noticed a little gong, incense and a holder. So someone else had been here. That made me feel better. I set the alarm of my travel clock, lit the incense, rang the gong, and followed my out breath. Down below I heard floorboards creaking, water faucets running, a toilet flushing. People were talking, getting ready for the seminar. Damn!

I kept dozing off or day dreaming. I'd jerk awake. Nothing happened. I didn't know what I was expecting. But certainly not nothing. It went on like this. The attic got hotter, the air more sterile. But I resolved I would do this for two weeks. Barbara thought I was absolutely crazy. Days passed. Still nothing happened. I did notice I was able to follow the breath for a longer time without being distracted. One afternoon I had dozed off but instead of jerking awake and blaming myself I began to witness my thought-dreams, my mind dramas. My head was full of cartoons. Little stories of good and evil, of injustice, of righting wrongs and the like. Suddenly it struck me what tied them all together—me. "I" was the central character, the hero, the good guy. In the stories I was either victorious or victimized, powerful or misunderstood and rejected. In one mind drama, I was a Sinbad the Sailor character, almost drowning. Then becoming Captain Marvel at a typewriter. God, what crap!

My legs and back started to ache. Weird, sometimes horrific, images came. I took them as a distraction. Gave them no energy. I went on following my breath. More days went by. Still nothing happened. It became a question for me—what did I want to happen? I didn't know. Just not nothing. I did notice my energy kept changing. It would be dull or peaceful, restless or vibrant. Sometimes the mind was quite clear, lucid. Mostly, it kept running out scenarios. I couldn't shut it off. Finally, I became resigned. I just followed the breath. No expectation, no hope, no nothing. It was after that I became aware of the breath. The experience was so light, so subtle. The breathing was happening of itself. I wasn't doing it. I realized then my mind had been controlling the breath all along. The body hadn't been breathing. The mind had been breathing.

Time slowed, dissolved, moved in a different tempo. Space enlarged. Days moved by quickly. Thoughts became slower, not as intense. Outside sounds were no longer so sharp, so stinging. They were no longer reacted to but absorbed. The mind seemed to have submerged in the body. One morning I lit the incense and rang the small gong. The sound rang out trilling and undulating through the attic, its vibration moving into finer and finer gyres until finally it, like the incense, disappeared into space. I continued listening. The sound returned, now more subtle, its vibration rising and falling, speeding and slowing, enlarging...until it, too, passed into pure space. The mind stayed still. Again the ringing of the gong returned, the sound now even more subtle. And for the first time I realized...*I am hearing the gong.*

The day was so delicious. I was in such a good place I didn't want to stop sitting. I was coming up on the final fifteen minute break of the day. I continued to sit. It had become customary for Rinpoche and the others to come up to the attic at the end of the day to meditate. Just as I thought I had better stretch my legs, I heard the familiar thump and drag of a man painfully pulling his weight up the stairs. The door opened and he hobbled in, the others trooping behind. He sat down hard in the chair, and laid his cane on the floor. The gong rang. The meditation had begun.

I had been sitting now an hour straight. And there were forty-five minutes more before I could move my legs. Almost immediately, my knees ached. I continued to follow the breath. The tendons in my groin had stretched taut like piano wire. The lumbar felt like a brick. I continued to following the exhalation. Needle sharp pains shot up my back. Neck muscles began to bunch. I felt like I was sitting in flames. The floor cut into my ankles. Voices shouted in my head. I kept to the breath. The pain increased. On and on it went. Just when it seemed unbearable—Rinpoche's chair creaked.

Thank God! Just before he rang the gong to end the meditation his chair always creaked as he bent over to pick up the gong. All my pain immediately disappeared. I had made it. I waited. But no gong! The pain returned like an angry cheated beast. The flames roared. The bones in my buttocks felt raw against the hard floorboards. Voices screamed inside. I tightened down my will. The body broke out into a sweat. On and on it went. And, again, just when the pain became impossible—his chair creaked.

And again, like magic, the pain left. I waited. Nothing. Not a sound. The flames shot up again. I vowed never to move. "Trungpa, screw you, you son-of-a-bitch!" a voice shouted out in my head. "Take this body. I don't need it."

Just then the gong rang.

My eyes opened. There sat Trungpa, looking at me. His face betrayed no thought. He picked up his cane, slowly got up and with great effort, hobbled away.

The seminar was drawing to a close. A few evenings later, before the final morning session, there was a big festive dinner. It was a high energy time with everyone letting it all hang out. Especially Rinpoche. He would hobble up to someone. His manner was quite serious, as if he had a special secret for them. The person's eyes would pop open. Rinpoche, his timing superb, would stick a deadly little black pistol into the person's beatific face—and give them a blast of his water pistol right between the eyes. Rinpoche, echoing gales of squeaky laughter, would hobble away like some crazy Oriental Quasimodo.

Kesang and I went for a walk later. She told me that when he first met him, Rinpoche had been "a very fearsome character." In its early days, the Scottish monastery had been very rigid and traditional. Then, in traveling to India, Rinpoche meditated in a cave in Bhutan. It was the same cave in which Padmasambhava, the man who had brought Buddhism to Tibet, once meditated. Rinpoche received the vision: If the teachings were to spread in the West, he would have to take off his robes.

"When he returned to the monastery, no one could believe it," Kesang exclaimed. "Practical jokes, chasing girls, gin bottles stacked up outside his door. Our 'holy man' had become a 'holy degenerate.'"

Later Rinpoche had married one of his disciples. "A sixteen year old, large breasted, upperclass English schoolgirl," Kesang recounted. "Her parents were of course furious. It became a scandal and made all the papers."

"But why does he have to drink beer and all that to spread the teaching?"

"Rinpoche decided to jump completely into the Western life-style," said Kesang. "There won't be any difference between what the rest of us live and what he lives. He's going to communicate straight out of our decadence."

We walked up the road a bit further. I couldn't understand it.

"Look," said Kesang, "he's a fearless crazy wisdom guru. He's not going to teach in an orthodox way."

Kesang told me that Rinpoche considered America very fertile ground for the teaching. "He says it's super samsara here—all materialism and convenience stores. America, Rinpoche says, is living in the 'thick black smog of materialism.'"

On the way back to the farmhouse, Kesang explained that Rinpoche thought the belief in materialism was so heavy here that the lesser teachings, the Hinayana, must be first introduced before the higher teachings, the Mahayana and Vajrayana.

"Some people want to start off meditating on sunyata," Kesang said, "That's the void, emptiness, what we all are. Rinpoche says that sunyata is a dangerous medicine. If you take it too early, it can poison you."

"We are all 'empty'? What's that mean?"

Kesang picked up a stone on the road and threw it into the steam. "It means the person is a construct. You know, made up. Remember what the Buddha said? 'Emptiness is form, form is emptiness.' There's no one here, you see."

"So who's talking to me, who's here listening?"

Kesang told me Rinpoche taught that the lack of discriminating awareness, creates the sense of "I," a sense of separateness. This "I" in turn creates ego which produces mind. The mind creates thoughts, and from thoughts come emotions and action, and the tight web of karma.

I stayed up thinking about Buddhism and The Fourth Way. I could see in this description the correspondence to Gurdjieff's teaching of descending and ascending octaves, the involution and evolution. It showed how the primordial intelligence, will and energy of the Absolute is successively stepped down through the various levels or worlds of existence. As it descends through the Ray of Creation the original vibration steadily becomes denser and slower, less intelligent, more egocentric and deflected. In short: more mechanical, closed, asleep. In evolving, ascending to higher and higher levels of being, I realized the person would experience lighter and faster vibrations. That tied in. Was there some level where the individual completely disappeared? Then there was only awareness. No person, no soul. Was this primordial awareness what Gurdjieff meant by real I? Was this the root difference between Buddhism and Christianity?

Mindfulness, returning the mind again and again to a simple, bare attention— that was the basic Tibetan practice. Some thought it was the same as Gurdjieff's self-remembering. Yet in descriptions of mindfulness no mention is made of coming to a feeling of oneself or the body. And what about Rinpoche's saying self-remembering created jealous gods? Did he really understand self-remembering? Rinpoche was trying to bring the way of the monk into the everyday world. The Fourth Way, what Gurdjieff taught, was rooted in the world. It used shocks and resistance of everyday living as a means of transformation. One teaching was from the East; the other from the West. Buddhism contended there was no soul, only emptiness, sunyata. Gurdjieff held that man had no soul but he did have the possibility to make one. He taught that soul could become a real and indivisible I, impersonal and immortal within the solar system. Perhaps it wasn't which was right—both seemed right to me—but which best fit the seeker and the times.

The following morning a blanket of thick mist hung close to the ground. It had rained the night before and the ground was still soggy. After breakfast, we all met in the living room. We were all a little bleary eyed from all the partying the night before. Rinpoche sat in a wicker chair by the windows, sandalwood incense burning at his feet, a line of wildflowers making a horseshoe pattern in front of his chair. Rinpoche's eyes darted around the room, going from person to person, nodding here and there, smiling, chuckling, seeming to recall the moments he had had with each person during the seminar. Then we meditated for five minutes.

"Could anyone say what you imagine *The Jewel Ornament of Liberation* is about...or what you found particularly interesting?" Rinpoche asked.

A long, stilted silence.

Finally, Rinpoche began prodding people to speak. Some cracked jokes, others went into long discourses, some argued with others, one man walked up and took Rinpoche's cane. Rinpoche only listened. He made no reply. When most people had spoken, Rinpoche looked at me. Did he want me to speak? How could I? I had been up in the attic. I hadn't heard the lectures or read the book. Rinpoche kept staring into my eyes. Suddenly, I knew the answer. He motioned to me to speak.

"Everything that's been spoken of in the book is all true," I said, my voice clear as a bell. "That is, as far as words can take us. But even at their best words are only a description, a map to liberation. So, all these words, though true, were only a 'jewel ornament,' a bauble, contrasted to the experiencing of real liberation."

The words had come out of me so quickly I didn't know what I said. No one spoke. I looked into the floor, afraid I was wrong. Finally, I looked up. Rinpoche was smiling at me.

"That's right," he said.

On the bus back to New York City, I told Barbara that Kesang had said Rinpoche was going to settle in Boulder, Colorado.

"Several people," I said, "have already asked if they could go with him, be his students."

"What are you going to do?" she asked.

"I don't know."

"You know," she said.

It was the beginning of August. We were to be married in October. We were planning a honeymoon we'd remember forever. Just before Tail, a friend at IBM had called and given me a free-lance job worth $7,000. A part of that money we decided to spend taking a month-long honeymoon, traveling to Vienna, Istanbul and Ephesus, then on to Athens and the Aegean islands of Hydra, Mykonos, Patmos and Rhodes. We'd gotten all the brochures and begun laying out our itinerary.

"Okay, okay," I finally admitted. "I do want to go to Boulder."

Barbara looked out the window at the passing farmland, the big sloping hills, worn down with age and use. She made no sound. But inside her I could feel something breaking.

"Barb, I could study with him. Do you realize that? What that represents?"

She nodded, not looking at me, her eyes on the old hills far away.

"Babe, this is my life," I cried, trying to explain. "What I'm living for."

Miles passed. The bus rumbled on down the narrow two-lane road, the gentle, open farmland giving way to the telltale signs of a town beyond. I had expected her to cry, to argue. But there was none of that. Instead, she said she did understand and if that's what I really wanted, well, then, go. There was no rancor in her voice, no bitterness. And when she added softly, "If I'm still here when you return, perhaps we can get back together." I knew she meant it.

I was free. It was as easy as that. I could go to Boulder now with Rinpoche. I could see us talking together, meditating together, studying the dharma together, and, yeah, even flying kites together. All that I never had with my own Father. All that I had hungered for all these years.

The bus speeded up coming out of the curve. I glanced at Barbara. Still no tears, no anger. She was so strong, so brave in her own quiet way. It was so easy to miss her. A deep feeling came over me. The same I had felt in church that day. *That's the girl you're going to marry.* And I knew then that I could never leave her. That she was a part of me. That I wanted to become conscious, yes, but I wanted us to become conscious together.

I leaned over, taking the long, fragile face in my hands, turning it toward me. I kissed her lips lightly, and whispered:

"After the wedding, babe—let's both go to Boulder."

"IT SEEMS LIKE A LONG TIME SINCE I LAST SAW YOU," SAID RINPOCHE, SMILING.

He was wearing a grey three-piece business suit and sitting in a luxuriously upholstered chair in a Manhattan apartment, just off Fifth Avenue near Washington Square Park. He looked like an Asian businessman.

"It's a wonderful disguise," I told him. He seemed quite pleased.

I told Rinpoche about our marriage and honeymoon and related a dream I had...

I am in a bookstore, talking with a friend who works there. I am telling him I have quit school. The coach wanted me to run in the last track meet and I was no longer interested. We argued and I was leaving.

My friend asks if there are any books I'd like. I choose two. One, a big ornate book of Salvador Dali's paintings; the other, a book of magic by Aleister Crowley, a black magician. My friend has left the store. I begin to leave. A woman notices me and screams, "Stop that man!" Instinctively, I begin to run, crashing my way through mobs of shoppers. As I'm running I begin to realize what this is all about. I have these books and I haven't paid for them. I hear a harsh male voice yelling: "Halt. Halt or I'll shoot!" I keep running, all the time wondering why I don't stop. I feel the bullet in me. Then I hear the gun sound. Everything goes black. I come to and there is Rinpoche shaking my hand, smiling. I look down and see my dead body at our feet. Says Rinpoche in a comical little voice: "See? I told you there was nothing to it. Now remember this next time."

"The body dies," Rinpoche said. He waited for me to say something.

I realized I was wasting time. Trying to feel things out. Did I trust Rinpoche? That was my question. If I was going to ask to go to Boulder, I had to trust him. There were a lot of rumors swirling around him.

"You said once there are many charlatans pretending to be gurus," I began.

"I know you aren't a charlatan...but are you a sex maniac? An alcoholic?"

Rinpoche came up in his chair. The eyes squinted. He seemed—for a split-second—stunned. I was stunned that I had said it.

"No," Rinpoche chuckled in a sweet innocent child's voice. "I don't think so."

We both broke into laughter. I loved him.

"Could Barbara and I come to Boulder?"

Just as I got the words out a name shot through my head like a meteor: *Lord Pentland!*

"Yes. I think we could work closely." Then he added, knowingly, "You would have to work with others also."

I could hardly hear his words. Why had that happened? I pretended nothing had happened. I told him that I wanted to leave for Boulder right away, but Barbara thought we should be more sensible and wait until next summer when we would have more money. Rinpoche suggested we come out now and see Boulder and make arrangements.

Kesang was by the door when I left. "Well," she laughed, "I see you finally made the decision...or rather it's been made for you."

I smiled appropriately and left.

I told Barbara about *Lord Pentland!* shooting through my head.

"Why do you think that happened?" she asked

"Maybe we really are Christians...maybe this isn't right for us," I answered.

SOREN AND MIRIAM WERE ONE WEIRD COUPLE. I LIKED THEM BUT DIDN'T understand them. I wondered what they would think of our leaving the Work to study with Rinpoche. One weekend they came for dinner.

Soren had come in, thrown his denim jacket on a chair and plopped down on the mattress on the floor. He sat as if he was always putting down a heavy load. Miriam sat beside him, her legs crossed, hands folded, her idea of the perfect little lady. Soren was dressed as usual. The same raggedy-ass boots, last month's jeans with holes in them, an old t-shirt; this one with the face of Jimi Hendrix. Miriam was wearing a cream-colored raincoat, probably from a Lower East Side church thrift shop. For footgear she had chosen (or probably Soren had, for he liked to dress her) high, lace-up black leather boots with big platform soles. She reminded me of some of the females Beckmann had painted.

Barbara asked if she'd like to take off her coat.

"No, no, I'd better not." She had that fixed eye catatonic look she sometimes got. Her voice was wispy, dreamy. She glanced furtively at Soren.

"You can do as you please, Miriam."

"Oh, I don't know. Gee, we had to schlep all the way from the subway. I'm so tired. Maybe later."

"Sure, sure," said Soren snidely.

It was hard to believe she had been an English honors graduate from Sarah Lawrence. Soren had gone to Berkeley, majoring in anthropology. He'd dropped out to do light shows for Bill Graham at the Fillmore.

"Are you sure you don't want to take your coat off?" I asked Miriam.

"Maybe later."

We showed honeymoon slides and looked at the artwork Soren and Miriam had done recently. His colors were vivid, the images violent, restless. She had a wonderful sense of color but they were painstakingly done and most were copies. What they shared was an emphasis on the sexual. I brought out some of my stuff. "You must have had some mother," commented Soren. His voice was understanding, resigned. He'd been an Army brat, the parents moving around a lot, Miriam had told me. It was a large family and he hadn't received much attention. His father was an inventor-type, a near genius. He was that rare type of person who was both good with his head and his hands. But he could never show much genuine feeling. There was too much fear. Soren was like that, Miriam had said. Her emotions were bottled up, too. She knew that. We had all discussed it many times. Her father had treated her as a sex symbol as she was growing up. She had had this hourglass figure from an early age. She looked quite mature. He had her dress in provocative clothes and on weekends would take her to Times Square, the two strolling around together for several hours before taking the subway back to Queens. So she had these two sides. "The temple whore and 'little Miss Prude,'" as Soren put it. I would talk about my invisible father and devouring mother and "Little Lord Fauntleroy." Barbara never said much. A lot of our talk was about dissection of these different sets of "I"s and how to see them. We never got any place.

Over dinner we talked about maybe going to Boulder, the opportunity to study with a holder of the lineage, to receive the direct transmission of the teachings...and then how at the crucial moment Lord Pentland's name had shot into my head. What did it mean?

Soren laughed. "LP's more powerful than you think," he said.

"You really think so?" Miriam doted on Soren's every word when it came to the Work and Lord Pentland.

"Take your raincoat off, Miriam."

"Don't mind him. He always gets a little nasty. It's just part of his nature. He can't do anything about it."

Barbara asked if Miriam would like to see the new dress she had just made. They both went into the bedroom.

Soren went over to the bookcase. He always checked out a person's books. He wanted to know what I was reading. I told him I wasn't. "Ha!" he sniggered.

His long fingers went quickly along the spines of the books. "Hey, this is a new one," he said. He wanted to know where I got it.

It was *The Art of Asha*. Ruth had given it to me just before we'd gone to Tail. She said Lord Pentland was lending it to me. He had spoken of how ancient, esoteric knowledge had been passed down through the centuries. As examples he had given the pyramids of Egypt and the Tarot. He said Mr. Gurdjieff's word for this was "legominism." I had asked after the meeting if chess were a legominism. Lord Pentland agreed. He seemed pleased that I had made a right connection.

A certain feeling inside me warned me about telling this to Soren, so I said I'd bought the book at Weiser's. Soren gave me a sly look, flipped through the pages and then laid down on the mattress with the book. "You play chess?" he quizzed.

Sounds of the girls laughing hysterically came from the bedroom.

"Not since college." I pointed to the large chess board in the corner.

He got up and examined the board. He saw the scuff marks of pawns pushed to the middle squares, a sign that the board had gotten a lot of use. He sensed I was bullshitting him in some way but he couldn't tell how.

"I saw LP playing chess once," Soren recounted. "You want to play the Big Banana?"

"That would be fantastic!" I thought of Bergman's film, *The Seventh Seal.*

"Well, maybe that can be arranged…"

Soren laid back down, stuck a pillow under his head, crossed his boots and began to read, first lighting up a joint. "Here," he said, sticking the joint in my face.

"Nah, not now. Maybe later."

He grinned and passed the joint to Miriam who had come back into the room.

Soren didn't play chess but I could see he was interested. The book went into the symbolic meaning of chess. And Soren was heavily into symbols, magic.

Asha, or chess, I told him, was known as the royal game, the Game of Kings. Some believe its origins lay in India about 5,000 B.C. The legend is that during a war the king's castle was under siege for many months and the queen—fearing her king would have no patience and act rashly—created the game to divert his attention. But, according to Persian legend, Zarathustra created the Game of Kings. It seems that King Vistaspa of Persia, having everything, had become extremely bored with life. He offered unlimited reward to anyone who could renew his interest in life. Zarathustra created the game for the King, teaching him not only to play but demonstrating through it all the laws of the universe and life.

The book examined chess as a conscious construct to represent the interaction of the laws and forces governing this world. The chess board, for example, is made up of sixty-four black and white squares. Black is symbolic of the denying, or tamasic force. Red of the active, or rajas force. The number sixty-four theosophically adds up to ten, a one and a zero, signifying all and nothing; as do the numbers nine and one, symbolic of the perfect manifest creation and the Absolute. The sixty-four squares are the result of the board having eight rows with eight squares each. Eight is the number of infinity and, turned on its side, constant return.

The primary elements of chess are time, space, force and material (the action and position of the pieces, and how many exist on the board). The white and black chess pieces stand for the cosmic and natural forces constantly struggling with one another. On the white side, the major pieces are the king and queen, called the Creator and Preserver; the two rooks known as Power and Peace; the two knights being Love and Work; and the two bishops, Wisdom and Eternal Life. Each of the pawns represents either a primary element such as water, fire and air or an expression of life such as man, food and joy. Meanwhile, the Black pieces represent the antithesis of these, the King and Queen being the Destroyer and Spoiler and so on. The white pieces, the Ahuras or cosmic forces, are led by Ahura Mazda, the Creator; and the dark, the Fravashis or natural forces, by Ahriman, the Destroyer.

Each game then is a microcosm of the archetypal opposition or battle between Creation and Destruction, between Good and Evil. Man is connected to both sets of pieces, both forces, white and black. He cannot be entirely separate. He is always, consciously or not, cooperating with either one or the other. To become a Man, to have a real I, one must struggle with oneself, with one's dark side. In so doing, like the pawn that advances to the opponent's eighth rank, he can then be transformed into any piece on the board, save the king. Thus, chess is a very pure reflection of an Archetype of Knowledge. Played consciously—in a serene state of sattvic empty mind—is to enter upon the threshold of that primordial Archetype.

"What melodramatic bullshit!" cried Soren, clapping the book shut. "You believe this garbage?"

He winked, trying to put out a double message. He stuck the book back in the bookcase. Suddenly, he became very excited:

"Hey, what's this?" He yanked a book out. "Why you goddam liar!"

He quickly thumbed through the book. "Miriam, you won't believe this!"

Barbara came out of the bedroom. Soren approached them like a lawyer at the bar. "Mr. Innocent says he knows absolutely nothing about black magic—right? Well, just lookee here."

Soren passed the cover in front of both their faces, then rifled through the pages like a Las Vegas card dealer. He turned to me. "Want to explain what this is doing in your bookcase, Mr. Pure?"

I looked at the book. Then I remembered sneaking out to Fire Island with a girl and buying something at Penn Station to read on the train. How could I have forgotten this? Did one "I" read the book and the other "I"s forget?

"Well, I only read half the book," I protested weakly.

"Hey, Barbara, you know what a two-faced weasel you've been living with, eh?" Soren joked.

I knew who Soren reminded me of now. It was the Scandinavian troublemaker of mythology, Loki.

"Soren," said Miriam, "maybe Pat has an excuse."

"Excuse? Excuse my ass! He's lied to his teacher."

"I really did only read half of it," I shouted. "And that was a long time ago. I forgot about it. I don't understand."

"Hey, ignorance before The Law is no excuse, my boy."

"Well, Soren, what about you!" exclaimed Miriam.

"Miriam. Button it."

He lit up another joint, his eyes flashing with glee, as he again thumbed through the book. "Well, pretty plebeian really. At least you could have read a serious book on the subject. But, in any case, you stand accused of not one but two big ass lies. One, lying about this book. Two, lying about seeing 'the Rimp.'"

I smoldered. Soren backed off, telling me I was too identified, couldn't have any fun with me. Miriam was faintly pissed at Soren. And Barbara had gone blank.

At the door, Soren became his charming, sincere self. He said what had happened tonight just showed how identified we all were. He included himself. He asked if I had ever heard of the game of *Chaturanga*. It was a Sanskrit word, he said, *Chatur* meaning four and *anga* meaning limb or component part. It was the original chess game and played with four players, each having eight pieces, king, rook, knight and bishop and four pawns. Each player's pieces were of a different color, green and black and red and yellow. To the north of the board were the black pieces; to the south, green; to the east, red; and to the west, yellow. The green and black players were allies, as were the red and yellow. The pieces were arranged in a swastika, the logo of the Self. A die was cast to determine which of a player's pieces had to move.

"Among the interesting differences between how the game was originally conceived and later modifications," explained Soren in a quiet, almost scholarly voice, "is that the king could be captured. And, sorry ladies, there was no queen. The appearance of the queen, it being the strongest piece on the board and, at the same time, the irony of the king becoming immortal, so to speak, were later derivations. Modern commentaries see these changes as signs of decadence."

Miriam looked on admiringly.

We all said goodnight in a low but friendlier key.

When we were in bed awhile, the large yellow moon outside lighting the room, Barbara turned to me and laughed, "You know what she was wearing under the raincoat?"

"Was she nude? Is that why you two were laughing?"

Barbara nodded and rolled her eyes.

"You're kidding me?"

"She said Soren made her do it. Told her it was good for her, if she did it consciously."

"You believe that?"

"Do you?"

"You know, Ouspensky talks about coming to a 'double crystallization.'"

I told her I'd read that if one remains theoretical too long and puts off really working on oneself then their "I"s can split into two definite groups of "I"s—one useful to waking up and the other indifferent, even opposed to it. All development stops then. And as everything is either ascending or descending, never staying the same, then retardation sets in. Or sometimes, Ouspensky had said, there is 'fixing before development' or 'wrong crystallization.' A person works to remember himself but does not take the idea of different "I"s seriously; he continues to take himself as a unity, as having a real I. The "I"s then become stronger. Crystallization, the fixing of elements, occurs on a wrong foundation, making development impossible. If so, like in *Peer Gynt,* the person has to submit to being melted down again. Could this be why Soren was always asking Lord Pentland whether or not he had a soul?

"Well, what do you think?" I asked.

But Barbara was asleep.

"Women!" I said and rolled over and went to sleep.

"Hello there luv," called the familiar high, lilting voice. "How you been?"

I was happy to hear from her, but I thought I heard a funny tone in Vali's voice. Perhaps, I thought, it was just the phone. But as she talked on, telling me of her plans to sell her art to galleries and friends here and her staying in a photographer-friend's loft in Soho, of making little love potions and all—there was an insistence, a demand I had never heard with her before.

Was she really a witch? Were witches real? I'd always thought witches only existed in fairy tales. That the witch burnings in Salem and the witch trials of the Middle Ages were simply mass hysteria. Now after Soren finding that book on black magic in my bookshelf—and me not having remembered I had read it—I wasn't so sure.

Vali wanted to see me. Barbara wasn't included. I couldn't think of an excuse quickly enough. We agreed to meet at her loft the next night. Was I imagining things? Or not? I didn't know. I felt embarrassed about telling Lord Pentland, so I called Vicki, Lord Pentland's assistant group leader, and told her about finding the black magic book and Vali calling. I needed to talk to her before I went down to Soho. We agreed to meet that evening at the Barbizon coffee shop. I had arrived early, had eaten and was watching the front door. A hand touched my shoulder. It was Vicki. She'd come in through the back door. "We'll be right along," she said and left. What did she mean—*we?*

In a few moments, Lord Pentland came through the front door. He greeted me in a soft, friendly voice and sat down. Vicki came and sat beside him. He said Vicki had asked him to see me. Had she told him? The way he looked at me I was sure he'd ask me to leave the Work. Instead he ordered coffee and an English muffin. She the same. I the same, once again. Then there was just this interminable chit-chatting. It went on and on. There were no empty spaces. Finally—I just blurted out the whole thing. "You were right after all. I did read a book on black magic. How is it possible that I could forget such a thing? How much else have I *forgotten?*"

Lord Pentland took his napkin from the table as if to put it on his lap. But then he put it back beneath the fork.

"That a person has no real I but groups of different 'I's," he said, "really goes much further than we suspect. One 'I' or group of 'I's may be antagonistic to another. Or they may not even know of the other's existence. Buffers separate them. One 'I' signs the check and another must pay for it. It can be quite a problem, if you see what I mean?"

"I was just reading the other day," put in Vicki, "about a man who murdered his wife and said he assumed he did it, because after getting angry the next thing he knew she was lying at his feet, her throat cut, and he was holding a bloody knife."

Lord Pentland looked at me closely. "You see, if I always say 'I' to everything that happens in me then I will be incapable of separating from my states. I will remain identified. When there is remembering, I am there in an entirely different way. I am in a position then to observe impartially and record, but if I become involved with my impressions—the observing stops. It means…"

"Heads up, now! Coffees, muffins, jam," barked the buxom bottle-blonde waitress, sliding the plates of muffins across the table.

"It says in the Bible," Vicki added, looking at Lord Pentland. 'Man's name is legion.'"

"I am distracted," he said, still looking at me. "I lose the thread then and become mechanical. I think I am observing but 'I am' is really asleep, if you see what I mean?"

"You mean part of me can do something then and the other parts, other 'I's, know nothing about it?"

Lord Pentland was busy buttering his English muffin. His movements were precise, sure, sensitive. "How many meals have we eaten and not known what we were eating, much less tasted the food?"

I was gulping down a glass of water as he spoke. I coughed but now tasted the water, felt it traveling down from my esophagus to my stomach.

"Sugar?" Lord Pentland asked, holding the sugar jar out.

I took the jar and poured sugar into my coffee. Vicki said something to Lord Pentland and I forgot I was pouring. I quickly put the jar down, poured in a lot of cream and stirred vigorously.

Lord Pentland and Vicki were chatting about *Jane Eyre*. Again, interminably. I waited. And waited. Finally, I just jumped in with the story about Vali.

Lord Pentland gazed at me a full minute before speaking—as if he were trying to mobilize and focus all my attention.

"When one begins to ascend," he said at last, "he will meet with many things. It's useless to do battle with them. One should observe them while remembering oneself. Look at everything." He watched to see how I was absorbing what he had said. Then he added casually, "You see, self-remembering creates certain connections with a higher center. At first, it creates subjective visions. You begin to see life in terms of allegories and symbols, people play certain parts, if you know what I mean?"

"Everything all right here?" boomed the waitress.

I was the only one to nod. She shrugged and left us.

"But can't I do something?" I asked. "I feel like this is very dangerous. That I'm being tempted in some way. Or is that making too much out of it?"

Lord Pentland put jam on his muffin. "It would do no good for me to tell you what to do."

He took a bite of the muffin and chewed and chewed, all the time looking at me. "You would either not understand...or not remember it when the time came."

The coffee was burning hot and sickeningly sweet. I felt a sense of hopelessness.

He took another bite and continued chewing. "No idea will help you much when you are in a situation like the one you describe."

He finished the muffin and pushed his plate away. Nevertheless, you must see it through, observe yourself—come to something within yourself. Do you follow me?"

The words sounded so pitiless. I opened my mouth to reply, but he called to the waitress who was charging down the aisle in the opposite direction:

"Coffee, please." His accent was decidedly English.

The waitress caught herself in mid-flight and returned to take his cup.

"Oh yes, won't you please give this fellow another cup, too?"

She looked at my cup. It was still full.

"He likes it with cream, not black," he said.

She stared at my cup.

"Doesn't like it cold either, I'm afraid," sighed Lord Pentland.

The coffee was still steaming. Lord Pentland beamed at her. She slowly picked the coffee up, a funny look on her face. Were these people for real or had they lost their marbles?

Just at the moment the waitress was going to speak, Lord Pentland leaned towards me and said in a confidential tone: "There is a time to be inconsistent. The most advanced people do not seem consistent."

I told him I didn't know what to trust in myself. How could I be consistent or inconsistent?

"You know what to trust." His voice was stern, uncompromising.

The waitress approached the table with the coffee. Lord Pentland looked honestly surprised.

"I think not. Could you please return that for us? Our schedule is such that we won't have time to drink it."

"Geez!"

"Sorry to trouble you," Lord Pentland called after her in a melodious voice.

She actually turned and smiled.

I was amazed. Even when Lord Pentland engaged in subterfuge, for whatever purpose, it could not be seen as devious or even bad manners. It didn't come from his person but another place. As I walked down Lexington, I saw how my behavior changed in his company. My attitude, bodily disposition, gesture and language all seemed raised, if that was the word.

The next evening I went to Soho. It was one of those in between nights where summer was long over and winter yet to come. I thought of not going, but I felt I had to face it. Just slipping away wouldn't break it with her. I'd always be carrying her. It had to be done in person. The loft was on Prince Street. The building's storefront served as headquarters for the Daughters of Bilitis, the lesbian organization.

The loft was one flight up. A weird guy, bald, burly, with dark searching eyes and a big black handlebar mustache wearing a lot of chains and studs passed me on the steps. He was taking two young Dobermans out for a walk. The door was one solid piece of heavy sheet metal. I could hear a jumble of voices and the incessant beat of bongos. The door's double locks were unlatched and there was Vali, shining green eyes, flaming red hair, tattoos and all.

"Oh, hello luv. Been expecting you."

Vali reached up, kissed me on the cheek and took my hand, leading me inside. I felt maybe I was making too much out of all this. Inside, the drumming boomed, the light was dim, hard to see, a heavy smell of incense and grass. The loft ran the whole length of the building. One wall covered with floor-to-ceiling mirrors. People jamming everywhere. Stretched out alone in their minds, kissing, confiding, coming on, shooting the shit, dancing, funked out. The whole Village was here. Rag tag street types. Hippies. Jiving blacks. Motorcycle mamas and their old men. Slumming uptowners. A smattering of weirded-out musicians, poets would-be artists, eggheads. A group of wild-eyed drummers beating the bongos to death. The place was rocking.

Vali led me to the rear of the loft. It was the living area. Big brass bed. Makeshift kitchen, bathtub, fridge. No chairs. She led me to the bed. We sat down on its edge. I could hardly hear her at first, the din was so loud. She was talking as if it were only a few minutes ago that we had last spoken. She told me in some detail about all her new loves. Males, females and even a young Chinese homosexual, Chan.

"I was his first girl, you know, luv?"

Vali gave me a little wink and nudge in the ribs, as if that one was particularly special.

She brought out her drawings which she kept beneath the bed. Gods, goddesses and denizens of an underworld region of the psyche, stylized images of Vali. Large, full nippled breasts, shaved, hot red pussies, seductive, violent, sometimes sinister, animal-like. This was no little girl on the bed beside me. And yet there was such a sweet child-like innocence to her.

Vali told me she earned her money selling drawings and making love potions. She asked in her sweet voice if I would like to buy a drawing or maybe a love potion for some little gal I was wild about.

I didn't. Vali didn't seem to mind. She said she'd make us dinner. She stood by the small two-burner stove making scrambled eggs, her bare feet keeping time to the music. There was a wild, untamed, primitive quality to her that I loved. And her sexuality was so direct. Nothing self-conscious. Inhibited.

"Whatcha thinking about luv?"

"You."

"Oh, that's nice." She did a little step. "I feel very close to you, too."

I froze. I was that easy to read for her. She gave me a shy, seductive look. She was maybe eight- years-old at that moment.

"You have a question about me?"

"Yes." I looked at her a long time. She waited, stirring the eggs. "Tell me, are you really a witch?"

She smiled to herself as if that were the funniest question she'd ever heard.

"Of course!"

"You really believe in it? In witchcraft?"

"Of course!" She smiled, knowingly.

Her directness flattened me. She was a witch. Of course. Why couldn't I accept it?

"Here come the eggs," Vali cried. "They're gorgeous. Hope you like them, love." She handed me a plate of scrambled eggs, toast and apple sauce, and sat down next to me with her own. She really enjoyed eating, as she seemed to enjoy everything she did.

At one point, she looked up and tenderly confided a secret: "I can hear it going in there all the time, love. You think too much. You're too serious, you know?"

"But, Vali, being a witch—doesn't that mean you follow the left-hand path?"

"What other path is there, luv!"

She jumped up and did a little hop, her ankle bracelets jangling.

"It's the best, you know."

I had read some of the literature on the tantric teachings. It was fascinating and powerful. But some warned that the deliberate arousal and use of sexual energy with a partner for purposes of transformation was part of the "left-hand path." Others maintained, however, that the teachings were meant for the Kali Yuga, our present age, considered to be the lowest, most vulgar and material of all the four Great Ages of humanity. Some of the Hindu and Taoist teachings also used sexual energy in this way. Gurdjieff spoke of being-Exioëhary, or sperm, being refined still further by means of a second conscious shock. The nature of this shock and the effort connected with it is not described. Ouspensky only says it is connected with the emotional life and is "a special kind of influence over one's emotions." I had read these words and, like the tantric teachings, I could repeat them. But I didn't know what they really meant. I didn't have enough material. But if it was a question of which path I was following, or wanted to follow, I knew that answer.

I told Vali I was following the right-hand path.

She sneaked a little look at me. There was still love in her eyes but pity, too. "What are you doing now?" she asked.

"Waiting."

"Waiting?"

I told her how I had "died"—I imagined it was something like what had happened to her in Paris with the drugs, and she seemed to agree—and now I had been "reborn" and I was waiting to see who I'd be.

"Be a warlock, love," her voice purred and her eyes rolled mischievously. "A lot of fun, not so heavy."

We both laughed and Vali wiped the rest of her plate clean with a crust of bread. The drumming had given way to the big stereo speakers blasting out The Doors' Jim Morrison doing "Light My Fire."

C'mon-c'mon-c'mon 'n love me babe. Don't yyya want to...

Vali held up a finger indicating that I was supposed to stay on the bed. She danced off and in a short time came back with a joint the size of a small cigar. She took a toke and offered it to me.

Lord Pentland had talked about how drugs weaken the will, burn up the fine energies of the body, create imagination in the higher emotional center, and keep one from doing the work. Sometimes, though, he said, they could show what the next step would be. "But one has to pay for it."

Vali held the joint out as if it was a special gift. I didn't want to insult her any more. I took a hit. She liked that and jumped up on the bed and told me stories of her early days in the outback with the aborigines and about all her favorite little animals back in Italy especially Foxy, a red-haired fox of which she'd made many drawings.

Up front a large screen had been pulled down from the ceiling and someone was projecting images using a three-screen projector. The stereo was blasting away with the Rolling Stones. Vali and I went up and sat on the floor to get a better look. There were a lot of hash pipes out now. The guy I'd seen with the Dobermans was using the projector. Vali told me his name was Irv. He reminded me of Stromboli, the puppet master.

They were his slides and quite professional. The color was good and he obviously had an eye for angles and drama. But as I watched I began to see that his images were all a little bit off. No matter how beautiful the image there was always a sickness. One slide showed a baby which he'd combined with another to make Siamese twins. Another was of a baby with a vagina on its inner thigh.

The music had moved off into a slow, slithering mood, falling off into the dark silences of space and then returning like a siren call. A big-breasted black girl stepped over me. She was wearing a sheer blouse, her full breasts jiggling with her movement, the budded nipples erect beneath the chiffon. Vali danced languorously in front of the mirror, soaking in the sound, completely absorbed with herself. In one corner a couple moved up and down.

There was a hand, warm and light, laying high up on my inner thigh. My penis shot to life. The hand was so warm, so alive. I knew whose it must be. Vali was stooping behind me. She smiled, curling around me, those rich, liquid eyes looking deeply into mine. I brought my attention into myself. I vowed I wouldn't make any move toward her. I wouldn't deny but I would not affirm. Such a heat came from her hand and her body. My body ached for her. I kept separate, repeating my vow, continuing to feel myself, observing. "Riders on the Storm" came on now, into the beat of rain and thunder on a lonely roadside and Jim Morrison calling...

Into this house we're born,
Into this world we're thrown.
Like a dog without a bone...
An actor out alone.
Riders on a storm.

Vali and I came together in the silence of our minds. Our eyes wide, neither of us moving, the music of The Doors filling the loft.

"You don't have to be afraid, luv," Vali whispered. "I'm just a little animal."

Let your children play
If you give this man a ride
Sweet Emily will die.
Killer on the road.

My body and groin were on fire and throbbing. But my mind was surprisingly clear. I knew only one thing: Vali was no ordinary woman and making love to her was going to put me on a road I didn't want to travel. I had to get out of that loft, and quickly. I stood up and went to the door, Vali following behind me. I thanked her. Bemused and perhaps a bit sad, Vali gave a little nod and smiled. "Goodbye, luv," she said.

On the way down the steps, I passed a young, slender Chinese boy, his face tattooed. I was very lucky. I went home and burned both the photo Vali had given me of herself and the black magic book in the kitchen sink. This was the fork in the road and I wanted to make it definite where I stood. Barbara had put down her knitting. She looked on, saying nothing. The fire whooshed up and crackled as it ate its food. The Jesus Prayer came to me and I said it to myself. Soon, there were only ashes in the sink. I put them in the garbage and washed out the sink. It all had the feeling of a ritual.

"TEMPTATION IS AN INTERESTING WORD," SAID LORD PENTLAND.

It was at the next meeting and he was speaking to Miriam's question and looking at me. "The real meaning of temptation isn't between doing this or not doing that for, you see, as long as we are mechanical, it is already known what we will do, for we cannot do otherwise. It is only when we begin to come to something real in ourselves that we can be tempted to descend to a lower level of being. So the temptation lies between levels, not within them, if you see what I mean?"

"But, gee, Lord Pentland," said Miriam in a bewildered little girl's voice, "I didn't think I was asking about that."

"You weren't," replied Lord Pentland. "The answer is always on a different level from the question."

I couldn't remember Miriam's question. I only knew he had answered my unspoken question.

When I passed him in the foyer at the end of the meeting, he stopped me. He said he thought perhaps I could look for work now. He suggested I become a court stenographer. I supposed he thought that would help me to listen. It would certainly put me into the black and white of life.

I got a hack license instead, driving the day shift for the 55th Street Garage, seven in the morning to four in the afternoon. I remembered in Maugham's *The Razor's Edge* that Larry, after his return from his search in India, had become a New York cab driver. The job didn't pay much, but it took me out into life again.

After a day of car-jockeying in the Manhattan traffic, I was bone-tired when I came home. But I was writing a short one-act play that had to be completed. Lord Pentland had asked our group to do a play on the Work ideas. I had volunteered to write it. I had the idea of building the play around the Ray of Creation. This was a key diagram and idea of the Work. It shows how matter evolves through levels of being, from the very lowest, heaviest vibration to the very finest and lightest, from the most mechanical worlds under the most laws to more and more conscious worlds having fewer and fewer laws. The higher the vibration the lower the density of matter. Every single thing, gross or subtle, has its place in the cosmic order, its specific level of gravity, intelligence, freedom. The lower the world, the less intelligence, less consciousness, the more influences and laws to which it is subject.

What really excited me was that the diagram showed the idea of relativity—how all things are relative to the world in which they exist. What exists in one world may not exist in another. What is visible at one level of vibration may be invisible at another. It accounted for how two ideas, seemingly mutually opposed, are resolved in a higher world.

To begin to understand the diagram I had to study the Law of Three, how the three primal and independent forces work in the Ray of Creation. The first force is active; the second, passive; and the third, neutralizing. The Law of Three, or the Sacred Triamazikamno, shows how these three forces manifest, how nothing can take place without the action of these forces.

The second great law of the universe, The Law of Seven, or Heptaparaparshinokh, shows how these forces move in one of two processes. One process is a descending octave (Si-La-Sol-Fa-Mi-Re-Do) of higher devolving to lower. The second process is an ascending octave (Do-Re-Mi-Fa-Sol-La-Si) of lower evolving to higher. "The higher blends with the lower in order to actualize the middle and thus becomes either higher or lower for the preceding lower, or lower for the succeeding higher," writes Gurdjieff in his intentionally frustrating style. As these processes proceed, there are lawful stopinders, or shocks, which occur between the notes mi and fa and after the note si, and which serve to intensify and keep the line or direction of the octave, given that the liberated energy is, of course, creatively assimilated and not identified with one of the "I"s; and, if not, which deflect the octave. My idea was to write the play based on an ascending octave, giving shocks where the stopinders come.

The group meetings were continuing. I felt as if they weren't going fast enough. It seemed everyone was asking the same question over and over again. The words were sometimes different, but the question was the same. And of course there were disagreements. It became clear watching myself and others that, just as the Work said, each of us perceived through different centers, or combinations of centers. A thinking type was hard put to understand a feeling or sensation type and so forth. This limitation, together with our prejudices and varying backgrounds, was enough to resurrect the age-old Tower of Babel. How to break through all this? How to ask a question I had never asked before? I hadn't the least idea.

In one meeting Lord Pentland focused on me. He was answering a question of Miriam's—he said she had "no organic shame"—pointing out how we had to see and struggle with features of ourselves, if we were to come to a deeper understanding of the Work. He turned to me slowly, like a gun turret on a battleship, saying:

"We have come to a point where we can see, if we would look, how our need to have a kingly attitude distorts and deadens us. We can see how this need to be the king of any situation or group keeps us from experiencing the moment, keeps us asleep."

Kingly attitude. The words blasted a hole through me. I had been sitting there tuning out. Miriam's question didn't interest me. He had caught me in a dream. And used it. I felt naked, exposed. At the same time—I really didn't know what he meant.

On the way to the subway, Paul, the fat guy, caught up with us. He was grinning.

"He stuck the sword of consciousness right into your heart, didn't he?" said Paul.

"He sure did," agreed Barbara. "Wow!"

I felt like a cannon ball had put a hole in my chest. I could only nod.

"It's a good sign. Shows that he thinks you can handle it." Paul patted me on the back and waved goodbye. We went down into the subway station, full of the roar and rattle of a passing express train. Soren and Miriam were on the other side of the subway tracks. Soren cupped his hands and called out:

"I give the Big Banana two ears and a tail!"

Winter had come again. A piercing cold sliced the streets. I'd go out sometimes without a jacket to build my body up against the cold. I turned over and over what Lord Pentland had told me. I really didn't see it. I certainly felt like no kind of king. I had quit the cab job and was working as a census taker. Taking the census, I saw that so many of the older people I spoke with in the tenements were hurt, broken, bewildered and frightened by life, buried in contracted little mind-worlds. With some the mind or feeling or body barely functioned. They were "dead" just as Gurdjieff said. It was like they all had abandoned ship and swum to this strange little island that was off the map.

One Czech woman I called on had all her furniture stacked up in the living room, afraid that neighbors would steal it out of storage in the basement. So she only lived in two rooms, the kitchen and the bedroom. The kitchen had a tub in it and had all these pictures of Jesus. Her son, Walter, was in the bedroom. He was in bed, the sheet pulled up over his head. Walter was twenty-one. He had been in bed for six years. He was an A student and a wonderful violinist. The woman upstairs was a witch. She didn't like Walter playing and warned him. One day when Walter was alone, the woman knocked on the door. When Walter opened it, she put a curse on him. He had been in bed ever since. I stood with his mother by the bed talking softly to Walter. His toes were wiggling. His mother pointed to the toes and whispered that this was a sign Walter liked me.

Later I went to see the local congressman's office to try to get help for Walter. But instead of helping Walter the police and social workers waited until his mother had gone shopping. Then they broke down the door with an axe and carted Walter off to Bellevue. His mother called me, hysterical. I understood then we really never know what our actions set in motion. I had meant for Walter to get some mature, loving care and here I'd put him in a looney bin! What was I to do now? With Walter's mother screaming at me in broken English like a wounded animal, it suddenly came to me: play a role! The different "I"s play different roles. Like Gurdjieff said, consciously play a role. The thought froze me. It called up some deep fear. I was messing with my identity. With who I was. Or, at least, who I took myself to be. It was like I had tapped into an unconscious taboo. All this study and talk about different "I"s and I—whoever this "I" was—demanded total loyalty. I must be Patterson at all times. Identification was like a deep underground stream. I'd never realized how deep it ran. It was more than mental. It had seeped into the bones and cells and nervous system. Identification was an infection that could become organic.

This recognition happened all at once, and wordlessly. This was knowledge in the real sense and I felt that to keep it I must act on it. Otherwise it would become more head knowledge. Mere memory.

I called the head nurse at Bellevue. I put on a deep, no-nonsense voice of a power-possessing being; the kind of "I" that instills fear and gets action.

"I'm Walter's attorney," I told the head nurse, my voice edged with contempt. "You're going to be party to a kidnapping charge if you don't let that boy out of there. And we want him out immediately—hear? Or there's going be big trouble!"

She licked my boots and agreed to set Walter free at once. I stood with a hand over the receiver, laughing and trembling.

About this time I'd been having dreams about Rinpoche. I kept going back and forth trying to decide whom I should go with. I couldn't shut my mind off. I would come to a decision. That would be it. Another few minutes and I'd be reconsidering and then reversing it. And this went on and on.

At one meeting Lord Pentland said, "Often it happens that people look for a place to rest because of the strain of the Work." Later he mentioned, "And people get sick because they can't decide whether to be in New York...or Bermuda." I knew he was talking to me. I had to decide once and for all. I decided to go to Boulder right after the play we were to perform.

The evening of the play was bedlam. We had practiced and practiced. Now people were unhappy with their lines and wanted to change them. We were all standing in the short hallway outside the meeting room where Lord Pentland and Vicki awaited us. Everyone was arguing. Finally, Lord Pentland gave a loud cough and that ended the rebellion.

I went into the room alone. Lord Pentland gave me a sly look as I turned off the lights. The room was pitch black, silent. In a few moments, Philippe opened the door. He slowly put a recorder to his mouth and blew the notes of the octave. Then he struck a match, lit a large white candle. Then he blew the first note of the octave, do, and Barbara appeared holding an unlit candle. Phillipe lit it and Barbara walked into the room and took the first seat in the first row of nine chairs.

One by one then, nine members of the group came to the doorway with unlit candles. The note they symbolically represented was played on the recorder and their candles were lit. The two people representing the two shock points in the octave had no notes played but they jumped into the entrance way and took their places quickly.

I sat off to the side of Lord Pentland and Vicki watching the play unfold. as each person entered the room with a lit candle. The idea had been that each person was to walk slowly, trying to sustain a sense of themselves. But, despite all our practice, it was so obvious that no one could remember themselves. They were only remembering an idea; there was no real feeling. They moved like automatons with this idea nailed to their foreheads. Some hurried, some walked too slow or somehow tripped over their own feet. Worse, their faces were set in this false purity. I began to feel physically sick.

Soon, everyone was in their seats and the room was aglow with flickering candlelight. When all were seated, Philippe was again to blow the different notes of the octave and the person, whose position corresponded to that note, would stand and say a few lines appropriate to their place in the octave. That is, I wrote their lines to accord with the "taste" and frequency of the vibration of energy corresponding to that point. In my mind I'd had an image of this incredible perfection unfolding. In reality, a living disaster began to play itself out.

Barbara spoke her lines well, but there was a lot of fear and her last few words were barely audible.

Helen stood up and went to Lord Pentland and handed him a five dollar bill which he rather reluctantly took. She said something, giving him that little pursed and knowing smile.

Lord Pentland turned and looked at me for an explanation. But the whole thing was her idea. None of it had I written.

Ruth had talked me into allowing her to play a tape she had secretly made of the group discussing the play. I'd thought it was a bad idea but I had let her do it, not wanting to appear too set in my ideas. She turned on the tape. All these voices arguing, interrupting one another, shouting. It was like a mad house. And the tape went on and on, Ruth sitting there with this supercilious goddamn smirk on her face.

Soren sat up for a moment, shouted his lines out, then defiantly stretched out in his chair again, smirking and shaking his head as if to say, "This is really stupid!"

Miriam was a bundle of messages fighting each other. Dressed in a short leather skirt up to the top reaches of her thighs and a long-sleeved white blouse buttoned up to the neck, Miriam spoke in a little girl's voice like she was talking to "Daddy."

Finally, thankfully, it came Paul's turn. He sat in last position at the place of the second shock. His voice boomed throughout the room—"All this energy! Glorious! What am I to do with all this energy?"

And with that the play ended. It was awful! The room got so small. The craggy bricks closed in on me. All the energy ran out of me. I wanted to leave, be alone, forget it all.

Lord Pentland acted as if nothing had happened. He was curious as to what we each had experienced.

Everyone spoke up. They accused me, the other actors and actresses, the play— nothing was any good. It was all wrong. And they knew all along it was wrong.

Lord Pentland listened with interest, but made no specific comment. When everyone had spoken, he remarked rather casually that he seemed to recall someone recently asking him about the chief impediment to their being conscious—that was me! I'd written him a letter.

"Look into yourselves now and come up with a specific impediment," he asked.

Nothing but silence. Blank silence. The room seemed very cold to me. A specific impediment? I could feel nothing. My head swam with accusations and images. By turns, I felt empty, then angry. Angry at myself. Angry at these assholes. It went on and on. And I could do nothing but watch it. In the watching it came to me where I was: *in the middle of the octave.* It had begun when I had turned out the lights and proceeded accordingly. I was caught. There was nothing to do but wait for the shock. Be conscious when it came. The octave wasn't an idea for me now on a piece of paper.

Not a person spoke.

Lord Pentland waited.

Suddenly, I knew what was for me an impediment. And immediately I felt this fear, this warning not to admit it. My heart pounded, my body vibrated. Finally, I took the leap:

"I want to be...I want to be...a god."

The words so small, so barely audible.

Lord Pentland looks as if he has awakened from a dream. He leans forward, apologizing, "I'm afraid I didn't hear you, Pat. Could you say that again. Please, for the rest of us."

Time has slowed but now it stops.

"I want...to be...a god."

The words still small, just above a whisper. My face flushes. A part of me, an "I," does not believe I am saying this. I go on:

"I think I have a right to everything."

Space expands. Only Lord Pentland and I am in the room now. Only two of us. The lights are on in room, but it seems dim, cloudy. My body isn't cold any longer. But it doesn't seem like it is breathing. I feel inside me Lord Pentland's silent urging, "Continue speaking."

But I am blank. I have nothing to say.

He persists.

Then it comes to me. This admission, it is even harder, more shameful.

"I want to have...all of...your attention."

Instantly—Lord Pentland and I are joined together in space. He is breathing me. I sense my lungs expanding, emptying, expanding again. I am not doing it. His chest seems immense. His upper body glows with that bluish-white light...

The image of Rinpoche flying the fighter kite—that came to my mind's eye. I ignored it. It became stronger. I tried to stop my mind, shut it out. I heard Lord Pentland saying something about "...and, so remember, we are not our thoughts and we should not believe in them."

I had gotten lost, gone to sleep. His words jolted me out of the mind...

Lord Pentland begins to speak in a general way about relationship—"Each of us must offer something," he advises. "Otherwise, it is parasitic."

His gaze meets mine. There is no judgment in his voice. He is speaking impersonally, simply as a statement of fact:

"You want everything…" He pauses, and then raises his voice an octave. "But are you prepared to pay for it?"

He takes a breath very deeply and speaks so quietly I barely hear him:

"One can be asked into the Work. Or they can come in. But in no case can they be dragged in."

"I feel like a hypocrite," I say.

He nods approvingly and smiles. "If you knew what it really means to say that…that would be a big thing."

And with that Lord Pentland stood up, tall as a tree, and left…

The following day I called his office. My call seemed to have startled or confused him. He didn't immediately recognize me. Then he put me on hold. I waited over twenty minutes. The old voices came. I didn't fight them. I hung on. Presently—

"Pat, is that you? Sorry you were 'forgotten.' What's on your mind?" He acted as if he had not heard from me for ages.

I said I'd like to see him. He had Joan, his secretary, hand him his appointment book. I heard pages turning. "What about next week?" he asked.

I agreed, but said I would like to see him sooner. I could come at any time, any hour, I told him.

"Hmmmmn…" He seemed to chew that over.

"I'd really like to see you," I said sincerely.

"This afternoon at four," he said and hung up.

I was there right on the dot. He had Joan show me to his office. He offered me a seat. This time I sat in the chair in front of his desk. He asked about Barbara. He asked if we were planning to have a child. I told him I didn't have a job as yet. He didn't see that as an "impediment" to starting a family. "It will all come together now," he assured me. He said he had told Soren and Miriam the same.

"But of course you haven't come here for all of this," he said. "What's on your mind?"

I told him about all that had happened with Rinpoche, about meditating in the attic and asking to go to Boulder and the voice coming and my realizing that maybe I was a Christian after all and how guilty I had felt and how I had brought it all on myself, that I had known I was crossing a line, mixing things up, but still I had crossed it.

"Remorse, yes, but guilt is not worth bothering about," he told me. "Remorse is something we so rarely let ourselves feel. You see, genuine remorse is purifying."

He went on to say that he didn't think Rinpoche would make any trouble. "He's an honest man," he said.

The way he spoke the word "honest" it was such a big and unusual word. It was as if so very few people are truly honest.

Lord Pentland offered me a piece of handmade candy.

It was like a gift, a reward.

BEING-PARTKDOLG-DUTY. CONSCIOUS LABOR AND INTENTIONAL SUFFERING practiced in daily life was a key tenet of Gurdjieff's teaching. "The Fourth Way," as Gurdjieff's teaching came to be called, was not to avoid or withdraw from life and practice tapas, discipline, and austerities as the ways of the fakir, monk and the yogi advocate. The Fourth Way was a radical break with these traditional ways of self-perfecting in that the ordinary conditions and circumstances of one's life served as the basis to remember oneself and observe. There was no artificial division created between spiritual and worldly life. The Fourth Way was a way in life. It was a way of the objective understanding of oneself and the cosmic laws that controlled life. After long study and many labors and sufferings, one gradually acquired the necessary material, inner knowledge and will needed for transformation.

Everyday life provided the necessary shocks to see ourselves but these were accidental. And there was no real demand, no conscious direction, no conscious shocks. It all just happened. To increase the pressure on what Gurdjieff considered modern man's malformed psyche and provide more intensive conditions for self-observation, everyone in the Work gathered together every Sunday to practice working with attention. These Work Days were held at an estate in Armonk, an hour's drive from Manhattan. The tasks were quite ordinary and involved taking care of the grounds and buildings, doing carpentry, laying tiles, house painting, and so forth, as well as working in cabinet making, ceramics, weaving, painting, translation and the like. What took it out of the ordinary was that everyone was to work consciously. One was to sense the body while working at their task and not become involved in the usual daydreaming, expression of negative emotions and other forms of identification. Of course one failed. And continually, if they were honest. But the ideal and the intentional striving to be conscious was enough to give the day a great force and tempo. So much so that after a day of hard manual labor or intellectual work, one left Armonk with an amazing amount of energy. More valuable was the rich set of new impressions of oneself working with others. For the opportunity of working with people whose sole intent, ideally, was also to remember and observe themselves helped to unearth quick and subtle impressions that simply could not be experienced in ordinary life (until one had come to a certain maturity) where everyone works, knowingly or not, not to be present—but instead to make their "I" rich or famous or, in some pathological cases, a failure.

The Sunday Work Days began at nine o'clock with a short meditation and a few words from Lord Pentland which would set the direction for the day. An exercise might be given or some general inner work would be suggested. A list would be posted assigning people to various projects. The day's theme would also be posted. For example, "The idea and experience of self-remembering." Or "Does the Work give a support in life or does it attack it?" Lunch would be served followed by a question and answer period. More work, and then a reading from one of the Work books.

I didn't like to work with my hands. I wanted to be on a team doing translation or painting so, of course, I was out breaking boulders. One Sunday I was put on a carpentry team. I was told to get a wing nut.

"What's a wing nut?" I asked.

Everyone stopped working and looked at me curiously. The project leader finally explained what a wing nut looked like while everyone roared with laughter. Humiliated, I ran off to get the damn wing nut!

My mind was shot full of anger. I blamed my Father. He hadn't taught me anything. He was good with his hands, but he never once asked me to do or learn anything. I was given everything. I had lived the privileged existence of a fool. I wanted to go home. What did wing nuts have to do with being conscious!

Later in a group meeting I related what I had experienced.

"This is a work with others," Lord Pentland said. "It's not a work in a ca-ve."

The way he said "cave" I knew he meant "apartment." I was living my life in an apartment, protecting myself from unpleasant shocks.

"You saw a great deal," he added with a smile.

I blew up like a peacock.

"But of course the moment you became identified, began to blame others...well, in any case, you were awake for a split-second."

"There was a moment," I said, "just before the reaction to the shock of the wing nut. It was like everything was still, everything stopped and—"

"Yes, quite right. The forces are separated in that moment. Energy is liberated. If there is identification, then one descends. If the energy is assimilated, then one is ascending. But at this point I'm afraid this can only be theoretical for us. To be able to be in the moment you speak of, that particular interval, requires many years of work on oneself."

It was so hard to look at myself. Time and again, I found I fell into anger and blaming. I'd be totally identified, and not see it. The buffers between the different "I"s, all my justifications, were so strong. I was full of anger for myself, my Father, everyone. Despite the clarity and energy that often resulted from the suffering of seeing what a two-headed, sleeping dunce I was...well, the impressions cut so deep that none of my "I"s ever, even in the best of times, looked forward to a Work Day.

"Although progress is rapid when one first enters the Work," said Lord Pentland during a group meeting, "the real lasting results of the Work do not come without long years of right effort."

"How many years are we talking about?" I asked. "Three years? Seven years?"

"One must not only know how to work but when and where to work." He stopped and considered me carefully for a moment. He continued with a chuckle, "Oh I should think fifteen or twenty years. Tell me, does that seem too optimistic?"

Once a year there were also Work Weeks. Being five or seven days in duration and the days often lasting from nine in the morning until midnight, these were incredibly intense periods with conscious shocks to the group and individuals provided at the appropriate time to keep a line of effort rising.

The first Work Week Lord Pentland invited me to attend was in San Francisco, and it was the week after the actual Work Week. He had invited several others from my group as well, explaining that this would serve as a "good introduction," as he felt the Work Week itself might be "too strenuous for us at this point."

When I arrived at the Foundation's house in San Francisco, I was immediately put to work whitewashing a wall. I noticed a young, intense woman in the foyer who sat rather fixedly staring into space. Her face was intelligent, but her dark eyes had an obsessive quality. I overheard Lord Pentland telling her in an exasperated tone, "Well, if you can't leave, then read the telephone book."

That evening six or seven of us along with Lord Pentland had dinner in the small dining room off the study. We were joined by a heavy-set, jowly man said to be a group leader in Los Angeles and a Tibetan lama, Lobsang Lhalungpa, who was helping Lord Pentland and some others translate anew *The Life of Milarepa*.

The conversation soon turned to the difficulties of translation and general comments about the book. I had read the book and was curious about the Tibetan perspective on omens. When the chance arrived I asked Lhalungpa about omens and symbols.

"Omens are a kind of symbol-reading," he answered, "that is possible in a certain state of awareness." He gave as an example when Milarepa left his teacher, Marpa, to meditate in a cave he gave him a gift of a copper pot. Marpa immediately filled the pot with food. "Had he not done that," explained Lhalungpa, "Milarepa would not even have had nettles to eat. So we must learn to manipulate symbols once we can read them."

The heavy-set man from L.A., asked about tumo, inner heat, and tantric teachings on the chakras. It was a long involved question and as he got into it he put a cigarette into his mouth. He went to pick his lighter from the table, but Lord Pentland took it and gestured as if he would light the cigarette. The man gave a quick nod of thanks and went on talking. He leaned forward bringing the cigarette to the lighter Lord Pentland held. He puffed to get a light. But Lord Pentland had not lit the lighter. Even so, he snapped back the lid as if he had. The man returned to an upright position, still talking about chakras and puffing to get a light.

In mid-sentence—suddenly he realized he was puffing on an unlit cigarette—he stopped. Stung into a moment of awareness, he looked sheepishly at Lord Pentland. There was a large hole of stunned silence. Finally, Lord Pentland said—"Sorry."

And with that the dinner ended.

The intense woman with a telephone book stood outside the dining room. Lord Pentland stepped by her, as if she weren't there.

"Lord Pentland," she implored. "Why is no one talking to me?"

"Sorry, not now," he replied, his voice barely audible.

"But I—"

He turned and looked down at her. His face was stone-like and his voice flat. "It would be best, if you went home. There is nothing to be gained by staying on, and much to lose. Your Work Week is over."

"I can't leave," she answered.

He looked at her a moment.

"No," she said.

He shrugged and went off. We cleared the table. Everyone ignored her. She seemed so lost. I felt sorry for her. She must have sensed that for she came up to me and asked, "Why is no one talking to me?"

"You refuse to do what he told you," I said. "Why don't you go home and then, if you like, come back tomorrow?"

"I've got to talk to you," she said.

We went into the foyer and sat on the couch. "My mind is going around and around," she told me.

"I can't leave."

"The telephone book—have you read it?"

"Yes, well, no, not really. I tried, but it doesn't do any good."

I thought of getting up but it was as if her energy was holding me there. She was a great swirl of energy, and her face kept changing as if she were underwater. Several times I tried to end the conversation, but couldn't.

Lord Pentland passed us by. The woman took no notice of him. He gave me a quick, sidelong glance. Some others passed by as well, looking at us curiously.

As we talked, my mind was suddenly filled with sexual fantasies. I resolved at once that I should do nothing. Otherwise, this all could explode. Finally, she calmed down and early in the morning she went home.

The next morning after breakfast Lord Pentland took me out by the movements hall. A steep hill led down to a small nursery that was being built. A huge mound of dirt was piled by the nursery. Lord Pentland told me to shovel the dirt into a wheelbarrow. He pointed to the ground where we stood, "Here—put the *dirt* here."

All morning I worked, sweating profusely, filling and pushing the wheelbarrow up the hill. At one point, I became aware of someone watching me. There she was sitting on the porch holding the telephone book. She stared at me with that same fixed gaze like she was trying to capture me. I felt like a fly with a spider.

I overheard Lord Pentland talking to someone. "Yes," he was saying, "the Irish have many good points, but they are naive. Gurdjieff said the worst person to have around was someone who was naive."

That evening Lord Pentland read a story to us by René Daumal. Its point was that consciousness gives the ability to say "No," and that the masculine principle is "No." He said that working on oneself liberates much energy but if we are going to let one of our "I"s leak it out in negativity or indulge itself in fantasies, sexual or otherwise, then that energy is lost. "We must work for the clarity and control that will enable us to step over the stumbling blocks that are thrown in our way," declared Lord Pentland. "Otherwise, all is for naught."

He said that if anyone wished to see him, he would be available the next morning. I made an appointment for right after breakfast and went to see him in his room in the back of the house. It was a small but well-appointed room with a low ceiling.

He had been painting some of the characters from the Tarot.

"I've just finished that one," he mentioned, pointing to The Fool.

I nodded perfunctorily. I didn't want to get side-tracked. He smiled and offered me a seat. I told him of all the guilt I felt. "Is self-righteousness just the reverse side of guilt?" I asked.

He didn't answer me directly but said, "We must transform our feelings of guilt, our inner considering, into the understanding of man's limitations."

"What are they?"

He smiled whimsically. "Hate, envy, lust, and so forth."

Yes, I saw and felt it now: it was lust I was feeling. Amazing how I could feel something and not be able to name it. What was the resistance? The blindness?

"You are an idealist," Lord Pentland said. "Well—good! It's brought you this far. But now you must go on. You must put everything into question."

That evening at dinner I was late. I was short of breath. I paused and settled myself before entering the room, breathing down into the body. I entered the dining room, looked at Lord Pentland, apologized, and sat down. His face remained impassive, but I felt like he was pleased. Later, he let me pour him a cup of coffee.

Lord Pentland suggested that as this was our last evening together perhaps we should have a brief meeting. We met upstairs in the library. We sat for a few minutes. I could feel his energy entering me. It was enormous.

Someone asked a question about emotions.

"Work on the emotions is difficult," Lord Pentland replied. "We must be careful not to work so hard that we overdo it and become sick. We must walk a razor's edge." He mentioned that when he was with Gurdjieff he noticed that he and most people had colds. "Elimination," he said.

"How is that Gurdjieff never talks about guilt?" I asked.

"He does—guilt is inner considering."

Lord Pentland left his seat and took Gurdjieff's *Views From The Real World* from a book shelf. He turned to the aphorisms in the back and read:

"If you have not by nature a critical mind, your staying here is useless."

He then asked for a bottle of Scotch and drinks were poured. We all lifted our shot glasses and Lord Pentland gave as a toast another of Gurdjieff's aphorisms: "Sleep little without regret," he said and downed the Scotch.

When I returned to New York, I went down to see Casey. The idea of symbols and there existing a whole symbolic level to life fascinated me. We talked a while but I really wasn't sure what he was saying. Finally, he searched through his bookshelf and took out a large art book.

"Here," he said handing me the book, "Beckmann really understood symbols."

"Who's he?"

"He was a post-impressionist painter, a German. He died in the fifties."

I leafed through Beckmann's paintings. I'd never seen paintings like these. They all had this direct, primitive quality; a tension and violence, a brutal, fearless honesty. The colors were sensuous. They shimmered with intensity and depth. The paintings themselves weren't pretty or beautiful. Many I found ugly, in fact; some cartoonish, even. But they commanded my attention. It was an encounter. They had an awesome power. And they exuded some quality, some mystery, I couldn't name. There was a struggle going on, a conflict between forces, between good and evil, that came out in many of them. I especially liked *The King,* painted in 1937; *Olympia* in 1946; and a triptych, *The Argonauts.*

Casey was throwing darts at a dart board. He came over, poured himself a cup of coffee and sat down at the long narrow metal lunch table covered with a red and white plastic checkerboard tablecloth. A primitive, shaman-like mobile hung from the ceiling. The wall behind the table was lined with bins of canvases. Mozart chamber music played lightly in the background. For a long time we didn't say anything. Finally Muffin, Casey's scrawny French poodle, jumped onto his lap, trying to lick his mustache. He pushed her off, nearly losing his glasses. Muffin tore around the loft, barking her anger.

"Thinks she's a human being," Casey cracked. "You know, a bad case of 'megalodoggia'?"

We both laughed.

"That's real doggerel," I told him.

"Standards-standards-standards," Casey chortled.

"Tell me about Beckmann," I said.

"You like him?"

I looked at one of the paintings, a torture scene. "No, I wouldn't say that."

"He's not somebody you hang on your walls, right? They'd be tough to live with," Casey said. He pointed to the use of black in the painting. "The most difficult color to use. It's so powerful it has to be used just right. Or else you overwhelm the painting. Beckmann, he was a master at it."

"But why does he mutilate people, have women carrying large fish or holding swords?" I asked. "What's he mean by it?"

"Symbols. Beckmann understood symbols. He was able to paint the mythological dimension. You know what that is?"

"No, not really…but I'd like to."

"Painting isn't a way to make a living, become famous. It's a channel, a sacred channel," Casey said, his normally joking manner now serious and intense.

"But—"

"To paint…to really paint…It can't be taught. I'm not a teacher. I don't teach. You might say all I do is *create the atmosphere.* The teaching, that happens by itself."

It was only then that I saw what was happening in the loft. Casey's studio was an "open space." Everything was permissible here. There were no rules. No right and wrong. Paint what you want—gods, demons, weird animals, humanoids, kinky sex scenes, ordinary mush—Casey was open to it. He would work with you. What was important was that you touched your real self.

He asked if I wanted to see some of his work. I was delighted. For all his friendliness, he was a very private person. He made a selection of paintings. They were large canvases at least six-feet in length. His early work was stark, raw, powerful. It went right to the belly. Great swashes of color. A lot of black. Figures quickly stroked in: an Indian chieftain, Jacob wrestling with the angel, a bereft woman. Everything in precarious balance; tremendous tension. All taken right to the edge. He painted that one moment where the opposites meet…where everything was about to explode.

He brought more paintings out of the stalls. It was as if he was showing me his life. With his later paintings the opposition and conflict appeared to deepen. I felt as if he was painting the moment after the explosion of opposites, for they both expressed and contained the opposites—contained those moments. And instead of using the entire canvas for a battleground, it was now placed within large, irregular shapes on backgrounds of flat color. At first sight, the shape simply gave the impression of being splotchy, a chimera of color. But as I continued to gaze, the foreground and background inside the shape would suddenly interchange. What was foreground would become background and vice versa. Then the whole shape would come to life with figures and animals. What had been opaque, or seemed a jumble of non-representational color and form, was now alive with form, situation, the questions of the soul.

I painted now at Casey's studio as much as three and four times a week. I couldn't get enough of it. Through him had come to me this new and incredible world. One day I went to his studio early. I found him puffing on his pipe, staring at one of my paintings. It was a large canvas of an old woman, sitting naked in a dark cavern, a small light behind her at the cave's entrance. Her shoulders were massive; bunched up with tension. Her body was strong but aging, worn down with having given birth so many times. Her hair was red and her body painted in blues, yellows and oranges. I called her *The Moon Woman*.

"What do you see?" I asked.

Casey smiled. "Keep painting," he said softly and went to make himself some coffee.

I got my paints out and screwed the canvas down on the easel and began to work. Casey came by a little later, just as class was beginning.

"Possessed by the anima," he muttered, barely above a whisper.

I didn't hear this immediately though. It was just sound. I was too far into the painting. But later on, when I had stopped painting and gone home, the words—*possessed by the anima*—came back to me. What did he mean? I had never heard that word "anima" before.

The next day I went to the studio early. He was sitting behind his old oak desk. On the wall beside it were shelves of books, framed photographs of Jung and Picasso, and a Dada-like art object, a shovel handle and, instead of a shovel blade, a phonograph record.

"What did you mean yesterday?" I asked.

He got up and went to one of the bins of paintings. He pulled out *The Moon*

Woman and stood her on an easel.

"See anything unusual?" he asked.

"No. Not really."

"See how big the figure is in relation to the canvas?"

"Yeah," I said. "It's practically the whole painting."

"The female figure takes up all the space."

"Yeah...?"

"The anima is your female side. The figure shows how large your anima is in your life."

I peered at the woman I had painted. "I don't get it," I told him. "She's just a big woman, isn't she?"

Casey went to his desk and searched his bookshelf. He brought me several books.

"These will give you a good introduction," he explained. "Take your time reading them. Let them seep into you." He handed them to me and pointed out a small photo on the wall of a sharp-eyed man smoking a pipe. "I've studied his ideas for many years. I corresponded with him before he died."

I began reading the books at once. They were by Carl Jung, the Swiss psychiatrist and early colleague of Freud's. He had broken with Freud to found Analytic Psychology, a process of individuation, of bringing the opposites together within the individual. I read where, according to Jung, the anima was the great feminine archetype of life. An archetype is an ordering principle, is reflected deep in the psyche, which mirrors the larger cosmos beyond us. It is in the patterns and influences of our collective and personal archetypes that we live our lives.

We can sense and see it in particular qualities of energy, events and symbols. There are many archetypes, but the two primary ones are the male, the animus, and the female, the anima. The archetypes, fused at the instinctual level when not differentiated in our consciousness, exist in everyone. Men usually manifest their animus energy and repress the anima; women do the reverse. Jung saw life as an interplay of archetypes, of principles which order and constellate our lives into different patterns. Besides the animus and anima, there are other archetypes such as the shadow, the trickster, the wise old man and so forth. In effect, all the gods and goddesses and demons are reflected in the psyche. Man's consciousness is their playground. While these archetypes, Jung said, are too great ever to be directly known by us, we can know them and how they function through reflection—through paintings and dreams, for example.

For Jung, each person carried within himself a personal and a collective unconscious. The personal has to do with all that had been repressed in the person because it is not accepted as part of his or her self; or it is thought of as being bad, antisocial and so on. The collective unconscious is our racial unconscious—those ideas, images and experiences that are part of the heritage of our race. In the West, the symbols of the Christian church are part of our collective unconscious. No matter our attitude toward it, we respond instinctively and intuitively to our psychic heritage, such as Christ on the cross. When an archetype becomes active in our lives we are filled with great tension and energy. It destroys our old world, our old patterns, and re-aligns everything, ushering in the new. As it does so, other situations and events are drawn into relation with it. These events are often quite dissimilar and seem to have no casual connection, but, if we are rightly attuned, we will see how they correspond to one another in a meaningful way. Beyond the will and purpose and causality in our lives there exists then another plane of reality, a plane of synchronistic events, of meaningful coincidence in which archetypes give our lives a numinous quality and a "magical causality."

Gradually, I began to see paintings in a different way. I saw them now as expressions of energies, symbols. We were all living in a sea of archetypes.

Casey cautioned me: "Don't think about painting. Just paint."

"But they have a meaning," I protested.

"Of course they mean something to you," he joked. "They're yours."

He adjusted his glasses and wiped his eyes. "You know that dream you told me about where you're in...what was it? that cave...no, the granite church."

I had forgotten I'd told him. "Yeah, yeah."

"Tell me..." Casey studied me curiously. "Have you ever had a bite of the apple?"

"The—apple?"

"Oh, c'mon. You know, for chrissakes—Adam and the apple."

"Yeah?" I stopped painting and faced him. "I don't get it."

Casey peered at me. "Whatever you do—you lose something." Then he added with emphasis, "You can't be right no matter what you do."

"But—"

"Just paint. *Paint* and stop thinking. Okay?"

GURDJIEFF AND ANOTHER MAN ARE SITTING ON A BENCH ALONGSIDE MY Grandfather Scott's house on Laketon Road. They are dressed in old Irish peasant clothes, dark and drab. They are clothes that have seen a lot of traveling.

The man with Gurdjieff is tall and lean. There is something seedy about him. His face has a peculiar look. I don't altogether trust him. Apparently, he is Gurdjieff's assistant for he is holding a brown valise and a stool.

"I'd like to speak with you," I say to Gurdjieff.

He agrees and gets up. He motions his assistant to hand me the stool to carry. We walk a few short spaces. Twice a soft blue light flashes. The light is soundless, like silent lightning. It washes the whole world in blue.

Gurdjieff and I are standing in a school yard. Suddenly Gurdjieff raises his right hand high over his head, his index finger pointing skyward. I watch, mesmerized. Then, in one swift movement, Gurdjieff's hand descends to the ground, his finger pointing to the exact spot where I am to place the stool.

I set the stool down carefully. Gurdjieff sits on it.

Just as I am about to ask my question Gurdjieff inquires: "Did you see the blue light?"

"Yes," I say, realizing that I had forgotten all about it.

At that moment the world, so solid seeming before, becomes very liquid, dynamic. All the forms and objects flow and mix together. Everything is energy. Energy moving in soft, undulating waves. I feel myself, my attention, being pulled into the plasticity. I force myself to refocus on my question. I can only remember that I had a question. I can't remember what it is. I keep wishing to remember it. Finally, dredged from the bottom of memory, the words form.

"How is it that the archangels could make such enormous mistakes in managing our planet?" I ask, adding, "It makes me angry. I don't really see why I should suffer for someone else's stupidity."

Gurdjieff bends down and reaches into the valise his assistant has placed by his stool. He takes out a copy of All and Everything. Gently but with great deliberation, Gurdjieff thumbs through the first few pages. The wordless gesture instantly stamps itself on my mind: I had read the book only once. To be properly understood, three readings are required.

Now I am standing at a distance from him. I am about to ask a second question, but I feel a chill. The air has become very cold. My body is shivering.

"Close the gate!" commands Gurdjieff.

I look around and see that many children are running through the gate to the school yard. I run to it, but just as I reach it a woman closes it. I look back toward Gurdjieff. He and the assistant have vanished. They have left their coats behind. I pick them up and run down Laketon Road and up the alley searching for them. In a vacant lot a crowd of people mill around a stage platform. It is decorated in the bright bunting customary for a political race. Among the men on the platform, I notice Gurdjieff and the tall fellow. They are dressed formally in black bowlers and waistcoats, the style of the 1920's.

A boy steps to the microphone and divides the crowd into three groups. Then he announces—"The People Races are about to begin!"

I feel now I have been accepted and am entering a new phase of The Work. ✗

LIONS AT MIDNIGHT

S WELL HIM AS ANOTHER
and then I asked him with my eyes to ask again yes and then he asked me would i
yes to say yes my mountain flower and first i put my arms around him yes and drew
him down to me so he could feel my breasts all perfume yes and his heart was going
like mad and yes I said yes I will yes…

Stanley Ravin, enormously self-pleased, smiled broadly at his campy falsetto,
rapid-fire recitation of Molly Bloom's soliloquy and told me that, yes, he had indeed
gone to Dublin one June 16th for Bloomsday, visiting the Martello tower where
Joyce and his Buck Mulligan had lived, walking around Eccles Street and St.
Stephen's Green and doing "the whole Ulyssesian tour." He had gone right after his
Paris years where he'd lived on the Left Bank, hobnobbing with artists, existential-
ists and the like and attending the Sorbonne and working his way through the
university, posing as an artist's model and dancing in the Follies—"Yes, I was such
a beautiful boy," declared Stanley Ravin, preening.

Ravin gave a high, choking laugh and eyed me, gauging the effect, his mouth all
smiles. He was lying and did I know it? How could I help but know it! There was
no way that bulbous nose stuck between those little dark eyes and the acne-scarred
skin could ever have been seen as beautiful. His body, too, squat and bull-like, was

no Nijinsky's. So why was he lying to me? And so obviously? He was daring me to try to disprove it.

"Ahh, the Jews, the Irish," mused Ravin changing course, his voice now deeper, more masculine, "they have a lot in common."

I nodded, remembering the quick sneaky little handshake he'd given me at the door. I wanted nothing to do with this guy. But I did need a job and Ravin was the publisher of a god-awful little trade magazine, *Quick Food,* that needed an editor. It was one of about thirty magazines his company published. All dogs, but money-making dogs. Ravin had looked through my portfolio, skimmed *In New York* and now, I supposed, this was his idea of selling himself to me.

"The Jews and Irish," repeated Ravin, speed-talking, "they both have a great need to be loved. Both very creative. And both guilty, of course." Ravin grinned and waited.

I smiled and nodded. I needed this job. But this guy was so manipulative. He pulled all the strings. He was so oddball charming and disgusting. I was both attracted and repulsed.

Ravin put on his bifocals and, not sparing the pomp and ceremony, went through my resume again.

"Very creative," he said, the beady eyes staring over the rim of his glasses. "You've got good experience."

"Thank you."

"But how much of it is lies?"

I forced a smile. "You can check, if you like."

"You been out of work a long time, William, *a very long time.*" The words and voice hit like a jackhammer.

"I've been free-lancing."

"Ahhh, two-and-a-half years you've been free-lancing," Ravin exclaimed, tossing my resume down on his desk as if it were a pack of lies. "Thank God for free-lancing! Covers a host of sins."

Ravin smiled knowingly, sure that we both knew what he meant.

I felt like I was turning purple. He wasn't going to let me off the hook. "I can put this magazine out," I told him.

Ravin weighed that, his head rocking back and forth. "Well," he said after a bit, leaning back in his leather swivel chair, clasping his hands behind his head, "tell me…whadda you know about food?"

"I've been eating it all my life," I joked.

"He's been eating it all his life!" Ravin suddenly slapped the desk, his pock-marked face reddening, his little bull body shaking with laughter.

And it was all a show. He didn't mean any of it. And he knew I knew that. And he went on with it anyway, forcing me to keep playing into it.

"Ever been to Fire Island, William?"

"Yeah."

"Cherry Grove?"

"Once," I said. "To do a story." Cherry Grove was a notorious gay hang-out. Why was he asking about that?

"Hmmm-hmm," Ravin grunted, quickly indicating I was probably lying about this, too. Then he told me, his voice full of affectation, a disgusting joke about two queens who had broken up and were fighting over a young French poodle, a bitch, as to who could love her better. Ravin went into both the faggot and dog sounds which he delighted in making as sickening as possible.

This man was crazy, outrageous, grotesque. But somehow, he had me laughing.

A young woman appeared at the door. "You want?" she asked holding out a pile of photos. "Oh, I'm sorry," she said a little too largely, as if she didn't know I was there.

"No, c'mon in," Ravin said, and gestured—"Sarah meet William. Sarah's editor of *Professional Cooking*. She's the best in the whole place. Trained her myself."

Ravin gave her a big grotesque grin. Sarah chuckled warmly.

She laid a stack of photos and some color separations on Ravin's desk and flicked a piece of lint from his shoulder, then stood back and smiled at me. There was something in her manner I liked. She was slender with a wonderfully full bosom and broad shoulders. Her face was small, delicate and oval-shaped with a large forehead, a strong nose, a slight rise in the center of the bridge, with thin lips, a little chin; the skin very white. The brown eyes were large and alert, hidden behind large glasses. She had short blonde hair, probably dyed, parted on one side. She was wearing a soft pink angora sweater, short tight skirt and red shoes with spike heels. Her look seemed to be giving a lot of messages at once.

"William's a burnt-out case," Ravin explained, "looking to make a comeback. Isn't that so?"

"Oh, Stanley, come on," Sarah kidded, "give the guy a break, huh?" Turning to me she said, wrinkling up her face, "Stanley's okay, really. Just has a big mouth."

"All the better to eat you with!" clowned Ravin, licking his chops.

"My God, Stanley, he'll never work here!" cried Sarah. "Would you?" She smiled at me, making a comical gesture, raising her shoulders and spreading her arms apart.

"Is he always like this?" I asked.

Sarah cocked her head pensively and stared at Ravin. The eyes behind the glasses were deer-like, sensitive and intelligent. They took it all in, missing nothing.

Stanley, like a child, waited expectantly and with a certain fear. Behind the audaciousness I felt a vulnerability. I felt sorry for him.

"Well…" Sarah gave him a big smile, "his bark is a lot worse than his bite."

"That's all! That's the best you can do?" challenged Ravin.

Sarah turned to me. "His heart's in the right place…"She turned to Ravin, "You have a heart, no?" She chuckled and gave us both a comical wave and departed.

"Well," said Ravin, nodding, "she likes you. That's something." His fingers tattooed the desk. He pointed out photos of his wife and family on his desk. "You got kids?"

"Not yet."

Ravin gave another cursory glance through my resume, his head rocking from side to side, and read off the names of the companies I'd worked for in a theatrical voice: "Weber & Heilbroner, J. Walter Thompson, BBD&O, IBM, hmmmn...*In New York.*" He made a long, doubtful face. Finally: "Okay, okay. You got the job, William."

Ravin reached across the desk and shook my hand, that same sneaky little grip. I asked about salary. He offered me half of what I had told him I wanted.

"Sorry," I said. "I can't accept that."

"Listen, you need this job," Ravin declared, the little eyes locking on me, the voice cutting into me. "You blew it. This is your chance."

"Sorry. It's not enough."

"You've been out on the street a long time. You say its 'free-lancing.' But everyone knows its bullshitting, okay? No one's going to want to hire you. You're too old. I'm taking a chance with you. You don't take this job, you go to the bottom again. Only lower...I know, believe me." His voice trailed off as if he spoke from personal experience.

Inside I was a mess. I had an impulse to hit him. Another to cry. Angry, vulnerable, scared. I wanted to get out of that office. I reached for my portfolio.

But now Ravin was on my side, his voice all soft, friendly and caring. "Wait a moment...look, I understand what you've been through. Yeah, you have talent. But, William—this city's full of talent. You gotta have a place to showcase that talent. Come here, stay a few years, you'll be ready to demand big money. But not now. Not from where you're sitting."

What he said was true. He'd read me completely. Stripped me bare. Without mercy. He was bringing up all these different parts of me, different "I"s. I felt the dog in me, the one that wanted to lick his hand. But I despised him, too, and everything he stood for. Something in me wasn't going to let him dominate me. Fuck the job.

"I'm worth what I'm asking and somebody will pay it."

Ravin jumped out of his chair, came around his desk. He was wearing a charcoal black suit. He put his hands on his hips, macho-style. His jacket parted revealing a cheap vinyl belt, a garish yellow. He pounded the desk, then pointed a finger at me—"Okay, okay. I'll go up $2,000. But hear? Not a dime more!"

"Sorry..."

Ravin looked bewildered, personally hurt. He reminded me of one of Rouault's clowns. A part of me, I saw, actually felt sorry for all this melodrama.

He went back behind his desk, fell into his chair, cracked his knuckles and then came right up in my face—

"No way, no way, William, am I going to up this offer!"

I stood up.

"Not to start with, of course," he quickly put in. "But later on..."

"I'll think it over." I was drained, sucked dry inside.

I described Ravin to Barbara saying he was neurotic, wounded animal putting on a big show. And both with that sneaky, sweaty handshake, grabbing your fingers and not the palm, and then squeezing and smiling. Why go through all that? Barbara thought I was making too much of it, that I needed a job, so take it till I found another. But as clear as she often was, I knew she never saw in dimension. It was always one level only. Something else was going on here. I felt as if I was being tested in some way. There had been Soren, Vali and Rinpoche. Now it was Stanley Ravin. I was painting at Casey's one day and spoke to him about it.

"Someday," Casey told me, "we all have to face our dragons. You're strong enough, Pat."

A few days later the phone rang. I was meditating and didn't answer. I knew it was Ravin. The phone kept ringing. Finally, I answered. The voice was deep and round—"Hello, that you, Bill?"

He told me he was Ted Spencer, Ravin's boss and president of the company. He wanted to talk things over. His manner was offhand, unpretentious. He told me he knew what I was feeling about Stanley, a lot of people felt like that, but Stanley knew his job and thought I was talented. I should come in for a talk. There was something compelling, ingratiating in Spencer's voice.

And it was the same in person.

"Call me Ted, will you Bill?" Spencer boomed, giving me a hearty, meaty handshake and gesturing me toward a chair by his desk. He was a big, lion-chested man with a flat, square face, heavily tanned, and silver hair and dark-rimmed glasses. He was dressed in an expensive dark blue suit with a blue striped shirt and a red and yellow rep tie. All very executive-looking. He took off his jacket and tossed it over his chair. This revealed thick, fire engine-red suspenders. The suspenders were another "I" entirely. He pulled his leather swivel chair from behind the desk so there'd be no space separating us.

"Hearing some good things about you, Bill."

The words just rolled off his lips. And the way Spencer said 'Bi-lll,' lengthening the end of my name, had a funny effect on my body. His words were acting on me somehow. I could feel myself liking him.

Spencer put my portfolio in his lap and went through it page by page. His manner was that of some likable farm boy, a yokel who had just happened to get lucky. Every time he turned a page, he'd stick out his tongue and wet his index finger. He must have read my thoughts for he said, without looking up:

"It's my page-turner, Bill."

He closed the portfolio. "You've got the goods. I can see that, Bill. Now let's talk turkey." He moved his chair closer to mine and pulled a toothpick from his vest and stuck it in his mouth. Then he parked his feet up on the desk by the in and out basket and for the next fifteen minutes or so we talked. Behind the cornball facade, Spencer was tough as nails. He picked up everything, all the nuances. We went back and forth a while.

Finally, he faced me, took me in. There was no nonsense now, no more dancing around the ring. He hit fast and solid—

"Okay, Bill, I've seen you. You've seen us. You do right by me, I'll do right by you. You and I strike a deal—it's between us, get that? Just you and me. There's problems with Stanley, you come to me. Now name a figure."

"Same as before." I knew he wanted me.

Spencer chomped on his toothpick and gazed up at the ceiling as if he were running through a long list of numbers. Then he got up, pulled a big black book from the bottom of his desk. Embossed in gold on its cover was the word "Budgets." He thumbed through to the right page and studied the figures. He'd throw out a figure of the total mailing cost of the magazine. "Get that," he said, like it was important. The cost of paper. "Get that?" The cost of printing and binding. "Get that?" It was like he was passing me the secrets, letting me in on just what it took to publish the magazine. But he never told me the salary overhead. Or gross or net profit. Nothing that mattered. I had this sense he was play-acting. Yet it was all so serious.

"Bill," declared Spencer in a big voice, looking up finally, confronting me, "no way we can start you at the full figure. Would if I could, but I just can't..."

Spencer studied my reaction. I was feeling my body, just letting my eyes go soft, taking in the whole room, not saying a word. Nodding but making no commitment.

"Bill, this is my Bible." Spencer's voice had gone into a higher register, somewhat perturbed.

"It's just not here, I tell you." He patted the book like he held the Tablets of Moses.

I nodded thoughtfully and made a slow movement to pick up my portfolio.

"But I can go within $1000 of what you want. This is a big opportunity, Bill. Listen, you do right by me, I'll do right by you."

There was no resisting Spencer. I'd used the salary not to have to face Ravin. Now I had no excuse. Especially as once again Spencer let me know he understood all about Ravin and, if it came to it, he would step in.

Spencer walked me out to the elevator, his big paw of a hand on my shoulder, telling me—"You'll never regret this, Bill."

I was just about to get on the elevator when Spencer called out, speaking in an entirely different voice, "Oh, Bill..."

I turned. There stood Spencer, holding a watch above his head, dangling it in his hand like a dead fish. I looked at my wrist. My watch was missing!

"Worked my way through college as a magician," Spencer boomed and chuckled, quickly and deftly replacing the watch on my wrist, and showing me once again onto the waiting elevator. As the door began to close, Ted Spencer gave me a big wave.

Gurdjieff had said that those who were strong in the Work were strong in life. I guessed this was my big chance.

STANLEY RAVIN'S FACE WORE A MINCING LITTLE SMILE. HIS SMALL BLACK eyes greeted me coldly. Giving a high, halting laugh, he cried, "How nice of you to join us, William."

Sarah stood by her cubicle. "He really means it. Don't you Stanley?"

"Well, of course! I'm surprised at you. I'm just kidding William, that's all. You can take it, can't you William. You're a big boy."

I forced a smile. Inside I was shaking with anger. I felt hollow, like I had no stomach. I tried to come down into the body, put my attention there, but I was too identified.

Ravin motioned me toward a vacant office. I went in, assuming it was mine, and put my briefcase on the desk.

"Oh, no," Ravin said. "I was just showing you the office you'll have if you're as good as Ted expects." Ravin pointed me to a cubicle next to Sarah's. Then he darted into his office and came back with a stack of *Quick Food* magazines and dropped them on my desk. "Look through these for background. Then come into my office."

I looked through the magazines. They were mostly fluff. The stories didn't say anything. They were all safe, boring, written not to offend. It was what a magazine became after it sold its heart. It was just a public relations handout. It was only called a magazine to attract advertising. I had to get out of here, but I had to give it a few months before I began looking for another job.

I went to see Ravin. He was copy editing a story. He looked up. "Took you long enough, William. Oh well, don't mind me. Look, I need a publisher's page fast. Write it and get it to me before the end of the day. It's for the next issue."

I stared at him, shocked.

"What's wrong? You do write, don't you?"

"Yes, but I don't know a thing about the fast food industry. I told you that."

Ravin put down his pencil and gave me that same crappy smile. "Ohhh," he said," I thought 'Stephen Daedalus' was supposed to be a 'creative soul.'"

"How can I write about what I don't know?"

"Then write about money," he said. "Saving it, protecting it, making more of it—whatever. Everyone's interested in money. And even if people don't read the piece, they know it's the right topic."

"I don't know anything about money," I said.

Ravin looked at me as if I was a complete fool. "Yeah, it's not a surprise, William," he chuckled. "Well, what *do* you know about?"

The raw hostility shot right into me. I couldn't think.

"Here—look," Ravin said, exasperated. He handed me a pile of magazines from his desk. "These are our competitors. Just pick an editorial and rewrite it."

"What?"

"You know, turn it around, take another point of view, make it sound different. And remember: don't say anything new. That's always dangerous. Everyone's more comfortable with what they already know. Just make it sound like it's new."

Ravin gave me another of his hyena laughs and waved me out of his office.

That afternoon he piled a stack of free-lance articles on my desk. I was to rewrite them too. They had been written for one of the company's magazines that had just folded. I scanned the articles. They were written for an entirely different readership. When I protested, he just shook his head sadly. "How long have you been around?"

he exclaimed. He whipped out a blue pencil, motioned me to his side of the desk, and line-by-line began blue lining any reference to the word "restaurant" and substituting "fast food," and changing any other telltale signs. In about five minutes he had edited the whole ten-page story.

"Here's your story, Mr. Editor." Ravin's laughter rang in my ears.

"Stanley, we can't do this!"

"Who says? You think advertisers read this crap?"

"But the readers…"

"Screw the readers. This is a controlled circulation book. The readers get it free. What do they care? They're lucky to be getting anything."

"This isn't journalism. This is—"

"Prostitution? William, this is—*business.*"

"But—"

"Business is in business to make money. *Profit!* Get it? Everything else is window dressing, get it? Now don't give me this high and mighty stuff about journalism. That's just lip service only suckers believe."

Ravin grinned, the little black eyes glaring, daring me to disagree.

"Stanley, this isn't how most magazines are run. We don't have to do this."

"Magazines are run by publishers, owners, the money men." Ravin lit up a cigarette with a flourish, like he was in a movie or something. "Bill," he said, "stop dreaming about how you'd like it to be and take a good look at how it is."

And with that Stanley Ravin pulled an ankle-length muskrat fur coat over his little bull's body, covered his balding pate with a black astrakhan hat and, with a multicolored, oversized umbrella in hand, sauntered to the elevator. He threw me a conspiratorial wink, calling a snide, "Good-night."

A moist female voice spoke from behind me.

"Some piece of work, no?" I whirled around. Sarah was looking out over her cubicle.

"Yeah…" I felt like Billy Budd had just met Claggart.

"I think he likes you, William."

"Likes me!"

"Well why would he have hired you, silly?"

"But he's so…" I wanted to say "cynical and corrupt" but caught myself.

"Stanley's been through a lot."

"Yeah, but he's…I don't know."

Sarah raised her shoulders and turned up her palms, looking heavenward. "So what can I tell you, William? Don't think like a goy."

"Like a goy?"

"You know—straight, linear?"

Peanuts posters "wallpapered" her cubicle. "I see you're a Charlie Brown fan," I said.

"My good man," replied Sarah, hands on hips in mock masculine aggression, "I will have you know 'Peanuts' is a very intelligent comic strip." Sarah gave me another of her sign-off waves and ducked back into her cubicle.

Two very long weeks went by. One morning Ravin summoned me into his office. He was very cordial, charming in a kind of kooky way. All my hostility dropped away like an old scab. Perhaps I'd overreacted. He was actually quite intelligent. Very sensitive, too, though he hid that. I had this peculiar feeling for no reason I could discern: I felt sorry for Stanley Ravin.

"Well, William, you've won your wings. I can tell you now the real reason why you were hired," said Stanley, pausing for effect. We're publishing a new magazine from scratch. It's called something real basic: *Food*. It's targeted at institutional foodservice. You're its editor. I'm the publisher. We have three months to get the first issue out."

I had already decided to quit. The chance to create a new magazine was too good to pass up. I stayed on. The three month deadline was absurd. We had no staff, no free-lancers, no art director. And neither I, nor as it turned out Stanley, knew a thing about institutional foodservice—volume feeding at schools, colleges, hospitals and nursing homes. We began to muddle through, but about a month later a terse memo from Spencer came around: Stanley L. Ravin had been demoted to assistant publisher of *Food* and Spencer would be acting publisher until one could be found. Sarah told me over lunch one day that Stanley had gone behind Spencer's back. He had tried to convince the owner of the company to stop a deal Spencer was putting together.

"Not many people here like Stanley," Sarah had told me. "But he's been Spencer's number one son. Everyone's afraid of him."

No more. Stories spread and Stanley sulked. People ignored him. In the initial weeks, Stanley had organized the magazine's departments and contributed some good, if routine, story ideas. Now he withdrew, spending his days behind a closed door or out beating the pavement for a new job. He had no more interest in *Food*. When I tried to talk to him about it, he waved me away or told me to see Spencer. Spencer had come up through sales. He knew nothing about the editorial side, and he was too busy with other projects. So I was free to do what I wanted. Stanley had hired Bobbie, a food editor. Not only couldn't she write very well, she knew nothing about institutional foodservice. She also wanted my job, telling me Stanley had promised it to her. He probably had. Stanley had also hired a free-lance art director who was good with type and designing brochures but knew nothing about magazine design. Did he have a death wish?

So I was not only going to have to create and write the magazine but design it as well. At least I knew what I wanted. I wanted *Food* to be visual, to look like a magazine and not a manual. I wanted to give it a consumer magazine feel, not look like a trade book, crammed with information, deadly dull and not saying anything. I could see what I wanted, so that was not a problem. I designed the magazine to have large two-page spread layouts with plenty of white space and use dramatic photos, artwork and typography. The problem was the articles. The magazine was going to professionals in the food field. Bobbie could get away with writing the food section, but the rest of the magazine had to have something to do with food as well. If I wrote about food, my ignorance would show. What to do? Weeks went by and the deadline for the first issue was fast approaching.

One day I was talking to my Mother on the phone. She was reminding me of how I disliked food as a child and time and again would push the food off the tray of my highchair. Suddenly, a story title came to me: "Food as a Weapon." Then the magazine's whole editorial slant came to me: *Food* would talk about food from the point of view of psychology and social issues. We'd target industry business issues and political sore points. We'd key on the maverick ideas, playing them off against mainstream dogma, define the issues, and let the readers decide. *Food* would be unique. It wouldn't talk about food!

The front covers of the competing food magazines were like their insides: totally boring, predictable, rooted in the prosaic: a cook in his kitchen, a plate of food, two people eating at a table, and so forth. Our first issue was going to be a theme issue devoted to nutrition which was just becoming a societal issue. How to illustrate that on the cover? One Saturday I was down at Casey's and we were looking through a book of Jackson Pollock's art and, again, the idea struck. We would use abstract art for the first cover. It would look like the body's digestion of food.

We introduced the magazine at the big industry food show in Chicago. It was an instant success with foodservice directors and advertisers. The magazine became the talk of the industry. Advertising dollars followed. And its success came without whoring—without catering to advertisers, without running advertorials. The name was a hybrid, two concepts that didn't belong together stuck together to get advertising. Advertorials were advertising sections disguised as editorial. The layout, type, photos and writing all imitated editorial articles so as to dupe the reader into thinking he was reading an objective article.

Spencer was overjoyed. Stanley glowered. He had somehow gotten on the good side of Spencer again. They both went to Puerto Rico to a publisher's convention and Stanley gave a slide show taking credit for creating the magazine. "It's just business, William," he explained, saying it made it easier to sell ads.

"How can you take credit for something you didn't do?"

"You're working for me," he told me. "I'll do whatever is necessary to sell space in the magazine."

"I'm not working for you. I'm working for Spencer," I told him.

"William," he said in a phony fatherly tone, "don't get involved in a battle you can't win."

From that day on Ravin and I battled.

The magazine got better and better. Prisoners of war were just coming back from Vietnam and I reasoned that they would be fed for a time in a hospital. What's a person eat after years of eating soup and rice, I wondered. We did the story featuring a San Diego hospital where the prisoners of war convalesced. The cover of *Food* showed a Vietnamese soldier marching emaciated American prisoners.

Ravin tried to get his power back. But I kept insisting I reported to Spencer, not to him. He must have gone to Spencer but got no backing. Now a pitched war of nerves began with Ravin trying to undermine the magazine by bastardizing the editorial. Time and again, he would promise advertisers special editorial treatment in return for ad contracts. I refused to go along.

"Goddamn it! It's just the way business is done," Ravin shouted. "Look around at the other magazines."

It was true. Spencer had made his money milking "cows," publishing second- and third-rate magazines. To exist at all, the magazines had to sell out their editorial to advertisers.

"Stop dreaming, Bill," Ravin told me. "Business is money. Journalism is a business. We're not here to tell the truth. That only gets you into trouble. It makes people think. No one really wants to hear the truth. Yeah, they're all the time talking about it but the truth hurts. People want comfort. You never know where the truth is taking you. People want security. They want to know where they're going. So journalism is just another way to make money by purporting to tell the truth but not really telling it. Got it? Now, William, some magazines are cash cows, some are sick, anemic cows, but we milk them all here. So pick up a pail and grab some teats!"

But *Food* was Spencer's first real magazine. He loved the new-found respectability. *Food* quickly became the company's flagship magazine and I was now Spencer's fair-haired boy. With the ads coming in and Ravin taking all the credit for it, he finally convinced Spencer to make him publisher again. Spencer, who ruled like a feudal lord, played us off against one another, taking the role of "Father" and loving it. I couldn't defeat Ravin. He couldn't defeat me. Many times I tried to call a truce, but, though he always agreed, he never stuck by his word. So there we were, locked in this incredible, senseless struggle. It was crazy. Ravin thrived on psychic warfare. He loved the crazy energy, the chaos, the lies and subterfuge, the negative emotion. He was in his element. That's what he fed on.

Without the Work, I would have self-destructed. I used Ravin as a reminder. Whenever I'd see him I'd come down into the body. The impression of him, myself— the utter disgust and contempt I felt—was so vivid as to actually hurt. I would burn up inside and, time and again, find myself in reaction, in judgment, in false personality. So the job became an extension of my work on myself, a living laboratory.

My only ally in the office was Sarah. She had a loyalty to Ravin as he had brought her to New York from the company's printing plant in Duluth, Minnesota. She'd only been a production clerk there, but Ravin had seen her potential and convinced her and her husband, Frank, to move to the City. Sarah understood and accepted his dark side. We took to going to lunch every day, usually at the Mayflower on York and 54th streets. She acted like a mother, trying to keep her two sons at bay, but, as she remarked over a Bloody Mary one day, "You two are like Cain and Abel. This runs too deep for just a battle over a magazine."

It was true. There was something almost mythical going on, as if two archetypes were playing out through us. To me, it was as though Ravin and I commanded opposing sides of a chess board. It was like *The Art of Asha*, the age-old struggle between Ahura Mazda and Ahriman. Could that be real? It seemed quite fanciful. And yet I sensed that on the deepest level this was what was going on. It was like Ravin was my "black teacher." I was learning on a whole different level, not theoretically but on the battlefield. Every misjudgment cost me directly. When I spoke of this to Barbara or our friends, there was only silence; that certain smile. Only Sarah and Casey seemed to have an understanding for the dimension on which this was being played out. To others, Ravin and I were just ordinary people—which we were. But when Ravin and I came together, something was ignited that brought the mythological into play. I had been cast in the role of "St. George," and he, the "dragon." Finally, I came to realize and accept the strange truth of that—that the myths, the Greek gods and all, are not an invention of an imaginative mind, but an actual living reality grounded in human life. So often I wanted to leave the absurdity of all this, but I understood that wasn't up to me. The leaving would take place in its own time. I sensed that something had to happen first, something had to be fulfilled between Ravin and me. Well, the question then, I supposed, was how to "slay" the dragon.

Meanwhile, *Food* had won national journalism awards. Spencer continued to boost my salary, though he always made me argue for every penny. He was a sly old wizard. I hated to talk money, to "bring things down to just a money level," but I began to realize that was simply an identification. It took me years to realize that if I hoped to get anywhere with Spencer, I had to speak his language. Spencer's language wasn't journalistic quality—he didn't give a hoot about it (unless it affected ad revenue). Spencer was all businessman. He lived for the action, cutting the deal, testing his powers against his competitors. Spencer was a priest of temporal power. And its stark, pitiless symbol was *m-o-n-e-y* in any form, be it in ad pages, lower printing costs, lower travel budget, lower salaries, whatever. "You gotta make the nut," Spencer would say. "Everything else is gravy." Spencer's nut was overhead. "Only three things you can do. Make money, save it, or lose it. And saving it is a helluva lot cheaper than making it."

Without the Work I could never have endured Stanley and Spencer. But it gave me a way of working with the situation. I used Stanley especially as a "reminder" to remember myself. I worked on identification, on negative emotion. I constantly failed but it enabled me to remain.

It had been two and a half years since Barbara and I had entered the Work. We were still in what Lord Pentland had called a "preparatory group." One evening, in a group meeting in March, Lord Pentland asked if the group would like to go to The Foundation. We were perhaps mature enough, he said, to enter a general group.

But many of our original group did not enter the Foundation. Soren had shown Lord Pentland a list of all the magic books in his library. He would never tell me what Lord Pentland said, but a few weeks afterward he had become angry during a meeting, shouting "I've had enough of this bullshit," and stalked out, taking Miriam in tow. Earlier, Lord Pentland had asked Phillipe to read *All and Everything* in front of the group. Phillipe had read several paragraphs when suddenly Lord Pentland demanded that he stop. Lord Pentland chided him severely for Phillipe, thinking that Gurdjieff wrote badly, had "edited" the book. Phillipe never returned. Paul, along with several others, had been transferred to another group. Lord Pentland had given Ruth a shock to her personality. Once the most devoted of the group, Ruth now spoke negatively to others in the group, trying to undermine their relationship to Lord Pentland. Finally, she left to study in Oregon with a woman teacher who had known Gurdjieff in Paris after the Second World War. Helen—whom Lord Pentland had advised repeatedly that "We can't go slow enough"—had become embroiled in an emotional triangle. She had finally married a painter-carpenter in the group and moved to Kansas City. They had a baby boy, but soon divorced.

There were many more people and activities at The Foundation. Perhaps as many as two hundred attended the Tuesday evening lectures in the main hall. We found a great deal of our time was being spent at The Foundation. One evening we would go for our regular group meeting. Another evening for a study group that read and discussed the Gospels. Another evening we went to practice the sacred movements—the dances and exercises that Gurdjieff had discovered, or created. Different movements evoked specific states of mental, emotional and bodily consciousness. And a fourth evening we went for meditation. Then we would spend all day Sundays at an estate at Armonk.

Barbara and I had our first child, a boy. I wanted to call him Cuchulainn, after the legendary Celtic hero, but Barbara wouldn't have it. "Heroes die young," she argued. We compromised, naming him John after Lord Pentland. Our one-bedroom walk-up apartment in Manhattan was too small and so after John began to walk we moved to a two bedroom apartment in Dobbs Ferry in Westchester which overlooked the Hudson River. Becoming a "father" now myself made me wonder about the early influences that had formed me.

"WRITE THE STORY OF YOUR LIFE," LORD PENTLAND TOLD OUR GROUP. "Tell of those events and people who have helped to form you. Try to separate 'essence' from 'personality.' That is, discriminate between that which you are and that which you have learned and become."

I had been one of the few in the group to take it seriously. Most just handed in a paragraph or two but I wrote about a thousand words. Lord Pentland gave me a privately published copy of Ouspensky's story of his life. Though I hadn't succeeded, the effort did call up many questions about my early life and influences. After a field trip for the magazine, I flew home by way of Pittsburgh to visit my roots.

It was a sunny, cloudless day when I drove through the Fort Pitt Tunnel and across the huge double-decker bridge. Ahead loomed the city of Pittsburgh, sitting in a triangle at the fork of two broad rivers, the Monongahela and the Allegheny. What had once been a smoky, grimy, soot-filled downtown was now a showplace of shiny silver skyscrapers, large fountains and green parks.

I drove into the city. Many of the old buildings were still there, as were the cobblestone streets. I took the F.D.R. Drive north along the Monongahela past the big rusting mills of J&L Steel, its tall cannon-like smokestacks still spewing black clouds. I rolled up the windows but too late. A familiar, heavy sulphur-smell filled my nostrils. Perched on the hillsides and spread along the gullies were the same row upon row of narrow, two-story workers' houses, stunted and dreary faced, covered with insul brick, a cheap imitation brick siding, wives in babushkas hanging laundry out the windows, old men sitting on stoops in undershirts nursing cans of Iron City beer. It was a scene out of a John Kane painting.

I drove on north to East Liberty and Shady Side and over Penn Avenue, following the old trolley tracks past the great lawns and fortress-like mansions of what were once the habitats of Pittsburgh's wealthy, until finally I came to Scotty's Diner, a throwback to the Forties, and just beyond it after the railroad tracks was my home town of Wilkinsburg. I drove around hoping to see the haunts of my youth. Finally, I pulled up in front of the old house on Laketon Road that my Grandfather Scott had built. The oleanders all in bloom, the old smells and images rushing in on me as if time had rewound itself. After a bit, I noticed the swing on the porch was gone and part of the porch had caved in. A young black school girl came by. She seemed very open and friendly. We exchanged greetings. Then I went up to the door and knocked. Pretty soon I heard this wonderful old voice growl at me—

"Billy! What you doin' around here?"

And there peering out at me from behind a curtain was a face I'd seldom seen but never forgotten.

"Bill! How are you?" I called out.

The door opened halfway and a hand came out and grabbed mine.

"C'mon, c'mon! Quick now," my Uncle Bill said, pulling me inside, checking up and down the street, then quickly closing the door and locking it.

It had been years since I'd seen him. He looked no different really. Oh, he had shrunk a little, but it was as if no time had passed. There was still the broad, flat gladiator's face, the steel blue eyes, clear and powerful, the bull neck, heavy shoulders, and the complexion still pink, like a baby's. He wore an old tattered white undershirt and dark, baggy trousers. His hair was all white now and I thought I saw a sadness, a hurt, in the eyes I'd never seen before.

He motioned me down the dark hallway into the kitchen. The large wall by the stairs which led up to the bedrooms was painted a deep red. I remembered my Mother telling me that when their mother died he had lain on her grave and wept and wept. They couldn't get him to come home and when he finally did he painted the wall a blood-red and then went to the dentist and had all his teeth pulled out. That was some twenty years ago. He must be in his eighties now.

He struck a wooden match and lit the old gas stove. He went to the sink by the back window and filled a kettle with water. Atop the sink a small mirror was propped up. I remembered that mirror and now it came to me that everything was just the same. The cupboards, the peeling wall paper, the linoleum, the round oak table, the tablecloth with the checked red-and-white pattern, the rusty old horseshoe nailed to the doorframe, the green and black Mellon Bank calendar, the heavy oak chest of drawers. Time hadn't moved here. Or so it seemed. And there was still a life here. Real people had lived here. Strong, upright people. "People," as my Mother said, "too strong for their own good."

I sat down at the table and my Uncle poured tea into the cracked white cups he had set out. I noticed his hands were shaking. My Mother had told me he had Parkinson's disease. He sat down across from me. There was a long moment of silence. I heard his breath then. The slow wheezing, the shortness of breath. The face was so bold, forthright, and virtually unlined except for the crow's feet by the eyes. Finally my Uncle asked, his voice deeper, more gravelly:

"How's yer mother doin' down in Florida?"

"Oh, I don't know. She likes it, I guess," I told him.

My Uncle took a slurp of tea. He shook his head.

"Well, I dunno, Billy," he said. "Don't really like it that much do they? Yer mother keeps talkin' of comin' back."

"Why do you suppose they left then?"

My Uncle laughed and coughed. "Nothin's back here," he said. "Everyone's dead…or moved off."

He took another drink of tea and barely got the cup back into the saucer. He shrugged. "Just me 'n Marie here now. Your sister 'n her family, they moved over to Glenwood." He stared out the window a moment. "Nah!" he muttered. "Nah, they're better off down there. This here…it's all past."

There was no sentimentality in his voice, no judgment. He was just speaking a fact. I nodded and we sat a bit more. Finally, I asked him:

"You ever see any of my friends around?"

He looked at me uncertainly.

"You know," I said, "Seibert, Gropup, Bill Drennings—"

"Nah! All long gone now, 'cept for Drennings. The older one. Lives up over the hill. Penn Township. Seibert, I hear, he's runnin' a movin' company. Over on North Side. Groshock, his mother Lillian, she moved to Cleveland after the old man got hit with lightning."

"He was playing golf, wasn't he? Churchill Country Club?"

"Yeah, yeah. Never seen 'em since. The boy…didn't the boy go up to New York?"

"Yes, he lived with me for a few months. But, no, I haven't seen him in years."

My Uncle looked around the kitchen but not at anything in particular.

"Billy," he said looking straight at me now. "This here, it's all past I tell ya." There was a long pause. "Ain't nothin' round here now 'cept the coloreds. Call 'em 'blacks' now. All came up from the Hill District when that was torn down and the new arena was put in." My Uncle looked aimlessly around the room. "There's nothin' here now but crime. Can't even walk down the street anymore. Even in daylight, I tell ya."

So that was what he was afraid of. I changed the subject.

"Did you see the Ali-Frazer fight?" I asked.

"Nah!" He took a slurp of tea and looked out the window. "Don't pay it no attention."

My Uncle had been a fighter. Battlin' Bill Scott was his name in the ring. I could hear my Mother telling me, "Why he could take you out with either hand. He hit like a mule. And he was fearless. Didn't care how big you were. The only trouble was our Bill wouldn't listen. No one could tell Bill anything. He never took the time to learn how to box. With him it was just get in there and slug it out and let the best man win."

My Uncle being a fighter was part of the family mythology. I didn't understand his lack of interest. I remembered all those Ring magazines stacked up in his room and how we'd talk about Joe Louis and Billy Conn, Zale and Graciano, LaMotta and Sugar Ray, Marciano and Jersey Joe Walcott. None of that mattered now?

"Bill, you don't mean it, do you?"

He drank up and took cup and saucer to the sink.

"But, Bill, fighting was—"

My Uncle wheeled around, facing me, that old look in his eyes.

"Billy," he said, his voice pounding out the words, "fightin' don't get ya no-where. Nowhere! Hear?"·

He eyed me a moment the way he must have when he was in the ring. The cup was shaking in the saucer. And in that moment I felt all his pain, his suffering, all the anger and bewilderment of his life. He put the cup and saucer in the sink and came back to the table. I laid my hand atop his. His hand shook under mine like it was attached to a small motor. I could still sense beneath the shaking the raw strength of his spirit.

He had had over seventy fights. Sparred with Jack Dempsey and Harry Greb. Then came the First World War and off he went to France, an infantryman. He boxed, winning his division and the Duke of Edinburgh gave him a medal. Then out in the trenches he breathed in a lungful of mustard gas. From that moment on his breath was rasping and wheezing. Big ugly boils the size of a grapefruit would well up on his back. Every few months he'd have to go to the VA hospital to get them drained. All my Uncle had known how to do was fight. Fighting was his whole life. The gas not only ended his career but, in a way, his life. He could never reinvent himself. He got married, had a daughter, sold insul brick, but his wife left him, di-vorced him. He kept to himself then, lived at home the rest of his life. His father had died in the fifties, his mother and brother in the sixties. It was only the three sisters and him who remained. He lived in the old house all alone. My Mother and Kate lived in Florida, Marie, the eldest of the daughters, lived next door in an apartment.

We sat together in the kitchen for some time without speaking. The silence was rich and alive. At one point, I felt a subtle change in the atmosphere. A shift of per-ception. My Uncle's face began to change, his features vibrating, no longer fixed and definite, but fluid, dynamic in appearance. He no longer looked like the Uncle I knew. I didn't know who he was. Faces came and went. None I knew. It seemed as though he, too, was aware of the shift. Suddenly, the moment enlarged. His face took on the visage of a Greek god. My body shuddered with energy. I came down more fully into the body. I could feel the pores opening. He reached over to me then, his big hand pulling me closer to him. He slowly turned his face to the side, and pointed to a badly mangled ear. And the gravelly voice repeated:

"Fightin'—it don't get ya nothing. D'ya hear?" He stared at me, trying with all his might to impress the knowledge of his life upon me. "Now ya remember that, Billy."

I nodded and smiled, a warm beautiful feeling flowing between us. From the silence we shared words came to me, words that told him how much I loved and respected him, how noble and brave he was. That he had been a fighter, a natural-born fighter. That had been his role, his destiny. And that his life had been full of suffering and misery that he had never understood, but that from it he had learned the greatest and last lesson a fighter can ever learn—that fighting leads nowhere.

I saw myself now when I was a child. I remembered Humphrey, the eldest of the two brothers, coming home at night from the railroad carrying his lunch pail with Batman and Phantom comic books sticking out from his coat pocket. Humphrey was so gentle and kind. His eyes were soft and intelligent, but so sad. I liked him a lot, but it was this Uncle, though he barely said a word to me, who had captured my imagination. Though I could not have put it in words then, I saw now that there was a force to him, untamed and pure, proud and independent, that attracted me.

We might never have spoken if some kid in the neighborhood hadn't whipped me in a fight and my mother, afraid that I was too sensitive and serious, that I might turn out to be a sissy, asked my Uncle to take me down to the cellar and "show Billy a thing or two."

I remembered my Uncle laughing and swooping me up in his arms like a feather and, holding me at eye level, and asking:

"So you wanna learn how to use your dukes?" His breath was heavy with a funny smell and his voice was rough and garbled.

I didn't understand him, but, bug-eyed, I nodded. I was too afraid to speak.

He laughed kind of crazy like and took me down the narrow steps to the old limestone cellar where he used to train. It was dark and cold down there. Dusty and dirty and very still. Sort of eerie. Years ago its rough limestone walls had been whitewashed but were black with soot from the coal furnace. The ceiling was low and you could see all the rafters and pipes and old spiders' nests. From one of the rafters hung a torn, battered punching bag. Near the coal bin were some rusted dumbbells, a barbell and a broken rowing machine.

My Uncle stood me in the center of the cellar and bent down till he was at eye level with me. "Gimme your hands," he grunted. He took my fingers and balled them up into a fist, curling the thumb around the outside of the fingers. It felt good. He did one hand, then the other. "Those are yer dukes," he told me.

Then he held my fists up, the left out a little, the right cocked back by the chin. "Now, Billy, ya shoot out the left. Once, twice. That's how ya jab. Now snap it out.

Twist your fist at the end. Yeah. Now bring out the right. Nahh!—keep yer dukes up. Okay now, ya start movin' side to side. Throw the jab. The jab. That's it. Now circle—stick the jab. Weave now. Circle. Jab, jab. Now throw the right!"

I'd been hitting at the air but now my Uncle held up this big thick meaty hand in front of me and ordered me to hit it. He kept the hand a steady target at first. Then began moving it. All the time he had me dancing around, shifting my weight, going into a crouch, tossing a jab, smacking that big hand, cracking the flesh, sending shots of electricity zinging through my body, the sound echoing in the old cellar.

"Attaboy, Billy! Attaboy!"

And then suddenly my Uncle sprang up to his full height. He towered above me like a huge tree. I felt this wave of fear sweep through me...

"C'mon!" he shouts. "C'mon."

He begins circling around me, puffing and wheezing like a locomotive, sticking the jab, measuring me, sticking and moving, those laughing steel blue eyes cold and strange now, fixing entirely upon mine, keen to the slightest movement, the slightest ebbing of will. It is just the two of us down here and he is very serious.

He weaves suddenly, breaking my attention and moving in, giving my midsection a drumming, slipping my right and letting fly with a nasty jab, and of course him never touching me, but me feeling the punches anyway as I step through my fear and stick and move, too, as my Uncle goes up on the balls of his feet and circles around the cellar faster and faster, catching phantom punches, keeping the head low, shooting the left, working the body, standing his man up with an uppercut, a hard left and finishing him off with a thunderous right cross!

And my Uncle standing there facing the blank limestone wall, his hands at his side, panting, wheezing, spitting, his bright eyes flashing and me laughing and dancing up and down and all this wonderful energy streaming between us, and the late afternoon light streaking in through the small cobwebbed windows and me feeling this great love for him...

I didn't know it then but that day down in the old limestone cellar he had shown me his animal. And his animal had evoked my own. For the first time, I felt my body, my own power and spirit, and I knew even before he said it, the two of us standing there both sweating and trying to catch our breath in the cool shadows of the old cellar, that it was true—

"Ya don't have to be afraid of anybody now," my Uncle shouted, a wonderful Irish smile on his face. "Nobody!"

Those words from the past shouted at me again as I sat with my Uncle in the kitchen. The time came and we got up from the table and went down the dark hallway to the door. We shook hands and smiled and I walked out onto the porch which creaked under the sudden weight. I waved goodbye and as I left I heard that wheezing, gravelly voice call from the doorway—

"Remember now. Hear?"

And then the door quickly closed.

Several nights after I arrived home this dream came to me:

I am standing in the kitchen of the old house. It is midnight. Out in the backlot I see a pride of lions. Very fierce looking. Some are fighting. Their roars go right through me. People begin pouring up the steps from the cellar, crying out, "I gotta get out of here!" An old chess friend from my Village days is at the front door. He looks haggard, worn. I go down into the cellar. It is as if I am entering an ancient crypt. It is cold and dark. A group of people sit meditating in half-lotus postures on the cement floor. I join them.

Suddenly I become aware that beside me there is this immense presence. A heavy thick animal smell fills my nostrils. My ears flood with the sound of its breath, the mighty ebb and heave of its lungs. I keep my eyes shut. But I know now what it is—a lion. Its enormous strength completely invades me.

I think of escaping, but realize it is useless. I sit motionless, the awesome animal totally dominating me. All I can do is stay still, not escape into a dream, take in the raw primal impression.

And then all the impressions crystallize. I am left with one staggering and numbing recognition: this lion…this lion is my death.

"CARE TO PLAY A GAME OF CHESS?" ASKED LORD PENTLAND OFF-HANDEDLY.

It seemed as if he had appeared out of nowhere. The two of us faced one another on opposite sides of a chess board; the black and white pieces set up and ready for action. Lord Pentland stood silently observing me in the glare of the hot afternoon sun. Behind him stood Soren, smirking, expectantly hopping up and down, making faces. I was startled and felt utterly stupid, ridiculous.

I was dressed in a black fez, loose Turkish pants and boots and a billowy white tunic belted with a brilliant red silk sash. I stood behind a row of tables covered with chessboards and pieces. High atop the row, blowing in the breeze, flew a big banner proclaiming—Play The Chess Masters of Persia Only 50 Cents! The chess booth was one of many in a bustling bazaar of colorful booths and tents that stretched the length of an entire block.

Overnight, following long months of meticulous planning, Lord Pentland's groups had transformed East 66th between Lexington and Park Avenues into a pungent and sumptuous Middle Eastern bazaar offering perfumes and pottery and carpets and candies and clothes and jewelry and belly dancing and fortune telling and story telling. The bazaar was a Work project whose purpose was chiefly to provide the conditions where we all might play a different role; the theory being that unique opportunities for self-observation would appear. In practice, my ego felt terrified, overwhelmed.

"Game of chess?" Lord Pentland inquired again, more spiritedly. He smiled at me, placed two quarters in my palm and sat down at the board.

Soren was doubled-up with suppressed laughter, giving me his cross-eyed ape face and sticking out his tongue. He had been by earlier. I hadn't seen him since he left the Work. He'd reminded me of my wanting to play Lord Pentland a game of chess. Earlier he'd asked, "Still want to play LP a game?" "Sure," I'd said, thinking it would never happen.

And now here this dream had suddenly become an uncomfortable reality.

It couldn't have come at a worse time. I felt so lousy! It was after midday and I'd been playing for hours already and was hot and sweaty and had lost practically every game. A Work friend, the other suffering "chess master," was doing a bit better, but we were both exhausted from the effort. The idea was that we would each play five games, simultaneously, moving from board to board, making our moves. I hadn't expected much interest but from the start our booth had been jammed, all the boards in play and surrounded by kibitzers, waiting their turn to attack us. Their ferocity shocked me. I hadn't expected anyone to take it so seriously. Maybe it was our costumes. But they were like hungry lions out for blood. The emotion and will of the crowd was overwhelming. It was as if I was playing one huge animal with many heads. I could hardly see more than a move ahead. I played like a *putzer*. I wasn't a very juicy meal. More than a few registered their disgust. Finally, "the lion" had its fill. The boards lay empty. The two "chessmasters" stood silently behind the boards, emotionally exhausted. I couldn't wait for the bazaar to end, to get out of this stupid costume and back into a familiar, trusted role. It was then Lord Pentland had appeared.

"Would you like white pieces or black?" I asked, still in a daze.

"White. of course," he answered, looking at me curiously.

Of course. What a ridiculous question. My hands and knees were trembling. My breath was shallow. It was hard to breathe. The recognition of the enormity of what was about to take place—*I was going to play my teacher*—astounded me. This was not going to be any old game of chess. I had only met him in his office and the group meetings where I'd asked questions and he had answered. Now I was meeting him on another plane and in another circumstance entirely. It was across a field of war, one where no questions could be asked. This was a test, I saw that. Though the outer focus had to be on the capturing of the white king, the inner one had to be on playing as consciously as I could, remembering myself, being present, not getting trapped in reaction, identification, on winning or losing. Otherwise, it would be a waste of a rare experience.

One by one, as though performing a ritual, I slowly set up the pieces on the white side of the board, then the black. I focused on the body, the breath, the space inside and out, feeling the weight and shape of each piece I took up in my hand, placing it in the center of its square, dividing my attention between inner and outer, doing all that I had practiced so many times before. But all those times, I saw now, were only preparatory. I could sense Lord Pentland's silent assent.

I stood back then. Neither of us moved. There was a stop, a silence, an incredible space. The board, the pieces, the two of us and the crowd around—all caught in a still image.

And then the game began, white advancing it's king's pawn two squares to the center of the board. In chess there are basically two openings. With one, the king's pawn is moved; the other, the queen's pawn. King's Pawn openings are a direct call to battle, to an immediate confrontation. Queen's Pawn openings are more strategic, more subtle and slippery, as they delay the confrontation. White, having the initial move, sets the basic line to be played. Black to choose the kind of game it will be.

There are two basic choices. The first is to meet white's pawn move head-on, advancing the black king's pawn two squares directly in front of the white pawn, thus blocking its forward movement, and maintaining the symmetry of the positions. This reply sets up an ongoing struggle for the center of the board. But as white has the first move, and thus the tempo, black is at a slight disadvantage. Another reply then for black is to lie back, to advance the king's pawn only one, not two squares. With this move the game enters what is known as the French Defense, a very cramped, somewhat stodgy game that often ends in a draw. Black playing either king's pawn move is very classical, going back to the early days of chess.

The second and more modern choice for black is to play an irregular, or asymmetrical, opening. These are moves that maintain parity on the board by the action of the pieces (they control squares not by occupying them—as in the king's pawn type of game—but by their ability to capture an opponent's pieces moving onto those squares). Among these openings is the Sicilian Defense. Instead of moving the king's pawn, it advances on the wing, moving the queen bishop's pawn two squares. As pawns capture only on the diagonals, it thus controls one of the center squares and maintains parity. It's an unorthodox opening known for its fighting spirit. As such, it inevitably leads to wild and explosive play, complex gambits, and sudden sharp attacks. It is a dangerous, tricky opening. To take the game into the Sicilian meant black was signalling it was going all out to win.

What should I play? A King's Pawn defense? The French? The Sicilian? I went back and forth trying to get a feeling for where I was, what kind of game I was in. I was thinking, too, of what kind of game would be most natural for Lord Pentland to play? It was likely he was familiar with the King's Pawn and French games more than the Sicilian. The unruliness of the Sicilian, its unpredictability, would run counter to his nature. Inside me, I could feel the energy massing, becoming more solid in a way, yet fluid, expansive. I went back and forth considering the various openings. Then it came to me. Dangerous or not, I just had to take the chance.

I moved the queen bishop's pawn out to attack the white center.

Lord Pentland was apparently familiar with the Sicilian for without delay he brought out his king's knight. We moved back and forth, playing out a variation of the Sicilian, each responding accurately to the other's moves, maintaining the balance of power on the board. Soon, the opening moves completed, the rival pieces faced one another in the deadly Sicilian formation. White, being strongly developed in the center of the board, massing for an attack. Black, giving way in the center, holding back from any direct and heavy contact, while developing its forces on the queen's wing, ready for counterplay. Prudently, both sides had castled kingside, removing their kings to the side of the board, giving greater security from capture.

The moves had gone quickly to this point. Now, with both sides fully developed, white delayed. Its next move would initiate us into the middle game, a deeper line of strategy and a new octave of play.

I looked away from the board. It was a beautiful day. The sky was a glorious cobalt blue with a bright sun and just enough summer breeze to give the air a fresh, light quality. I breathed slowly into the body, feeling each part and limb, the "sound" flowing in me. The word must have spread quickly, for crowded about Lord Pentland were many familiar faces from the Work.

White moved. I looked down at the sixty-four black and white squares. A rook had been relocated to the queen's file in the middle of the board. This was the beginning of the white attack. The rook threatened capture of my black bishop. I'd either have to move it or defend it with another piece. If I moved the bishop, white's tempo would be strengthened. I could defend it as well, but that would lock in my pieces a bit. The position was already tight. Protecting the bishop would only give a more cramped configuration of pieces. What to do? Neither move had much to offer.

I breathed through tension, reestablishing myself, relaxing more deeply, and gazed at the board. No other possibility showed itself. It was either move the bishop, or defend it. But there was a dim feeling that there was something there on the board; some move I had yet to see. I went deeper, focusing completely into the matrix of black and white squares. As with painting, I found I had somehow "stepped into" the board, experiencing the tension and possibilities of the pieces. I could sense the beginnings of another perspective, a new thought coming to life, one that had been totally hidden to me. It suddenly took form in words: *What if I didn't move the bishop!?*

White would take it, of course. But what then? I had never looked at that. The thought of sacrificing a major piece so early in the game for no discernible advantage seemed ridiculous, silly, not worth thinking about. And so I had never investigated what would happen. Unwittingly, I had trapped myself in the usual categories of thought. Now summoning everything in me, I tried to visualize what the sacrifice of the bishop would mean. It would free me to move. But what move could I make that would compensate for the loss of such a valuable piece? I scanned the board again and again, but the board didn't speak to me: I saw no such move. This line of thinking produced nothing. And further, whatever black's move, the capture of the bishop would put a white rook on black's second rank. Rooks are like tanks. Once they break through your front lines, they are a menace difficult to drive back. They set up powerful outposts from which devastating attacks can be launched. The play of defending pieces is usually distorted defending against them. Strength is slowly sapped as the position becomes more and more cramped.

No, it was either move the bishop or defend it. Sacrificing it meant a certain loss of the game.

A tug-of-war broke out between my intellectual and emotional centers. The one urging me not to be foolish, the other to keep open, to go deeper. The pressure built. The resulting tension—the mind on one side, the intuition on the other and the witnessing of same—became unbearable. It was just coming to an end when suddenly: a moment of vision. I saw it. The forced mate of the white king! And the wonder of it was that the whole sequence of moves began with the innocuous movement of a kingside pawn that threatened nothing.

I'd never seen this deeply. And it was all so vivid, so simple. I was overjoyed. Could it really be true? When I came back to the board to recheck the sequence I found I couldn't remember it! It was as if my memory was camera film. The shutter had opened and I had recorded the whole image—all the individual moves as one image. This had been imprinted upon the film in memory. But instead of giving me a positive print I could see, I had only a negative print, the black and white parts reversed. I couldn't read it in the "normal" way. But I knew I had seen it. It was like a vision. I had to find some way to "develop" a positive print. With film, it passes through a chemical solution. What, then, was the "solution"?

I tried to force-remember the sequence. Brute power. It was painful. The mind resisted. It was tired. But I knew I had seen a forced mate. Now I had to act on that vision. But still my rational "I" wanted to make sure. It willed the mind into focus. I began with the first move. I could remember that. And the second move, mine and all of white's possible moves, as well. But with the remaining moves it was like going along a dark path at night—I could only feel my way along. Several times I almost had the entire sequence, black and white together. But like a house of cards, with the last card, it would fall apart, taking all the cards with it. And I would have to start at the beginning, again. This happened time after time. It was like trying to hold onto a handful of water—it kept seeping through the fingers.

I was going to have to play it "in the dark." But had I seen everything? If that intuitive vision was off only slightly, it would mean a quick and certain loss. Of that much I was sure. My rational "I" kept going back and forth as to what to do. But another "I," a deeper, intuitive one, knew what had to be done…I had to take the leap, chance it, risk defeat, bet on my inner vision. Slowly, painfully, the "I"s disappeared and the naked recognition emerged: *I had to give up knowing.*

I breathed and steadied myself, wiping the perspiration from my forehead. I focused the mind on the "sound" and breathed slowly and fully into the body, all the time pretending to be still looking at the board. When I felt balanced, I carefully reached out and moved the bishop's pawn on the kingside, thus leaving the bishop unprotected. Immediately, a strange empty silence emerged. Everything stopped. Time had frozen.

I watched Lord Pentland's face. He could not hide his surprise. Leaving the bishop defenseless was totally unexpected. He had looked as I had looked and seen there was no advantage in doing this. So what had I seen? He sat there, that tall, perfectly still figure, and studied the board. Lord Pentland's upper body arched forward, bringing his face directly up on the board. I could feel the strength of his attention. It searched the board relentlessly, working out the moves, probing, looking for the trap. He stayed for a long while in that position, totally motionless. A good ten minutes must have passed. He sat back then, a small breath passing through his nostrils. He had not discovered the forced mate. I thought he might move then but, no, something else happened. Though his eyes remained on the board, I could feel his attention focusing on me. It went all over me, slowly probing, searching me, looking for a sign of tension, trying to gauge my state. It was so strong. I had never felt anything like it. I didn't move. I hardly breathed. I emptied out and just stood, the mind merged with the "sound." After a bit, he sighed. He recognized he was going to have to gamble, make a bet as well. Either I had miscalculated, made a bonehead move—or I had seen a weakness in his pieces. He stayed with the question for what seemed an interminable time. I stood still, empty, my eyes affixed to the board, feeling every breath, my heart beating erratically. Finally, the moment came: with a looping graceful motion his hand took up his rook and reached down the board to capture my bishop. The rook was now deep inside my territory.

The crowd gave a little murmur. The bishop gone, the white rook on black's second rank, deep in its territory with no possibility of getting it out, they were sure I had blundered. I could feel their judgment. It had no effect. It was eaten up in my atmosphere. A strange mixture of sorrow and joy welled up in me. I did not want white to lose. My legs began to tremble again. I couldn't let my attention touch that feeling. I sensed my body anew and refocused my attention, peering deeply into the board. Deliberately, I advanced a second pawn, this one attacking the white king knight. He had no recourse. He had to move it.

The sacrifice of the black bishop had given black the move. Though the pieces were still dark colored, the sacrifice had changed the nature of the pieces. In effect, black was now white; that is, it had become the active force on the board, white the passive.

As expected, the white knight retreated. I could feel the crowd. Black's moves had surprised them. They were no longer so dead sure.

Black moved again, jumping its knight forward into white territory.

The move threatened another piece of white's and at the same time opened up the diagonal squares running across the board for the black's fianchettoed bishop on the diagonal. The game was all forced now, determined. There was no way out for white. The deepness of the trap, its inexorable quality, came up on the board now. Seeing it, a short spurt of air shot involuntarily from between Lord Pentland's lips. But otherwise there was no reaction. He played the white side out, not giving up, and allowing black to capture the white king. The crowd made no sound. Lord Pentland rose then, an enigmatic look on his face—

"Very good," he said to me in that same tone with which he had first asked to play. He nodded and added, "Perhaps I'll return later when you are more tired."

When he had disappeared into the crowd, Soren stepped forward. "And you thought he was so great, heh?" he said.

I looked at Soren. The anger in his voice startled me. I liked Soren, respected him in some ways, pitied him in others. Something had happened between him and Lord Pentland. I didn't know what. But this was ugly. Soren cursed and stalked off.

The crowd dispersed and I was left alone at the boards. Waves of people streamed past the booth laughing and shouting and talking, eating baklava, drinking Turkish coffee, shopping through tents and booths full of candies and pottery and copper and bronze work and antiques and Persian rugs and paintings or listening to storytellers relating the comical adventures of Mullah Nassr Eddin or having their palms or Tarot read, while in the background could be heard the soulful sounds of Middle Eastern music. People came and played chess now and then and I did much better. The day slowly wound down. It was nearly six o'clock now. The crowd had begun to thin out.

IT WAS LATE AFTERNOON AND THE BAZAAR WAS CAST IN LONG SHADOWS. The heat of this mid-summer's day had abated only a little. There were no chess challengers. The boards were empty. My tunic was damp with sweat and I was exhausted. Though Lord Pentland had said he'd be back to play another game of chess, I supposed he wasn't coming. However, I no sooner left the booth when I became aware of this tall erect figure stepping through the crowd, moving deliberately, as if he had an appointment to keep.

Lord Pentland approached me directly. "You look tired, Pat," he said, his voice low and kind. "I'll take your place at the board, if you don't mind?"

"Of course," I replied, standing up. Damn! Why hadn't I believed him? Why did I always fall back and take him on an ordinary level?

Lord Pentland stepped into the booth. Almost immediately a challenger came forward. He was a well-built man in his mid-forties. He had a hard, unforgiving warrior's face, broad forehead, square jaw, glasses and sharp direct eyes. I had the impression that this man had "crystallized," but narrowly so. He was dressed casually in a beige sweater, dark brown slacks and loafers but there was nothing casual about him. His manner was aggressive, cocksure, even defiant.

"Game?" the man asked.

Lord Pentland nodded, somewhat resignedly I thought. It was as if he knew this man, or this type of man, and had played him many times before. Lord Pentland silently set up the pieces, placing the white pieces on his side of the board.

"You always take white?" snapped the man.

Lord Pentland smiled benignly, but made no reply. He moved his king's pawn two squares to the center of the board as he had before.

The man's eyes glinted. Instead of countering on the wing with a pawn move, he immediately blocked white's advance by advancing his king's pawn two squares. He pushed up the sleeves of his sweater, snatched a pack of Benson and Hedges from a pocket, took out a cigarette, crushed the pack, tossing it on the ground. He brought the cigarette to his lips, flicked a light from an expensive gold lighter, inhaled and awaited Lord Pentland's reply. He gave off a strong animal energy. His movements were confident, powerful. There was a "knowing" about him, but of a certain type. He was, to use Gurdjieff's phrase, a "power possessing being." And as they played the initial moves, the game evolved into the Four Knights game, the symmetrical variation, a solid and conservative game. It was obvious the man was no newcomer to the game of chess. He commanded his pieces with authority.

Inexplicably, some seven or eight moves into the game, Lord Pentland blundered away a bishop. At once, like an eagle, the man's hand darted out. It swooped down on the board, capturing the bishop and putting his knight in its place. The knight smacked down on the board like a rifle shot. The sound hit me right in the stomach.

Lord Pentland, at least outwardly, remained impassive, apparently studying the board. But I felt inside he was working with his energy.

A bishop down now, white had to go on the defensive and so the tempo was black's. He didn't throw away the opportunity. He quickly built up and consolidated his position and then mounted an attack right into the heart of white's pieces. Fortunately, Lord Pentland had castled his king, but such was the force of the black attack that its forward momentum could only be stalled by the sacrifice of several pawns.

Given black's material advantage in pieces and its board position, there seemed little hope now of white even managing a draw. White looked doomed. I thought it would be best to concede quickly rather than go through the ordeal of playing out a game that was clearly lost; and particularly so with this man. Why give him the satisfaction? But, instead, Lord Pentland played on. I supposed it was in keeping with the Work.

Someone found a large comfortable chair and set it down next to the board for Lord Pentland.

"Would you like a chair as well?" inquired Lord Pentland politely.

The man made no reply. He was bent over the board, bracing his body with one hand, the other on his hip; he did not even look up. He had his win, and he wanted it. He was not going to be distracted. Lord Pentland sat down.

There was a sense in the air that something unusual was happening. Soon, a large group of people, many of them Lord Pentland's students, were gathered around the board. No one spoke. All eyes were on the conflict.

At one point, having moved, Lord Pentland attempted to engage the man in a little conversation. Instead, the man held up his forearm, checking the time on his large watch. His manner signaled his impatience. In a clipped, implacable tone he stated:

"Have to be going soon. Let's get on with it."

He resumed his position, hovering over the board. For some moments, Lord Pentland continued to look at the waiting man immersed in thought. Then he nodded once, twice, three times to himself. It was as if he were coming to an inner agreement with all the parts of himself, galvanizing his will and energy, bringing up his full attention to the total acceptance of the fierce struggle that awaited him. For though chess looks harmless enough, considered by most a game, it is in fact a symbolic and magical rite capable of evoking primordial forces, the highest manifestation of what Gurdjieff called the Sacred Triamazikamno, or Law of Three. I noticed a sobriety cross Lord Pentland's face, a resolution and seriousness appeared such as I had never before seen. It was the face of a real warrior, a great and ancient warrior.

But it was all lost to the man. He would not know a subtle but dramatic change had taken place that took the game to another height entirely. No, he gave all his energies to the board. He would have his win. And certainly, looking at the board, white's position appeared beyond the power of any quality of will or intelligence to change.

Black had driven a deep vee-shaped wedge straight into the heart of white's forces, the lead black pawn standing only two ranks from white's last rank. White had erected a blockade with his own pawn, but how long could it hold? Should it fall, the ensuing black invasion would make it a rout. Black was deeply inside the center of white territory and as such could quickly shift its attack from side to side; the effect being, as white countershifted to meet the threats, that the communication, or ability to work as a unit, between white's forces would loosen and break. This was exactly black's strategy. It swung the game from side to side, feigning attacks on the flanks, laying traps, offering sacrifices of pawns, even a bishop, always with an eye to bulling its way through in the center—but nothing worked. Somehow, white held.

Lord Pentland's play, his every move, had to be precise. Or all was lost. His situation was so desperate that he had to play not just a good move, but the absolute best move. His pieces had to counter yet maintain pressure exactly…contesting, giving ground, creating obstacles, minor deflections. And the timing had to be perfect. His opponent was relentless, his play deep and cunning. Somehow, Lord Pentland managed to maintain the integrity of his defenses. The pressure was enormous. Yet many moves later the essential position on the board remained the same: black's pieces were massed in a dagger-point formation cutting into the white center, while white blockaded the center and artfully warded off attacks to his flanks.

Black's attacks being blunted again and again, a frustration welled up in the man like an angry wind. He was running out of ideas, his will and energy were flagging. His physical posture was hardening and constricting.

Lord Pentland seemed to sense that. He looked solemnly at the man. but said not a word. Finally, the man felt his gaze and looked up. Said Lord Pentland softly: "Perhaps it's only a draw."

"I've got a win here, I tell you!" shouted the man. He glowered and vowed, "I'm going to win."

Lord Pentland smiled wanly, patiently. He understood the man's dilemma. He did have a won game. And yet little by little that win had disappeared. It didn't seem to be on the board any longer. But the man had seen it. His win was there! I could almost hear him shouting the words.

Now Lord Pentland brought both his hands to the level of the board. He turned them palm up toward the man. It was as if saying he was sorry but this is how life is. What is here at one moment is taken at the next. Whether just or not, the reality and the fact now was that the board showed a draw. The gesture and its execution were extraordinary. I got shivers over my whole body. But the man only snorted. Some ancient deep anger, hatred even, surfaced in him. He would have his win and nothing else would do!

Summoning all that was in him, the man studied and restudied the board. Throughout the game, I could feel the will, the resolve, in each of them building. Going up one level, then to another. Each matching the other. But this seemed the final twist of the screw. He was giving absolutely everything that was in him.

The play went on. To no avail for black. Yet now the pressure told anew on the man. The tension of holding the polarities of energy so long in precarious balance within himself, the effects of such an ego-effort began to make themselves felt. At first it revealed itself in little, almost imperceptible ways. There was a feeling only...the sense that the man's image of himself, so crystal clear before, was now blurring. A certain melting was happening on the edges. And with that his posture and facial expression became less fluid, more contracted. Then the movements themselves began to fragment, becoming jerky, almost impulsive. But the man was a fighter. He fought it all down. He somehow kept control of the building chaos within himself. The additional effort must have come at great cost. I sensed the energies at work within him. It was like he was holding apart two angry snakes. I felt like the enormous effort of will he was making had begun to eat at his mind, tipping its center, interfering with his vision, eroding his concentration—but ever so slightly. But just enough, perhaps, to make a small but fatal miscalculation. Several times the man's head shot up from the board and his feet shifted back and forth as he tried to steady and seal off his will and mind from all distraction.

With Lord Pentland there was no such strain. Quite the contrary. In fact, if anything, he appeared to have gathered strength. Though the stress of such combat must have sapped him as well, he seemed relaxed, contained. At one point, he took out a cigarette, lit up and took a long inhalation, his eyes not once leaving the bent angry figure across from him. He closed his eyes then, cocking his head to the sky, and exhaling a long funnelling draft of smoke.

Suddenly, then, the man moved. It was like the move jumped out of him. It was born more from desperation than logic or inspiration. It was the kind of move a man makes when the pressure of active and passive energies inside him becomes intolerable, when all he wants is to get it over with, when unconsciously he gives in to the tamasic dog in himself.

Lord Pentland came up quickly in his chair, moving closer to the board, studying the implications of black's move. Time passed silently. Finally, satisfied he understood it, Lord Pentland very deliberately placed his lit cigarette, only half-smoked, on the street, slowly extinguishing it beneath his foot. Then, looking toward his opponent, he asked in a friendly way—"Would you like one?"

Lord Pentland extended his hand across the black and white board, offering the man a pack of cigarettes. Either the man could not speak. Or would not. In any case, he refused, shaking his head adamantly. Though the "game" had gone on for over two hours, he would not indulge, not take the chance on letting anything other than the desire to win predominate.

Lord Pentland nodded, understandingly, and returned to the board between them.

A slight gust of wind swirled up, blowing the awnings of the booths and lifting the vinyl cloths covering the long narrow chess tables. The sun had gone down. It was a twilight that muted even the bright colors of the bazaar.

Lord Pentland rechecked his position. The man's move, though quick and awkward, did not appear to be a blunder. Perhaps it wasn't his best move but, under the circumstances, he could likely afford it I thought. But perhaps I was wrong.

Not countering the move, Lord Pentland advanced a pawn, attacking a piece of black's on the wing. It caught black in a weakness as its pieces were overextended on that side. Not having adequate counterplay, black had to retreat the piece.

Then Lord Pentland jumped a knight on the other wing and again black had to defend it. But that in turn left a weakness on the opposite side. As black's forces had become so locked up far inside white's territory, he had no flexibility to regroup and quickly defend the white attack on the wings. He had to give up a pawn. Still, it didn't seem too serious. White's attack seemed sure to peter out.

But then a silent scream went up at the board. The man suddenly saw what that abrupt move earlier had cost. Another black pawn had to be sacrificed or he would lose a major piece. Even so the capturing white pawn now threatened another of black's pieces. Black had no time to untangle himself. But white kept advancing on the wings, driving now into the center behind black's forces, attacking its soft underbelly.

And then the impossible happened—Black was mated.

A long deathly stillness hung in the moment, the man leaned over the board in shock, Lord Pentland quietly looking on from his chair. Finally, Lord Pentland stood and extended his hand. The man had fought well and bravely, calling on all of himself. He had nothing to be ashamed of. But the anger that fueled his desire to win now turned on him. He could barely bring himself to shake the offered hand. He did so without looking at Lord Pentland, turned, and quickly walked off through the long shadows of the near empty bazaar.

The skies had been darkening and now, as if on cue, there was a great rumbling in the clouds. It was as if the gods were talking. Lightning flashed and cracked between the buildings and the heavens opened. The hot street was suddenly awash in torrents of water, the rain coming down in bucketfuls, the applause of the gods for The Art of Asha.

"C'MON, BILLY—HE'S IN HERE."

Aunt Marie tugged on my arm and led me into the viewing room. A large, dark mahogany casket had been stationed just to the left of the entrance. The lighting was dim. The stars and stripes was draped over the lower end of the casket. Vases of flowers stood at either end. My Uncle Bill looked so small in the big casket, as if he had shrunk to half his size. But the massive head was still there, the gladiator features. He looked the spitting image of his father. They were the same type of man. No wonder they fought. As I drew closer I saw the undertaker had touched up my Uncle's face with makeup. It looked ridiculous, decadent. This was a fighter, a warrior, not a dandy.

"Now don't he look good?" Aunt Marie said, staring into the casket, clucking her tongue. She seemed so small, compressed. But the face was the same—broad, direct with large eyes that seemed on the verge of popping from their sockets. She was heavily rouged and wearing a mink stole. Her black hair, probably a wig, cut short, curly at the ends, in a 1920's style. She, the eldest of the five Scott children, two boys and three girls, laid a hand at the back of her brother's head.

"Ain't it a shame now?" she said. "I mean he was so active 'n everything." She paused, making another inspection of the corpse. "Makes ya wonder."

She looked about the room. "I mean there's a mystery here," she whispered, her elbow nudging my arm. "There's a mystery t' life none of us knows about. Odd, huh?"

She stepped closer and really took in the corpse in the coffin.

"Nahh, Billy! It ain't him. Ain't him at all. Mr. Turner, he did a good job though. You can say that for him. Made our Bill look real nice."

Aunt Marie put a gnarled, liver-spotted hand into the casket and tickled her brother's cheeks as if he were a baby.

"Ahhh!" she exclaimed. "This is all that's left of Bill!

I drove her home then. We drove down Braddock Street and came around past the old railway station, boarded up for years now, onto Wood Street. Aunt Marie's tongue made that familiar clicking noise and the wattle-like jowls of her heavily rouged cheeks shook with disdain.

"Certainly has changed here, hasn't it?" she said. "Who would know the place now with all the coloreds?"

My aunt began clucking again like an angry hen biting off the black boys' heads.

"No one goes out at night anymore," she observed. "Not safe."

I noticed Warburton's Used Furniture was still at the corner of Coal Street. I remembered tossing a brick through Warburton's window one night. I must have been fourteen or fifteen. I was walking home from a movie. I couldn't remember why I'd done it. I was always considered a "good boy." I never smoked or drank, cursed, played hooky or got in trouble with the law. "He's never caused us any trouble," my Mother would say. I grew up in an atmosphere that was very black and white. My Father was always talking, when he did talk, about "having high principles." The idea of lying, cheating, stealing was considered really low. I never did anything wrong.

"What's wrong, Billy? Why you lookin' at that old store?" asked Aunt Marie.

"Oh, just remembering some of the old times."

"You are a strange duck," my Aunt said, laughing and clucking.

I parked the car outside the old house next to the four family apartment house Grandpa Scott had built just before the Depression. Aunt Marie made me promise I'd check things out before I opened her door. Then, gripping her mink stole, she rushed across the street to the apartment. Nearly out of breath, she cried up into my face:

"Oh, I'm glad, I tell you, my dad and poor mom didn't live t' see all this. It would've broke their hearts it would."

At her apartment my aunt made a bed for me on the couch and turned off the lights. I couldn't sleep. I had tapped into a whole flow of images and memory. My Mother used to tell me how every night after dinner her family would gather in the living room and grandpa would take out "the big book," the King James Bible. He'd begin to read in that thick deep Scotch-Irish brogue and, with the fire crackling in the fireplace, he'd begin treading back and forth, "talking the words of the Lord," as my Mother would say. I remembered my Mother showing me the rug in the living room, pointing to where it was threadbare from his walking. "Oh he could put the fear of God in you," she told me, still marvelling.

Every Sunday, she said, he'd go back by Chekwigin's Grocery and read aloud from his King James. He had a strong delivery and an even stronger conviction which attracted churchgoers, some of whom stayed on for his explanation of chapter and verse. His flock threatened, the local minister complained. So my grandfather took his preaching up into the woods behind Chekwigin's. The minister continued to howl and so at the prodding of his wife, Mary, a gentle soul who did her best to stay clear of trouble, he took to sitting on the porch Sunday mornings, reading aloud to passers-by. "It's my property," he said, "and God called me to read, Mary, and that's what I'll do! Hear now?"

My only memories of Grandpa Scott were of him sitting out on the front porch in the summer in a rocking chair in an old undershirt and trousers held up by thick workingman's suspenders and atop his head a big Stetson hat, grey with a black band. At his feet lay a yellow cane. He'd been hit a few times by "horseless carriages" as he refused to move fast enough. One leg was now shorter than the other so he had to walk with a cane. The sole of one shoe was bigger than the other to even out the legs. What I remembered most was his face. It was enormous, unmoving, like a granite mountain. The features were bold. Big jaw, strong nose, high forehead and steel-blue eyes. The eyebrows were thick and bushy; all white now just like his crew-cut. He was a little fearsome even then. But he would give me horsey rides on his knee and "sing the old country songs."

I don't recall his dying. I just remember one day going by the old porch and it was empty. Even the old rocker was gone. My Mother told me that when he died he was one hundred years old.

LIFE HAD LED ME OUT OF MY NETHERWORLD, OUT OF THE MIND-BOG, AND if indeed I had been dead, I was in the process now of being reborn. Not so very long ago life for me had been looking out of an apartment window for hours on end. Now those days were only memory. It was a new time now, a new tempo. My life was filled with people and ideas and possibilities I'd never imagined. There was Gurdjieff, Lord Pentland and the Work. Jack Casey and painting. Jung and archetypes and synchronicity. Barbara, my wife, and my son, John. And a new job, too. Editor-in-Chief of *Food*. And, yes, Stanley Ravin.

Never had I met anyone like Stanley Ravin. Sarah, somehow, seemed to understand him. It was always a big topic of conversation between us.

"The two of you—it's like watching some ancient, unfinished combat," Sarah said one day at lunch. We were having lunch at the Mayflower on First Avenue in the Fifties. We'd been there so many times it had become "our place."

I shook my head. "But why can't we settle this? Come to some agreement that he'll stick by?"

"That's obvious," replied Sarah. "You've gotten too big for him."

"He never expected I'd be any trouble, did he?"

"No, he thought he could control you like everybody else."

We laughed and clinked wine glasses. She pulled out a pack of Marlboros, tapped the cigarette on the table, lit up and leaned back, exhaling a long draft of smoke.

She seemed so much more self-assured now than the "Sarah" I first knew. And those awful glasses were gone. She wore contacts now. And no more stacked heels. She had lovely hands, long strong sculpted fingers. The fingernails were painted red now.

"You know, I could never figure out why Stanley chose you," Sarah said. "The people he hired before were always kind of, you know, 'ballsy.' Maybe not so much in how they looked but how they acted. But you…"

"I wasn't powerful?" I mocked.

"You! You were like a ghost in his office that day. Hunched over with your head bowed in some kind of perpetual humiliation."

"C'mon. I wasn't that bad!"

"I'll never forget that day in his office. There you were with your head down. You wouldn't look at either of us. You sat with your legs crossed and—this I'll never forget—as he's talking to you the toe of your shoe is rubbing back and forth on his desk. My god, I bet the scuff marks are still there."

"You're kidding."

"I said to myself, 'Good heavens! What's wrong with this poor man?' I'd never seen anyone who so resolutely refused to live life."

Harriet came with the special-of-the-day.

"Here y'all go," she said in a modulated Texas twang. Harriet was a dancer from Dallas come to New York to make it. She'd gotten as far as a jazz trumpet player in the Village, but was still hoping.

"How y'all today?" Harriet asked. She expertly placed the two dishes of meat loaf, mashed potatoes and green beans before us. "You folks still going to Mexico City?"

"Sarah is. Not me," I said.

"Oh, you should go. I was there once." Harriet caught me looking at Sarah. She smiled. "Great pyramids. You'd like them."

Harriet went to pick up another order. Wonderful calves, cut full and long. Thin ankles.

"Mr. Patterson," reprimanded Sarah, catching my thoughts. "It is true, is it not, that you are married, a new father…"

"Aye, that it is," I replied, putting on an Irish accent. "But I'm a great admirer of beauty in all its many permutations."

"A rogue, I'd say."

"A friendly eye would never see such faults. Now, c'mon. Back to Ravin."

"Well, anyway…you were so quiet, withdrawn. And, yes, so sad. That's it. Very sad. I wondered why he hired you."

"Didn't you tell me he was looking for 'a man with a halo'?" I put ketchup on the mashed potatoes. Barbara couldn't stand me putting ketchup on mashed potatoes. I motioned to Harriet for two more wines, the house red for me, white for Sarah.

Sarah put out her cigarette. "That's what he said. But he never would say why."

"Maybe he figured I might be gay," I said, winking.

"Well, you do have a baby face, soft features," laughed Sarah. Her eyes, so large and doe-like, grew bigger. She made them flutter as if she were astonished anyone could ever think that of me. She was so easy to kid with.

"You know, I think the bastard actually hates me," I said.

"No, it's not you so much as what you stand for. I don't think he's ever run into that." Sarah sipped her wine. "The real fight between you two is still to come, I think."

"You don't think we've been fighting?"

"Oh, you've been a surprise." She took out another Marlboro and lit up. "You won't like to hear this, William, but my feeling is he still has you in his pocket. He still owns you, in some way."

"Ahhh!" My hand flew up and hit the small conical light that hung over our booth from a long cord attached to the ceiling, sending it moving back and forth between us like a clock weight.

"Is he getting violent, dear?" called Harriet, looking up from totaling our check.

Sarah nodded expansively, and drank up.

Harriet came over to the table with the check. "Say, I'm curious. Just what are your signs, anyway?"

We had asked each other so many questions, but that had never come up. Sarah was a Capricorn sun sign with an Aquarius ascendant; I was just the opposite. We were mirror-images of one another.

"Holy cow, that's a first for me," exclaimed Harriet.

"First for us, too," I said.

Back in my office, Stanley buzzed me. He still couldn't believe I didn't want to go to Mexico City. It was a five-day foodservice conference, a real boondoggle, all expenses paid. Was I sure I didn't want to go? Sarah was going and all the editors in the industry. I was too busy, I told him. I would send Bobbi in my place. It would be a nice way to thank her for the good job she was doing with the food section.

"You aren't that nice, Bill," Stanley said and hung up. He couldn't figure it out, but he wasn't buying my excuse.

For me it was an experiment. For months now, I could feel the attraction between Sarah and me building. I had flirted too much. I liked female attention. I'd kidded myself, as usual. "It doesn't mean anything," I'd tell myself. But our bodies knew otherwise. They were starving for each other. I had carelessly started something I didn't want to finish. I loved Barbara. I had a family now. I knew if Sarah and I went to Mexico we'd be in bed within two minutes. I felt as if it was fated that we would sleep together in Mexico. That there was no way out. I'd taken a bite of the apple. *I was damned if I did, damned if I didn't.* Then I got an idea: Lord Pentland had always talked about taking a scientific attitude towards life, not to live in belief systems or superstitions, but to test things. So I thought that If it was true that we were fated to make love, then I could do anything and it still would happen. So I turned down the Mexico trip. I never told Sarah, but she seemed to have some sixth sense of what was going on. Whatever, she never said a word about my not going.

And it certainly looked as if I wasn't going. Bobbi had left a few days earlier for Mexico making a few stopovers on the way in order to do some stories. She got as far as Dallas when Stanley phoned and told her to come back immediately. When she did, he fired her. He didn't even ask me. He explained that he had received a letter from an advertiser complaining about an article Bobbi had written.

"She just had to go, William," Stanley said, his voice full of mock seriousness.

"Look, every magazine gets letters like that. What's the big deal?" I argued.

"It was from a very big advertiser. Let's face it, she's only doing a mediocre job."

"You had no right to fire her. She was part of my staff."

"Let's get this straight. I run this magazine, not you. I do the hiring and firing here. Now you have to go in her place. That's all there is to it."

I went to see Spencer. He played it on both sides of the street as usual. He would talk to Stanley, he promised. He wasn't to fire or hire anyone without my knowledge. But in the meantime, as Bobbi was gone now, I had to represent the editorial side of the magazine in Mexico. Stanley would represent the business side.

A week later Sarah and her husband picked me up at our apartment to take me to the airport. Barbara stood by the stoop, cradling John in her arms, waving. I looked at Sarah and her husband. We were all smiling. It seemed so weird. I felt that on some level all of us knew what was about to happen.

Sitting in different rows, Sarah and I didn't talk much on the plane. She read Colette's *The Vagabond.* I was rereading Ouspensky's *Tertium Organum.* Gurdjieff told Ouspensky when they met that if he understood his own writing, he would be Gurdjieff's teacher. How is it possible, I wondered, that the intellect could be clear enough to write or speak coherently about something, yet not really understand it? What was understanding? Gurdjieff had said it was the result of both being—one's sense of self, the level of vibration at which one lives—and genuine knowledge. Understanding could only increase with the simultaneous growth of being and knowledge. There must be a proportion. And whereas knowledge can be the function of one center, understanding is the function of three centers: thinking, emotional, moving.

That seemed clear enough on the level I was taking it on. But it didn't explain how, if I was right, the four of us knew what was going to happen. We just couldn't admit this to ourselves; the suffering would be too great. Ouspensky's theory of eternal recurrence explained it. The theory held that we had all lived our lives before. Our lives seemed new only because we lived most of our lives in sleep. Moments of self-remembering leave a mark, have a certain taste. Such moments exude a subtle familiarity.

Ouspensky saw life in terms of dimensions of reality. When a person only lives in three dimensions, he does not remember himself. With the fourth dimension comes self-remembering, the realization of one possibility of each moment. The fifth dimension is a repeat of this. Only with the sixth dimension is there the realization of different possibilities. Change is only possible for man, then, in the sixth dimension.

Dunne's book, *Experiments With Time,* gave an interesting explanation as well. Dunne's theory was that though we experience time and space sequentially, in actuality, time-space exists as a complete unit. We think we are moving through time because events appear to happen one after another. Dunne believed that our lives exist as a complete unit, birth to death. We simply "activate," so to speak, the particular time-event by our presence. During sleep or meditation, when the soul could leave the body and travel backward or forward, we could experience our "past" or "future." Whatever, I was interested to see how this would all play out. I had the sense of entering an entirely new domain.

MEXICO CITY SWELTERED IN THE DEAD HEAT OF AUGUST. SARAH AND I caught a cab from the airport to the downtown Hilton. The smog was stultifying. Dull-eyed peasants stood along the roadside waving packs of tissues for sale. Once checked in, we agreed to meet at the pool. I quickly changed and was stretched out in a lounge chair, Marguerita in hand, thinking that maybe I was kidding myself about all this…when across the courtyard I saw this cream white figure in big dark sunglasses and a jet black bikini, cut high at the hips, long legs, bare and white, moving toward me, the large full bosom jostling with her gait. The image was incredible. My blood thundered with new wild life. I had only seen her in street clothes before. Sarah gave a little nervous wave. I couldn't move. She stopped suddenly, tossed her towel and sunglasses on a chair, and ran and dived into the bright sunshine, disappearing into the dancing water. I went to the side of the large pool, trying not to rush. The clear blue water shimmered and sparkled in the sunlight, making gentle lapping sounds against the edges of the pool.

She had dived deep. Way down, I could see this black and white image rising to the surface amid a flurry of bubbles. She shook the water from her face, smiled now, and swam in mid-pool, alone and still, gazing up at the sky. She looked like a strange and magical seabird. She swam toward me now, her feet sending long sprays of water into the hot sultry air, her arms reaching out before her in long sweeping motions, sharply outlining the mounds of her breasts.

The black and white image blazed in my mind and I dived into the water and swam to her. We joked a bit and, obeying a not so innocent impulse, I picked her up in my arms and carried her about the pool, threatening to dunk her...all the while feeling her wet smooth flesh against mine. The contact sent a shock of electricity through me. And recognition, too. We had crossed a threshold. Our eyes and bodies spoke. Nothing needed to be said. We soon were back in her room. It was the first time we had ever been alone together. She tried to appear natural. So did I. But all our movements were so self-conscious, awkward. My body ached but my mind was frozen in fear. I was married. What was I doing?

Sarah puttered about. I sat down on the edge of one of the two beds. She was leaning over her luggage, searching through the clothes. The top strap of her bikini had fallen down. As she turned toward the chest of drawers her breasts jiggled slightly. Her skin had an ardent rose-like glow on the chest and top of the thighs. She lit a Marlboro but with none of the sureness that she did at the Mayflower. She put a towel down on the bed and sat across from me, cross-legged, casually smoking, becoming more relaxed. Though the talk was brittle, with many long questioning pauses, our eyes searched one another, imploring. But we could still stop. We didn't know, couldn't know, where this would lead. We could still stop.

There was a confidence to her I liked. Something even a bit brazen. The cigarette hung from a corner of her mouth, its thin serpentine column of smoke caressing her face. She was perfectly still, her eyes peering into mine, no longer questioning, defending, a faint flame trembling on her cheek. The moment was there. Another crossroad. Slowly, wordlessly, I reached out across the space between the beds separating us and touched the black bikini, my fingertips running lightly along the contour of her breast. Her body gave a little jump under the skin. Goosebumps. Yet her eyes, large and moist, never left mine. I moved from my bed to hers. She opened to me now like a flower, some ancient chemistry flaming and flashing between us. Thoughts tore at me, one "I" accusing another. Sarah moved away, her eyes searching mine. We could still stop. We didn't have to go on. Or did we?

And then the telephone rang.

Like a police siren, It cut through the room, shocking the space, contracting and closing it. It rang and rang. Someone knew the room was not empty.

Finally, Sarah smiled and cleared her throat. She picked up the receiver. Just as she did I knew who it was.

"Oh, it's you," said Sarah, chuckling and rolling her eyes.

"Stanley?" I whispered.

"Yes, Stanley, it really is muggy," she agreed. She shrugged.

The conversation was inane, about nothing, but it went on and on, Sarah making faces, trying to get off the phone, Stanley hanging on. I felt both the anger and the desire coursing through my blood.

"Why am I laughing?" Sarah said. "Oh, I don't know, Stanley. Good heavens! Mexico is certainly a strange place. The people you meet here. Why they're altogether different than in the States, don't you think?"

We smiled at one another. I reached over and closed her eyelids.

"Sorry, I must go now, Stanley. See you later…"

That evening in the lobby just as we were going to dinner—

"Well now, where have you two turtle doves been! Hmmm?"

We didn't have to look around. Stanley was right at our side, as if he had been waiting for us. He cackled and licked his lips and fawned over us. "You two certainly do look absolutely smashing together," he declared. I wondered if he knew what had happened. I felt a cold chill. But Stanley went on talking, laying on the charm, the flattery, the small talk. He left no holes in the conversation. There was no getting away from him.

"I know Mexico City real well," he said. "I lived here for a few years. Where are you going for dinner?"

I took out a piece of paper. "The El Coyote," I said. It was a restaurant Mexican friends of Barbara's mother had recommended.

"Well…" Stanley replied with a big grin, "mind if I come along?"

In the cab he took over completely. In pidgin Spanish he argued with the driver about how to get to the El Coyote and then with me in English about going there at all.

"Horrible, William. Ab-so-lutely horrible." Stanley cried. "I know a much better place. After all, Mexico is like a second home to me."

I didn't care that much where we ate. And Stanley was more familiar with the place, so why not? But Sarah nudged me in the ribs. She looked at me as if to say, "Wake up!"

"No," I told Stanley, "we're going to the El Coyote. Maybe we can drop you somewhere, huh?"

"Anywhere but there!" Stanley declared. He folded his arms and fumed.

"Where should we drop you?"

"Don't think you're getting rid of me as easy as that. I'll come. I don't want you two going around this town alone."

"Now Stanley, don't be like that. Be nice to William," said Sarah.

"Hah!"

Stanley cursed the whole way in Spanish and English, warning me, "It had better be good, William!"

It was about nine o'clock when we arrived. El Coyote was beneath ground level. We went down the stairs. It was very quiet, too quiet. The restaurant was completely empty. Not a soul at the tables, the small stage curtained. Stanley was vindicated. He whooped with delight.

"How nice!" Stanley observed. "We have the place all to ourselves." He sat down next to Sarah and grinned at me.

I felt lousy but managed a smile. I picked up a menu. It was oversized with countless dishes.

Stanley snickered. "Always the sign of a great restaurant," he said. He snapped the sides of his menu together. They looked like the jaws of an animal.

When the waiter came Stanley questioned him at great length about different dishes. His Spanish was now much better than the pidgin variety he had spoken in the cab. Perhaps he really had lived in Mexico. He was an arch trickster. It was hard to know what to believe.

"Stanley, let's order," said Sarah finally.

"Well, now tell us, William—what are you having?" he demanded in a campy voice laced with poison.

"Number seven," I said. It was a combination plate of tacos and enchiladas with beans.

"Very good for gringos you put numbers on the menu," Stanley told the waiter. "But, no, William, you must, absolutely must, change your order. Believe me, you wouldn't like it." He turned to the waiter, "Give our 'gringo' here number twenty-nine." He clapped the menu together authoritatively and stuck it in the waiter's hand.

This was crazy. What was he doing? Whatever, I really didn't care what I ate. For the sake of peace, why not let him have his way? What was the sense in arguing? Just make matters worse…I felt a kick in the ankle. Sarah was staring at me. I had fallen asleep again. I came down out of the head and felt myself in the chair, my feet on the floor, and slowly breathed. The waiter was about to leave.

"Number seven," I said quickly.

The waiter dutifully began to erase the old order.

"No! He's having number twenty-nine. Got that?" Stanley shouted at the bewildered waiter. Stanley glared at me. He seemed very powerful. I felt myself go very weak. Did it really matter that much what I ordered. After all—

"William! Order what you want." Sarah's voice was definite. "Don't let him do this to you," she whispered, leaning toward me.

But Stanley heard her. "Do what?" he challenged, acting the aggrieved soul. "I was just trying to help the poor boy."

"Seven!" I shouted at the waiter who was looking at us very strangely.

"They're both loco," confided Sarah to the waiter.

"Si, senorita, si," he said.

Finally, "the battle of the orders" over, Stanley launched into tales of his boyhood escapades in Mexico. Perverse sexual tales. When we protested, he just told a more sickening story. There was no stopping him. He seemed to delight in our disgust. It was all lies and he loved the sound of lies told as truth.

I felt chest high in muck. I remembered about not expressing negative emotions. I came down into the body, breathed into the sensation, and vowed not to get sucked into this: to say nothing. I watched him, listened and felt the body. In time, Stanley finally calmed down—he had talked as if he were possessed—and presently the food appeared. It turned out to be very good. Even Stanley, though begrudgingly, had to admit it. Even worse, El Coyote was soon packed. Not a table empty. The curtains parted, the spotlights came on and a mariachi band started up. Costumed dancers flooded the stage. It was like another world entirely. The whole place had been transformed. Stanley went into a funk. Sarah and I danced.

"You fall into his traps," she said. "You can't do that."

"I know, I know," I said. I noticed Stanley looking at us suspiciously.

The next day we went to the conference. After the luncheon we had a free afternoon. Stanley was busy making himself known and didn't notice that we left. I rented a car and we went to see the pyramids. They were supposed to be no more than an hour or so out of the city. We hadn't had a chance to speak seriously of what had happened at dinner.

"He's got some kind of power, hasn't he?" said Sarah adjusting the straw hat with a red brim she had just bought for the outing.

"Yeah, and he acts on you without your knowing it."

"He controls people, you know?"

"Yeah. By guilt, intimidation, flattery—any way he can."

We were out of the city now, going through a mountain pass. The air was a lot lighter, easier to breathe. Soon, we were down in the plains now. The land was so hard, barren, scorched by the sun. Hot as hell. You could cut the heat with a knife. I was thinking about Stanley when Lord Pentland came into my mind. I recalled him saying that self-remembering in quiet neutral times was good practice, but only preparatory. "A very high vibration of emotional energy is needed," he said, "to discover what the real meaning of self-remembering is." What was demanded was that we have the energy and will to remember and observe ourselves in "the heat of conditions." That is, when the instincts and emotions are raging—that is the time to remember oneself, to stop the momentum, to create real will. Then all of one's previous efforts crystallize in the intensity of the moment and a real foundation is laid for self-remembering. "This requires," he said, "a very big payment." I remembered him once quoting a line of T. S. Eliot's poetry to me in his office. *An unattended moment in and out of time,* he said, explaining that self-remembering was "a moment of will, a stop that takes us out of time." At first these moments would come to us because we have "remembered with the mind but then, after long practice, the body remembers." I could see him looking at me. "The moment to make the effort—and it's actually a non-effort and we must be very quick to make it—is when we are about to be caught up in the moment." He paused and sighed. "That's the real meaning of surrender."

"You want?" asked Sarah holding out a pack of gum.

"No."

Sarah took out a cigarette, tamping the end down on the dash. Her movements were so sure. She had such an intriguing mixture of feminine and masculine.

UP AHEAD WE COULD SEE THE REMAINS OF THE CITY THE AZTECS HAD CALLED "Teotihuacan." It was a straight shot now to the pyramids. Nothing is known about the original inhabitants, but the name Teotihuacan means, "The place where one becomes a God."

Sarah put out her cigarette, sighed, and flipped the ash tray closed.

"Better watch out for him, William."

"What do you mean?"

She paused. "He always says, 'I'm a survivor.' And he is. He'll do anything—anything—to survive."

Sarah sometimes had a taste for melodrama but I did feel Ravin was capable of *anything*. But, then, what could he do? He'd already tried to have me fired. Spencer had stood by me. So what else could he do? What was Sarah trying to tell me?

We parked the car and bought tickets. Ancient ruins held some kind of fascination for me. The first I'd seen was Tulum near the seacoast of the Yucatan jungle. Barbara and I had flown into it from Cozumel. Then I'd gone to Chichen-Itza and Uxmal. On our honeymoon we'd gone to Ephesus in Turkey. Now here I was again. All these places had some special feeling for me. They lived for me in a certain way I could never describe. As though the spirit of those people, those times, could somehow be contacted, if you were quiet, sensitive enough.

The city had been built in a broad valley rimmed with volcanic cones, many of which are still active. Before its destruction by volcanic eruption, the city's population numbered 25,000. It was laid out so that a two-mile long ceremonial boulevard bisected its center. It was known as The Street of the Dead. It was lined with palaces, temples, pyramids. The Pyramid of the Sun, located about half way down the street, and the Pyramid of the Moon, at its end, are the largest outside of Egypt. As the two of us entered I felt odd, as if we were stepping into a dream together. I felt we had been called here that our coming to Mexico and the pyramids was no accident. Sarah and I stood before the fearsome Temple of Quetzalcoatl. The staircase was lined with huge grotesque heads jutting menacingly out into space, their mouths open, baring six tusk-like serpent's teeth. The head was wreathed in feathers. As serpents don't have feathers, I wondered if this was then a symbol of transcendence? And to come to a higher order of being—in Quetzalcoatl revealing a part of himself—the god ate you.

I noticed that the serpent heads of Quetzalcoatl alternated with the strange, almost robot-like masks of Tlaloc, the rain God. Connecting the two heads was the long undulating body of the feathered serpent, Quetzalcoatl. This motif repeated itself over and over. Rain, is a symbol of grace, anointment, nourishment. The serpent that of wisdom and kundalini, the sleeping power lying at the base of the spine, guarded by the dragon, our fear of really living. The people the Aztecs called "Teotihuacan" obviously knew about how to raise the kundalini. Was this why this street was called The Street of the Dead? The person had to die to himself, die to the ordinary perspectives, identifications—die to the imaginary "I." It was here that he could pass from being a human being into the being of a God. But how? I suddenly became aware that I was "reading" all this without thinking about it. With that the reading stopped and I was left peering into the stone mouth of a serpent.

Sarah just looked but made no comment. We made our way along the street, past the various temples to the Pyramid of the Sun. It was built, I had read, so that its axis is in line with the evening sun as it passes its zenith. It was an immense structure. The people who had climbed to the top looked no bigger than toy soldiers. I found it disorienting to stand at the base and gaze up. It seemed as though the pyramid was not vertical but instead a bridge to the heavens. We climbed the steep steps and, panting and perspiring, sat down at the top which wasn't pointed but flat at its top. The view of the whole countryside in all directions was stupendous.

A wind gusted and blew the straw hat off Sarah's head, but she caught it just in time. A gentle breeze came up, soft and caressing. It was a glorious day, the sky a rich azure blue, cloudless, with the hot Mexican sun high in the heavens. We sat for a long time gazing into the panorama of nature. It was a weekday and there were only a few people at the ruins. They were so far below us it was as if we were alone in the sky. I had this feeling that we had known each other for a long time. I felt like Sarah was my sister, or had been so in another lifetime. There was the sense, too, that we had unwittingly passed through a gate, one neither of us had known existed. It was as if the world had stopped, and we were sitting amidst a gigantic still life. There was a presence all about. The silence just opened up and took us into it. In my ears, flowing like a strong brook and the buzzing of bees, was what I called the "sound" but, as I had learned, it was known as the audible sound current, *shabd* or *nam*—the root vibration of the universe. We sat atop the pyramid for a long time before, slowly, in a soft voice, Sarah began to speak of the magnificence around us and inside us that we shared. Then she began to tell me of her life, her dreams and her fears. I told her mine as well. I mentioned the Work to her and what it was about. I wasn't sure she understood, but it didn't matter. We held hands, the red ribbon of her hat dancing like a banner in the breeze.

"God!" Sarah exclaimed. "It's like you can see forever."

Sunset approached. I stood atop the pyramid. To the west was the descending sun. To the east rose the moon. And here where I stood was the earth. The triangulation suddenly lived for me. And I realized: I was seeing the Ray of Creation! There were the three octaves as physical fact: Absolute to sun, sun to earth, and earth to moon. I'd taken the Ray to be a metaphor, but it was a concrete fact as well as a great intellectual intuition. Yes! *The Ray of Creation could be seen!*

"What is it? asked Sarah. "What's happened?"

I wished I could share it with Sarah but it would take too many words. "I'll tell you later. I promise," I said.

We were about to leave when an intuition flooded me. Magnificent but did I dare it? Where would it lead? I couldn't know. I had to take the chance. The "sound" hummed strongly in me, my vision opened. I asked her to turn and face me, sitting cross-legged. For a moment, Sarah looked at me strangely.

"Don't you think we should be going?" she asked…

"Just sit," I say softly.

She does. I sit opposite her, legs crossed in a half-lotus as well.

"Allow your thoughts to stop," I say.

Behind Sarah, down below, is the Street of the Dead leading to the Pyramid of the Moon and directly behind it Cerro Gordo, the Fat Mountain. And all around like a necklace, a range of old mountains looking soft and billowy, their colors muted in purples and dark blues with touches of crimson. Suddenly, again Sarah looks like that magical seabird I'd seen in the pool.

"Now just sense and feel your body. Experience the stillness and the inner warmth."

She does and I do as well, the surrounding horizon deepening and lengthening, a small breeze flowing through the space.

"Just allow yourself to open. Gaze at me now, not looking or staring. Let your eyes soften, take in the space, continuing to sense and feel yourself at the same time."

I feel Sarah's body relax still deeper, the tissues magnetizing with attention, opening to life. The rhythm and quality of her breath evens and fills every cell. Softly, I chant *Aum* and soon Sarah does as well. The air becomes light, the space magnetic.

Sarah's breath coarsens, the eyes fix. She is holding onto something. She is beginning to panic. The moment is enlarging, going beyond what she can take in. She is jamming, fighting the energy.

"Just relax," I say. "Allow it to happen." My voice is rumbling, guttural, coming from a great depth. Almost inaudible. "Come into the body. Don't get locked up in a thought."

Sarah's eyes are as big as moons. The consciousness—behind thought, behind fear—appears. I smile. She smiles as well, relaxes. Her face begins to change form. It is no longer static—no longer fixed in shape and form—but dynamic—pulsating with energy. Gods and goddesses appear. Egyptian, Persian, Hindu, Chinese. Then witch faces. Old ladies. Animals. Humanoids. Suddenly, all the faces disappear altogether. Only blackness. Then radiant and numinous light

My attention deepens, expands. I focus gently on my centers, front and back, one by one, slowly passing along "the stairway," my attention taking in the "sound" and the radiant, luxurious warmth.

"Focus your attention," I murmur, telling her where the centers were located.

We breathe in the same rhythm, a bridge of energy linking us together, our faces no longer static but dynamic, the moment stopped, no separationall was timeless *being*, the energy moving between us in a flowing circle of light. ⚡

COLUMBINE'S CARDS

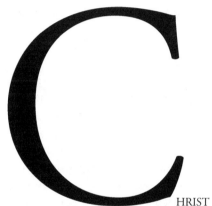

C HRIST ON THE CROSS looked Nordic. He reminded me of the Norse god, Balder. But as I painted the features began to change into those of a Hindu. A Hindu Christ! What did that mean?

Before Christ stood an androgynous petitioner, his hand outstretched, palm up. It was a moment of possibility and danger, for between the petitioner and the Christ loomed a bottomless abyss. The petitioner stood on the edge of that abyss. One insincere feeling, one false word—and he would be plunged into deep darkness.

To one side of the petitioner cavorted a grotesque prehistoric bird with a long penis. On the other side, stood a robed, white bearded man, an Ancient-of-Days, holding a forked staff and a large book, *The Book of Life*. These figures appeared within a ring of boulders with a narrow entrance way where the boulders parted. Beyond the boulders, a burly, blond man, a devil character, looked on, in his hand a dead goldfish which mocked Christ and the sacredness of this time beyond time. Behind these five main figures were groups of mourners and ancestors, witnessing and praying.

I called the painting *The Petitioner*. It was almost finished. I'd started on the painting before Sarah and I had gone to Mexico, before the chess game with Lord Pentland. I'd begun it out of the frustration I had felt with the Work's study group and the material we were working with, the New Testament Gospels. Though Lord

Pentland had created the study group he did not attend any meetings. Instead he appointed a moderator. Within a half dozen meetings it had become obvious that none of us in the group could get beyond our backgrounds, our prejudices. We could not take in the material directly, impersonally. It was all being filtered. We were all speaking from the formatory mind.

And, on its own terms, the Gospels were a problem. As we studied and researched, we found that the earliest Gospel had not been written until 64 A.D., or even later. Worse, scholars maintained that it was compiled from a series of notes, a document they arbitrarily called "Q," and oral tradition. Later, the Gospels had been glossed, or changed in places, so as to reflect better the social and political positions of the Church. So in studying the material, how could we know what was Christ's and what the Church's? What was sacred and what was simply worldly? We couldn't know. We were time-bound, too far away from the events.

One Saturday at Casey's the luncheon discussion turned to Jung and his theory of the collective unconscious. Jung's idea was that each person carries within himself ancient symbols and knowledge that, existing at a deep level, remains uncontaminated by our present personality and historical time. Jung, like Casey, thought painting was a sacred channel, a means of approach to the unconscious. I was mulling this over, not connecting it to the problem with the study group at all, when the thought suddenly flashed: *what if I painted Christ?*

The idea of doing this—me doing it—seemed absurd. I loved to paint but I was no painter. But what if I painted it as an experiment. Without planning or preparation. No thinking. I'd just begin and let the brush do its work. Paint on feeling, intuition. Stay out of judgement, wrong and right. Let the canvas speak to me. Could that take me beyond time, beyond "Patterson"? Could I intentionally access the collective unconscious?

I bought a new canvas, gessoed it, and put it up on the easel. I had a paint brush under my arm as I did this and it had made a mark on the canvas. I was going to paint it out. But, no. All right. That would be the top of the cross. And so in that spirit, I "entered" the canvas. Below Christ on the cross, for example, suddenly appeared two men, both with oddly shaped faces, one holding a mallet. It wasn't until I saw the mallet coming through that I knew who they were; the men who had nailed Christ to the cross. And between the petitioner and Christ appeared a huge abyss.

So much was happening on the canvas but once I stepped back out I could never put it into words. And if I tried to do so while painting, or in some way to remember the intuitions, I was taken right out of the canvas, straight down into the formatory mind. All the while, I kept wondering: what was the petitioner asking for? No answer came, not even a glimmer. Perhaps that wouldn't reveal itself, if at all, until the end of the painting. *You are the music while the music lasts,* I remembered Eliot writing. I was having a bear of a time with the background and the devil figure. Finishing the painting seemed like a long time off. It all kept changing on me.

My relationship with Sarah deepened. It was like it had a life of its own. I felt in another life we must have known one another. An energy was coming through us that was so strong and fluid that it could only be primordial. There was this awesome sense of vibration and fusion. This incredible dance of magic. We weren't doing it. We were only taking part in it.

Still, I was feeling a lot of guilt. I didn't want to hurt Barbara. Yet I didn't want to end my relationship with Sarah. In fact, I knew I couldn't. It had become too strong, too fast. We were riding a wild bull. I didn't think about it ending or where it was leading. I only took care to insure that Barbara wouldn't discover my unfaithfulness. At one meeting Lord Pentland looked straight at me, and asked: "What would it be like if one day we got into an automobile in Manhattan and went the length of the island and made every green light. We'd say of course that would be impossible and yet the "impossible" is happening. How to observe that?" That was exactly how it felt: every light was green.

One afternoon in a hotel room in the Village I sat in bed watching Sarah, nude, lighting up a cigarette. She was standing by the window, holding the blinds back a bit, watching the comings and goings on lower Broadway.

"What are you thinking about?" I asked finally.

"You...you and Stanley." She sat down in the chair, crossing her legs and leaning forward, her elbows on her knee. The late afternoon light streaked in through the cracks of the blinds giving her body a chiaroscuro effect of dark and light. "It's not getting any better, you know?"

"Yeah, that's right. But you and he, you seem to get along pretty good."

"Yes. I suppose that's because there's never been anything between us." She parted the blinds at the edge and looked out.

"I hope to hell not."

"C'mon now," she said. "For me Stanley has always been, you know, asexual...so there's never been any lust or aversion." Sarah took a long drag and exhaled. "And in a funny way"—she looked up and smiled at me—"he was kind of my 'Prince Charming.'"

"What!" I sat up. "You're kiddin' me?"

As a child she said she had always dreamed of living in New York City. Her parents had laughed at her. There they were down in Greenville, North Carolina, surrounded by their whole family. No one had ever left, much less to go to New York. But then, just a few years ago, one bright Spring day Stanley had showed up at the printing plant and offered her a job. "A few months later there I was in Manhattan," she said. "Dreams do come true."

"Look, you knew about production. He knew nothing. You were intelligent and loyal. But you were no threat. He knew he could mold you. He didn't do it for you. He did it for himself, for Stanley."

Sarah nodded.

"He told me once," Sarah said, "and these were his exact words: 'I'm a 'made-up man.'"

"Made-up or not, he's hurt a lot of people."

"You know, William," she said softly, "you do have an abiding interest in people. But you don't always listen to them, especially when it's not what you want to hear."

She had a wonderful way of saying hard things softly. She was so easy to talk to and followed with interest my ideas on practically anything—"I don't buy all your bullshit," she joked, "but even at its worst, it's always interesting." I expected a red light but it never came.

Months passed. She had detected a certain similarity in my ideas and began to probe me. Finally, I began to tell her about the Work. Perhaps I was a kind of messenger to her. That's what all this was about. She was interested. So I spoke to Lord Pentland and asked if I should give her one of Gurdjieff's books. I wanted to tell him about what was happening, but I didn't. It was all too new. I was calming myself with the idea that it would one day end and no one would be the wiser. He told me to give her *Meetings With Remarkable Men.* Sarah immediately came alive to it. So all our Mayflower lunches were now taken up not so much with Stanley, but with Gurdjieff and the Work ideas. And then she began to meet now and then with Lord Pentland.

THE PETITIONER PAINTING WITH ITS HINDU CHRIST HAD BEEN STARTLING, but it hadn't given me any new understanding of the Gospels. Like everyone else in the study group, I wasn't saying anything. The group's moderator was no help. He was a dry, unimaginative sort, very controlled, into having things go well.

Then at one meeting it struck me—*why hadn't we talked about Satan?*

The word have never been mentioned. It was like an unconscious taboo. And yet Satan played the central part in Jesus' crystallization. Were we too sophisticated to believe in him? Perhaps not as an entity but what about as a quality of mind? A certain type of attitude or energy? Yes, we had discussed Christ's birth and flight from Egypt, the role of John the Baptist and his baptism of Jesus, the parables and the Sermon on the Mount, Pilate, the Jews, Judas and the Crucifixion, the Resurrection—but never once Satan!

I began to research Satan. I found that the name appeared in the Old Testament as both a noun and a verb. The noun usage was taken as being earlier, as the verb form, *s´a-tan,* appeared only in later texts. Was he then considered by the Hebrews to be a being, an archetype? The word "satan" (*stn* in Hebrew, *diabolos* in Greek) meant to persecute, be hostile toward, to accuse, slander, to be an opponent, a stumbling block. So Satan was the persecutor, the pursuer, the provoker, the accuser, the liar. His role is that of the tempter, the adversary.

Whether he was an archetype, energy, concept or personage, Satan certainly enjoyed a long history. In the Old Testament his evolution could be seen evolving from Genesis through Job, Zechariah, Chronicles and Numbers. But it is in the New Testament that he becomes fully fleshed out, being cast as the adversary not just of good men like Job, but of those who would become Christ conscious.

What would happen to the Jesus story if we deleted Satan and the temptations?

Wouldn't it simply be a story of ignorance, not evil? Without Satan, it was simply a story of people being asleep. Satan's conscious denial of Jesus and his deliberate obstruction and temptation gave the story real spice. More important: Satan also served to crystallize Jesus in a higher body.

Gurdjieff spoke of good and evil in many ways, but principally he connects it with the idea of evolution—the creation of a real I. "Good" and "evil" then are relative to the individual's awakening: what keeps him asleep is "evil"; what awakens him is "good." To actually sin—to deny and subvert the Holy Ghost—one had to be conscious. Otherwise, there could be no responsibility. Lucifer's denial of God's command to worship Adam, this unconscious piece of clay, is conscious. Yet Lucifer, the brightest and most far seeing of all angels, is blind to God's vision and plan. He had to have faith. Instead he rebels. It is only later when he actively obstructs God's plan by becoming a serpent and tempting Eve (the emotional side of Adam's nature) that he becomes Satan, the Prince of Darkness.

Ouspensky once asked Gurdjieff if there is a "conscious force" that pits itself against spiritual evolution. "From a certain point of view," Gurdjieff replied. He then described two processes, the involutionary and evolutionary, or the descending and ascending octaves. The involutionary, he said, begins consciously in the Absolute. At the first elaboration, mechanicality enters into the descending octave. It increases as the octave successively manifests down through the Ray of Creation.

The evolutionary, or ascending octave, begins half-consciously at a coarser level of manifestation. It becomes more conscious as the octave proceeds upward through finer and finer densities of vibration. Only in this evolutionary process can conscious opposition appear at certain moments. Here, the process of the development of consciousness must proceed without interruption. Any interference strong enough to alter the ascending octave aborts the process and causes a separation. These separated fragments of consciousness can unite, can live for a certain time, by struggling against the evolutionary process.

Where in the Ray of Creation, I wondered, would Satan exist? Ouspensky pointed to the interval between Do-Si in the lateral octave. So in the ascending octave man would meet Satan at the Si-Do interval, the place of the shock. At this juncture, the crossroads of psyche and being, at the outermost region of man's psychology, would be Satan's home ground. The shock of Satan would have to be assimilated. None but the pure could pass this satanic judicial eye. So it is Satan who plays the pivotal part in the development and maturing of objective consciousness. And in the New Testament it is Satan's temptations that provide the necessary shock and spur so that Jesus' consciousness can crystallize into that of the Christ.

So what was it that sealed our mouths about Satan?

At the next study group, I felt the urge well up in me to speak about Satan. I felt the deep fear, too: *it was dangerous in some way*. By uttering his name, did you call him into your life, call him to challenge and test you? I choked off the voice inside me. The meeting droned on and on, counting the same angels on the head of a pin.

"WE TALK ABOUT GOD—HOW COME WE DON'T TALK ABOUT SATAN? WHAT stops us?" I asked with a lot of force.

Satan. The word froze the group. It was like I'd tossed a rotting animal into the middle of the room. Everyone smelled it. But no one was letting on.

I hadn't wanted to cause trouble. But I'd had enough of going through the motions, pretending to think. If thinking, as Ouspensky said, was "thinking in other categories," then thinking was dangerous. It upset and challenged the familiar categories. And who knew where it led…?

I'd just been sitting quietly, listening to my formatory mind and everyone else's when a vision ripped through me. All the questioning I'd done about Satan and his relationship to Jesus, all the information I'd stuffed myself with—suddenly, it all took shape, formed a pattern. It was too big to remember. Like with chess, I realized I could only remember by acting, giving it voice.

"Instead of directly talking about Satan let me ask a question: what kind of world do we live in?"

The initial shock worn off, some people began to listen.

"Don't we live in Caesar's world where 'might makes right'? As Ouspensky once said, 'The history of man is the history of crime.' Who rules man's world? Man? According to Gurdjieff we're just part of organic life whose primary purpose is to feed the moon. So if we don't rule this world—who does?"

I could feel the anger well up in the group. It was like a silent hailstorm hitting my body. I wasn't stopping. I'd crossed a line and I was taking them with me, like it or not.

"So let's consider the idea that this is Satan's world. That may be hard to stomach, I know, because everything is kept so nice and orderly down here, at least in this country. Progress, science and all that. But remember Gurdjieff's story of the magician and the sheep—all this slick veneer just to hypnotize us so that we never really question who's in charge here."

My tone of voice had a quality I'd never heard before. An "I," or something, was speaking that was not familiar.

"There's the idea that we live in a fallen world—that's a very Gnostic idea. Is it true? We won't really know until we can objectively see this world. And to do that we have to begin to awaken. Yet the fact is the whole world is set up to keep us asleep.

"We are conditioned to buying into societal mind games, to living in our heads. The body is taboo. Hence, the great preoccupation with sex. But we have mind-sex, not body-sex, not spiritual- sex. Sex is just another form of mental domination. No wonder that the Work says that sex is this world's center of gravity. Sex—not sacred conscious sex but mechanical sex—this is the primary motivating force behind all our sleep. Mechanical sex is a power trip and it's one of Satan's most hypnotic suggestions.

"Now sex and temptation are words that are very much linked in our minds, so let's look now at the temptations of Jesus. Before he goes into the wilderness, Jesus is conscious but he isn't crystallized yet. His real I isn't permanent yet. He can still fall asleep. So how does Satan tempt him? First he asks Jesus to prove he has actual power, that is, can he make stones into bread? A very cunning question because if Jesus makes bread from stones he obviously violates the laws of this world—Satan can then brand him a mere magician.

"And, mind you, Satan has a very personal stake in this question. For Satan is not asking Jesus about temporal power. No, he wants to know if Jesus has real power. Power in dimension, power capable of transforming the world—power strong enough to break the laws of this world.

"Jesus understands just what Satan is asking. So he answers—not in his own words—but by quoting scripture. Why? He wants to avoid the ego-trap of speaking from ordinary mind or, what Gurdjieff calls, 'formatory mind.' Also, in answering from the scriptures, he puts himself squarely within the line of tradition.

"Satan then asks if Jesus has complete faith in God. If he really is the Son of God, Satan says, he should prove it by leaping off the pinnacle of the temple. Again, Jesus answers—not from himself—from scripture. He says that to do so would not be God's will but his own will, his earthly will. He is drawing then a distinction. Are there two or three wills? Is there God's will, man's will and Satan's will? Or are there two wills—that of God's and that of Satan's? Or is there only one will? Or is it a question of relativity, of levels, of what world you find yourself in? This question of Satan's existence—is it relative? That is, above a certain level on the Ray of Creation does he have no existence? While on lower planes he does? And if so—what planes?"

People coughed, moved uncomfortably, stared at the wall. I could feel the mental censure, the energy building to shut me up. I sensed someone was about to speak, to deflect my line of thought. I had to hurry. I talked more forcefully, faster now, trying to get it all out.

"So now, having passed the first two temptations, Satan recognizes Jesus has actually realized genuine consciousness, a living awareness of what he truly is, of what this world is. This calls up all Satan's cunning. He says to Jesus: 'Okay, the game is up, you see through it. But look, look around. It's beautiful here. If you agree to worship me, you can have it all. All these kingdoms on earth, they're all mine and you can have them.'

"Think now of what Jesus is being offered. All he can see, smell, taste, touch, conceive and imagine—it's all his. And what else is there other than what your senses tell you there is? Seeing is believing, right? But Jesus knows the difference between consciousness and its contents. Jesus reminds Satan that it is written: 'Thou shalt worship the Lord thy God, and him only shalt thou serve.' Jesus is a Son of God, not a Son of Satan.

"Now let me ask—*can you give away something you don't own?* If Satan tells Christ he will give him all the kingdoms of this world that must mean he owns this world. (Remember: creating and owning are different. God may have created it, but the Prince of Darkness owns it, governs it.)

"Now it might be that Mr. Satan only pretends he owns it. He certainly isn't above a little deception. Looking at the evidence of mankind's history, of its near continual practice of war and allegiance to egoism—doesn't this show us where we live? It is the Land of Lies, the Land of Satan. The more unconscious we are of it, the bigger Mr. Satan's influence. We're sheep hypnotized to think we are lions. Unless we wake up…"

I stopped, looked around. Barbara glanced at me uneasily, her eyes fearful. Utter silence. Not a word from anyone. Not an eye would meet mine. I was a fool. Finally, the moderator checked his watch.

"It is something to think about," he said, coughing. "While some interesting things have been said, I'm afraid it is…well, time to go."

And immediately everyone got up and left.

They must have sensed, as I did now——*I was asking for it.*

SARAH WAS ASLEEP, LYING NAKED BESIDE ME IN A ROOM IN A MID-TOWN Manhattan hotel that in its day must have been a showplace, but had long ago fallen from grace. The room was large with a high white ceiling and fancy molding. The windows were barred and the brown carpet stained and threadbare. A dank, musty odor permeated the room. I stared aimlessly at the peeling strips of discolored, lime green, floral wallpaper, hanging out like hideous animal tongues.

What the hell was I going to do with her?

Somehow, she had gotten lost in the energy. She couldn't keep making the shift, keep the separation. What we'd experienced on one level, she wanted to make permanent on another. That wasn't possible. Why couldn't she see it? The freedom had been too much for her. She wanted security. All of me. She had kissed me and whispered—"I want your soul."

The remark stunned me.

Only then did I realize how dangerous this was. I was so naive. Blind. I had thought we could share this, explore, but make no demands. Mexico seemed so long ago. What was it two years? I couldn't remember. I only knew: now she wanted me to leave my wife, my family. I couldn't do that. But there was no half way with her. Once it had been all light and energy, the vibration so intense that there was no longer a "Sarah" or "William." We had gone from the physical to the mythological. It had all seemed so natural, so right. And, yes, I'd imagined it would last forever.

Now "William" and "Sarah" were here in full force…and they weren't letting go.

I looked at the naked figure lying beside me on the rumpled sheets. Her body was curled together, lying on its side, the knees drawn up to the chest like a baby. The skin, so white. The face was so strong. But fragile, too. The shoulders were broad like a man's. The breasts full and supple, almost muscular. The rest of the body was much smaller, not as developed. It was as if half of Sarah was masculine, half feminine.

I looked back into the wallpaper again. *What the hell was I going to do!*

Suddenly, I felt my perception shift. The wallpaper's elaborate floral design was filled with primitive, vegetative lime green faces, malevolent and dangerous. It had happened enough times that I knew I'd changed dimensions. I'd gone from the physical to the psychic.

"Where am I?" asked Sarah with a start.

"You're in Africa," I told her.

"What?"

"C'mon, you know. We've been here before."

Sarah sat up and looked around the room.

"Ohh," she said.

But she wasn't here. I could see that. Her eyes had a glassy, far away look. There was an odd quality to her look; as though a part of her still remained outside, a part that hadn't made the re-entry.

"Time to leave?" she asked.

"Soon."

Once she had left her body and couldn't return. We'd been attending a food conference in Phoenix. We were in her room meditating together. She had left and hadn't come back. Her speech was drowsy, drawn-out, as if she was speaking from a distant galaxy. It was as if only a thin fragile cord connected her to the room, to the earth, this plane of existence. And that cord could easily snap. I didn't know what to do. I had kept talking to her, appearing unconcerned, making it seem like only a matter of time until she made a re-entry. But she didn't. Or couldn't.

What if she didn't come back? We had both been playing with all this energy, all this fire. It had never seemed dangerous. It wasn't dangerous, but you couldn't identify. Otherwise, you went into that identity, that world. Like Zeus taking the body of Leda, the swan. Only for Zeus the act was intentional. He hadn't been grabbed by the unconscious.

I didn't know what to do, and so I had gathered all my energy and silently and earnestly prayed.

An idea came. I remembered that Sarah was studying belly dancing. I shook her. Her arms shook like a doll's. I began asking her questions about belly-dancing. At first she didn't answer. I persisted. Finally, she moved her head. Even that took effort. I knew I had to be very gentle. I kept talking, slowly and evenly, but insisting on a verbal answer. She answered but her tone remained distant. I asked if she would show me one of the movements. No, no interest. I kidded her and got up and moved my hips. "No, that isn't how you do it," she said. She got up and danced, moving like syrup through space, me gently clapping and singing, kidding her…until finally, the dance reconnected her.

"What did you mean…I'm in Africa?" Sarah asked.

"Sarah, what you have been saying, this stuff about getting married, wanting my soul…it doesn't make any sense. It's all imagination. A dream. Why are you suddenly insisting on what can't be?"

"You don't understand," she answered. She rolled over, pulling the covers around her. She buried herself in the covers. Then she sat up, crying— *"Why won't you understand?"*

"Let's not get into that again. I've got to catch a train."

"Oh, really? Of course. Mr. Patterson has to catch his train. I should know by now."

"For chrissakes! Let's not get into that, okay?"

"Okay."

We dressed and hurried to Grand Central. Sarah caught the train to Yonkers. I just made the 8:20 to Ossining.

The train was empty. I took a seat. The car looked so stark, inhospitable. The fluorescent ceiling light glared. How the fuck had I got myself into this! She wasn't letting go. It was over. No, I didn't want it to be over. I cared a great deal for her. But she couldn't see it. I couldn't leave my wife. That was never part of the bargain. Our son, John, was two years old now. And last month Barbara had had another baby, a boy, Matthew. I loved them. I'd never considered leaving. Never mentioned it.

The train went by Riverdale. I remembered one meeting with Lord Pentland looking at me curiously and saying, "When we are caught up on the horns of a struggle between a 'yes' and a 'no' in ourselves—we should see it. See the struggle and see how we lose energy, see how the "yes" and "no" come together and a decision is made."

Was I seeing it? No. I was totally identified. Why couldn't I come to a decision? There was this "Yes" in me, and this "No." One group of "I"s wanted to just get it over with—Goodbye. That's it. It's over. But another would shout—No, you can't do that. You really like her. You can't treat her that way. I am strung up between the two of them. I felt like I was being cut in two. I loved Barbara, my family. And, yes, I loved Sarah, too. But not in the same way. Why couldn't she understand that? Or was I just being a dumb unfeeling man? No, I couldn't just let her fall through space.

Space? I remembered Beckmann's last canvas, *Falling Man.* He had painted it just before he died. His pictures had always been so crowded. Here was this bigfooted man, man of the earth, falling upside down, through blue space. No, I couldn't let that happen to Sarah.

A thousand goddamn times I had been through it with Sarah. But she wouldn't listen. I told her I was not—not leaving my family! Didn't she understand? I told her I felt we were all—Sarah, Barbara, myself—karmically connected. Jesus, did she crack up over that one. Well, it sounded like bullshit, but it was true. Or was it?

Whatever, there was this unspoken battle now raging between us.

It had become a question of her will or mine.

I could see it from her side. I'd taken her into a world she'd never known existed (and neither did I). She'd given me everything. We were so good together. We understood each other. Her sense of humor was so keen, her mind so quick. But it was almost as if we were too good together. There was nothing to work out. It was like we were brother and sister.

There was paranoia, too. "I" felt she was trying to trap me. For example, that lunchtime Sarah had taken a shower. Her fingers were soapy and her wedding ring slipped off. Fell down the drain. She screamed. I ran into the bathroom. She was kneeling down in the tub, still wet and soapy, trying to pry open the drain screen. She seemed as if she was in a dream. I freaked out. Her wedding ring! Was this a sign? Was it my marriage, too? She kept working and finally got the screen off. She came out of the bathroom, a hotel towel around her head, smiled and opened her hand. There was the ring. She said it had gotten caught in some hair...

"Isn't it interesting" Lord Pentland had asked, "as one travels down a road with all sorts of danger signals cropping up...that we continue traveling in that same direction? What is it, I wonder, that prevents us from stopping? Why don't we simply turn around?"

Just what does it take to turn around? To break the momentum? I couldn't come to any place in myself that was real. I couldn't sit. I couldn't remember myself. My body said one thing, my mind another. I had gone to "Africa" as well.

It was late. We passed Sing-Sing Prison and the train lumbered into the station.

BARBARA OPENED THE DOOR, HER FACE BROAD AND SMILING IN THE FULL bloom of motherhood, cradling Matthew in her arms, John by her knees, pulling on her skirt, sucking his thumb and calling, "Poppy! Poppy's home Mommy!"

Barbara, so beautiful and innocent, so unsuspecting, so glad to see me, and not even mentioning my being so late. She put Matthew back in his crib and went into the kitchen to make me a sandwich.

Somehow, I felt she knew. She had to know, but she didn't want to know.

"Have a good day at the office?" she asked.

"Oh, yeah," I replied weakly. "You know, Stanley's up to his old tricks."

"What else?"

"Well, *Food* just won the Neal award. The Best Business Magazine of the Year. Can you believe it?"

"Another award?" asked Barbara.

"No...?"

"But you told me you won that award last week."

"Ahhh, what do I know?" I said and ducked into the bathroom. In the tub by the drain was this huge black spider. It was trying to scale the wall of the tub, but it was too sheer. I washed my hands and watched. The spider would almost make it out—then fall back to the bottom. No crash. No sound. But there it was at the bottom again. There was no way out for it, but up. And it must be losing strength. Only a matter of time until someone drew the water and down the drain it would go. I went to the living room to get a newspaper it could crawl onto. Then I'd carry "Charlotte" outside.

Barbara said she had put all the papers in the trash outside.

What had I gotten myself into? I loved women but I never took them seriously. Women were capable of such tremendous feeling. I loved this feeling, reveled in it, but gave it no respect. I sat down at the table and had my fill and then got up and went off. I thought I could go on this wonderful sexual spree with Sarah and it would have no consequences. I never took her feelings, Barbara's feelings, seriously. And so I could play and never have to pay the piper.

By the time I returned with a newspaper, I heard the water running in the tub. I rushed to the bathroom. There was Barbara bent over the tub and the two kids splashing around in it.

"What happened to the spider?" I asked.

"What spider?"

"The spider that was just goddamn here!"

"Pat, calm down. I didn't see any spider."

"There was a spider here, all right?"

"Okay, look. I'm sorry."

The kids started to cry.

"Jesus!"

"You're frightening the children. Lower your voice. Why are you making such a big deal over a spider?"

"Look, I'm sorry, okay? I'm going crazy at the office. I don't know what to do, and it's getting worse. An explosion is coming and…"

Barbara splashed water softly on the kids. "Can't you talk to Spencer? He must know what is going on with Stanley. Why does he protect him?"

"No one knows. Spencer has a big ego and Stanley drools all over him."

"Maybe you should 'drool' a little bit," said Barbara laughing.

She shined with love.

I turned away and walked into the bedroom and looked in the mirror, snorted, and fell into bed exhausted.

I am playing a board game showing a map of the world with an older woman, in her sixties. The game is Risk. The idea is to occupy enough countries so that the world is eventually dominated. The woman is dressed in a black sequined dress, early 1900's vintage. When it is my turn to move, she lays her fan across the board. It is studded with expensive jewels cut in the shape of Risk pieces. They are beautiful, but the fan prevents me from seeing the board.

"It's unfair!" I cry. "I have no chance to win."

She smiles sweetly. She has very long teeth, canine teeth. "You don't like to lose, do you?" she tells me in an accusing tone.

"You didn't sleep last night. What's wrong?" Barbara asked.

I told her about the dream.

Barbara was nursing Matthew. She looked up and laughed, "Well, it's true. You don't like to lose."

"Some things you can't afford to lose. They're not trivial."

"Babe, why don't you talk to Spencer? He must know what is going on."

"We all know what's going on. We just keep ourselves dumb, asleep. Seeing the truth of how things really are hurts too much, or so we think."

"Well, try to lighten up. Remember your father saying you take life too seriously."

"He did?"

"You told me that."

"I forgot. Yeah, too serious. No, I don't take it seriously enough."

At work Sarah was tight and becoming hysterical. She had an argument with Alice, my managing editor. Stanley had pushed me into hiring Alice about a year before. Alice fawned over me, playing the good, obedient daughter. Like Stanley, she knew how to feed the ego. Sarah thought I was interested in Alice. She saw her as a threat. But it was all projection. Alice drove Sarah up the wall. Stanley was calling Sarah into his office now for long closed-door talks. Sarah looked sucked out when she left.

"Why talk to him?" I asked.

"I have to. He's the boss, remember?"

"You haven't said anything, have you?"

"About what?"

I didn't reply

"Don't worry, William. I'm not going to shatter your little dream world."

"Sarah, c'mon. Don't be that way."

"Now what 'way' is that, my good fellow?"

"Sarah, for chrissakes! We're in the office, all right?"

THE WOMAN REMINDED ME OF *COLUMBINE,* BECKMANN'S FEMME FATALE.

She had appeared one morning dressed all in black, her dress pulled up above the knees, revealing two enormous, beautiful pink thighs. She wore a small black hat, its veil covering her face, a red rose adorning the side.

His anima figure, his woman, was masked and huge of body much out of proportion to her small head. She was dressed in a black petticoat, her legs spread aggressively at extreme right angles from the pelvis. She was wearing black stockings. But they stop just beyond the knees so as to reveal the pale flesh of her massive thighs. Between her thighs, some cards have been thrown; two face-up, two down. A game of fate. The past known, the future to be turned up. The painting has a kind of daring, a threatening sexuality, but a destined, inexorable quality, too. Beckmann's *Columbine* is a woman, or an intense emotional state, a man meets only at a major crossroads. Jung says that two of the primary qualities of the female are binding and loosening. Which was she? I wondered how the image had come to Beckmann. Mine had come to me during a morning meditation.

To strengthen the connection between my dream woman and me, I knew I had to paint her at once. The paint was hardly dry when I received an invitation from the Spanish Olive Commission to tour the olive groves and factories of Spain with a group of food editors. I felt it was *her*. I knew I had to go but Spain didn't really interest me. Then the thought came to fly to Ireland afterward, visit my roots. And it would be good to get away from Stanley and this situation with Sarah.

The feeling kept coming to me that I should visit the Museum of Modern Art. At lunchtime I hurried over, wandering around, wondering why the hell I was there. Then I came upon Beckmann's *Departure*, a gigantic triptych. I just "stepped into" the painting. It was the first time I experienced it with someone else's painting. My formatory mind shut off and I found myself "reading" it with my feelings. Beckmann had painted a modern day Garden of Eden...*Departure* represented Adam and Eve, cast from the Garden into the world of formatory thought and feeling. He depicted them on their return voyage of redemption.

The center, I saw, is where everything begins, so I looked at the middle panel first. It showed a royal family in a boat. There was a King, Queen and, in her arms, their blonde-haired baby. Guiding the boat was a helmeted warrior-oarsman holding a huge fish between his hands. The fish, symbol of Christ, was the soul. A strange trickster, only half his head showing, peered over the Queen's shoulder. In the foreground, by the boat's side, was a net with a large catch of fish. The bearded king, wearing a golden trident crown, stared off into the distance.

The king was looking into the future toward the new land to which they were rowing. He was looking off into the right panel. So the left panel represented the past. This panel showed a weird, gruesome scene of bloody torture. It was composed of a small table with some larger than life-size fruit. A phallic-looking green pear, a bunch of purple grapes and a big red apple, lying on its stem side, highlighted with a phallic brush stroke.

Four figures dominated this panel: a torturer, two males, and a female. In the foreground was a woman in a tight corset and slip. She was on her knees, bent over the lid of a garbage can. The torturer stood between the woman and the two men in the background. One male was nude, his genitals shielded from the viewer by the torturer holding a mallet with a fish face. The man was gagged and bound to a Grecian pillar. His hands are cut off. He was helpless. The other man, facing into the second of three pillars, has his back to the viewer. He was not seeing what was happening. He was clothed, his wrists bound, but not gagged. He stood in a garbage can.

All the figures represented parts of the psyche. The torturer, the brute unconscious. The man in the can, the intelligence. The handless man and corseted woman, the male and female energies. The intelligence was being tortured because he had not had the courage to see what was happening, and had allowed the man and the woman to taste "the forbidden fruits."

In the right panel, the future, a woman walked up flights of stairs. She held an oil lamp and carried a man bound to her left side, upside down. The soles of his feet in the air, his head hanging only inches from the ground. Beckmann had reversed the roles. The female force will lead the way.

Close behind these two figures was a man in a parade costume, a hat pulled over his eyes. He carried a large fish. He was its guardian. In the foreground, a man beat a big drum. The drum beat was the heart's beat. No, this departure was not just any journey, but the journey of the soul. The woman is the soul's guide. The feeling was guiding the head that could only see the ground and had no perspective, no idea where the journey was leading. Only at the journey's end will the upside down man be loosed, much wiser now, to stand right side up again.

My eyes wide and still, It suddenly came to me—Beckmann, this powerful fearless German poet of the night, was painting the archetypal story of an updated Adam's sin, punishment, and his alchemical journey to redemption!

I felt transported by Beckmann's colossal imagination. So often imagination is used in a negative way, especially in the Work. But creative imagination, which in its true sense is spiritual, that is, it connects things, removes the "psychic space," is a great joy. It's not personal at all, not an indulgence of fancy and day dreaming. It was the highest of the powers of man and therefore the most misunderstood and abused for, in essence, it is feminine, receptive and intelligent in nature. Hence, all the talk of "muses."

Beckmann's imagination, his imaging-inward, was able to see beyond the physical. His imagination was therefore metaphysical in the best sense. He worked in the symbolic and mythological realms, marrying form and color with a purity that gave the gods a chance to channel and speak. Through the power and fearlessness of his inner sight, Beckmann was able to enter the world of the archetypes and have revealed to him the ancient patterns of going forth and return, death and rebirth, that guide the human soul. To do this he needed a special passport and that passport was only given upon the death of "Beckmann." This inner death completely freed and empowered his imagination, taking it beyond identification.

So imagination had to be seen for what it was. The highest and lowest power of the human soul. Max Beckmann lived at the top of his imagination.

HOTEL ALFONSO XIII, SEVILLE, SPAIN, A PERIOD PIECE BUILT IN THE YEAR OF the crash, 1929. As a special treat on the last evening of the Spanish olive tour, we editors had been driven to a private 16th century villa on the outskirts of Seville for dinner. We were greeted by our hosts and taken inside. At a signal a group of gypsies began playing that mad, insistent, hypnotic music, the women singing and clapping and dancing a wild flamenco. One gypsy woman pulled me out to dance with her. Her hair was long and thick and brilliant copper, just like Vali's, and she wore a black and white polka dot dress. I had felt all along that something would happen to me on this trip but nothing had. Now, dancing with this laughing gypsy woman, I felt as if a door was opening.

Later that evening we had dinner in an ornate dining room, filled with candles, mirrors and gilded antiques. It was so sumptuous and romantic and a bit depressing as well, for I had been seated next to a woman editor from one of the large ladies magazines. Slender, sickly-looking, dressed all in black, she reminded me of a starved bird. Her skin had an unhealthy pallor. It was dry, bloodless, like a plastic flower. Her face was plain, rather sorrowful. She wore no makeup. Her short brown hair was thin and lifeless. I'd noticed her a few times during the trip. She reminded me of someone or something. Suddenly I had it—"Have you ever heard of Anne Boleyn?" I asked.

She looked at me. I felt a strong intelligence and sensitivity. "You mean the princess that was beheaded?" she asked. Her voice was small, measured.

I nodded, thinking to myself—why had I let myself say that! The candles flickered and shadows danced everywhere. I saw us reflected in one of the large mirrors.

"Yes, I know what you mean," the woman murmured, digesting the idea. She stirred her tea. "I have always thought I was at the edge of doom," she answered evenly.

Had she said what I heard? Did she actually mean that? Fortunately, she went on to talk at some length about Anne Boleyn. She was quite familiar with her life. She hesitated a moment at one point and then asked me in that small reed-thin voice:

"Do you know why Henry was able to have Anne beheaded?"

"No, not really."

She minced a smile. This was a little secret.

"Anne had web hands..."

I looked at her, putting down my wine glass.

"...and an ugly cyst on her neck," the woman informed me.

I didn't get her point. I must have showed it.

"In that day," she said, "those were telltale signs of a witch."

"Hmmmn," I said, cutting my steak. "Tell me, what do you think a 'witch' is?"

A very queer look passed across her face. She hadn't expected that. She looked away into the mirror and then scanned the room. Finally she placed her fork and knife on her plate and leaned toward me:

"A witch is someone who knows more than we do," she said.

Her reply somehow stunned me. It was so direct, precise and, I felt, true.

The woman did not wait for a reply but instead turned away, striking up a conversation with an editor to the other side of her.

I thought of Vali. She certainly knew more than most people do about wicca, the bending of energy. Witches, I supposed, used energy the way others used words or logic. It was a means of influencing. Its special power and the fear it evokes, I saw, is because of its invisibility. It can't be seen. It can only be felt.

The dinner went on. I wanted to talk to the woman but she was engaged. I thought those might be our last words, but at the end of dinner the woman leaned over and confided in a tone of voice quite candid yet impersonal—"I have no skin, you see."

I looked at her skin. It didn't look alive.

"Living is very difficult for me," she continued. "You see, all my nerve endings are hanging out. I can feel everything."

I nodded sympathetically though I had no feeling for what she might be conveying. "It is...such torture," she said. There was real emotion in her voice.

I didn't know what to say. Finally, I ventured: "But if you can feel what another person feels, wouldn't that help you to come together with them?" I was trying to look on the bright side.

She looked, her face drawn and blank. "We are all alone in life," she replied. "There is no coming together."

"But people do come together," I insisted.

She pondered that. "Yes...I suppose for a time," she said rather wistfully.

"Well then...?"

"But it's only for a few moments...oh, perhaps for a bit longer. But this coming together, you see. It's always temporary. And then...then there is such sorrow."

The way she uttered "sorrow"—it was with such a sense of resignation. The word dropped on me like a dead weight shattering whatever constructs I had. The energy was all over. I couldn't contain the energy. I reached for the bottle of chardonnay.

"Would you like a glass?" I inquired.

She demurred and instead lifted her small yellowish hands spreading the fingers wide on the pink table cloth, curling the tips as if she were holding onto the table.

"I feel everything," she said, her voice almost a cry.

I had raised my wine glass but returned it to the table.

"I feel so alone. I'm always grasping too much...much too much. But I can't seem to let go. It's not possible. I'm too afraid of the pain."

I wondered if that was how it was with Sarah. She knew it was over but couldn't let go. The suffering, she thought, would be unbearable.

Back in the hotel I packed for Ireland and fell into a deep sleep.

GURDJIEFF IS ABOUT FIFTY YEARS OLD. I AM ALONE WITH HIM IN A DIMLY LIT *hotel room. The light casts the room in long soft shadow. We are sitting on a sofa. He needs a shave. His clothes are drab, rumpled.*

We are talking. I am finding it so easy to talk with him. He is very kind and seems to understand completely what I am feeling. Several times he looks directly at me. I feel the incredible force of his being. I feel, too, his strangeness, unpredictability. I notice that his dark eyes are bloodshot and have a grey cast.

He is telling me a story about himself. He ends with—"And that is the way it was the first time I lived."

I understand this to mean that during his first life he had died consciously to himself, to all his "I"s, and so he is living now for the second time.

"Would you like to die in this way?" Gurdjieff inquires, peering at me.

"Yes."

He ponders for a moment, weighing the situation. "It will take about three years," he says at last.

"But at the Foundation—"

"The Foundation is only preparatory. It is a unique and powerful preparation, and one that may last a long while, but still—only preparatory."

I am confused. "The Foundation is everything to me. I—"

"In itself it is nothing."

I see what he means. The Foundation exists to prepare one to die consciously, but the undergoing of one's death to this world is an individual matter; one that each must experience alone.

"Tell me," asks Gurdjieff, his voice sharp and direct, "do you really want to die in this way?"

"Yes," I tell him.

He leans toward me, his eyes entering mine. I could feel the full force of Gurdjieff's being pouring into me.

"It will cost you," he warns. "You must make a payment."

I nod, but what kind of "payment" does he mean? Isn't suffering through my identification payment enough?

"Fifty thousand dollars!" exclaims Gurdjieff. "That's what it will cost you to die."

"Fifty thousand dollars!" I had never supposed the payment to be in money.

Gurdjieff draws nearer. "You have to be able to live for three years."

I nod but am confused.

"You know—you have to be able to pay your taxes," he tells me, chuckling. ✗

DEEP DIVING

ELLO THERE," CALLED
the smiling man with the small mouth organ. "now what would you like to hear?"

"Oh, anything you'd like to play," I said.

The man smiled and extended his hand to me. He had a small shamrock tattooed on his thumb. "The name's Markum Hanrahan," he said.

I told him my name and he asked where I was from. His dark eyes seemed remarkably alert, though his breath was heavy with alcohol.

"The States," I told him and he began to play "Yankee Doodle Dandy."

I had just arrived in Dublin and was walking along the quay beside the River Liffey when I heard this Irish jig music coming from the other side. I crossed the narrow pedestrian bridge and found this curious man sitting on the steps playing on a small mouth organ. He was in his forties and had dark curly hair and liquid eyes, full of life, though his face showed a lot of wear.

When he finished playing "Yankee Doodle" I dropped a few coins in his hat and was about to go, but something told me to stay.

"Been a sailor most of my life but now I'm a bum," said the man in a lovely Irish voice. "But I've no shame about it. I live it to the full."

I nodded and pulled my coat around me. A cold wind had come off the river and my legs were quivering.

"Doesn't everyone have to be someone now?" he asked, his eyes twinkling.

I laughed. "That's true," I said.

"I was born in the States you know? Las Vegas, would you believe? That was, oh let me see, over forty years ago. Left when I was five years old and haven't been back. Say, where'd you say you're from?"

"New York."

He considered that awhile. Then played me another jig. The tunes were simple and lively. It was as if I was hearing the spirit of Ireland.

"Say," he said, looking up, "would you be having a drink with me now?"

"I would." I said.

"Grand!"

"But I've bought a ticket for a play."

He looked about for a moment. "Where'd you say you're from?" he asked again.

"New York City," I said, feeling strange repeating the answer. It reminded me of that first meeting with Lord Pentland. Was he expecting a philosophical answer? His mind was probably gone from all the booze. I was going to leave.

"Tell me," he inquired, "what are you doing here?"

"Ohhh," I said, "I'm looking for 'the other world.'"

"Are you now? Fancy that."

He smiled and picked up the mouth organ and played another jig, this one very fast and intricate. The interweaving of melodies reminded me of a Celtic design. I put a few more coins in his hat.

"I'm a deep diver," he confided, putting his pipe in his jacket. "Been all the way to the bottom of the sea."

I felt very close to him in some way. Like we had known each other a long time. I nodded and smiled.

"Now say—are you sure now you wouldn't be having a drink with me?"

"Oh, I've got to go. I'm sorry. I'll be late for the play."

He seemed sad at that. I didn't know why but there I was then pulling the red Western scarf from around my neck and handing it to him. Just as I did there was this funny feeling: *I shouldn't do this!* But he took the red scarf immediately and had it tied around his neck before I could say a word.

"I've heard," I said jokingly, "you can get in touch with someone if you have a piece of their clothing. Is that true?"

"Aye, that you can," he agreed and winked like the two of us shared a common knowledge.

I couldn't believe what I had done. I felt like an idiot. I didn't even know this man. What had gotten into me?

"Where'd you say you're from?" he asked.

"The States," I said. "Goodbye."

I hurried off then to the Peacock Theatre to see Ionesco's *What A Bloody Circus.*

I was early as it happened, so I read the playbill:

> The play exists on many levels. The unusual suddenly springs from events that seem ordinary, comedy merges into tragedy before reverting to burlesque, realism is overtaken by caricature. The play portrays the horror of sometimes existing in a universe both overwhelming and oppressing, where matter and substance are worn away and objects proliferate. We are witness to the gradual disintegration of objects and characters.

I smiled. That certainly seemed the way my life was going. Watching the play, the sense of this only increased. The character of the bored wife (I associated her very much with Sarah) first appeared with a large animal skin, its head, legs, tail and all, draped around her. By the second act there she was in a black dress and a black hat with—of course!—*a veil and red rose*. By the last act she had become a magician's helper. The black hat with a veil and a rose—it was just like the dream. How could this be? I remembered now my room at the boarding house up the quay where I'd left my bags. It hadn't registered then. The wallpaper there—it was all red roses. And the vase of plastic roses by the nightstand. What was going on?

On the way back from the play I mused about how I came to be at that boarding house. It, and this whole trip really, had a fated quality. I'd first checked in at the Royal Hibernia Hotel on St. Stephen's Green. I wanted to meet the real Irish people and I wasn't going to meet them there. So, trusting to luck, I'd picked up my bags and wandered off, following my feelings. Finally, I'd come to the River Liffey at O'Connell Bridge and walked along the river until I came to a chalkboard sign offering bed and board. The address was 36 Wellington Quay. I rang the bell. No answer at first but soon I heard footsteps hurrying down a flight of steps. Presently, a small dark-haired man, needing a shave, opened the door. But only part way.

"What'd you want?" he demanded.

"A room."

"You a Yank?"

I nodded and smiled.

"The Mrs. don't like Yanks," the man announced flatly.

"Why not?" I asked.

"Too pampered," he said.

"Why?"

"Like to take hot showers. And all that."

"Not me," I told him.

"Is that so?" he said and shut the door in my face.

I heard him quickly clamoring up the steps. A deep female voice boomed out—- "Who's that?"

"Some Yank," I heard the man say.

"You know I don't like Yanks."

There was silence. Then I heard the man say, his voice softer, "Respectable chap."

"Well, now...we'll see about that!" the woman shouted.

There came more clamoring of feet down the stairs but slower, heavier. Again, the door opened—this time completely. And there she stood, this huge battle-axe of a woman. An Irish Valkyrie. Large, square face. Very direct. The eyes hooded, big and blue, but sharp, challenging. She wore an old print dress that long ago had seen its best days, with a badly stained apron tied round her middle.

She sized me up, first with her eyes and then questions.

"Where was it you say you're from?" she asked, her eyes not leaving me for a second.

"The States."

"And how'd you get here, may I ask?"

"You mean to Dublin? Or here right now?"

She looked at me like was I trying to put one over on her. "Here. Of course," she said and stamped the floor.

"I was just wandering around, looking for a good place to stay."

"Is that so?" Her eyes squinted. "And what is it you want?"

I smiled. "A room," I said. She rubbed her chin.

"What did you say your name was?"

"Patrick Patterson." I said. "Named after St. Patrick."

"Oh really? Would you be Irish now?"

"Scotch-Irish. A little English and French."

"Humph!" She rubbed her chin a moment, looking me over head to foot again. "All right!" she roared at last. "You can have a room. But, mind you—this is a cold water working man's flat." She turned to go up the narrow stairway, but then thought better of it. "We don't indulge people here," she declared, her eyes giving me fair warning.

"I understand," I told her.

She looked at me like I might be a sly one. "My name is Mrs. Clarke," she stated, putting an accent on the "Mrs." Then she led me up the stairs and into a large room, the kitchen, dining room and living room combined. She showed me to my room which was on the same floor and overlooked the River Liffey. Mrs. Clarke took up a post by the door while I looked about. The room was narrow, barely large enough for the single bed. A single bare bulb hung from the ceiling. The floor was covered in linoleum. By the side of the bed where travelers got into and out of bed, it was worn nearly through. I put my bags down and nodded to her that the room was okay. She stayed at the doorway, watching. I shuffled around waiting for her to leave. I supposed she wanted to see what was in my bags. Was I an IRA gun runner? A CIA spy?

I play acted long enough, taking no notice of her, that she at last gave up. She blew out a few gusts of air and informed me of her thoughts of the moment. "African boy used to take this room," she mused. "Nice boy but had no conscience."

I turned. "Yes?"

She paused. "Got a girl in trouble."

"Really?"

"An Irish girl she was. To get rid of her what do you think he does? Why he puts her through a meat grinder, of course. Makes nice and neat mince meat of her, he does."

"Is that so?" I said, wondering where this was leading.

"Why not a soul has eaten mince meat in Dublin since!" she boomed.

I just stood looking at her.

She looked at me as if I were a bit daft, then continued: "Studying to be a doctor, the police said. Seems he was in the wrong field. Why what with his talent the lad should've been a butcher!"

We both laughed. I got her point: she didn't want any trouble.

"Breakfast" she said pointedly, "is from seven to eight-thirty. You have that? No exceptions."

"Fine," I told her.

"Now, Mr. Patterson, what time do you suppose we might be expecting you?" Mrs. Clarke said brightly.

"Well," I answered, considering a moment, "why don't you wake me at seven and I'll have breakfast at eight."

My answer completely threw her. She cocked her head to the side and repeated it slowly—"Wake him at seven and he'll have breakfast at eight?" Her voice was skinny and her eyes suspicious.

"That's right," I told her.

She looked at me as if I were another "strange one." I could see where her mind went. She couldn't quite figure me out—but she no doubt she would.

The following morning Mrs. Clarke had banged on the door, hollering the time to me.

"Seven o'clock, Mr. Patterson. Seven o'clock."

I roused myself and began my meditation. A second call never came, but I had set my travel alarm. When I appeared in the big room for breakfast Mrs. Clarke, by the stove in the same dress and apron, was waiting for me.

"Ahh, now this is Mr. Patterson, gentlemen," she announced to the line of workingmen seated at the two dining tables. "He's a Yank that's found his way to us."

All the men laughed. Mrs. Clarke put a pan down on the old horse of a stove and came toward me. She placed her hands on either hip.

"Tell me now, Mr. Patterson..." she called out, her voice sweet with poison for she knew well the ancient Irish art of guilt-making. "Just what is it you've been doing in there all this time?" She turned to the men to explain. "Why I woke him at seven," she said, "and here he is—a good hour-and-a-half later!"

All the men turned to look at me. Mrs. Clarke's massive face glowered, daring me to be man enough to confess and get it off my back.

The implication in her voice and manner could only mean one thing in these circumstances—*You've been jacking off in there alone, haven't you?*

Such was the power of her words that the moment stopped completely. I was stunned but I hadn't gone blank. The observer was still there. A quiver of energy began to rise. I knew if I let it spread, identified with it, put a thought to it, the energy would become guilt and, mechanically I would either be in a rage or turn tail. But this recognition was not of the mind. Ordinary thought would have been too slow. It came from a much deeper level which, ordinarily, I was not aware of. It was a level of subtle stirring before manifestation.

And so, in this sense, it was instantaneous that a separation between personality and essence—a separation of "myself from myself" in Gurdjieff terms—happened. I, the observer, stood "outside" the happening, the content. I was "the seeing" as Lord Pentland said. That's where the value was placed, and not on the contents.

Out of that place I found myself taking a step toward her. I mirrored her hands-on-hips image.

"Now Mrs. Clarke," I said, my voice catching some of that Irish lilt, "if that were any of your business…now wouldn't I be telling you?"

A shock wave went through the room. Total stunned silence. And then the whole room burst into laughter. Even Mrs. Clarke, the tables so deftly turned, was forced to laugh.

"Ahhhh, boys! We have a live one here, don't we?" she said appreciatively. She motioned me to my spot at the table. "Sit there, next to Mr. Solon. He's one of my better boys. He's licked the bottle, he has, and is an example to us all!" She looked the remaining men up and down, inviting and daring a refutation.

"Twice he has! And more power to him!" one voice roared once Mrs. Clarke had turned about.

Everyone laughed but Mrs. Clarke who spun around like a tank cannon and spat: "Now that will be enough out of the likes of you!"

The room quieted down and Mrs. Clarke returned to her station by the stove. Mr. Solon, an old grey-haired man, grizzled and mostly bald, told me a story about the "Mrs." here coming upon two burglars one night and her chasing them all the way down the stairs with a poker.

"Met the wrath of the Almighty," one man said.

"Worse!" put in another.

"Made the paper it did," declared Mrs. Clarke, beaming. "The telly, too."

She hurried to me then, carrying a hot plate, her hand wrapped in a dish towel. There was one egg, sunny side up, three little hot dogs (not sausages), potatoes, toast and coffee. This close, I noticed Mrs. Clarke wore a hairnet. But there straggling across the white and yellow of the egg were two long strands of her hair. Thinking I'd best say nothing, I just cleared them away.

Mr. Solon gave me a quick smile and began to tell me stories of his boyhood in County Mayo.

One by one the men left the tables for work and soon I was alone with Mrs. Clarke. She brought a pot of tea to the table and also a framed letter for me to read.

"No," she said. "Not to yourself. Read it aloud," and sat back to hear it anew.

It was from Winston Churchill. It commended her for her work in the Aliens Department during the war.

"Oh, Winny was a tough one," she declared, her voice now rich and sonorous. "Me, a young Irish girl in England during the bombings working at Number 10 Downing Street! Can you imagine that?"

I laughed and handed her the framed letter.

"Told me, he did, that I was 'too cheeky.' And if I didn't 'straighten up' why he would send me 'back to Ireland—to eat shamrocks.'"

Mrs. Clarke roared to the ceiling while casting a sly eye to see how it was going over.

"Would you be married, Mr. Patterson?"

"I am. And have a family, too," I said. I had started speaking with an Irish tone.

Mrs. Clarke considered things a moment.

"You look too young for the ball and chain. But...well, I suppose it does as many good as naught. You haven't come to court an Irish lass then?"

"No, I've just come back to see my roots. I hope to hear an Irish storyteller, if I can find one."

"Well, tell me, have you ever heard about 'Paddy and Molly'?" Mrs. Clarke asked toying with her tea cup.

"No."

Mrs. Clarke stole a look out the window, coughed and began: "Paddy and Molly, you see, had dated for some thirty years. You know, we Irish don't do things rashly. Specially not tying the cord. So one time after the Saturday night dance, Molly gets Paddy to drive off the highway onto the old dirt road. The one they used to always take before the new road came. Well, before long, they come to this old oak tree standing all alone in a green meadow and just peering over its branches way up in the night sky is a full moon as big as a mountain.

"When they both were in high school this was the very tree where Paddy had carved into its bark a big heart. And in the center of the heart he carved the names, 'Paddy & Molly.' Now here these many years later the two of them are standing there looking at this heart and the names inside it.

'Do you remember?' asks Molly.

'Ahh, yes, love.' Paddy replies, a bit wary.

'Well,' says Molly, 'it was a long time ago, you know?'

'That it was,' he says. 'That it was.'

'Well, don't you think now,' suggests Molly, 'it's high time we be getting married?'

"Paddy, caught by surprise, stares at the ground, his one foot pawing at the roots of the tree. He shakes his head and stares up into the black of the night sky and soft beams of the moon. And finally he declares with a sad eye—

'Ahh, yes, love...but who would have us!?'"

Mrs. Clarke slapped the table. And we both roared with laughter.

"Now tell me! Isn't that an Irish joke? Have you ever heard anything to beat that in all your life?"

And so it went. I had found what I was looking for.

THE NEXT MORNING I WAS OFF TO THE WEST. AT BREAKFAST, MR. SOLON had recommended I stop at Ballintubber Abbey in County Mayo, about seven miles south of Castlebar. Pilgrimages to the holy mountain of Croagh Patrick began at the Abbey, he said, "Ballintubber" meaning "well of St. Patrick." Cathal O'Connor, King of Connacht had it built to repay the kindness shown him while he was in exile. Mass, he said, had been held there continuously for over seven hundred and sixty years. I wrote down the name, thanked everyone and went to get my bags. It was a joyous goodbye with everyone laughing and hollering.

I packed the car I had rented and went to Trinity College to see the Book of Kells, an illuminated manuscript of the four Gospels written at the end of the eighth century. The illuminations were glorious, both innocent and filled with understanding. My attention was particularly drawn to the *Portrait of St. Matthew* and to *The Man*, Matthew's iconic symbol. I was off, then, to see the rest of Ireland.

It was a fine and brilliant October's day. I drove first to the north of Dublin to Tara, the royal site of the old Irish kings. Along the way I passed caravans of tinkers pulled off by the side of the road. At the ancient hilltop nothing remained but the view—the soft rolling land stretched out in all directions was magnificent. The feeling of total space. Studding the blue vastness canopied above, there hung layer upon layer of clouds filled with animal shapes and human faces, a riot of imagination worthy of the gods. I had read that to be a high Irish king you had to be able to go to "the other world." At what had been the home of Cormac, the high king, instinctively I felt the urge, and turned about in the space three times, silently asking for blessing. I had just opened my eyes when, it seemed out of nowhere, charged this big black Labrador. He was on me before I could move, jumping up on my chest and nuzzling me like an old lost friend. The greeting over and without my saying a word, he lay down at my feet. A good thing, for I found this blessing was a mite too real. I was close to a heart attack.

I went on to Kells and stayed the night. The next day was October 3rd, the anniversary of Barbara's and my marriage, five years earlier. I sent her a kiss and then found myself thinking of Sarah. Whenever I thought of one, up came the other. A fight was going on in me. Two sides, two groups of "I"s, at war. My mind told me one thing, my body another. I—whoever that was—was getting torn to pieces. How was this all going to end?

I soon found myself at New Grange, a passage grave, an enormous stone burial mound overlooking the Boyne River and valley. Stooping down, I crept along the small narrow passageway leading to the chamber. On several of the huge stones at the entrance and now in the chamber I noticed, carved into the stone, circular lines in a swirl. There were three swirling circles reminiscent of the Law of Three. The shaft and the chamber were in the design of a cross, but carbon dating placed New

Grange at least 2000 B.C. Local folklore had it that the passage graves, like New Grange, were the homes of the "little people," the leprechauns, but they must have been sleeping. I said a prayer and went on to Monasterboice to see its famous High Irish Cross. I drove along an old dirt road to a church and in its graveyard came upon this towering stone cross, a good twelve feet high, elaborately carved with biblical scenes. The atmosphere, like that at New Grange, was so silent and still I stayed on a few hours making sketches in my notebook and diary. That evening I wrote a letter to Barbara. I felt like a hypocrite.

I traveled on to Clonmacnoise in County Offaly. The soft radiant scenery was as beautiful as the name of this old monastic site, its ruins standing alongside a slowly flowing river. Several round towers and small churches still stood and there were two High Irish Crosses. I made more sketches and wrote my impressions in the journal. Like Tara and New Grange there was a presence, a feeling of it all existing outside time. I felt as if I was in transit now, traveling between two different times. The past was gone, but where I was going was not yet in sight. My moods and energy had been up and down since leaving Dublin. I didn't feel like myself, whatever that was. Sketching one of the crosses, I stopped and looked out over the valley. Thoughts stilled. Feelings of death and decay came. Then they jelled into one thought: *Ireland is a Land of Death.* The whole country smelled of death, of ceaseless suffering and grief. The people and the land were beautiful, but both were so wounded and scarred from centuries of conflict. It was entombed in its past, frozen in memory. *Ireland was the Land of The Mother.* I remembered James Joyce telling about Ireland's three mothers, all quite deadly, if not rightly taken. There was one's own mother, the Mother Church and Mother Ireland. It all began to fit: the woman in black with a red rose who came to me in a dream, Beckmann's *Columbine* and *Departure.* All foreshadowings. I had been called home, home to the ancient Mother. I had glimpsed something of her reflection with Barbara and Sarah and now—what? I didn't know.

I meditated for a while at Clonmacnoise. There was such a peace and serenity there. But the mind wouldn't relax. It kept ping-ponging back and forth between Barbara and Sarah. It was mid-afternoon and getting cool. The sky had turned slate grey and lifeless. I drove on into the West. I was tired but more lonely than tired. My mind kept chewing on yes-and-no between Barbara or Sarah. One "I" proclaiming, then another. Both absolutely sure. Suddenly I realized—*it hadn't been my question at all.* It was Sarah's. In her continuing insistence that I choose between them, I had unconsciously accepted it as my question. The mind had accepted it and now was convinced it must find an answer. But oddly this recognition had no power. The mind kept eating on it. I couldn't stop it. Every brain cell felt overcharged. I felt raw, without atmosphere, like that "Ann Boleyn" I'd met in Spain.

My mind blank, exhausted from the struggle between "I's," I drove through village after village. They all looked the same. School was letting out. Coming around a bend there stood a young girl, no more than thirteen or fourteen, in a Catholic school uniform, a little thumb up in the air. I had no energy but I felt like talking to someone. I stopped the car. She didn't get right in but first peered through the window to see if I was okay. She got in but was very shy. I tried engaging her in conversation but nothing. She wouldn't speak unless I spoke, and then only a few words. She kept a knapsack of books and homework placed securely over her lap and kept her face straight ahead.

We drove a long while not speaking, both of us staring out the window. The road narrowed to two lanes and soon we were out of town and into the open country, the lanes bounded on either side by long walls of piled stone which the Irish use to divide their property. The whole countryside was cut and divided by stone into neat squares and rectangles. It was the mind's way of dealing with nature, and man.

The silence in the car was heavy, psychological. I wished I hadn't stopped. I felt too raw, too open. I felt dull, enervated, frustrated. I wanted to go to sleep. Then, quite suddenly, for no reason that was apparent, and so all the more frightening, a mad "I," seized my mind, whispering…

Stop the car. Take the girl behind the stone wall—and do it.

The "I" was so strong and strange, so insistent. It felt so alien, not "me." But then what was it? Was this an "I" long buried that had just surfaced? Or was it somebody else's? Something I had picked up? Was it her fear I was picking up and turning around? Was it Markum's? I had given my scarf to him hadn't I?

Stop the car…

What "I" could I trust? What "I" could be believed? The stark and obvious recognition, one that I had really always denied despite so much glib talk, was that there was no "I." I was nothing. Nothing.

The mind raged in frenzy. "I"s warred and screamed.

Was I going mad? The body was growing hot, tense. I tried to remember myself, to come into the body. But the effort was too mental, the attention too thin and jumpy, the "I"s too powerful. The strain sapped my remaining energy. My God! what was I going to do?

Then a shift. A peculiar quiet descends upon the car.

An inner voice, very distinct, speaks to me: *Do not take your hands off the wheel. Do not take your foot off the gas pedal. Do absolutely—nothing.*

A colossal battle breaks out. First one voice—*Stop the car!*

Then the other: *Do nothing!*

I hold the wheel tight, my hands turning white. I keep driving, my eyes not leaving the narrow road. Up and over the green and yellowing hills we go, passing through valleys and climbing hills. Fluffy sheep stand mindlessly in meadows. Cows on hillsides indifferently chewing away. Little homes of stone, whitewashed clean, with thick straw roofs like beards dot the landscape.

Stop the car!

My legs tremble. I am perspiring. The mind is a jungle of "I"s. The schoolgirl is keeping still, very quiet, not saying a word, hoping to become invisible. Some part of her has sensed the danger. I sense her apprehension, her dumbstruck fear that what she has been warned about is about to happen.

I have read about people who commit some hideous crime and say afterward that they don't remember doing it, but they admit they must have for the knife or gun or whatever is in their hand. Gurdjieff says one "I" acts, the others pay for it.

I must stay conscious.

Stop the car. Do it!

"Here!" she cries.

I hit the brake immediately. The brakes lock and the car screeches to a halt on the black asphalt.

Goddamn it! Do it!

She is out of the door like a cat and off and running down the dirt road, flying at full speed, her knapsack swinging side to side. And at the bottom of the road standing in the doorway of one of those tidy little whitewashed homes is the girl's mother...

I didn't drive off immediately. I couldn't. I was eaten out inside. Near delirious. I felt utterly alone, unprotected, stripped of the veil of familiar, of any notion of self-identity. I felt as though I was living inside my unconscious. That I had unwittingly entered the 'other world' or some dangerous in-between world. There was nothing to lean on, hide behind, put between myself and the world. And here I was, thousands of miles from home, clear across the ocean, a mad machine, as Gurdjieff said, who, might go out of control at any moment and with no one in charge!

As I sat, my mind stunned into stillness with the gravity of what had just occurred, I saw the truth of an obvious fact: consciousness is intentional. It must be why Gurdjieff talked in his *Third Series* about wishing. To be conscious, I had to first wish to be conscious. Of course, it might come. But that was a gift. I needed to make being conscious my wish.

And now I realized something else: that all this practicing of self-remembering and self-observation had been only that—*just practice*. It was all only a preparation for the day when the door would swing open and one would be fair game, a mere mortal to be tested and judged in what Beckmann had referred to as "The Palace of the Gods." Here existed all the fruits, ripe or rotten, of one's personal and collective unconscious. Or perhaps the better word was "subconscious," as Gurdjieff had said. Conscience was there. But one had to wish for it, fight for it, fight to be worthy of it. A fight between what he called the non-desires and the desires. And the battle took place not in the ordinary world walled off into neat little fields by the mind but in the other world, the world outside the mind, the world where anything goes because everything is and isn't, all at once. It's only on this ground where the ancient combat takes place—only on this archetypal ground where the I's wrestle in the court of Being. And whatever I-desire dominates, that I takes root in you. That he never spoke about.

It was impossible for a teacher to prepare a student for any specific situation, for all situations were possible and all subject to change. Hence, the only practical preparation, the only sensible way to navigate through this maze of the unimaginable, was to remember oneself. And no matter how many times one was taken, went to sleep, the attention short-circuited, it was to train the attention to return to the body, to start anew, so that whatever befell one—one grounded inside oneself. One worked to be present. Present to give assent, to deny or ignore and therefore to take human responsibility for whatever god, goddess or malignant force would have its way among humankind, would test its God-given humanity in its striving for objective reason.

I could only thank God. I had been blessed. Without such training and without grace, I might just as easily be cowering behind a stone wall, horrified and wanting to kill myself for such a debased and brutal act.

I started the car and before long found myself up near Sligo. I stopped at a bed 'n board on a hillside overlooking a long natural lake with little islands scattered through it. There wasn't a house or a farm or a fence for miles. I sat on the porch pretending to look at the lake and the landlady brought me tea. She was lovely and caring in a quiet, simple way.

"You've come a long way, haven't you, lad?" she said, her voice so soft and moist with feeling.

I nodded slowly and smiled weakly for I could not speak.

"Well, a good night's rest will do your soul a world of good. You'll see," she said. She stood a moment and we both looked out into the broad landscape. Two strangers on a hillside at dusk. But I could feel her, feel the moment. "I'll leave you be now," she murmured finally and went back inside.

I sat on the swing gazing at the dark forest and the broad lake with its little islands of trees, the whole lake in the late afternoon light now a slate of shimmering liquid steel. The Mayans, I remembered, thought of lakes and ponds as eyes of God. I wondered what the old Celtics thought? I felt myself now. The fever, or whatever, had passed. The psychic assault was over. In the Middle Ages they'd say some devil had entered me. But I had struggled, I'd had a taste of real conscience. Strange, how what had happened had been prefigured in a way with Mrs. Clarke and what she had told me about the former tenant of my room. Did my giving the scarf to Markum have anything to do with this? Or was I trying to make excuses? I didn't know. Truly, I didn't know.

The next morning I woke up feeling like I had slept a hundred years and was still tired. It was a dreary, drizzly day with the fog so thick I couldn't see the lake. A good day for a funeral but little more. I was off early to Sligo to see Yeats' grave. Drove up through Collooney, past a black cat on the road, still writhing in its death agony. I thought of driving over it, but did not. Without difficulty I found the Drumcliff churchyard. And there was Yeats' gravestone. I took off my cap and read the inscription:

Cast a cold Eye
On Life, on Death
Horseman pass by!

The poet's last words. He spoke right into me.

Heaps of flowers lay at a nearby grave, newly dug. I took a long red carnation and gave it to Yeats and then drove away. I wasn't far south of Sligo when my mind was suddenly seized with another tug 'o war between Barbara and Sarah. I drove on, locking the doors, vowing to pick up no one. Signs for Galway appeared. I pulled over and fell asleep, only to awake and find the thoughts, like knives, still slashing at me.

Go with Sarah!

Stay with your wife!

And they weren't thoughts now—but voices. My head thundered with these voices. I couldn't stay separate, just listen. They were too powerful. But they didn't take me completely. Something in me remained watching. All the years of self-remembering. That had all been practice. Now I had been stripped down. All that was left was the wish. And I saw that was so small, so feeble.

I prayed right there in the car.

All I wanted was to do what was right. I would do whatever that was. But I had to be told what to do. I couldn't choose. I could see that. I wasn't free. I wasn't conscious. I was asleep. Now I was on the edge of a cliff.

The image of Mr. Solon came to me. I remembered him telling me about Ballintubber Abbey. That was it! I had to go there. I checked the map. The Abbey was in between Ballinrobe and Castlebar. A good thirty-five miles or more back. I'd always hated driving back to any place I'd passed. But I did. It wasn't easy to find. The guidebook said St. Patrick baptized his converts here. The foundation of the church was said to date back to the time of St. Patrick, about 441 A.D. The Abbey had been built in 1216. It had been razed by fire and newly built, most recently in 1966. It lay in a field of rolling hillsides with Croagh Patrick looming up in the distance.

As I approached the Abbey a heavy wind came up. It thrashed the trees, forcing them to bend, and then, just as suddenly, died out and all was quiet again. The doors to Ballintubber were solid oak and huge, at least twice my height. I put my hand on the door ring to open it and just as I did the wind gusted up again, the strength of it actually blowing me inside. If I hadn't had hold of the ring, I would've been flat on my face. The interior was painted all white. It was spare with little ornamentation. I lit candles to Gurdjieff and to both sides of my family, the Pattersons and the Scotts. I sat in a pew near the front and meditated. My mind was too tired to have thoughts. The silence felt so good. Healing. I don't know how long I sat there, but dimly at first and then more clearly I became aware of an inner urging: Go to the pulpit. I did so. The large Bible was open. It was turned to the twenty-seventh Sunday. The reading was from Matthew. It spoke about God having vineyards that had produced only sour grapes and how God had made woman from Adam's rib. A disciple had asked Jesus about divorce.

I knew now why I had been brought here.

The disciple said that Moses had said divorce was acceptable. Jesus told him that Moses' answer had been due to the state of the people of his time but that now we could hear the real truth. And this was that a man is joined to a woman in marriage for them to become one body, one soul. To separate them then is to commit adultery.

I had never understood what adultery really was. I'd thought it was only social morality. I never realized it had a spiritual dimension.

I looked up into the arched wooden ceiling above my head—

"All right!" my voice thundered and, like a judge's gavel, I saw my fist pound the Bible. Ballintubber had spoken.

I had tasted Casey's apple—damned if you do, damned if you don't. It had almost killed me.

I stepped outside into the wind and the Irish countryside. I felt like a new man. The air tasted so sweet and crisp. Saint Patrick and The Mother had given me life again.

I was thirsty and went to the small country tavern across from the Abbey. An old alcoholic was at the bar. He asked the barmaid to give me a drink. It was on him, he said. I declined and bought my own but we talked awhile. I asked about storytellers and he told me of Eamon Kelly, quite famous in Ireland. But there was one even better, he declared. That would be "Sonny Lacey" but the problem was he was in a nursing home in Clifden, about fifty miles west of Galway, in Connemara. We talked a bit more and the man took from his wallet three pocket-sized pictures. One was of Mary, another Christ, and the third, an Italian priest, a stigmata in the palm of his hand. The priest's hand reminded me of my *Petitioner* painting. The man wanted to give the pictures to me. I'd already given a scarf away to a stranger. I wasn't about to accept a stranger's gift; perhaps, a stranger's burden. I bought him a drink and gave him a few coins to win my release.

"HAVE YOU EVER HEARD OF THE TUATHA DA DANAAN, THE CHILDREN OF the goddess Diana?" boomed the stout rosy-faced man with the crop of snow white hair and riveting blue eyes. He couldn't believe I had never heard of them. What kind of Irishman was I anyway? Well, he didn't understand these times or these strange new types but seeing as how I was a Yank perhaps it could be excused.

The man was Sonny Lacey, the storyteller, and it was the day after Ballintubber Abbey. I had gotten up early and driven further west, by-passing Galway and traveling along the sea coast into the Connemara, a craggy, rock strewn, windswept terrain with a haunting desolate beauty. It was like driving on the moon, the autumn light ever shifting while overhead the great grey clouds blew by. I'd come along a narrow road, a hard and windy drive with many quick cutbacks, to the village of Clifden in search of Sonny Lacey. I had found the nursing home without trouble.

"Is Sonny Lacey here?" I asked the nurse at the reception desk.

"Oh, yes, of course," the nurse said, as if she knew him well.

She led me back to the mens' quarters, a dreary place at best, and pointed in the direction of an old duffer sitting alone on his bed like a bag of last year's newspapers. Perhaps, I thought, I've come too late. I walked up to him and asked:

"Are you Sonny Lacey?"

He said nothing but just sat there all piled in upon himself. It took several hollers but finally the man looked up out of his dream, his eyes all glassy and dim.

"Yes, I am," he said.

While I had his attention I quickly explained why I'd come to see him.

He nodded, again. It seemed he understood, but then he fell back into himself. A few beds down sat another man. This one more alive.

"Are you Lacey?" I asked.

"Of course not," he piped. "Everyone knows that."

I looked about the room. It was like a big boatyard of landlocked seamen in from the storm. Riders of the sea who had taken their last ride. Men on cots like skiffs staring into the past their bodies still functioning, their minds like watch springs all run down. I was about to leave when a deep voice, full of timber, boomed out—

"I'm the man you want, Sonny Lacey! And who might you be?"

I turned around. The man facing me was a man to be reckoned with. He was totally there and sure of himself. The face was thick and powerful; the blue eyes, clear and sharp, with hooded eyelids; the nose long and slightly hooked. The complexion was rosy and fair like a baby's but the face was that of a warrior. This was a man only the foolish took lightly.

"A man at Ballintubber told me you were 'the finest storyteller in all of Ireland,'" I said. "Is that right?"

"I won't deny it," Lacey answered, a bit of mischief in his eyes. "Or admit it, either."

"Would you tell me a story?" I asked.

"No, no—not here!" Lacey acted as if I were a bit daft. "This is not the place for that." He grabbed me by the arm. "Look here. I'll be out in six weeks or so and we'll have a drink together at O'Malley's. That would be the place."

"But I have to leave tomorrow."

"It's not possible here—don't you know?" Lacey's blue eyes nailed me.

"Could we talk awhile then?"

"Of course, of course," he nodded and sat down on his bed, offering me a seat as well.

"How'd you become a storyteller?" I asked.

"My mother, God rest her soul, had the sweetest voice in all of Ireland. It was her that taught me all the old songs and stories." He paused and, nodding to himself, said softly, "She gave me The Gift."

"Where'd you live?"

Sonny Lacey motioned in the direction of the sea. "On the Arrr-an," he said. "Inisheer."

Inisheer was the smallest of the three Aran islands that lay thirty miles off the coast of Galway.

"I'd still be there fishing, lad, if I could," he said. "I'm only seventy-two, but I tell you it was ha-rrd out there. Ha-rrd."

I could hear the roll of the sea in his voice.

He hit his chest a few times with the thick of his hand. "Everything else can be cured," he roared, "but not this. The asthma did me in."

He coughed a little and bent toward me, staring me straight in the eye. "Tell me," he asked, his voice almost a whisper, "you proud to be Irish?"

"Yeah," I said. "Sure." I didn't understand what he meant. I had never thought about it really.

Sonny Lacey sat straight up on the bed, the bulk of the man turned toward me—"You mean to say you've never given it a thought?"

"Well—"

"We're Christians!" he rumbled. "Have always been Christians—and never cowards. Do you know what I mean now, lad?"

"Yes," I said, not wanting to offend him. But still I had no good idea what he was talking about.

Lacey searched me over outside and in with stone eyes. There was something important he thought I should know and be completely clear about. And when finally he spoke it was as if he were calling down a long corridor of time. His words were slow, definite and even—

"There's never been a coward among us. We carry good blood."

He paused to see if I finally took it in. Satisfied now, he smiled, and with the eyes friendly and voice soft, he continued:

"You're a respectable man. Not a con man."

Our eyes and hearts touched.

"Always be direct and open, and you'll do all right, lad," he said.

The power radiating from him was immense.

"Tell me now..." he inquired in a deep rumble that broke over me like the waves of the sea, "would you be knowing how the leprechauns came to be?"

"That I would," I answered, hearing the Irish in me. I smiled.

Quick as a cat, he grabbed my elbow and pulled me over closer, checking the room for eavesdroppers. "Now this isn't a story," he told me. "...It's the truth!"

Sonny Lacey's blue eyes opened wide. His face, that wonderful cream and roses complexion, changed and loomed before me and in a few moments, as if some magic door had opened, he had taken me inside the story with him, the stream of words flowing over me like water, creating pictures and feelings and great wonder and gratitude at the beauty and goodness and mystery of his gift and the gift of language itself.

"The Tuatha da Danaan, the children of the Goddess Diana, were huge giants of men who had valor every bit as big as they were tall. And they were a good seven, eight, nine, even ten feet tall. Incredible giants of men, they were, and they had to be; for it was them, the Tuatha, that defeated the men of the bogs, the Fir Bolg, those that had first conquered old Erin way back before history itself had a beginning.

"The Fir Bolg were just as big and valiant as the Tuatha, but now you would never guess—and neither did the Fir Bolg—and that was their downfall, as sure as we, ourselves, know we are here. For you see, the Tuatha were a race of magicians as well. And it was for this reason that the mighty Fir Bolg, first conquerors of all of

Erin, tasted the bitter dregs of defeat.

"And so the Tuatha, the children of the Goddess Diana, reigned supreme over all the land for centuries upon centuries, with all the ordinary folk around looking up to them and saying their prayers to these mightiest of mighty heroes, the Tuatha—the children of the Goddess Diana.

"But as Life would have it, nothing can be forever just as it is, and so in time from across the sea came the Sons of Mil. And do you know what? In a battle the likes of which the world had never seen and will never see again, those strangers from across the sea, the Sons of Mil defeated the Tuatha da Dannan! Oh! the rage of that battle. The strong swords clanging against shields, the sound of death screaming and fields all red and sticky with blood, the living and the dead all so bathed in it that if the living weren't standing and the dead lying, I tell you, it would be difficult for even the keenest eye to tell the living from the dead. Such a sight! And such a sorrow! So many killed and hopelessly maimed...

"All about the land, from seacoast to seacoast, lay the bodies of the noble Tuatha so that barely an inch of the precious sod of Erin was not stained with the blood of the slain. It was a sight so bloody as to even bring pity into the glory-swollen hearts of the victors, these strangers that had come by sea, the Sons of Mil. They now who stood exhausted, panting, soaked through with the magical blood of the Tuatha, with only themselves now standing upright and all about them this horrible sight and silence, the eerie stillness and stop in time that precedes every rightful new movement of the day—- well, it was then at that very first moment that the new conquerors of this sacred soil put away their weapons and spared but a few of the remaining Tuatha, those that still had a breath to draw.

"It was a different day from then on for the once mighty Tuatha...for as people are, they always act. The ordinary people acted as all ordinary people always act. No longer did they revere the Tuatha, but now gave all their attention instead to the Sons of Mil. That very same attention, mind you, they had once so lavishly given to the now fallen children of the Goddess Diana. And so a curious thing began to happen the likes of which the world has never seen again. These Tuatha, great giants of men—well, you wouldn't believe it maybe but, all the same, it did happen. The Tuatha, these giants of men, began to shrink, growing smaller and smaller, and smaller still. Until, you know what? These giants passed right out of sight. They disappeared, they did, to the ordinary eye.

"But now sometimes, if your vision is good and your heart pure, you can see the once mighty Tuatha, for they exist now as they have these many long years. They are known as 'the little people!' 'Leprechauns'! They are the 'good folk' that dance and delight and make fun and sometimes, yes, do mischief. They are there to take you to 'the other world,' the invisible one that exists right behind this one you're looking at. But, lad, better watch out! For if you go with them, if they take you there to their world, why they may not bring you back. For you see the only thing lacking in that wee world is that the wee people cannot procreate. And so they have to replenish their number now and then, by occasionally, not very often, failing to return a person or two that's been foolish, or brave enough, to 'cross the line'...the line, you know, that separates the world of the big folk from the world of the small folk, the good people, the mighty and noble Tuatha da Dannan, the children of the Goddess Diana. But if you cross and come back then you have known the kings of the past and are a rightful king yourself, for you have known bigness and smallness, victory and defeat, and won the secret of all secrets—that all things in themselves are nothing."

Sonny Lacey was full of the story, his eyes were liquid light, his head bobbing up and down like a cork in windy water. We sat a while in the beauty of the space. And after a while a bell sounded. It was time to say farewell. We stood, the two of us, and shook hands, strong and full and right to the bone. The shaking of hands of two Irishmen.

"I hope we meet again, and soon," I said.

"If God wills it, we will," he declared. Then he added so softly, his eyes shining like a warrior of old, "And I hope we do meet again, lad, I hope we do."

The next day I was on Inishmore, the northern most of the three Aran Islands. All around me, like great beached whales, lay slabs of fissured grey stone. The landscape was all rock and grass, nearly treeless. And above, the sky, great rolls of clouds and now and then the long groaning whistle of winds whipping across the rock. There was something else here, as well. Something I could feel but not name. But after a bit the secret formed into words. What was most striking about this island was that which was most deafening—the silence. I had never heard anything like it. It was all around me. Everywhere and nowhere, this invisible stillness.

I'd come on the morning ferry from Galway and taken a room and had hiked off to see Dun Aengus, a prehistoric fort built by the Fir Bolg. The island was all limestone, I had read, and the soil had come from generations of farmers spreading seaweed, sand and animal manure over rock. The fields were terraced and partitioned with loose stone walls. Inisheer was like a fist in the sea. On the island's western side, its sheer cliffs towered three hundred feet and more in height. From here the terrain sloped down to nearly sea level on its eastern side. I'd walked out from the village and crossed from the narrow road into the fields, picking my way through the rocks and climbing up to Dun Aengus atop the highest cliff.

Not much remained for the eye to see: only a high wall of stone shaped like a horseshoe, its open side facing the sea, an inner belt of sharp stone spars set closely together, and some large stone slabs. But the place was alive with sound. The wind was tearing about, giving out long shrill whistles and blasting me in the face while down below, at the cliff's bottom, the waves of the sea crashed ceaselessly. Sea gulls squawked. And off on the western horizon the sun was saying its farewell after a long day's ride in the sky, its light now fading and streaking through the darkening skies. I stood inside the fort's ancient grey stone walls, gazing out into the sea and the majesty of nature, trying to imagine what it might have been like to live here back at the time of the Fir Bolg, when from inside me there came this voice:

Go to the edge and look over.

It was the last thing I wanted to do. I had a fear of high places, having nearly fallen once, so I hesitated a bit before finally walking out to the edge where space met rock. I got within about four feet of the edge and, with the winds still howling and smacking my face, I looked down into that great whamming explosion of undulating wave as it swelled and rushed forward into the hard, unyielding rock. It must have been this way since the world was formed. Looking down into this world I felt I was peering into the primordial. The human story ended here. Here reigned the elements, the impersonal. One had to be very pure here.

Go to the edge.

My legs wouldn't move me another step. The space had become overwhelming. I couldn't stand taking in that sight any longer. I sank down on my knees, my body spreading out flat against the limestone, feeling its support. I gathered my remaining strength and carefully crawled out to the edge and again peered into the primeval—

And there's never been a coward among us!

And there I was clinging to the rock like a frightened little boy.

Never been a coward among us!

I thought of standing up. But looking down into that abyss of nature I had no confidence. I was no hero, no warrior. I was no fool, either. My life was worth too much to me to trust to luck. Just a little irregular wind, a tipping forward—and down I'd go.

As I shimmied back away from the edge, the sound of Sonny Lacey's laughter filled my ears.

OUT FROM BEHIND A BLACK ELM TREE SUDDENLY DARTS THIS FIGURE ALL dressed in black. He sticks out his thumb. I have no intention of stopping, yet I find my foot putting on the brake. A man in a black raincoat runs up to the car. The door opens and he slips into the front seat beside me.

I can't believe it—"Markum!" I shout. It is the bum I'd met by the River Liffey, the one I'd given my scarf to.

"Aye, that it is," he says with a smile.

"It's you!"

"Yes, me," he agrees.

"What are you doing down here?"

"Same as you."

"What?"

"Looking around, of course."

We both laugh. I think: Could I be imagining this?

"You know," I say, still in shock, "if I ran the odds on us meeting here, two weeks later and on the backroads some hundred and fifty miles south of Dublin—why they'd be a billion-to-one!"

"Oh yes," he says. He looks out the windshield and shrugs. The drizzle had turned into rain and the windows were awash with rivulets of water and were beginning to steam.

"How do you explain it?" I ask.

"I can't," he replies. "And yet, all the same, here we are…"

My mind took over. I looked at him closely. He was clean-shaven and had a haircut. Not so scruffy as in Dublin. Perhaps he lived around here. He was much more slender than I remembered.

This was absurd! What was going on? Was I dreaming this? I really didn't know any longer.

"Markum," I said, "let me touch your arm, okay?"

He laughed, extending a forearm for my inspection. I felt his forearm, gripping it tight.

"You're real!" I said.

"As real as you are. Of course," he remarked, unbuttoning the top of his raincoat.

"I don't understand it."

"I know. Neither do I," he said. "I think we better be going now."

And so off we drove while I told him a little of my trip. He had a beautiful way of listening. I felt he was right there with me sharing the experience.

"It's been a strange voyage for you, but a good one," he said, a little laugh in his eye.

He told me it was good that I'd been to New Grange and had seen the High Irish Crosses. "You should see the Moone High Crosses at Kilkenny before you go. Quite unusual. Like none of the other crosses," Markum mused. "Always a message in that."

I was feeling more relaxed. "Would you still like to have that drink?" I asked.

"There's a pub up near Bennett's Bridge. Turn there," said Markum.

About a quarter of a mile further there was a small bridge over a roadside creek and on the other side a country pub. We crossed to the other side and parked the car. The name of the drinking house was John Locke's Pub. I had to laugh. I'd studied philosophy in college. John Locke was a nineteenth century British empiricist, famous within philosophy. But like his contemporary, David Hume, a Scottish philosopher whose thought went to a much higher level, Locke was little known outside it. Both had had a tremendous influence on the way we perceive and think about things. I was feeling a burst of new energy from the shock of meeting Markum and so when we opened the pub door I just had to say to the bartender—

"Hello, there! Is this really John Locke's Pub?"

"Oh yes," he replied in a sing-song voice, swift as an arrow. "He sleeps here."

"Well, then—where is Hume?" I laughed.

"Upstairs, of course!" replied the man straight-faced.

"And Blake? Would William Blake be around?"

"Oh yes…but in the cellar!"

I couldn't believe it. How many barkeeps would know those names! I waved my admiration and Markum and I took a seat in the corner by the stained glass window. We ordered two pints of Guinness. I noticed Markum's hands. He had, I saw now, not one but two cloverleaf tattoos, one on each thumb.

"Well now," Markum asked, "what brought you to Ireland?"

I thought I'd only mention a few things, but pretty soon I was getting into the whole damn story of Sarah and Barbara. He listened and I felt like he was a friend I'd known all my life.

"I talk too much," I said at last, taking a long swig from the mug.

"You don't talk half enough," Markum declared. "Not half enough."

We sat for a while and then I said: "You know, Markum, I feel like I'm in some kind of transit state. It's odd."

"How's that?" He wasn't sure what I meant.

"You know…I don't feel like 'me' anymore."

"Aye, I think I know what you're talking about. You feel like there's a charm about you, do you?"

I would never have put that word to it. But he was right. And "charm" was a much better word. "Charm" cut both ways, personal and impersonal. "Transit" had such a technological, impersonal feel to it.

At the door a priest appeared and went into the dining room.

"What do you think about the Church?" I asked.

"The Church is getting larger, the priests fatter and labor thinner," Markum observed coldly.

"There's an expression that 'Ireland is the old sow that eats her farrow.'"

"Aye, that says it as well."

"Well, what do you think about Christ?" I asked. "Who do you think Christ was?"

He thought a while, looking into his pint. It reminded me of how a gypsy would read tea leaves.

"Oh, he was a person who knew a bit more than the man of his day," he said.

That was practically the same thing as the woman with no skin had said about witches—that they know a little bit more than we do.

"But—" I began.

"I don't believe he rose from the dead," Markum said. He took a small draught of the warm black beer, matter of factly adding—"No, when you're gone, you're gone."

I ordered a second pint. Markum was still working on his first. If he was an alcoholic, he wasn't drinking like one.

"What's an alcoholic?" I asked.

He paused a moment. He smiled and raised his pint. "When one is too much…and a hundred not enough."

It wasn't original but he said it so simply, so honestly. No sentimentality. No trace of self-pity. And this, despite all the suffering, the humiliation, drinking must have caused him. My heart opened to him.

"We all have many selves," he told me.

What was he saying? That he was an alcoholic on one level, not on another?

"Say," he asked, "have you ever been to Ireland before?"

"No. This is my first time."

"Strange, that is. I'm sure you and a Swede picked me up several years ago down south."

I shook my head.

"You're sure now?" asked Markum.

"Well, not absolutely," I laughed. "Not anymore."

"Good," he said and we drank to that.

I told Markum about what had happened with Lord Pentland, "the sound" and the books on black magic and how I had sworn I had never read any and yet there in my bookcase I had found two that I had forgotten I had read.

"It was like you'd been in a dream with the books," Markum reflected, "a dream you couldn't remember." He gave a knowing smile, as if it had happened to him many times. "We always get in a little deeper than we expect."

"Yes," I said, thinking of what had happened, "we certainly do."

"Have you ever been involved in witchcraft?" he wanted to know.

"No, not as far as I know. I remember once just touching a book by Aleister Crowley and my stomach turned over."

"Gurdjieff—was he into it?"

"No. Some people, I guess, might think that." I told him that Gurdjieff had an unusual way of teaching. He said there are two ends to a stick and if he took the good end, then you'd have to take the bad. So he took the bad intentionally. "In Sufism it's called The Path of Blame."

Markum listened, taking it in, but making no comment.

We finished the pints and got up to go. Markum pointed to a two pence piece lying on the floor by our table.

"It's yours," Markum said. He was quite emphatic.

The coin wasn't mine. I knew that. But I picked it up anyway. I felt he wanted me to have some tangible memento of our meeting so there'd be no doubting later.

It had stopped raining and the day was starting to clear, though it was still very grey and cold. In the car I showed him the diary I was keeping and my sketch book. He liked the drawings of the crosses.

"It's good you're doing this," he said, handing them back to me. "It all happens so quickly and it's so easy to forget otherwise."

I nodded and started the car.

"Good to keep a record," he said. "Especially if you're a deep diver and want to drink the cup to the bottom."

We drove a short bit and he pointed up ahead to another bridge, saying I should drop him there.

"I'll be seeing you again one day. You can be sure of that," he said as he got out of the car and closed the door. He said something to me, but I couldn't hear him. I rolled down the window.

"What's your Christian name?" he asked.

"William."

"That's a good one," he said. "Would you have an address?"

I opened my wallet and passed him a business card. We shook hands through the open window, his index and middle fingers touching the veins of my wrist. I had to smile. It was like a secret grip. We were part of the same brotherhood.

"Remember this now," Markum Hanrahan advised. "You don't talk half enough, not half enough."

He stepped back from the car then to let me go on. He pulled the black raincoat tight round him, giving me a nod and a wave. I waved as well, knowing that Markum Hanrahan was leaving my world now, probably forever. I watched him in the rearview mirror walking off and for a long while I drove with the tears streaming down my cheeks, like the water on the windshield.

I JUST WANTED TO GET HOME. I WAS RAW. ALL THESE WORLDS I WAS LIVING through, the physical, symbolic, mythological—it was like being stuffed into a cosmic washing machine. It had stripped me right down to the skin.

The skin! That was it. I felt like I had no skin. That editor in Seville, Mary or whatever. Her words—"I have no skin"—had been a foretaste of this whole crazy time. How could that happen? She could not have known, or even cared, what would happen to me. It was as if she had lines to say.

I drove with that a while and then it came to me: the only choice I had was to wish to remember myself. The wish to live it all as consciously as possible—that was the only freedom. What would change then was not the events—they could not be changed. It was the quality, the speed and intelligence with which events were lived. Whether they happened all in a blur or would be lived through with my eyes open, yes: *When all things are lived through to the end, there's no sadness, no regret, no false springtime; for each moment lived pushes open a newer, wider horizon and there is no escape—save living.*

Yes, real living could only be conscious living. It was not to be someone else, to play another part, to elude one's fate. Every role in the play was needed and had to be acted out. You either suffered your part consciously or walked through it asleep. The part, the character, the actions and the lines were already written. All the crucial events had to be fulfilled. But could "the play" be rewritten? Within limits, I guessed so. Perhaps as the octaves of one's life played out, if you were really conscious, not justifying, not feeding the momentum, you might have a forefeeling of where the shocks would come. Then, assimilating the energy, you could "move" it to higher ground; a higher level of vibration.

To be awake in the interval, to assimilate the new energy that the shock releases, to be conscious of more than three dimensions and so intuit not one but the many possibilities given by the moment—then perhaps, if you had the necessary will, it might be possible to act in another way.

So determinism and free will existed. Not one or the other, but both. But at different levels of consciousness, in different worlds. The idea of the relativity of all things intrigued me. The idea that the Absolute and the relative could exist at one and the same moment, that one dimension was the "absolute" for a lower dimension, the higher interpenetrating the lower. The idea that nothing is static; everything is in movement, busy being born or dying. Everything is reciprocally maintaining everything else. The one force becoming the three forces, affirming, denying and neutralizing. All in a dance. Moving up and down the Ray of Creation extending from the Absolute, all and everything and no-thing, all the way down through our lateral octave to the earth and the moon beyond. All the dualistic arguments were resolved. It wasn't a question of one or the other being true, but both being true, depending on place and location—what world was being spoken of.

When I'd first read about Gurdjieff's idea of relativity I couldn't get my mind around it. I didn't have the material, the experience, even to remotely understand. But now it began to live for me just as the octave had when I'd seen the sun, moon and earth from atop the Pyramid of The Sun. So what was causal within one dimension was synchronistic within another.

Another idea was time. Gurdjieff called it "the unique subjective." I had noticed how the mind kept slipping back and forth between the past and the future. But then when I came to myself either through thought, sensation, feeling or vibration, or when the sudden force of circumstances shocked me into a relative presence...there was only the hereness: that still quality of being present. But there was no present moment. For each time I became aware of the present moment, I was in the head, in the past. The present moment could be lived but not as a thought; for that kind of thinking immediately put me into the past. So when there was "hereness," I was out of time. There was no present, no past, or future either. It was all a construct, an abstraction of the mind. I would find myself shifting between the deep past, the immediate past and the future. It was all a mind trip. Then, seemingly out of nowhere, would appear this quality of relative hereness, a sense and feeling of presence. And it was then that I realized the incredible fact: *Consciousness had no time.* At least not the time we ordinarily experience.

I remembered that first time I had telephoned Lord Pentland. Though I didn't know it then, that was my first taste of the shift. I was never present as long as I was identified with an "I". For all "I"s were concepts. Reactions to hereness. The "present" had already become past. I was only here when "I" wasn't here. Weird.

These ideas and so many more were raining in on me as I traveled the back roads heading north toward Dublin. The day was foggy, drizzly and overcast. The windshield wipers were swishing, but I couldn't see more than a car's length ahead. A god-awful day in some ways. But a relief, too. I couldn't take any more of "Ireland." The fewer the people, the impressions, the better. I was raw. My bones were coming out of my skin. Every sound came right into me. I had no atmosphere around the body, no "ozone layer," to absorb the radiations. I'd become too sensitive. My brain was still smoking, like a field in flames still smoldering the day after. I just wanted to get back to Dublin and home to Barbara and the kids.

I spent the next to last night in Athy and the next day found the Moone High Cross in a cemetery. It was true. It was unlike any I'd seen. The cross was carved in biblical scenes like all the rest but, instead of conventional images for the apostles, there were these bald men with round big domes a la Gurdjieff. They looked like men from the moon. Or perhaps, the little moon, Toro. Maybe Karatas. In his book *All and Everything*, Gurdjieff anchored the story to Hassein and his grandfather returning in a spaceship from a sojourn on earth to their planetary home, Karatas.

I felt myself drawn to one of the trees. I stood for a while but couldn't make out what was so special here. Then I looked down and there by the tree's roots were about thirty or forty little people, all dressed in medieval garb, dancing and frolicking, doing cartwheels and all, just as if they were at a country fair. They couldn't be more than an inch high. I thought I must be imagining so I closed one eye and then the other, even looked away. But there they were, the magical people, the Tuatha da Danaan, the children of the Goddess Diana.

I was in Dublin soon after, staying the last night with Mrs. Clarke. We had a lovely time, she wanted me to go gambling with her but I was too tired. I told her of some of my adventures. She was all ears. I asked about the roses on the wallpaper, in the vases—what did they signify to her? "It's the rose of austerity," she told me. The next day as I was taking my bags down the narrow stairway she called out, chuckling—

"Mr. Patterson, do you know we're six hundred years behind the times here? And we like it that way! Goodbye, Yank. God bless."

Driving to the airport my mind kept turning on the notion of time. A book came to mind, *Living Time*, by Maurice Nicoll, a disciple of both Jung and Gurdjieff. Spatial objects, he said, existed in three dimensions. The fourth dimension was time. The three dimensions existing in time gave extension and uniqueness, for time was always changing the object. The "Ireland" that I had known I could never come back to, except if I changed my notion of time to be like space. That is, took time to be a solid entity like space. The space between New York and Dublin existed and was made up of a certain number of miles, towns, people and so forth. Time existed, Nicoll suggested, in the same way. The past and future were all here in the present. The present was to be experienced not just in a flat three dimensions but in four, five, six and seven dimensions. When we could consciously move back and forth in our time body, we would understand that everything is again-recurring. That time is circular. Our past is ahead of us. Time isn't visible or experienced in the same way space is.

The airport appeared ahead. Towering mountains of pearl-white cumulus cloud surrounded it. I boarded the jumbo jet and collapsed into my seat. Music was coming over the plane's loud speaker system. It was very familiar. I was sure I knew it. But the name wouldn't come. I hummed along but couldn't remember. Finally, I tapped the gentleman in front of me to see if he knew it.

In halting English he apologized, telling me he was German. A few seconds later he turned about, saying with a smile and a heavy Teutonic accent—
 "Amazing Grace."

I TOLD BARBARA ABOUT MY AFFAIR WITH SARAH. IT WAS LIKE I HAD STABBED her in the heart. I felt anew what had not been in my own heart for a long time: my great love and respect for her, and for her strength and quiet dignity and the wonderful family she had given me. Her face wet with tears, I told her about the answer I had asked for and received at Ballintubber Abbey. I told her that the affair was over. The two of us felt so close then, and I realized what I had risked. The impact of that impression and recognition flooded through me and I began crying. After a while, she wanted to know the details. But I refused, knowing that it would only give her mind something to gnaw on. That we were both in the Work was a great help.

I then told Sarah. She was quite brave and understanding. She said she'd known this was coming once Barbara became pregnant with Matthew. I tried to convince her that I was genuinely fond of her, but she couldn't seem to accept that. I was going to say something to Lord Pentland but before I had a chance to, he put Sarah in our group. Barbara was furious and, after a month or so, wrote him a letter telling of the rage she felt whenever she saw Sarah. At the next meeting Sarah was gone. "There are some letters we shouldn't write," Lord Pentland said, "and if written, they should not be posted."

Then trouble started between Sarah and Stanley. He was sloughing off as usual, just doing what he had to get by, but recently he'd begun to knock Sarah's magazine to advertisers. They'd both gone to make a presentation to H.J. Heinz Company and Stanley had openly promoted my magazine and criticized Sarah's. They got into a big row about it and she went to see Spencer several times. It got worse and worse between them until one day—and Spencer truly liked Sarah—Spencer fired her.

Soon after Sarah had called me, saying she was at the Martha Washington Hotel. She'd taken a room there, had left her husband and…did I want to have lunch? It put me in a panic. She was throwing over her whole life all at once. I'd finally spoken to Lord Pentland about us and he had told me that "the disentanglement process" requires a lot of time. I knew she needed to see me and I owed her a great deal. She was in a fragile state. I had to go.

We met at the Mayflower. Sarah was very bright and cheery, telling me about the Martha Washington. There were all these old ladies, she said, sitting in the foyer with their timeworn stockings, the old rooms with the flowery wallpaper turned all dusty gray over the years. She'd gone to an employment agency. They said she'd have a good job in no time. Tomorrow she was looking at an apartment on Fifth Avenue, a darling little studio. Lord Pentland had even mentioned one might be available only a block or two from the Foundation.

Sarah was beautiful that day, almost translucent. She was hearing "the sound," she told me, the soft humming and waterfalls, and when she meditated she felt herself enveloped by a soft light. The night before she was going to leave her husband she'd had a dream. "When I woke up there were all these crows sitting in a tree outside my patio. They looked so silent, so ghostly," she said. Still she packed her suitcase and left, taking the train to Manhattan. "That image of the crows was so strong," she recounted. "But wait, I didn't tell you about the dream. The dream was of being in the city, of getting up to go to work and on the way I pass this hot dog stand. You know, the kind you see everyday in New York. It was early but I stopped and now the hot dog man changes from just an ordinary looking man into an Oriental in gold and red robes with a tall red silk hat and a long thin beard and tiny mustache. That was weird, but I still ordered a hot dog. But he says, 'You don't want this. This is what you want.' And he holds up this small yellow book with a red mandala on its cover. And, you know what, I ran away. Okay, end of scene, end of dream, huh? But that's not all! Today, just an hour ago, I go into this bookstore—and what do you think I see. The book in the dream!" She reached into her purse and, holding the book up, said, "See, *The Secret of The Golden Flower*."

I looked at her, marvelling. Sarah looked so radiant, beautiful. She was playing every card. Columbine's cards. And I did love her. And I didn't want to hurt her and I didn't know what to do. I had asked at Ballintubber for a decision to be made and it was made and now we had to live with that.

I finished my Bloody Mary and I told her hard that I was in love with my wife and my children. That I could not leave them. That I could not see my sons grow up fatherless. "You're forcing this," I told her. "You're insisting on something that can't happen."

My words startled her. She told me she understood, that she wasn't doing this to trap or trick me or to force me in any way—"I am doing this for myself," she said. "I want to be free, free of the dreariness, the sameness—"

"Sarah, I know you mean what you're saying, but—"

"No, I haven't come into the city for you. I've come for a new life. Don't you understand that?"

She was trembling with anger and fear, coming apart and I was watching it and I was afraid for her. I wanted to tell her she was lying to herself, that she couldn't see where she was or what she was really doing. But I knew, too, she couldn't hear it. She was in the throes of an incredible energy. Completely identified, at the mercy of an "I" that has no mercy.

She had taken a letter from her purse and put it on my plate. "I knew you wouldn't understand," she said. "You're too hard, obtuse. You love your mind too much."

And she slid out of the booth and walked out the door.

I opened the envelope. It was not a letter. It was a typed excerpt from Colette's *The Vagabond:*

You didn't make so much fuss when love swept down on you and found you so mad and brave. You didn't ask yourself, that day, if it was love. You couldn't mistake it; it was love indeed, first love. That was and never again will be…

Later, I heard that Sarah had gone back to her husband and had left the Work and moved upstate to Brewster. I felt like she had moved up there to "die." She had told me at the end of that last lunch—"Ours is the story of the gods acting out their fantasies through poor helpless mortals. And now they demand a sacrifice and I guess I'm to be the sacrificial lamb. Thanks a lot."

THE GOSPEL STUDY GROUP HAD STARTED UP AGAIN. IT WAS JUST AS DRY. EVERYONE mentally going through the motions. No one challenging their own thinking. Finally, I brought up Satan again—"We don't know anything until we know his role in this," I declared. But, again, I was cold shouldered. I knew plenty of people in the Work capable of thinking, but this group all played it safe. Maybe that was my role here: to goad them into thinking about the "dangerous." But I had, too, this sense: *I am asking for it.* I better stop this.

After the meeting that night Barbara and I returned home. Upstairs, lying on our bed, I noticed two cards. Something told me immediately that these weren't just any cards. There was something strange about them, as though they were a message of some type. I saw the image of the cards lying between Columbine's thighs.

One card lay face up on the bedspread on my side of the bed. The other, on my pillow, was face down. They were small cards, no bigger than the palm of my hand. I picked up the card on the bedspread. It was an Old Maid card showing the Big Bad Wolf. I picked up the card lying face down on my pillow. Another Big Bad Wolf. This was absurd what I was thinking. All the same my stomach went queasy.

Barbara had been undressing for bed but was watching me.

"What's wrong?" she asked.

"Funny. Did you notice these cards?"

"They're Old Maid cards. The kids must've been playing here."

"Oh."

"What are you thinking?" she said, pulling on a robe. "They're just cards. They don't mean anything."

"Right. Probably not."

"Oh, c'mon. Let's not go through this again," she said and went into the bathroom.

"Yeah. You're probably right," I said and got undressed and went to bed. I knew Barbara couldn't understand. She hadn't entered the psychic world yet. But I knew these cards were symbols. I had that feeling. And I had "read" them immediately. The cards were on the bed. The bed is the trap-door to the unconscious. Very personal, intimate. Both cards were on my side. The message was for me. The wolf was a symbol for the devil. Double wolves. Whatever is coming is going to be really powerful. The wolf face up meant something will happen to me, and soon. The wolf face down, that wolf will come later.

Barbara went to sleep but I stayed awake. Did I actually believe in Satan? If not as a "he," as a diabolic energy? I got up and went downstairs and sat in the darkened living room and thought about Gurdjieff's teaching about "good" and "evil." His thinking was many layered. He taught the unity of everything, unity in diversity, the only true difference between things and worlds being in the level of vibration. Therefore, the notion of "good" and "evil" existing independently outside the essence of beings was what he termed a "maleficent idea." There were no such personalities or entities as "God" or the "Devil." He saw the world in terms of forces which in relation to one another can be termed "Good" and "Evil." The active force which strives "to blend with the cause of its arising," that which strives to be objectively conscious, is Good. Though it is vivifying, its action is denying in relation to the passive, or Evil, force. The nature of this second force is always to flow outward to the next event, experience, person. So to evolve one must *in*-volve, return to themselves. So what looks to be active is really passive, what is passive is actually active—but *only* if the goal is consciousness.

From the clash between these two forces emerges the third force. Its nature is to reconcile. Its energy is very sensitive, subtle, intelligent. We are usually blind to it because we're so gross, so hypnotized by the other two forces and the inherent conflict between them. In spiritually evolving, Gurdjieff said, conscious opposition can appear at certain moments in the process. This opposition comes from those that have stopped evolving toward consciousness. They are very powerful in that, having a bastardized consciousness, they can use any means to destroy. Whereas, those striving to be conscious, to come to conscience, are more limited. In this view, Satan would be an evolved consciousness whose perfection had been aborted. He provided the test, the necessary shock, for the evolutionary octave to continue. Ouspensky had said he existed in the Do-Si interval of the octave. So some shock was coming. And, given the cards, it would be an incredible shock. There was nothing to do but wait.

Outside I heard birds singing. It was dawn. I'd been up the whole night. It was Saturday morning. I caught the train from Ossining into the city and went to Casey's. All I had to do was finish the faces of the Petitioner and the Ancient-of-Days and the painting was done. I took the old creeping elevator to the sixth floor. The door banged open. Casey had just gotten up. He excused himself and went into the back of the loft where he, his wife and daughter lived. In the early morning light, his studio was very soft-looking, all the colors subdued. The only brightness was the play of light streaming in through the long bank of windows at the front of the loft. The light nipped the tops of the dark brown easels. They were arranged in a half circle around a green shag rug where the day's model would pose. Most of the canvases had been put away. A few remained leaning against a wall, propped up on a locker, or stuck off in a corner. Paintings of faces, landscapes, wild birds, snakes and wild abstracts stood in various states of gestation, each revealing a world of emotion struggling to express itself, to break through the grid and grip of the head. There was always a wonderful quietness here at times like this, a presence. It was if the studio stood still in space. It contained us all, all the energy and ideas, all the crazy emotion, and yet it remained untouched.

I hauled *The Petitioner* out of its stall, hoisted it up on the easel and screwed it into place. I opened my paint box, took out some tubes and squeezed the colors into little curly blobs on the palette. I began to paint and almost at once stepped into the canvas. As I painted the faces of the two figures, I noticed a queer feeling in my stomach. I stopped and stepped back to get another look at the painting. There where the petitioner's face had been I had painted in my Father's face! And the face of the Ancient-of-Days—that was my Grandpa Scott, my Mother's father! What was going on? The petitioner (my Father) was standing at the edge of an abyss. I quickly painted out the faces and repainted them. Still, they bore a resemblance. I painted them out again, completely changing them.

Casey came out from the back, combing his hair, still tucking an old wool shirt into his baggy, unpressed trousers. He made us both a cup of the bitter coffee he liked and we sat at the long lunch table. He took out a red tin of Prince Albert and filled his corncob. Neither of us rushed to say anything. It was just nice here at this time of morning. Very quiet and soft. Class wouldn't begin until eleven o'clock. Seymour, then Joel, would come trooping in about ten-thirty, new people coming at eleven and Martha, Babi, Judy, Kathleen and the others dribbling in about noon.

"Well," said Casey finally, "covered with paint again, I see."

"Yeah. I must like the stuff, huh?"

More time passed. Casey lit his pipe. It was always going out on him. I wanted to tell him about the painting. But he brought it up first.

"Interesting perspective there," he said, nodding in the direction of the painting.

"What do you mean?"

"That's the first time I think I've ever seen that," he said.

"What?" I still didn't know what he was talking about.

"You know. Usually the viewer looks up at Christ on the cross. Look, you've painted it so the viewer is above Christ."

"What? I don't see it."

"Where are we looking from?" asked Casey. "It's like we are on a hill—we're looking down on Christ."

It was true. Obvious. But I'd never seen it before.

"What could that mean?" he said, blowing out a great gob of smoke.

"I didn't mean to."

"If you did, it would be nothing. It's what we don't mean to do and still do— that's what's interesting."

We walked to the easel.

"What are you going to do up there," he asked, pointing to the top of the cross.

"I don't know yet."

Casey blew a draught of smoke. "Well, you know, you could paint the grain of wood in circles. That's how it is when a tree is cut. The horizontal grain you only see on boards after the logs have been milled."

He was right. That would tie it all together. The grain was realistic, and sym-bolically it would represent the wheel of life, the whole round of birth and death. In a word: time. I saw the figure of Christ was tied to time!

"Jack! Did you take Muffin out?" It was Casey's wife, Judith. She was standing by the door.

Muffin came around the work bench and jumped up on Casey's lap. She was a mangy French poodle, scrawny, dirty and a pest. If Muffin wasn't barking at Mozart, the neurotic cat (who usually hid and scratched anyone who touched him), she was barking every time the elevator door banged opened.

"Yes, I think so," replied Casey, smiling beneath his white mustache.

"He thinks so," Judith said looking at me. "Well, Jack, she's just puddled the floor again." Judith glared. She was small, slender, with high cheekbones. Quite striking, especially when she was upset. Her eyes always reminded me of those deep, alive, darkly intelligent ones Beckmann gave many of his women. I'd always wondered if Casey had seen that.

"You want me to wipe it up?" Casey asked, not moving. Finally, he tossed Muffin onto the floor. The mutt immediately took off after Mozart, the two of them chasing madly around the easels.

There was a decided pause. Then Judith declared—

"Oh no, Jack. Of course don't wipe it up. Let's put chairs around it and sell tickets."

Casey laughed a bit nervously, made a face and mopped up the puddle. Judith prepared to go shopping. "Sometimes I think that dog believes she's a human being," Judith mused.

"Don't we all?" murmured Casey, putting away the mop.

"Oh, I forgot," declared Judith, looking at me. "'God' is here."

"God, schmod, just another concept," said Casey.

"Hey, why don't we go to dinner tonight?" I asked. "Barbara could drive down, bring my clothes, I'd get a shower here, we could go to Raoul's in Soho. Or maybe…I don't know…"

Judith liked the idea.

"Well…?" She looked at Casey.

Casey looked trapped. "What about that Middle Eastern restaurant down the street?" he suggested finally, cleaning out the bowl of his pipe.

"You see?" Judith said to me. "You see what I have to live with! A grown man who can't go more than five blocks from his home."

"Well," I said, trying to ease the tension, "Joyce was that way, too."

Casey gave me a large, conspiratorial wink.

"You're disgusting, Jack," said Judith. "And you, too. Both of you. Now where is that damn elevator?" Judith was dressed in high black boots, grey wool skirt, sweater and a colorful French scarf—she always dressed meticulously and decidedly "uptown." She lit up a small cigar. The elevator doors banged open. "Wouldn't you know it? Well, I'll let you 'big boys' figure out what we do for dinner. Muffin! Stay there! Jack, call her, will you?"

"Muffin!" called Casey. The dog was barking and whining.

The elevator door banged shut. Casey ran a hand through his shock of white hair and adjusted his glasses.

"Hmmmn. Close call there," he joked and coughed a little. "Now, where were we?"

I told him what happened with the faces appearing in the painting. What did it mean? He didn't seem to know. We talked about Rousseau. He was a primitive and Casey thought I was in that line. At one point he asked, coming back to *The Petitioner* painting—"How is it between your father and you?"

"You mean how do we get along?"

Casey nodded.

"Okay. We're pretty close. When I go down at Christmas, we always go out for these long drives. We've done our talking and there isn't much more to say. It feels good just being with each other."

Casey peered at the painting, chomping on the stem of his pipe.

"You mean as a kid?" I asked. "How we got along then?"

He nodded.

"Well...it was like I never had a father. He was 'the man who wasn't there.' The invisible Father. Hardly ever said a word to me. I remember once hitting a grand slam home run. We were three runs behind, bases loaded, with two outs—can you believe it? It was a real Frank Merriwell. A once-in-a-lifetime home run. He's there but doesn't say a word to me. Can you believe it?"

Casey smoked on that a while. "The father...the father is the law giver," he mused. "He tells the son how to live. He sets the bar."

"Sets the bar?"

"You know, the high jump. He puts the bar up. Tells you how high you're going to have to go to succeed...in his eyes. He affirms or denies your effort." Casey relit his pipe, and looked at me closely—— "Your father never told you anything?"

"Well, he was always telling me to 'get commercialized,' 'to not be so serious,' 'to get my feet on the ground.' That was about all he ever said...when he said anything."

"My father was a pain in the ass, too. It was a relief to get him out of the way. Still, it was quite a blow when he went. It took a full year to get over it, to get a sense of humor back."

"You think my Father is going to die?" I asked. "Is that what it means?"

Casey struck another match. "I don't know. Maybe he's going to have some big experience. Meet a world he never knew existed."

"How did you get along with your dad?"

Casey pondered that a while. "It wasn't that I didn't love him. I did. The books he read and introduced me to—why he had me reading Nietzsche, Hume and Blake when I was fourteen. It was just that life was all over for him. There he was out in New Jersey, weak and sick and just hanging on. Death was a relief."

Casey took a drink of that horrible coffee. "Of course, once it happened...well, then it was a different story. God had taken my father. I lived with the fact of his death for a year. It was all over the place, stinking up everything. I couldn't even paint."

He looked me over for a few moments, deciding whether to go on. "I'd already killed him, you know," he said point blank. "You have to 'kill the father.' It's the son's duty. Not physically, of course. That's gross. But kill him by doing better than him."

I cringed. I knew what he meant—but *kill the father?* The idea was right. But it sounded wrong. I looked at the petitioner, then at Christ up on the easel. If the petitioner was my Father—what was he asking Christ for?

"You know, Picasso's father was a painter. He taught his son to paint. One day he saw what his son was doing. He never painted after that. He gave his son his brushes."

"Why would he do that?"

"Picasso's father knew he was a beaten man. And he was man enough to admit it. And man enough to give his son his full support. Imagine how Picasso felt. Is there any greater gift a father can give a son?"

The elevator door banged open.

"Well, there they are. Two peas in a pod," called Seymour with Kathleen and Babi right behind him. Judith followed calling out—

"Well, have you two geniuses figured out where we're going for dinner?"

MY FATHER. LYING THERE IN THAT HOSPITAL BED. MY FATHER SO SMALL now, so fragile and frail. His skin pale and yellowish, drained of life. His hair, so thin now, snow white. Only the blue eyes behind the glasses still alive, still the Father I remembered. My Mother, standing by his bed, fighting back the grief. Reaching out now, like some fearful acolyte, placing a cup of tapioca pudding beneath the face of the gaunt silent figure laid out on the bed.

"Bill…honey, eat this. Please. It's good for you." She speaks the words so gently, as if she is speaking to a child.

The head moves slightly. A glance at the pudding.

"I'm not hungry," he says. "I'll eat later."

"But Bill—you've got to eat."

The figure on the bed makes no reply. He has returned to that border zone between two worlds. My Mother keeps calling him back.

"Here, Bill," she says, more insistent, bringing the tapioca to his eye level. "I made it myself. Just the way you always liked it."

There is a slight nod of the head, a thin ironic movement to the corners of the lips. Nothing more. She dips a teaspoon into the tapioca and brings it to his lips. The face turns away but he smiles now. She is just like his own Mother trying to feed him when he was sick as a boy, and he doing the same, turning away.

"But Bill—" She is pleading now.

"Now, Mabel…" he says. An edge of irritation. He begins again, "Mabel, you certainly can make a mountain out of a mole hill." It was a phrase he often used. My Father, hearing himself, has to laugh a little and as always, too, a hand cups in front of his mouth so as not to show his teeth.

My Mother, having brought him back, strokes his hair now, telling him how much she misses him at home. She relates what the neighbors and mailman have said, how the doctor says he is going to get better. "But only," she declares, "if you eat something."

In the doorway a young, dark-eyed nurse appears. The long dark hair is shiny and thick, her skin tanned and supple. The epitome of youth, health. She smiles cheerfully to my Father and nods as well to the beer-bellied bald man in an adjacent bed, sitting up, chewing on an unlit cigar, surrounded by three fat dutiful sons, all middle-aged.

The nurse comes over to my Father's bed. A big wonderful smile. Red lips and bright white teeth. She shakes a thermometer in the air as if it's a magic wand. She beams and tells him: "Now open wide."

My Father obeys, without hesitation.

My Mother's eyes glint, giving him a sly look—"Why you old fox!"

The nurse goes about tidying up the bed.

I watch my Mother's face—she isn't quite sure how to take this "other woman." But she says nothing.

Across the way, in hushed tones the sons are talking to the fat father. Something about business. He listens, but his eyes follow the nurse's every movement. He whispers to his sons. They turn in unison, stealing a quick look. Yes, the nurse has a great ass. They give a family grunt and fall back into discussing some business scheme.

"Right on normal, Mr. Patterson," the nurse says, deftly taking the little mercury wand from my Father's mouth. "The doctor says all your life lines are A-OK." She looks at my Mother reassuringly and then to my Father: "Why you should be up and out of here in a few days."

"But, nurse, nurse," implores my Mother—"Tell him, please—*he's got to eat something.*"

"I'll eat later, Mabel," my Father promises, a bit weary. She goes to say something but he holds up both hands in a sign of surrender. "Probably for dinner," he says.

I notice his cheeks. There is some color now.

My Mother sighs. "You know," she says to the nurse, "you just can't do a thing with him when he gets this way. Once he makes up his mind, he won't change it come hell or high water. He just won't listen then."

"There's really no reason to worry. He's being fed intravenously," explains the nurse.

"That's what you say!" my Mother snaps.

"Now, Mabel, don't—"

"I don't care what anybody says. Who's to say what will happen? Who's to say? You've got to eat real food—and we all know it." She looks at me. "Isn't that right, Pat?"

"Yes," I say, "and—"

"*Roots* on TV," bellows the fat man, still admiring the nurse. The sons, clones of the old man, are still circling the bed. "Anyone for seeing it?" he calls.

My Father shakes his head. The fat man shrugs. They all fall back into a huddle. The nurse leaves. My Father asks me to prop him up in bed. I slide my hands beneath the shoulders, lifting him up. He's like a feather. Nothing but bone. His chest has been shaved clean. The face still has the white stubble of a first day's beard. He looks like a plucked chicken.

"Let me see your arm," my Father asks, looking up at me.

"Oh c'mon, Dad."

But he is serious. "G'wan," my Mother says. So I stretch out my right arm.

"Roll up the sleeve," he asks.

I feel the embarrassment but I unbutton the cuff of my shirt and roll up the sleeve. My Father's hand rises from the blanket, the fingers touching my bicep, squeezing it, kneading the flesh. The fingers are really feeling the arm, taking in the whole tactile sensation, the total impression. They withdraw then and feel the bicep of his own arm. Nothing there. The muscle is nearly all gone. Just wrinkled skin, pale, lifeless, hanging from the bone.

A wry smile appears on my Father's face. The hand reaches up and explores my bicep again. The manner is detached, scientific. No self-pity. No fear. Simply the comparison of the arm of an eighty-two-year-old body with that belonging to a middle-aged body. The whole experience happening between us is without words. There is something ancient, timeless, here. A father and son come to the end of the road, all masks off. Our eyes meet. I see there is still someone there. Before he was barely here. We gaze at one another. No thought, no pretense, no defense.

"Funny…" my Father muses, his voice speaking not from feeling but fact, "what happens to us."

A peculiar but knowing smile crosses his face like a shadow, his head slowly moving at the wonder of it all.

"Dinnertime," calls the dark-eyed nurse. She wheels in a shiny aluminum cart. It is loaded with trays of food. She slides one out and places it on my Father's lap. His eyes examine the food. Each portion of food is wrapped in plastic or aluminum foil. My Father views it as he did my arm. There is that same detachment, same direct attention.

My Mother stands silently by, waiting, her brow knit and jaw tense. Her face hides nothing. I can see what she is thinking as she looks at the food on the tray. The food so colorful but waxen looking, the life cooked out of it. The food nice, neat, embalmed. But if he will eat it, fine.

My Father finally shakes his head, saying softly, "I'm not up to eating right now, I'm afraid. Maybe later."

My Mother's face, already drawn, becomes longer. She moves her head back and forth in dismay and then stares vacantly out the window into the night. What can she do if he refuses to eat?

A buzzer blares, splintering the moment like a stone cracking against a mirror.

My Mother embraces my Father tenderly, assuring him we will be back tomorrow, that she will bring him something good to eat, and then she joshes him, speaking in a tiny Irish accent—

"And you'd be eating it, or there'll be trouble, I tell you."

My Father smiles and pats her hand. "Don't worry, Mabel," he says, trying to be reassuring. "My appetite just hasn't come back, yet. But it will."

My Father and I shake hands and my Mother and I begin to leave. The fat man is busily feeding his face, watching Roots.

At the door, I look back.

My Father is watching us, his eyes large and fixed, an odd look on his face, one I've never seen before. What is it? I guide my Mother along the corridor. Suddenly, I know that look—we are leaving his world, this may be the last time he sees us. I feel a sense of his aloneness; the complete and utter sense of being alone. Or is it the last look? The look of goodbye? No, it couldn't be. The nurse—hadn't she said he is going to be all right? And I am back in my head again thinking...

MY MOTHER AND I WAITED AT THE ELEVATOR. THE FAT MAN'S SONS CAME down the corridor, still telling each other "how great, how clever the old man is." He still contained them. He was still their god. I thought of the conversation with Casey. I heard my mind whisper to them: "It's time to kill the old man." One of them must have caught it. He woke up. Gave me a funny look. Then he fell back into the jabbering.

My Mother and I walked out of the hospital. She held my arm tightly, like it was the edge of a raft and she had fallen overboard. She seemed so small, defenseless, vulnerable.

"Will he be all right?" she asked.

"Mom, his life lines, the life support systems, are fine. That's what the doctor said."

"But, Pat—he's not eating," she insisted. "You have to eat to live."

I started up the engine of the old Hornet. My sister, Louise, had bought it for them a few years ago. The engine gave a rumble or two and finally sputtered awake. My Mother huddled silently, sinking far back into the seat. She was staring straight ahead. I tried to keep her talking. But I couldn't catch her attention for long. Finally, I asked about Louise—

"How's she doing? I understand the antique business is going good."

"How should I know? We haven't spoken," answered my Mother. "Or haven't you heard?"

The anger in her voice shocks me, brings me back to myself. I mumble something and speed up the old six-cylinder station wagon. We are almost home when she says as if in a dream:

"I feel like a truck's hit me. It came out of nowhere. He was fine a few days ago."

"Mom, he'll be all right. Really."

"Pat—can't you see? *He doesn't want to live anymore.* Can't you see that?"

Could that be true? That he didn't want to live? Was this all fated? I saw my Father's face on the petitioner. It did no good to repaint the face. It was a forewarning. And a day after, it was the late afternoon, my Mother had called. She had been trying to reach Louise and me all day. She said she'd gotten out of bed and he was there flat on the floor, right by the bathroom door. He had gotten up to go to the bathroom she supposed and had fallen. Her voice a scream, she told me—"Daddy was lying there in his own filth!" She had tried but couldn't move him. So she cleaned him up as best she could and covered him with blankets. She had called and called but couldn't reach anyone. The whole day had passed with him there on the rug. "Call the hospital," I told her. But she wouldn't. "He's mine, all I have," she cried. "I can't let him go."

I had caught the red-eye special that night. It was three in the morning when I arrived in Miami. I had an immediate sense of unreality. The enormous red-carpeted terminal was virtually empty, all space and no one there. Like the scene of yesterday's big party. One that had played itself out. Only the dank smells and litter left. Crunched up newsprint, spills of popcorn, empty soda cans, straws, wadded napkins, ashtrays packed with butts and here and there some drunks and night people slunk down deep in chairs asleep or staring off into space. The place had an eerie quiet. Like a graveyard. The only sound the churning of air-conditioning. Somewhere, the faint noise of machines at work. I come upon a squadron of sweepers and waxers manned by a sullen, robot-eyed night crew of blacks and Hispanics. I felt I was on some night journey.

Outside, I walked into a wall of air, hot and sterile. It just hung. Sucking you out. Not moving. I picked up the rental car and drove north to Fort Lauderdale. The air-conditioning was out, so I rolled all the windows down. For long stretches I was alone on the road. The highway lights looked like tentacles rising out of the earth. Their orange glare against the black umbrella of sky looked ghoulish. Along the way huge dancing neon night animals sprang up into the night, lining either side of the road. Alligators, giraffes, pelicans, mermaids, busty chicks all flickering, beckoning, promising a good time at night lounges, peep shows, motels. My outside matched my inside. An "I" was ranting— *Why didn't she call the hospital? Why is she hanging on to him? His life is over. He's been dead for years. If he doesn't die then we'll just have to go through this again.* From long experience, many failures, I knew to stay separate from this voice. To not put the feeling of I into it. Not to judge it, either. Or fight with it. Just see it, witness it. It was in me, yes, but I was not this "I." But good lord! It was so negative, heartless. It began to get to me so I turned on the radio.

Some radio evangelist, a cracker with a sharp twang, was thundering about "Comin' to Chr-ist Gee-sus!"

I switched to rock music. Up came "Mr. Tambourine Man" sung in that familiar nasal voice, defiant and clear:

> *I'm not sleepy and there is no place*
> *I'm going to.*

I turned it up loud and shot on down the highway.

> *Though I know evening's empire has*
> *returned into sand.*
> *Vanished from my hand.*

I'm alone on the night road, going like crazy, the wind whistling, my hair blowing and Dylan's words cutting through the thick humid air.

> *I have no one to meet*
> *and my ancient, empty streets*
> *too dead for dreaming.*

I let Dylan out full blast, a wall of sound.

> *In that jingle-jangle morning*
> *I'll come following you.*

Several times I got lost and had to backtrack. Though it was only forty miles or so to Tamarac, the little tract town west of Ft. Lauderdale, I didn't arrive till just before five in the morning. I was stiff and exhausted. A small silent figure stood in the doorway waiting for me.

"Hi, Mom," I said, trying not to show what I was feeling. Her face had a yellowish cast. The eyes looked out at me from hollow sockets. She looked lost, disconnected.

"Pat, he wouldn't go to the hospital, not till you came."

My Father was lying on the living room floor, blankets piled over him. He was all hoary white-looking, bloodless. He made an effort to rise and gave a little embarrassed laugh when he couldn't. I knelt down beside him.

"I'll be all right now," he said. "I'm glad you've come."

"Dad, we've got to get you to a hospital."

"Okay. Get a few hours sleep first. I'm okay. Just drive me there. Don't waste money on an ambulance."

I left for the hospital to make arrangements. When I returned I found my Mother bent over him, whispering into his ear. His head was arched back on the pillow, his mouth wide open, his dentures out. She was like a mother hen feeding her young.

We stood him up on his feet. He hung on my shoulders, and I supported him with my arms while my Mother, piece by piece, dressed him.

He shook his head and gave a little laugh. "The last time this happened was when I was a boy," he said.

"Yes, you were spoiled rotten, daddy. Raised with a silver spoon in your mouth," my Mother said, tying a shoe lace.

"Hmmnnn...I suppose I was," he agreed.

My Mother had dressed him all in powder blue. Blue was his color. But the effect now was jarring. He looked like a corpse in clothes. We had to get him to the hospital quickly. We began to walk him to the door, one small step at a time. It was only five feet away. But it took forever.

"Now take another step, daddy," my Mother coaxed. "That's right. Move the other leg now. Good "

We were getting there but within two steps of the door, he stopped.

"What's wrong?" asked my Mother.

"Ohhh, my," he said sheepishly. "Better stop here, Mabel."

A faint unpleasant odor tainted the air. To undress him again would take too long. I asked my Mother if she had any scissors. She understood. She took down his trousers and cut the underwear off him.

Finally, we got to the door. The Florida sun was already scorching. Its glare near blinding. I felt as if we were stepping into an inferno. Their Hornet was the closest car, just five or six feet from the door, but by the time we got him there all of us were dripping with sweat and out of breath. We got him into the back seat and drove to University Hospital. An orderly with a wheelchair waited at the emergency entrance. An intern checked my Father's condition. No immediate danger. He would have to wait for Dr. Cohen to admit him.

My Mother's face gave a funny twist. "Does that mean he'll be my husband's doctor?"

"Yes," said the intern.

My Mother whispered to me: "I don't like him. He doesn't care about people."

Presently, a short boyish figure appeared. He was outfitted in sneakers, jeans and a loud Hawaiian sport shirt. Around his neck hung a stethoscope like a necklace. With much gravity, he introduced himself as "Dr. Cohen."

My Mother and he were obviously old enemies. Neither looked at the other.

"Of all the people," she muttered under her breath just loud enough for him to hear.

There was dehydration and inflammation of the chest, Dr. Cohen informed us. Nothing to worry about. The only thing of concern was whether or not the kidneys had suffered any damage. That could be ascertained only with a more thorough examination.

An hour or so later we were allowed to go to see him. He had been put in a special room with a sealed door. The room was dim, morgue-like, painted pale green and grey. The blinds were down. The thin rays of light coming through cast a lattice work of shadows on the linoleum floor.

My Father was fast asleep, his mouth hanging open. My Mother went about making the room more comfortable. She adjusted the drapery and the blinds, letting in more light, poured a glass of water and placed it on the night stand and straightened the blankets on his bed. One of his arms was askew, the hand hanging off the bed. She took it gently in her own and carefully placed it beside him, patting it softly. Around the wrist was a name bracelet. She stared at it a moment and shook her head. Taking his hand in hers again, she bowed her head and closed her eyes, and silently prayed. He was given up to the hospital and now there was only prayer.

Outside an angry tropical storm suddenly blew up. The room darkened, became more forlorn. Human life seemed so small. Rain and wind beat wildly against the windows, the giant palm trees outside thrashed back and forth, lightning flashed and thunder cracked. It was like the gods were announcing themselves. Again, there was this eerie feeling. I sensed my Mother felt it as well, but neither of us said a word. She continued tidying. Soon, the storm passed and the room lightened and we left.

"I DON'T CARE WHAT THE DOCTORS SAY. THEIR THINKING DOESN'T WEIGH much," said my Mother. "I tell you: *He-Is-Not-Eating.* Do you understand?" She stared out the window. "To live a man has to want to live," she said and then pushed the half-eaten tuna sandwich aside and stalked back to the bedroom.

I heard the dresser drawer in the bedroom open and close several times. Then the shouting began and I went back. She was moving around the room like a ball of energy. She was only five-foot-one but seemed much larger.

"You know why I didn't want him to go to that hospital?" she asked. "I'll tell you why? Because when they take you up there, you don't come back! That's why."

She could really work herself into a state. "But Mom—"

"I know what's going on. You don't have to tell me. I wasn't born yesterday. I've seen what happens…how people go to that place…just for a checkup or something…they put them in bed. 'It'll only be for a few days,' they say sweetly…but I'll tell you that's one bed they'll never get out of. The only way you get out of there is when they wheel you out—in a coffin!"

She was fighting and flailing away. Her arms were rigid and her little hands were balled up into fists, the knuckles white with tension. Her face was a mask of contempt and hatred. Her words came like great swelling waves, rising and crashing.

"And they think they're kidding us—all those little boy doctors over there. They want nothing but your money! They're not interested in you. No! Not one bit. It's just the money. It's not like before when they knew you, and talked to you, knew your family, knew your friends. Now who do they know? Only the Almighty Dollar, that's who! They don't have the time. 'Too busy,' they say. Yes, all they have time to do is to take your money and your loved ones."

I felt the energy draining from me. Eating me out, sucking me dry. I felt like I was asleep—I am asleep—with my eyes open. And from somewhere comes the recognition that it has always been like this. I don't want to see this. There's nothing I can do. No way to help her. I want to run, hide. Any place but here. And I feel this tug-of-war going on in me. To be here. To run. I force the thoughts away, repel them, give them nothing to hold on to. I guard the mind from all associative influences, and a strong wish comes to be present…

There is no appeal, no protest or reasoning—nothing that helps when she gets like this. She is taken over. An energy, an "I" comes up from the depths and she is powerless. It totally eats her. Totally obliterates her. It is so absolute, so primitive, without a thread of mercy or feeling…I had never stood and seen it so directly before. Or what it did to me. Louise usually got all this. Sometimes my Father. But I had been always been spared. I only got the white side. I could see them now, my Father and Louise. Sometimes Louise would fight. But it would do no good. You either escaped into the head or made yourself invisible, as my Father had done. And I had done the same.

My Mother goes into the bathroom to change. When she returns she is another person. The anger is spent. She glances at the beds. She runs her hand over the spread on his bed. Wistfully, she says:

"Funny, this is the first time—in how many years?—that Daddy won't be here."

She points to a large dark spot on the green shag rug.

"That's where he fell," she says, strangely remote like a disinterested guide. "Right there. Had to lie in his own filth all night."

But the way the word "filth" shoots out of her I know another seizure is coming. I steady myself with the breath, breathing into the different limbs. I am not going to identify.

"That damn dentist!" she cries. "I should never have let Daddy go to him. He didn't want to go. Our anniversary was the next day. But ohh…I made him do it. Yes, yes, it's my fault. Yes, my fault."

This is a different devil. This one doesn't beat other people. It beats her. Lashes her with guilt. I watch. The energy is colossal, primal, and black with rage. I remember Gurdjieff saying that you block the associative influences, but not to fight chemico-physical ones. Instead, you allowed these vibrations to pass through you. So I hollow out, become empty and passive. I simply watch.

My Mother is going on and on. She can't help herself. Suddenly it strikes me who is speaking. It's her father. He's living in her. All the devils, the inferior sides, he couldn't or wouldn't deal with. A terrible, poisonous "I." He and that whip hanging on the kitchen wall had nearly frightened her to death.

"Did you see his forearms?" my Mother demands. "All those ugly bruises and cuts. He had been stumbling for the last year or so, then falling. He'd just be walking and suddenly he'd go down. I was afraid he would break his arms. But what could I do?

"I thought it might be an infected tooth throwing poison into his system. So I called Dr. Infante and made an appointment for him. He didn't want to go because of the anniversary the next day. That dentist! He tried out a new drug on Daddy, can you believe it? Didn't tell him until later. Daddy was fine when he came home, but then on Saturday he began to get woozy. Oh, I don't want to think about it!"

I stare at the dark spot on the rug. How ironic given his dirt and germ phobia. The doctor's prophecy that he would die before he was forty was a curse that haunted him all his life. This was when he was a young boy and had been bedridden for two years with tuberculosis, peritonitis and rheumatic fever. "They brought him home on a pillow," my Mother had told me. "He was all bone. You couldn't touch him." No one, I guessed, had ever touched him…

My mother was determined my father would eat. She brought him a large straw basket of fresh fruit and slices of homemade cherry and apple pie. We found him sitting up in bed. He looked much better. The skin had some color now, the face was fuller, less drawn. I sat in the large leather chair at the end of the bed and my Mother stood by him, speaking in hushed tones, gently stroking his hair. He was listening to her, smiling…

I am smiling, too, but it is a mask. Inside I hear that voice again. *He's going to get better. Why? To go back to sitting out his time on the patio? I'll just have to come down again some time then, go through the whole damn thing again.*

I stand there listening, not running, not judging, not giving it any fuel. It rants on and on. I sense the body. Separate the consciousness from the sensitivity. Just stand there. Start to expand. The voice, the "I," keeps talking. It lives only for itself. I, myself and me. It's my "Little Lord Fauntleroy."

My Father is being very affectionate with my Mother. They've been married fifty-seven years now. He acts as though he really understands her, accepts her just as she is. Their energies come together, talking and laughing like old friends. I notice around him a thin, bluish light. The same kind of aura I had seen around Lord Pentland.

My Mother is telling stories now, acting out all the different parts. My Father is listening, only adding a wry and telling comment now and then.

My Father smiles and pats his leg, just as he used to do when a story tickled him. My Mother quickly puts his robe over his shoulders and motions me to help get him up.

"Now Bill, you know you just can't stay in that bed all day—it isn't good for you. Tell that nurse she has to help you out of bed in the morning."

My Father is smiling at my Mother's slyness. "God broke the mold when he made you, Mabel," he says with a chuckle.

We help him to a chair. He still has not eaten anything but he is obviously in such good spirits, thinking that he would be home shortly, that the worst is over…

Later, I took my Mother home. She was as much relieved as I. The nurse had said it would only be a few more days till he came home. I was going to stay till then, but my Mother insisted that I go home. "Your family needs you," she said. "That's where you belong."

The following morning I packed. I'd taken the rental car back, so I called a cab. At the door my Mother and I embraced. She seemed so small, but her heart was huge.

"Goodbye, Pat," she said. "I don't know what I'd have done without you."

I whispered into her ear, "Remember what Dad said—the Lord broke the mold when he made you."

A cab drove up and out jumped a burly, energetic cabby in a beat-up red baseball cap. I gave her a last hug and got in the cab. A large cross dangled from the rear view mirror.

"Well, now, how ya doin' today?" called out the cabby in a downhome twang and off we went. Along the way, he told me he was a World War II fighter pilot. He had been saved during the war, had given his life to Jesus.

"Yup," he hollered into the backseat over the traffic noise. "Ran out of gas over Indonesia and nothin'—believe me—but the Good Lord could put me back on the ground. Been walkin' in the Spirit ever since."

He held up a big Bible like it was a million dollars, and looked at me over his shoulder. "A lot a people who ride with me have come to Christ, too."

He adjusted the bill of his hat and checked me out in the rear view mirror to see how that had gone down, the cross still swinging back and forth from the last turn.

"Yup, there was one fella needed the Good Lord real bad. So ya know what? Why I jist pulled this cab right off the road 'n right there in the middle of traffic we both of us got down on our knees 'n prayed for the Holy Spirit to wash away his sin 'n give him a new life. Yup, Life in Christ Jesus! Amen!"

I told him what had happened with my dad and how I saw this blue light around him, how he seemed so peaceful now. How was that possible? My Father had never showed any interest in church though he would speak about having a "pipeline straight to God."

"'Strange are the ways of the Lord.' Romans 2:10," the cabby called back, eyeing me in the rearview mirror.

"Doesn't make a lot of sense," I said.

"Why don't ya know, young fella, it's not for us to question the wisdom of the Lord. 'No man shall come to the Father but by me.' Matthew 4:10."

He told me he was a singer, sang at festivals, and asked if I would mind him singing me a song. So there we were in South Florida in the heat and the traffic and he's singing at the top of his lungs—

Amazing grace, how sweet the sound
that saved a wretch like me.
I once was lost, but now I'm found,
Was blind but now I see

He pulled up to the curb in front of the airline and hopped out.

"Goodbye," he said and gave me a big bear hug. "Now don't ya worry none. Your mom is walkin' in the palm of the Lord, I tell ya."

I took my bags and asked if he would drive my Mother back and forth to the hospital every day.

"Of course," he said. "Be more than glad to."

At the door I turned and he called out—"Goodbye brother!"

I passed through the door and called back— *"Amazing Grace!"*

Cock's Rainbow

OUR FATHER'S RUNNING OUT OF gas," Dr. Cohen says. "better come as soon as possible." The words flash through me, cracking open the mind. The pores of the body open, energy pouring out, the mind jams, unable to comprehend. But there is nothing, nothing to take in. My Father, he is going to die. The meaning of the words finally registers and a feeling that is more than feeling, more than mere stillness makes itself present, and in that presence all separation dissolves, everything merging, interpenetrating in the enormity of the mysterious truth of death.

I hear myself asking a question. Not that an answer matters. "When did it happen?"

"Earlythismorninghiskidneysfailedyourmotherisholdingupokay."

The words sound like a secret code. Finally, as if on a delay, they are re-heard: "Early this morning his kidneys failed. Your mother is holding up okay." And then—"Better come quickly."

"Yes," I say and replace the receiver.

I sit back in the swivel chair and gaze out the office window. The sky is an empty sheet of blue. So vast, soothing. I can taste the blue in me. There are no thoughts. Just impressions. I feel like a child looking out on a kingdom of cement.

The red across the street. The apartment building, it's red bricks. The strong morning sunlight makes the bricks shimmer, their redness descending in value as they pass into shadow. The building itself painted into large areas of light and shade. The windows, all empty, silent. Except at one window, cast in shadows, a nameless old woman, her grey hair in a bun, wearing only a pink bra, rinsing her breakfast dishes. Bowl, cup, saucer, a single spoon. A solitary figure alive within a massive brick structure. Edward Hopper come to life.

Down below on street level, angry honking. I pull my chair closer to the window. A crush of Manhattan traffic going nowhere. Into view comes a shiny aluminum hot dog cart with a red and white umbrella. A stumpy old man chewing the end of a thick unlit cigar, pushes the cart alongside the line of cars and small trucks, talking to himself, angrily. The light has changed and traffic roars on. A long-legged young woman toting a large black portfolio spies a cab and waving anxiously darts into traffic. A yellow cab stops, its tires screeching. Getting into the cab's backseat, the model's short black skirt hitches up showing a long expanse of white thigh. Two men gawk, mesmerized, and quickly pass on, smiling at their shared fantasy. A weirded-out wino bellows at God. The traffic light changes.

I hurried to Grand Central to catch the 10:20 A.M. train back to Ossining. I ran to the train. The car was nearly deserted. The seats and floors were littered with the morning's newspapers, empty coffee cups and old sour smells. Graffiti was scrawled everywhere. Soon, the train lurched forward, pulling itself down through the dark tunnel. An old scene replays.

I'm ten, maybe twelve years old. I'm at bat. A high, hard one zips right down the middle of the plate. The meat end of the bat meets the ball flush on. It's a perfect meeting of bat, body and ball. I feel this incredible rightness. A loud thwack! I am half-way down the first base line when I look into left field. Out there a tiny dark object is sailing over the treetops. It's a ninth inning grand slam home run. We win the game. My Father is there. He's been up in the car waiting to take me home for dinner.

I cross the home plate, the roar of the crowd, of my teammates, in my ears; but my eyes are on the green Ford coupe parked on the street. A hand from the car's window waves me to hurry. I get my glove and run to the car, jump in, breathless, my heart still pounding wildly. My Father is in a business suit. He has just come from work. He coughs, mumbles something about having to get home for dinner, and pulls out into traffic.

Home is only five minutes away. I sit and wait, wait to hear what he has to say. But he is lost in his thoughts. A voice is screaming inside me—*Did you see it! Did you see it!* But he is off somewhere. And now we are pulling into the driveway. He shuts off the engine without a word.

"Dad," I shout. "Dad, did you see it?"

"What?" he says, startled. "What did you say?"

"The home run. The grand slam!"

"Oh, yes. Yes, that was a good hit." He pauses, adjusts his horn rims and coughs, that little cough he always made when he was uncomfortable. "All this stuff is okay for now. But it won't mean a hill of beans later on. You've got to come out of your dreams, get commercialized. That's what counts in the world," he says and gets out of the car.

Something breaks in me right then. I can't help it. It just breaks. I know I will never again let him into my world. I wasn't going to care what he thought. I would be the ghost to him that he was to me.

I'd paid no real attention to him after that. It wasn't a strategy. I wasn't hoping he'd notice and begin to talk to me, take me into his world. No, all that was over. He had waited too long. I wasn't angry with him. I didn't hate him. There was no strain, unfriendliness. Nothing. I never thought about it, never put it into words. But some place down deep something had cracked and the fact was accepted: *There would be no relationship.*

An "I" had been born then. An "I" that had protected me but sealed me off as well. And it was an "I" that had exacted a great and horrible tribute, for from that moment on this "I" had secretly dominated my life without my ever realizing it.

The train began to slow. Out the window I saw the familiar gun turrets and solemn guards with loaded rifles, the high forbidding Kafka-like grey walls, the long jangled river of wire with jagged teeth. Sing-Sing Prison. Punishment castle of The State, the secular world's Great Father. Inside, the sons this Father had banished from sight. Rebellious sons, those who refused to live by the Father laws. Exiled, cut off, sentenced to humiliation, pain and suffering—forced into a truncated life designed to remind forever that the Father had withdrawn his love, his protection, that they were on their own now in a hellhole of a dark and loveless world.

The forsaken, faceless men warehoused behind these walls—they were breathing symbols of a failed relationship with the secular Father. And what of their natural fathers? Had they been abandoned or rejected in childhood and so became outlaws?

And what about Lucifer? He had refused his Father's order to worship this motley new creation called Man. His understanding was not great enough. Pride confused and poisoned his faith. So Lucifer, great angel of the morning star, resisted, refused and ultimately rebelled, becoming a cold-blooded serpent with the aim of subverting his Father's creation. Opposing the will of the Father, this son had sinned against the Holy Ghost, and so bright Lucifer became Satan, Prince of Darkness.

Secular and religious criminals—they had killed the father in themselves.

And I saw now that, unwittingly, I had done the same.

But instead of being banished from the Father world, I had banished him from mine. Casey had said you "killed the father" by being better than he was. That was one way. Acceptable and healthy. But another was by putting up a wall around myself. That made for a wound that would never heal. For as no one can jump out of his own shadow no one can disown his own blood.

All these years, wasted.

My Father had realized his mistake. But I had grown up. It was too late. For both of us. What was done could not be undone. I forgave him. Many times. I loved him. I understood. But the "I" that understood was not the "I" that had been hurt. Once on a quiet afternoon drive I even told him about the home run and how I had felt. He pulled on his pipe and looked at me strangely—he didn't remember. He didn't know what I was talking about.

As the years passed, we did grow closer. But, somehow, the wound never healed.

Being the invisible Father, he had never "set the bar," told me how high I was to jump. There was nothing I had to equal, to live up to, to surpass.

The train pulled into Ossining. I hurried off, ran to my car, tossing my attache case into the backseat and driving up the hill. The air tasted good and fresh. But the space had a different feel. I didn't feel any sense of time in it. It all seemed to be of a piece.

In my mind's eye I saw us all sitting together on the couch, my Mother on one side of my Father, me on the other, looking at all these photos of my Father's family. One old photo, crinkled at the edges, showed my Father as a child. The eyes looking out from the scrapbook were sensitive, intelligent, heavy lidded with dark circles beneath. They seemed to be looking out from some remote place. There was a certain sadness, too. Another photo showed him crouched in a three-point stance playing tackle on the high school football team. Another dressed in an Army uniform. Another in a suit and vest with a large pocket handkerchief. He looked quite handsome, confident, maybe something of a dandy. He kept staring at the photos of himself as if he had never seen them before, studying them, searching for something. Finally, he looked up. It was as if he had come up to the surface after being down in the ocean of time. He gave a muffled laugh and shook his head like a man does when he's been asleep a long time.

"That fella's got the stuff," he declared. "He had it in him to really go places in this world."

"Oh, now, Bill. Don't talk that way," my Mother put in. "You did well enough."

My Father, too, had been wounded early as well. All that sickness and female pampering. The idea that he wouldn't live past forty. He had never understood the power of thought, of suggestion. That Dr. Powell, the family doctor and a cousin, the Father as a professional, who had put a scientific curse on him. He had lived with his own death all these years.

"I don't know what happened," my Father said reaching for his pipe. "I suppose I lost confidence somewhere along the way."

"Bill, now," my Mother said, "that's no way to think." She bent her head forward and looked over at me. "No one's complaining. Are we, Billy?"

Another image replays.

My Father was sitting there on the patio down in Florida in the thin evening light, drawing on his corncob pipe. He was looking off into space, going over and over again the same old ground, trying to make sense of it all, trying to see where his life had stopped, see where he'd gone wrong.

"I've lived a long time," he said, shaking his head, "and I still wonder…what's it all about?"

"WILLIAM PATTERSON?"

"Oh, you must be his son," said the nurse behind the desk. "Here, let me take you to him."

I am led down a corridor. Past an old man in a wheelchair. Room after room, their doors open, patients watching TV, talking to visitors, resting. The nurse stopped before a closed door, opened it and gestured me inside. In the far bed in the shadows lay a gaunt emaciated form, all bones, purplish and sickly yellow, more reptilian than human.

"Here," murmured the nurse. She motioned me to the bed by the door. It was blocked from view by a heavy white vinyl curtain that hung from the ceiling. She switched a light on over the bed and slowly drew back the white curtain…

There before me the image, the unimaginable image. My Father. On his death bed.

My Father is propped up high on the bed with pillows. Everything is very neat, white and clean. Everything perfectly still. It is as if he has been put on display.

His head lies half-cocked on the pillow, the empty eyes looking into the ceiling. The skin is waxen, without blood. From his nostrils and wrists run a jangle of ugly yellow tubing.

I hear then this horrible sound filling the space. A deep guttural rasping noise. Pushing. Sucking. Pushing. Sucking. The sound of a machine breathing a man. Forcing oxygen into his lungs, forcing the old out. In through the nostrils. Out through the nostrils. This mechanical sound going on ceaselessly, mindlessly. A sound only a machine could make. So monstrous, inhuman…and my Father— helpless and alone.

The nurse gently takes my hand. She leads me over to the bed.

"The last thing to go," she whispers, "is the hearing."

She leaves, pulling the curtain around us. I take my Father's hand. A faint warmth. So fragile. The skin is paper-thin, as though it would just come off the bone. There is nothing in his hand. No desire, no resistance. Only feeling. The vibration of "the sound" is so strong in my ears.

I bend toward him.

"Dad…Dad?" I call. "Can you hear me?"

No response. The eyes remain lost in space. The face is unshaven, a sickly yellowish-grey.

"Dad? Dad?" I call again.

Nothing. No sign of hearing. No movement.

But I can feel him. Something is still there, taking it all in. He is still conscious.

"Dad," I say softly, "I want to talk to you. Please?"

His head begins to move on the pillow, though so very slightly. The eyes come down out of space. They come to mine. The blue eyes I am seeing are total space. No thoughts to distract. No dreams, no pain or hurts. No expectation. That is all gone, all over with.

He is still conscious. He still has the power of recognition, of action.

"Dad...I love you. I really love you."

A tear, a single tear, rises at the corner of his eye. It grows until it spills over the edge, slowly winding its way down the side of his face through the white stubble of his beard. And then the head falls back onto the pillows.

He had made a supreme effort of will, of love.

Into the silence comes again the vulgar sound of a machine breathing a man. We had left it behind. Now it roars loud in my ears like a hungry lion. It fills the room completely in a sound wall of rasping.

The curtain parts and from behind me comes a saccharine sweet voice:

"Oh, it's you! We're so glad you're here, Billy."

I turn and nod. It's May, my cousin.

"My—" she says, "doesn't he look bad?" She is peering at him as if he is a museum object behind glass.

I say nothing.

"Now who would've ever thought?" she whispers.

I look at her.

"Oh yes, I understand," she says knowingly, patting me on the shoulder. "You'll want to have some time alone with him."

She withdraws quickly. I close the curtain and step close to the bed.

My Father and I are alone now. I bend down close to his face and whisper into his ear: "Dad, Dad, I love you."

I feel his forehead. It is damp, a little sticky. I look into his eyes. I feel there a deep wordless fright. I have seen the eyes before. They are like those of an animal caught in a trap so strong there is no hope of escape. There is only soul and consciousness now. Innocent and bewildered, frightened and waiting.

My Father is on the razor's edge, standing on a cliff. I stand by his side, waiting with him, the two of us out there on the precipice, framed in a welter of silence. Father and son. No sentimentality. A moment without time. And then slowly, down deep in me, I feel a subtle stirring and something rising and taking shape in the mind, the words forming—*What does he need to hear now?*

I look into my Father's face. He is between two worlds, the living and the dead. What to say? I feel my total ignorance. Yet the question remains. It is him and me alone and he is going to leave soon, leave forever, and I am without words. Yet the question remains—*what would be useful for him to hear?*

And down deep I feel another stirring. There is a rightness to it and I go with it, I let it speak through me....

"This is the real thing, isn't it, Dad? You are right there are at the edge. Between this life and what happens after."

The voice inside me stops speaking.

The breathing machine rasps on.

I'm filled with a shuddering emptiness. A yawning gap. As if a primeval mouth had opened.

Once more the voice begins to speak. It is much stronger now.

"I love you, Dad, but I'm not afraid for you. I know you are afraid, that you are suffering. But I don't think you are in any pain. It is just the newness of this, the fact you feel yourself so totally helpless."

Again, it stops. I stand mute, observing, waiting. Again, the voice:

"Can you feel yourself being breathed? Don't avoid it. Just feel it, come into it. Relax into it. Yes, that's right. Don't be afraid of that sound. That's it. It's all right to be breathed."

The respirator goes on. Suddenly, all at once, I feel what it is that needs to be said and I watch as it is put sequentially into words.

"The mind was holding on there. Now, can you see your suffering? Can you see what it is that is suffering? It's very subtle like the breath. Only much more subtle. Dad, if you can see it, then that suffering can't be you. Like the breath, accept it, relax into it. But don't identify with it. You are not your suffering. Do you hear me— *You are not your suffering. You are that which sees. You are consciousness.*"

His breathing becomes less harsh, the body more relaxed. Or was I imagining all this?

I'm in my head. I refocus, redistribute the attention out of the head and into the whole body, hearing the "sound," breathing, steadying myself in the space of the moment. And I wait in the stillness. What should my Father hear now? What would be useful?

And again, I see it and then watch it form into words:

"Dad, I'm going to give you a prayer that was given to me. It's the Prayer of the Heart, an ancient, sacred prayer. A Christian prayer. Now repeat to yourself after me: *Lord Jesus Christ, have mercy on me. Lord have mercy...* Keep repeating this prayer. Focus all your attention, all your consciousness, on the words. Really feel them."

I place my hand on his forehead. I press my thumb into the center of the forehead, just above the eyes.

"And as you repeat to yourself *Lord have mercy...Lord have mercy...*bring all of yourself, all of your attention, right here." My thumb presses hard against my father's pineal gland, and as I do, I feel more words forming. I hesitate. Should I let them be said? They are dangerous words. But I feel their truth.

"Now, whenever you're to be separated from the body...whenever Death comes...and I imagine it'll be a total shock to your body—just come out of the body through here."

I press my thumb hard into the third eye.

"Come out through the forehead. Leave the body through here. Leave through the forehead."

I withdraw my hand. I stand and gaze at the figure lying on the bed. I come down into the body, grounding myself, feeling the centers, letting the mind dissolve into the sensation, opening the pores of the skin and pouring all my energy into him.

I sit down on the bed, taking his hand in my own. And I pray, the respirator and the "sound" in my ears. Like hundreds of bees in flight. I get up to go then.

"You'll be all right now, Dad. All right," I say as I pull the white vinyl curtain around his bed.

At the far end of the hospital corridor, filled with nurses wheeling patients in wheelchairs, doctors rushing in and out of rooms, I see a small crumpled figure leaning against the wall. I recognize the blonde beehive hairdo. It is my Mother. She looks lost, like a homeless waif. The overhead fluorescent lighting whites out her features. It is only the eyes I see. Eyes half-dead with hurt.

"Pat," she whispers, as if out of a grave. "You've come!"

We embrace. She buries her face in my chest and sobs.

"Oh, Pat, how is he? Is he going to be all right?"

"Everything is fine, Mom."

"It was so sudden, Pat. He was getting better. Your Aunt Kate and May, they were over to see him just last night. He was laughing, joking with them, talking old times. And then...then...I don't know what? He took a turn for the worse. The doctor called this morning. I've been here ever since."

We walk down the corridor. I am supporting most of her weight. In the rooms we pass the patients are still watching television, reading, having visitors. For them, it is just an interim stop.

My Mother stops in her tracks. "Pat, what am I going to do without Daddy? He's all I have. The nurses, they said he didn't want to live anymore. I can't believe it. *Not want to live anymore?*" My Mother's face is a crinkled mass of pain.

We walk a bit more. I can feel her questioning something. Something doesn't feel right to her. She stops again.

"You don't seem worried," she says. "There's something different about you."

"Ohhh, there you are!" cries my cousin May. "Why we were all wondering where she'd gotten to." May had just come out of the small waiting room by the front desk. Aunt Kate is there. So is my sister Louise.

"Billy!" cries Aunt Kate. "Why, I haven't seen you in years. How are you?"

"Fine," I say, "and how are you?"

Aunt Kate's in a fox fur wrap and an expensive black suit. She's dyed her hair jet black. Dark flashing eyes. All the Scott features, the broad chiseled bone structure. She is sitting very straight in her chair, like a grande dame at a salon.

May is in a simple print, the good daughter's dress. She sits down beside her, a lady in waiting.

I smile and nod to my sister Louise and everyone. It is as if we are at a school picnic. A lot of idiot smiling and chattering. All a little forced. For this is a picnic at which someone dies.

My sister is sitting in a corner close to the wall. Her legs are crossed. Bill Scott's funeral was the last time we'd seen each other. She looks encased in stone. Gray skirt, gray long sleeved blouse. The face immobile. A bronze mask. Still wearing that heavy pancake make-up. The hair is bleached blonde. Wearing it up in a beehive.

"Well, tell us, Billy, how is New York?" asks Aunt Kate, sitting back and unleashing a long stream of smoke.

"Kate," my Mother says softly. "His name isn't—"

"Oh yes, yes," answers Aunt Kate, flicking an ash into the ashtray. "You call him 'Pat' now, don't you? Well, 'Pat'—how is The Big City? I understand you have a good job."

"Oh, Mother, he doesn't want to be talking about that now," interjects May.

"Can you get over that, Mabel? My own daughter ordering me around. Well, that's what happens when you get old and are left alone."

Louise crosses and recrosses her legs.

Aunt Kate checks her watch. The gesture is emphatic. Like a police sergeant.

"Better take your mother home now, Billy. We've all had a big day," declares Aunt Kate. "Get something into her."

"Mother! His name is 'Pat,'" May tells her.

"Now what's a name mean at a time like this, I ask you?"

Aunt Kate and May get up to leave. My Mother, Louise and I sit silently. My sister and Mother. A wall between them. Each in her own space.

"Billy, let's go back and see Daddy," says Louise finally.

"You haven't been back?" I ask.

"I just got here," she said.

"Okay. We'll be right back Mom."

My Father's room is dark except for the light above his bed. The sound of the machine breathing him—it is as if we were in an engine room. I pull back the curtain. That image again. He looks like a life-size waxen doll.

"My God, Billy" gasps Louise. "My God!"

Instinctively, my sister and I hold each other looking on at the unspeakable image. "Oh look at him!" she whispers. "Billy, I just can't believe it."

She goes to his bed and strokes his hand. She leans over him. "Dad? Dad? Do you hear me? This is Louise. *Dad? Lou-ise!*"

No response.

Finally she turns toward me, holding his limp hand up as if it's a dead fish. "He's in a coma," she declares.

"The nurse said the hearing is the last to go."

She turns back to him, clutching the hand and calling out at the figure on the bed. "Dad! I'm here now. Daddy, it's me. Lou-ise. I'm here."

No movement. No sign of recognition.

All the while, the machine mindlessly does its duty, filling the lungs with oxygen, emptying the lungs, filling, emptying. On and on.

My sister puts his hand back on the bed, collects herself. This is another "Louise."

"I'm all right," she tells me. "You take Mother home. I'm going to stay the night."

I go to his bed now. I feel his forehead. A faint warmth. I bend down and kiss his cheek. I press my thumb into his forehead. I whisper to him, one word at a time:

"Dad, remember: 'Lord have mercy.' Repeat it over and over again. When it's time, remember—come out through the forehead."

I take my Mother home.

She boils water for tea and makes me a tuna fish sandwich on whole wheat with mayonnaise, lettuce and tomato. I am not hungry but I eat.

Before going to bed, she goes around the house like a sleepwalker, tidying up, washing the plates in the sink, changing the towels in the guest bathroom, turning down my bed, checking if all the doors are locked. Habit has its uses.

"IT'S SOME GIRL," CALLED MY MOTHER, RAPPING ON MY BEDROOM DOOR. "Says she's an 'old girlfriend.'"

"Old girlfriend?"

"That's what she says."

Who could it be? I checked the clock. It was six forty-five in the morning. I was groggy. I had meditated before going to bed, visualizing my Father, sending him all my energy. Then I'd fallen asleep exhausted. The body was tired but the mind kept waking up. All night long I was waking and falling back to sleep. I remembered once I'd awakened with a start. I'd sat straight up in bed, my body trembling. I'd looked at the clock. It was five in the morning. The thought came: *Go to the hospital.* But I'd rationalized and fallen back to sleep.

I pulled on a robe. Went down the corridor to the kitchen. The fluorescent light glared. My Mother stood by the wall phone holding the receiver. She looked like a fragile angel. Her face was drained, heavily wrinkled. Deep dark circles under the eyes. Yet there was such a beauty to her, such a stillness. There was a quality, yes, of holiness.

I rubbed my eyes and took the phone.

"Hello," I said, still wondering what girl would be calling me.

"I didn't want to upset your mother," said a young girl's voice. It was soft and watery. Who could it be? "So I pretended to be an old girlfriend."

"Ohh," I said. Still a little woozy.

"Do you understand?"

"Yes," I said, "I understand." But I didn't really.

There was a hesitation. Then quickly, factually, the voice said:

"Your father just passed away. Your sister is still here and would like you to take her home."

My Father. Dead.

A great gaping space…

"I'll be right there," I mutter and hang up.

"Who's that?" my Mother asks. She is by the stove boiling water for tea.

"Oh, just the nurse at the hospital. Louise's tired and wants me to come relieve her."

"Well," says my Mother taking the kettle off the fire as the steam whistles, "what's this 'girlfriend' business then?"

"Oh, you know, Mom. These young girls. Always playing around."

I dress and start up the old Hornet. The engine rumbles and sputters and finally shakes itself alive. I back out the driveway. Down the street comes a strange-looking skinny man with a little white beard and pork pie hat. He doesn't look like he belongs around here. There's something special about him. His eyes are alert, twinkling. We take each other in, but say nothing.

The sun is just appearing over the top of the trees, robed in clouds. At the far end of the street is a dusty open lot dotted with bunches of tall grass. There is an inner urging to stop. I pull over, get out of the Hornet and face directly into the radiant softness of the sun. I open to it, raising my arms wide, its heat and light, its intelligence washing through me. I stand amid the panorama of the sky world witnessing the great wonder and mystery of its existence. Painted in glorious golds and pinks, soft oranges and blues, its centerpiece this great globe of shimmering light, once a planet like the earth itself, set now like a jewel amid billowing mountains of cloud, a testament to the evolving world and the great scale of creation. Birds are heralding the new day and through the vacant lot, sweeps a strong wind, the tall grass softly hissing its pleasure, eddies of dust swirling like tornadoes. Then it dies and all is still. I feel like an ancient sun worshipper. I feel a voice stirring in me. Standing with arms still outstretched, I say seven times aloud, my body resonating with each word...*In the name of the Father, the Son, and in the name of the Holy Ghost, please have mercy on my Father, protect him and lead him to the Truth.*

At the end of the seventh recitation I suck in a great breath and cry out onto the heavens above:

"Dad! Dad, I love you! I have always loved you. Don't be frightened. There's nothing to fear. I love you, Dad. Good-bye. Good-bye...."

Some birds flutter in the trees. Otherwise the whole world is cradled in silence. Soft, radiant and deep. I give my gratitude to the sun world and leave the lot, the Hornet's tires crunching over pebbles and rock, as I drive out onto the smooth paved road.

"OH BILLY," SHE MURMURS, AS IF TELLING AN AWFUL SECRET. "YOU'LL NEVER believe it...what he looks like. Our Daddy!"

My sister has been waiting for me by the information desk, her green night bag by her feet, packed and zipped shut. Her face is puffed and her jaw set. She stands up and we embrace. She is soft in my arms, exhausted from the vigil.

She motions me down the corridor and sits down to wait.

His room is dark and the air chilled. The white curtain is still drawn around his bed. The far bed next to the window is empty. The gaunt man has probably died as well. This was the room of death. The window shade is down. I raise it to let the sun light the room. Then I draw aside the heavy vinyl curtain.

There is my Father.

He is lying on his right side, half-turned, the head fallen almost to the edge of the pillow. The eyes are open, fixed in a stare. I lean down and take in my hands my Father's face, his final face, his death face, the last I will see until the circle converges and again we recur. The blue eyes are bereft of consciousness, no longer able to register the world of form. The face is without color. Only a whitish-yellow cast remains like a thin wash of watercolor. The nostrils look like black bullet holes. The white stubble of his beard makes the sheets look grey. Even the lips have no color. Just two quick pencil strokes. The mouth is turned up slightly at one corner in a smirk as if his last thought was, "So, this is it. This is what Death is like." A tuft of hair, I notice, protrudes from the right nostril. So, his final exhalation, the moment when death struck, the breath came through the right side. I stand now and put a hand on his forehead. It is hard, cold. Like stone. I press a thumb into the forehead.

"Goodbye, Dad," I whisper and leave.

MOTHER IS WAITING FOR US BY THE DOOR. SHE LOOKS SO SMALL IN THE doorway. Everything is in her eyes. It's as though her body has just dropped away. It still functions but she's not in it. My sister takes her hand and leads her to the couch.

"Mom," she says softly, "we have something to tell you. Daddy passed away this morning."

Mother screams a terrible cry, like a fatally wounded animal, and falls back into the couch.

"No, no—it can't be!" she cries. "It can't be!"

Her face explodes into a river of anguish and tears. Her hands cover her face, the sobs coming up from the depth of her being. The worst has come true. Her husband of nearly sixty years is gone.

After a while she looks around the room, amazed. "We would sit right there— together. In those chairs. At the table there. Here on the couch." she says pointing to the various pieces of furniture. "And now? Now, never again…?"

My sister tells her that she had stayed up all night praying beside his bed. At five in the morning he had worsened. An alarm had rung and nurses and orderlies ran in with special equipment to try to keep him alive. "He lasted until quarter to seven," Louise says.

"Was he in any pain?" my Mother asks.

"No, he wasn't in any pain."

Mother stares into space, her mouth agape, trying to take in what has happened, but somehow the simple enormity of it is beyond her mind.

"I wish someone would wake me up," she says at last. "I feel like I'm asleep."

That afternoon I went out to arrange a funeral. My Father had always told me, "Just send me out on the cheapest train. No use making the undertakers rich." I was going to have to bargain, and I had never bargained for anything. I either paid what was asked or walked out. I'd had this idea, like my Father I supposed, that money was dirty. I didn't believe that any more, but I could still feel the resistance. "I" didn't want to bargain. The "yes" and the "no" of it kept going back and forth in me. I stayed separate from it. It came to me then, as I drove along, that day in the coffee shop with Lord Pentland when he told me about acting otherwise, not being consistent, how we had to struggle against our conditioning. Okay, okay. I would do as my Father wished. But when I arrived at the funeral home a friend of my Mother's had suggested, Kennings on Commercial Boulevard, the fear and resistance and all the rationalizing resurfaced. Fortunately, I felt some anger, too.

Kennings was the Florida con job at its most innovative. Like Southern California, Florida is a developer's culture, a mindless mishmash of utilitarian make-a-buck architecture or gaudy grandiose imitations. Kennings was a masterpiece. It had tried for the ancestral Boston Brahmin look, but had more of a kitsch Presbyterian-in-Athens feel. It was a two-story red brick building with a steep angled roof fronted by two towering white Greek Doric columns. Serene, ethereal statuary led the bereaved to an oversized and intimidating mahogany door appropriately punctuated with a big golden doorknob and golden doorbell. I cleared my throat and spat into the manicured hedges before entering the portico.

I rang the doorbell. Inside a mellifluous chime sounded. Presently, the great door opened inward. There stood an unctuous, skinny young man with pop eyes and thick glasses costumed in the classic undertaker's serious dark suit and expensive but inoffensive tie. With great ceremonial solemnity, a touch of knowing sadness, he bid me to enter.

If the portico was foreplay, the foyer climaxed the whole icky dream. High domed ceiling with a skylight, pristine virginal white walls, garlands of stucco flowers, large white temple vases, on pedestals life-size neo-Greek statuary—Aphrodite, Iris and assorted nymphets with little girl breasts; young muscled athletes, genitalia discretely hidden; philosophic wise men, wearing serious expressions and flowing togas. Certainly here among these classic representations the bereaved might conjure up the true spirit of the recently deceased. And if imagination failed, well, certainly the company in which they abided was upscale.

My instant and no less diffident friend gave a moment's pause for the drinking in of the great display before motioning me onward down a softly-lit, sumptuously carpeted hallway. Passing two small chapels, we arrived finally before a vault-like door which opened onto a large, low-ceilinged office having the ambiance of a formal but restful bedroom, all done in polished woods and indirect lighting. The centerpiece of the room was a massive and altar-like mahogany desk. My friend took up a position behind the desk, motioning me into the wine red leather chair. He then sat down in the same type of chair, but his somehow put him at a higher level. He placed his elbows on the desk, cupped his hands at chin level and asked in a rich officious baritone:

"Now, tell me…how may we help you?"

"I need a funeral," I said point blank.

"Yesss," he replied. "And may I inquire…whom it is for?"

"My Father."

He sighed and made a helpless gesture with his hand. One reeking with understanding. "Yesss," he said.,

A moment's pause and then he was down to business. Name of the deceased, date of departure, address of next of kin and so forth. He noted it all on a long legal-sized form.

"How much will it cost?" I interrupted.

My friend's head gave a quick pitch. His brows furrowed. After a long moment, he nodded, assuring me, "We will most certainly get to that, but for the moment…"

"I'm on a tight budget," I explained. "Let's talk price."

Visibly shocked, even a mite horrified at my lack of respect for the nature of the occasion, the undertaker's pop eyes stared into mine: I must be the cruelest, most heartless son-of-a-bitch on earth. But such judgments did not sell coffins. He took off his glasses and wiped his eyes. Then he looked at me like he really did understand—my father must have been a real son-of-a-bitch.

"Burial or cremation," he said briskly, falling in with what he took to be my let's-bury-the-bastard-cheap attitude.

"Cremation."

He x-ed the sheet. "Large chapel or small?"

"Small."

"Full service, with us supplying the minister?"

"We'll supply our own."

"The deceased—how many days on view?"

"For the service only."

"Chauffeur-driven limousine to the crematorium?"

"No. We'll drive."

"Now, the casket," he said. "You'll be needing a casket—"

"Why?"

"For the service."

"Right. Make it the cheapest."

"Yesss. But of course," he muttered acidly. He sharpened his eyes on me. "The most economical we have is six hundred and ninety-five dollars."

I thought about that. "We won't need one for long. What about renting a casket?"

He swallowed, nodding gravely. I was a most peculiar client. "Yes, I do suppose we might rent one."

"How much?" I was loving this.

"Three-hundred and ninety-five dollars." His tone was crisp and clipped. That was the lowest he'd go.

I mulled that over. "But he'll only be in it a few hours."

My friend no more, he sat with that, his mouth zipped into a tight smile, the rodent eyes sharp upon me.

"By law," he informed me, "the entire insides of the casket must be taken out, and replaced."

"Can I see the rentals?"

"By all means."

He'd won his point. He stood immediately and led me down the hushed darkened hallway by another route, past some imitation Monets, to yet another door with a large golden doorknob, this the size of a small grapefruit. He flicked on the light and out of the darkness a great ornate tiered showroom of bone boxes came to life, overhead spots highlighting coffins of special interest, and price. He flicked yet another switch and the sound of harps filled the space.

The salesman now gave a tour of the product line, delineating the special features. I let him romance me for a while but at last I interjected:

"I'm sorry, but I really don't have much time. Where's the cheapest one?"

The word "cheap" cut him to the quick. Chilled by my brazenness, but still out to make a sale, he silently but with resignation motioned me to a far corner.

There tucked to the side of two masterworks sat the "no frills" model. It was just a step or two above a Dodge City pine box. I ran my hand over the gaudy cloth interior. I shook my head as if this wouldn't do.

"Wait—wait! Your father was a veteran, was he not?"

I nodded.

"Well, do you realize that the widow receives about six hundred dollars from the government for his burial, heh?"

"My Mother...yes, we were counting on that...but she'll need every penny now just to scrape by." I kept my eyes down on the pine box, not wanting to chance blowing it all.

He drummed his fingers on one of the masterworks, with a floral design of whites, silvers and golds. "Well," he asked conspiratorially, "do you have to show him?"

"Whatever is 'best.'" I replied.

"I have an idea!"

He took me by the arm and led me into another corner. Here was the Boot Hill shipping carton. I'd finally arrived. He looked at me as if we were committing a great crime together, but so be it.

"Only two hundred ninety five dollars," he whispered in exclamation. "And if the casket is going to be closed, well, we can drape a flag over it. Who's to know the difference!"

At once I agreed and we both marched out of the showroom, now sealed in darkness again, the Muzak harps silenced. In his office, he quickly calculated the bill. It came to thirteen hundred and ninety-five dollars. He looked amazed.

"Do you know the average funeral comes to twenty-five hundred dollars?"

He passed the form to me with one hand and a gold pen with the other.

"Just sign at the bottom," he directed, giving me a pop-eyed smile. Yes, the two of us had put one over on the old bastard, hadn't we? A dirt cheap funeral and who would know the difference!

I laid the form down on the great altar, neatly placing the pen at a diagonal across it. He froze. "I'll need my Mother to okay this, first," I murmured.

He could have killed me then, but ambition and greed are wonderful control mechanisms. He bit it all down and walked me to the door, my giving him every assurance that I would be back and he, if I could judge by his inner face, relieved I was getting the hell out of there.

I was exhilarated. I decided to do some "comparison shopping." I turned into Mason's. It was a funeral home just a few long blocks from my Mother's home. A pleasant looking, square jawed man with a deep drawl answered the door. We went directly to his office, a small cubby hole right off the doorway. I told him I wanted "the cheapest funeral I can get." Without any bargaining, he offered me the same funeral as Kennings, minus one or two extras, for six hundred and eighty dollars.

THE NEXT DAY WAS CLEAR, CLOUDLESS AND SO BRIGHT THAT WHEN WE stepped from the sharp hot glare of sun into the cool womb-like darkness of the chapel, it was like stepping into a Rothko painting. There was only inky blackness. Then slowly, out of the apparent emptiness, silent forms and figures appeared amid the pews. My Mother, dressed all in white except for a mink stole, walked up the center aisle alone, my sister and me following. Her step was unhurried, unfaltering. She walked with the dignity of someone who had a sense of herself and the moment. People looked as we passed, but her eyes were focused on the end of the aisle. There, up a few steps, lay my Father's closed casket, edged with flowers and draped with an American flag. It was softly lit and shimmered in the surrounding darkness. The pulpit stood off to the side. My Mother knelt down at the bier, folding her hands and resting them atop the casket. She prayed silently, tears trickling down her cheeks. At the end of her prayer, she whispered aloud: "Oh Bill…Bill, I love you. I'll *always* love you." The words were so direct, so whole. They echoed through me. She prayed again before sitting down in the front pew between my sister and me. I held her hand. It was so still. She was there but barely breathing.

In moments the Pastor came down the aisle carrying his Bible under one arm. I could feel the wake of his energy as he passed. He strode to the pulpit and opened his Bible. He looked out into the darkness for a moment and then over to my Mother to whom he nodded, and then he began as he must have begun so many times before: "Dearly beloved, we are gathered here today…"

As he spoke the image came again of my Father and me traveling the old dirt roads together. The roads were straight as a ruler and hard-packed and, in places, deeply rutted from the rains. We would drive for miles and miles into the flat, grassy Florida marshland, the only sounds being the rumble of the tires on the rough roads and now and then the cawing of crows. It was all just endless grassland except for an occasional gnarled old tree or a lone egret hunting for fish. It was so quiet and peaceful and away from the world. That was why we liked it though we never talked about that. We would drive for miles and miles, not saying a word. They weren't needed here. My Dad would be smoking his corncob and pretty soon I'd light up a Tiparillo. Sometimes he had one, too. We'd talk sometimes. Usually about my job or the family or whether they might ever return to Pittsburgh or not. But once I had asked him:

"Do you remember Nancy Smith?"

He thought for a few moments. "You mean that little dark-eyed gypsy girl?" he asked, smiling to himself.

"Well," I said, "she wasn't a gypsy, but she could have been!"

I glanced over at him and rolled my eyes. We both laughed. And I told him a childhood tale of a sexual escapade.

My Dad had gotten a big kick out of that story. He had slapped his knee and really laughed.

We drove deeper into the marshlands, and then headed back. I could tell he was still thinking about things. Finally, he tapped out the remaining tobacco in his pipe and repacked it from the tin of Prince Albert. I got the feeling that this was a ghost he'd been living with a long time.

"I don't suppose it would mean much nowadays..." he said. "But back then it did."

My Father was a good man. He had meant well. But circumstances had been too heavy for him. He had been kept locked up inside himself. He hadn't been able to get free, to get beyond personality, beyond a belief in the world. But at the end a miracle had happened. He did get free finally, free on his death bed.

And I will dwell in the house of the Lord forever. Amen.

Afterward while Mother was sleeping, Louise and I took a walk around Vanguard Village.

"Mother is really holding up well," I said. "I was so proud of her at the funeral. She had a real sense of the moment. She acted with so much dignity."

"I know Mother thinks I'm awful for not coming when he first fell," Louise said, "but you were here and he seemed to be getting better, Billy."

"I called Daddy on Sunday, you know," Louise told me. "We had a long talk. Do you know what he told me, Billy?" There was a real surprise in her voice. "He told me he had seen God."

"Did he say what he meant?"

"He said there was this light in his room everywhere, and that I shouldn't worry. Everything would be all right." She took a deep breath. "But he...I don't know. You see, he didn't want to live any longer. I don't understand it. Why wouldn't you want to go on living?"

"Did Dad leave a will?" I asked my Mother the next morning at breakfast.

"No, never said a word about a will," my Mother answered.

"That's funny," I said, knowing what meticulous records my Father kept.

"If he did, I guess it would be in the strong box at the bank at Margate."

After breakfast we got into the Hornet and drove to their bank, about ten miles north. It was a somber day, a sheet of grey sky, and you could feel in the moistness of the air an imminent rain. Just outside Margate my Mother pointed out a small diner.

"That's where he'd go for doughnuts and coffee," she said. "He'd tell me he was, 'Just going out for a paper.' And a few hours later he'd come back acting like it was no time at all. What a guy."

The skies had turned from grey to black as we drove. Soon a hard tropical rainstorm beat against the car and flooded the streets with water, the heavy winds bending the giant palm trees, their fronds thrashing high above our heads. It was like the storm when we first took my Father to the hospital. It had felt like an omen. We parked in the bank's lot and waited. But the storm didn't abate. So we made a run for it, covering our heads with the morning's newspaper. We were dripping wet and laughing like kids when we reached the door of the bank. All the while a handful of old folks huddled under the awning at the entrance. They stared at us as if we were crazy but said nothing.

"Did you see them, Pat? They must think we've got a big pile in here," my Mother chuckled once we were inside the bank. "No one hurries down here. Everyone's just passing time."

The bank was one great space whose high ceiling, long vertical windows, inlaid marble floor and sturdy fixtures all gave testimony to the belief in and worship of security and power. Its parishioners were virtually all senior citizens, solemn and long faced, whose heavy silence stood in marked contrast with their colorful youthful rain gear. Young polite acolytes spoke to them individually in hushed tones of their worth, the recent deposits, accrued interest and withdrawals, all that lay between them and the vagaries of the unforeseen. This secular sacredness was broken now and then by the mechanical sounds of the punch and screech of calculators and computer printers or, as the brethren departed, the squeak and slosh of wet rubber against marble floor. Otherwise all was silent with the high seriousness of the moment.

My Mother and I waited outside a knee-high, wrought iron gate which separated us from the holy of holies, a mammoth, highly polished steel vault and beyond that the safe deposit boxes. A young, self-important woman buzzed the gate open, having first meticulously checked our identification. She escorted us to a large room, stacked floor to ceiling with steel boxes. She inserted her key and ours into box seven hundred and thirty-two and withdrew an impersonal steel tray, about the size of a long loaf of bread. Still without a word, or our eyes meeting, we were motioned inside a narrow cubicle where she closed the door behind us.

We sat down, our clothes dripping, and I opened the tray. It contained packets of papers, all neatly bundled and held together with rubber bands or string. My Mother thumbed through them, feeling their texture.

"It's funny," she mused, "your Father would come up here every six months or so."

"Why would he do that?" I asked.

"I don't know. He was a very private man. He kept everything inside."

"You don't know what's here?" I said.

"No," she murmured. "I suppose the mortgage, that sort of thing."

I took a deep breath and began to go through his papers. They were just what my Mother had supposed. Mortgage papers. Financial statements. Warranties. Income tax receipts. Some stocks. No sign of a will. Perhaps that was just as well. Out of a batch of papers slipped a small photo of him, very serious. He was dressed in a business suit. He looked stern, no-nonsense. My Mother wanted to see it. She held it about an inch from her eyes. "He always liked this photo," she said. "I don't know why."

At the bottom of the tray was an envelope with *Louise* written in a heavy black pencil. It wasn't sealed and obviously had been read over many times. I had a general idea of what it might say. I distracted my Mother and slipped it in my jacket pocket. I had gone through all the papers and still no will. Yet I had the recurring feeling that he had left one, so I rifled though the papers one more time. I came across several sheets of paper with crosshatched blue lines. That was the accounting paper he used at Westinghouse. I unfolded it. It was written in a large sculpted backhand that could only be my Father's.

"It's the will, Mom," I said.

"I knew it," she answered. "I just had that feeling. Read it to me." My Mother bent closer in my direction.

I could read it easily but I said, "It's tough to make out, Mom. Let me read it to myself first."

> *My biggest regret is that I am ashamed of my record—*
> *as a youth, as a man, as a husband, as a father. I know*
> *I had it in me to go places and make you happy and I didn't*
> *begin to try—why I'll never know for I loved you all*
> *very much in my own peculiar way. I was looking*
> *for the rainbow when I had it in all of you all the time.*
> *Forget the past. You're in the new world—*
> *get going and enjoy it.*

At the bottom of the will was the signature—*William B. Patterson.* He had signed his name four different times. Each signature was dated. The first was the year my magazine went bankrupt. The next was two years later. Then another two years. Then three years. Two years after his final signature he had died. A total of nine years. In that time he had to have read the will at least four times. It was as though with each reading he acknowledged that the intervening years had not changed his mind about himself—that the truth of these simple and awful words remained:

> *I am ashamed of my record—*
> *as a youth, as a man, as a husband,*
> *as a father.*

All those years I had brought my family down for Christmas, all the times together on those backroads, and he never said a word. He lived the whole time with the conscious recognition of this shame.

This wasn't a will. It was a confession.

"What's it say, Pat? What's it say?" my Mother asked.

My biggest regret, I began...

The words stunned my Mother. She, too, had no sense of the guilt he was living with. She shook her head slowly, her face a mask of utter disbelief. "My God, I never knew he felt that bad about things, I never knew."

"Mom—"

"Oh, Bill..." she cried. "Oh, Bill." It was in that same wounded voice. She hung her head and prayed.

I reread his words to myself. These were the words for me of the Father, the Father I had never known. I could feel him there with us then. Not there for our tears. Not there for our sympathy or surprise. But there for the revealing, the unburdening, the final laying down of the cross he had borne. In that moment I thought of *The Petitioner.* It came to me that what the petitioner, my Father, was asking for was to be relieved of the burden of living with the knowledge and shame of the Father. He was asking for new life, a death to this life.

"Read it again," my Mother whispered.

I looked at the words written in that large, handsome but self-conscious backhand and I realized that he had written no salutation, no closing. So as I read the will again for my Mother. I added, as I knew he would want me to, the words *Dear Mabel* and at the end *Love, Bill.*

That evening after dinner my mother and I sat talking about what she would do now. I wanted to bring her back to New York with me, but she insisted on staying in the house, living alone. May and Aunt Kate, she told me, had agreed to help her get back on her feet. I didn't think it was practical or healthy to stay in the house, but she said she had made up her mind. Something must have been said. Some trigger must have been pulled for all of a sudden out of me came this enormous anger—

"The selfish son-of-a-bitch!" I cried. "He didn't give a damn about anyone. Only himself."

"Pat! Don't ever talk about your Father that way. Don't ever!" My Mother jumped up out of her chair, her little hands balled up into fists.

"Well, he was! And you know it."

"He was your Father. *Your Father!* Do you understand? Don't ever let me hear you speak about him that way. Why you're his own flesh and blood."

"Mom—"

"Honor thy Father and Mother—" she shouted raising her fist to me.

"Mother, I'm sorry. I didn't mean to."

"Has the world come to this that a son speaks like this about his own Father!"

All the years of silent screaming had finally come up in me. I couldn't keep it down anymore. He was weak. And whatever excuses I might find for that, the fact still remained—he was weak. A weak Father. A Father who was no Father but ever remained a son. And a Father like that is a wound that each of us, mother, sister and son must bear. That was our family karma. What we each had to do was to finally acknowledge that, to understand and to work with that. But how could I explain this to my Mother?

"So that's…that's what you really think of him?" said my Mother. She sat back down in her chair. She looked so bewildered.

"Mom, I'm really sorry. I—"

"You said it and you meant it." Her body was shaking in the chair.

"Yes, that's true. But, Mom, please…I didn't mean to hurt you."

"Hurt me? You hurt him! You hurt yourself! Don't you understand? Has the world gotten so crazy that no one understands anymore?"

"Mom, I've carried this pain all these years. I've never said a word about it." I stood up and walked around and sat back down again. "And I'm not trying to hurt anyone. But yes, I admit it. I finally admit it—there is this anger in me. Mom, don't you see? I can't deny that any longer."

"Your Father was a good man, a kind man. A real gentleman. A gentle-man," she declared. "I don't suppose you know what that is."

"He was, Mom. He was. I agree."

"He had very high principles."

"Yes," I said. "He did."

"He sacrificed so much for you, Pat. Did you know that we even borrowed against our furniture so that you could go to college—get the chance he never had! The house was already mortgaged and so all that was left was the furniture. And now…now this is the thanks he gets?"

"Mom, please, don't do this to yourself."

"You've had your say. Now let me have mine. Yes, your Father knew he didn't give you enough attention. But, Pat, what could he do? When he realized it, you'd already grown up. It was too late. It was all water under the bridge."

"COCKFIGHT! COCKFIGHT!" A MAN SHOUTED. "SEE THE COCKFIGHT!" IN THE CENTER of a ring of men two enormous green roosters with gila monster bodies fought fiercely with beaks and long talons. Suddenly, the one rooster lunged, its sharp beak gripping the other's neck. It was a fight for life. A terrific test of wills. Slowly, little by little, choking to death, one gila-rooster was forced to the ground, the victor absorbing all its vitality. The big bird now stood erect, its dead opponent at its feet, its chest full and puffed with energy, feeling supremely alive, alive with the life of another.

The dream was so vivid. I knew at once who the gila-roosters were. I had killed my Father. And I could feel now that by some strange, archaic transmission what had been his was now passed on to me. I could feel my Father in me. He had given me his strength, his life.

At breakfast the phone rang. My Mother answered. It was Louise calling from Pittsburgh. My Mother and she talked awhile about Thomas, my sister's husband. He was legally blind like my Mother and had now come down with diabetes.

She hung up and sat down. Her face gave off a great sadness.

"I've never had a daughter," she said.

"Louise loves you, Mom."

"Mother, sit up straight in your chair," I say softly. "Put your hands in your lap and close your eyes."

"But why?"

"Oh, c'mon. Just as an experiment. I want to show you something."

She sits up. I ask her to close her eyes, to relax her face, and get a sense of her body sitting in the chair. I ask her to watch her thoughts, let her mind slow down, then come to a simple sensation of the different parts of the body. I ask that she slowly breathe into them, grounding herself in the awareness of the sensation of her body. She does as I ask and soon the tension begins to release. A healing stillness appears and settles throughout the room. After a while I ask my Mother to repeat after me, "Lord Jesus Christ, have mercy…have mercy on William Patterson."

An image of my Father comes to me. He is smiling. My Mother's weeping is in my ears. The tears are good tears, tears of release and acceptance. Everything is going to be all right now. I can feel it. She is giving her husband up to God…

Later that day, my bags packed, I was about to leave for New York when my Mother went into the bedroom and brought out a book and a money bag.

"Here, Pat," she said. "Your Father wanted you to have these."

I took the book and the bag. The book was *The New Man* by Maurice Nicoll, a close student of Gurdjieff and Ouspensky. I had lent it to my Father years before and had forgotten about it. The bag was heavy.

"All his old coins are there," my Mother said. "Every coin he ever saved from I don't know how long."

I emptied the bag on the dining room table. There were groups of envelopes, each marked in my Father's backhand script: "Old Lincoln pennies without mint marks," "Indian head pennies—rating good," "Barber half-dollars," "Walking Liberty half-dollars," "Dollar bills with 'In God We Trust' omitted." There were smaller bags of loose coins and rolled zinc pennies, buffalo head nickels, old dimes, quarters and half-dollars.

"I don't know how much they're worth," my Mother said, her voice just above a whisper, "but your Father wanted you to have them."

I hugged and kissed her. She was so strong, so generous and noble. There was something so good and true inside her that when I felt it, I knew my love for her would carry beyond all time. That no event or words, no matter how hurtful, could ever break this bond. And I knew at that moment that my sister Louise had probably never felt that. It was true for her also. But the roots between them had turned so sour that their relationship had become virtually all personality. It was all surface and no depth. Old wounds hadn't healed. They were too afraid to feel around one another. Essence remained untouched.

"About the book…he kept telling me after he went to the hospital to make sure I gave it back to you."

Outside, the cabby was honking. We walked to the door and she said:

"I don't know what I would've done without you, son. May the good Lord watch over you and keep you."

"Mom, I love you. I'll call you soon."

On the way to the airport I looked at the book. I'd first read it shortly before Barbara and I were married. That was eight years ago, almost to the day. I thumbed through the book. I came to a passage I had underlined:

"To act from faith is to act from beyond oneself—to act beyond self-love and its interests. It is just the same in the case of thinking from faith. To think from the knowledge and ideas of faith is to think beyond one's ordinary mind, beyond all ordinary ideas and ways of thought. To think from faith is to think in a new way: to act from faith is to act in a new way."

I took it as a message for me. I had had no words for what was happening.

I got on the big jumbo jet and sat by the window. The plane was nearly empty. Only a few travelers. A tall, bird-like stewardess came by with a stack of magazines. She held the magazines up one by one for me to choose: *Time. Life. Fortune. Money. Sports Illustrated. Popular Mechanics. The New Yorker.*

I smiled. The magazines were like little worlds. I shook my head and she passed on.

Soon, like awakening dragons the jet turbine engines roared into life, carrying the huge silver plane out from the terminal and onto the tarmac, its wing tips dancing softly in the hot dazzling sunlight. Another roar and off we went down the runway, traveling faster and faster, until all at once gravity lost its grip and off we lifted, and what was once earthbound was now airborne, hurtling into the great expanse of cerulean sky like a well-thrown spear. Out the window and down below, I looked at the receding ant-like world of cars and houses. I took off my shoes and stretched out and closed my eyes.

MY FATHER. LYING THERE IN THAT HOSPITAL BED. MY FATHER SO SMALL, SO fragile, frail. The skin just hanging from the bones. The machine breathing man. That ugly horrid rasping. My thumb pressing into his forehead. My telling him: "Come out through the forehead. Leave the body through here…"

I feel this deep urge to know, to know that I have not been imagining it all, to know that I have acted rightly. A voice calls out inside me, "Lord, Lord, please tell me. Please tell me."

The "sound" is roaring. I open my eyes and I look out the small window. The plane is approaching a towering cloud bank. It's so white and lustrous, filled with shapes and faces, all appearing and disappearing and recombining before my eyes.

And then I see a great arc of color thousands of feet above the earth—*A rainbow!*

All the years I have been flying down to Florida to see my parents never once had I seen one.

And then—*a second rainbow.*

And—*a third rainbow!*

And with the third rainbow my Father's last words sound again…

> *I loved you all very much*
> *in my own peculiar way.*
> *Looking for the rainbow,*
> *when I had it in all of you*
> *all the time.*
> *Forget the past.*
> *You're in a new world—*
> *get going*
> *and enjoy it.*

WHO ARE YOU, STRANGER?

S UDDENLY THE HUGE METALLIC bird descended from the clouds and up from below rushed a great erection of towering vertical forms, the angularity of their shadows sharp and unforgiving on the smooth faceless sheets of steel and concrete which gave the city its form. Here was New York, city of the temporal word made flesh, the secular logos, the secular father.

I'd first come to Manhattan eighteen years ago. It had captured me immediately. I had stood gawk-eyed at Lexington and Forty-Second staring up at the Chrysler Building, the traffic, bumper to bumper, roaring by, shrieking, the endless swarms of people pushing past, the crazy jacked-up energy and jangled sound, the raw worship of money, power, ambition—what was the word for it? I had none. I'd never experienced anything like it.

Out the plane's window I saw Rockefeller Center. That's where I'd first met Lord Pentland. All that had happened at my Father's death bed and afterward—none of it would have been possible without him and the Work. My blood Father had died, but my spiritual Father still lived. As the plane banked and headed for La Guardia I felt the lack of relationship I had felt with my Father was a pattern I was repeating with Lord Pentland. There was this rent in my psyche. Emotionally, it would not heal. Intellectually, I realized it was projection. I'd observed it so often.

But the "I"s that protected it continued to entangle me. These "I"s were like a vine that sucked at my roots.

The air traffic was heavy and we had to circle through the cloud banks and wait. An image of Lord Pentland came to me. I saw him getting out of a cab in front of the Foundation. It was a surprise. He had had a heart attack and almost died. Eight months had passed. It wasn't known when or if he would ever return to the Work. I was a block away when the cab stopped and this tall, erect figure got out. I felt elated at first, but then I turned away, pretending not to see him. I both respected and feared him.

Another image. Lord Pentland standing alone against a bare colorless wall. He gives me that "empty look." My feelings burst in reaction and I greeted him effusively, yes, too much emotion, too much personality…and that look burns me into cinders.

It was just a few days after I'd seen him get out of the cab. There had been a Work day on Sunday at Armonk, Lord Pentland opened the day. In his absence other teachers had given the morning talk but none could articulate the Work, either in words or presence, as he could. We met as always in the large dining room with the massive hand-built stone fireplace. After everyone had settled, Lord Pentland entered the room and sat down in front of the fireplace. A bright winter's morning sun was streaming in through the tall windows. He looked a bit drawn, more slender perhaps, but he was still "there" in that incredible way, devoid of all semblance of personality. The room crackled and then settled down, the silence becoming very lush and strong. He hitched up his trousers and slowly took everyone in. Then he began to speak. And though his voice was very low, it carried throughout the room.

"This is a work in life," he said. "It is not done in a monastery or ashram but rather out in the ordinary circumstances of life. That is our laboratory. That is where we find ourselves and too often lose ourselves. Most of us here have practiced the Work long enough that we have the force necessary to play consciously a role in life…to take an active part…to use life as a means to awaken.

"Many years ago my grandfather gave me a piece of advice. He told me: 'Whatever you put your hand to, do as well as you can'. To really do anything well one has to be inwardly free, not identified with oneself or what one is doing. So we must work well but be free in the work. For this is The Fourth Way. It is distinguished from all other ways in that it is a work of transformation in life.

"Such a work is not, and cannot be, for everyone. It is a way of understanding that creatively uses the shocks and sufferings of our ordinary life to come to Life. The Work is not well-known, and when it is, so often the result is misunderstanding. The Work functions on a much deeper level than ordinary life and so cannot be understood by values and motives which serve mechanical life.

"The Fourth Way, being esoteric, and originating from what has been called 'The Conscious Circle of Humanity,' is a tradition which stands outside tradition, as it is commonly regarded. One of the characteristics which distinguishes it is that it works with what is usually disregarded: negativity.

"We find it alluded to, however, in some ancient and traditional texts. In the *Bhagavad Gita,* for example, we find this sutra:

"'Both renunciation and holy work are a path to the Supreme; but better than surrender of work is the Yoga of holy work...'I am not doing any work,' thinks the man who is in harmony, who sees the truth. For in seeing or hearing, smelling or touching, in eating or walking, or sleeping, or breathing, in talking or grasping or relaxing, and even in opening or closing his eyes, he remembers: 'It is the servants of my soul that are working.'

"Let those who wish to experiment today with the understanding which the *Gita* points us toward..."

Afterwards, I saw Lord Pentland standing alone in the hallway. I went straight to him. Either he hadn't seen me coming or pretended not to. I stood there, shaking inside, so glad to see him. Finally, he looked at me and we shook hands, lightly. I just looked at him. There was a pause and then he said matter-of-factly:

"I understand you've been away."

Me? He was the one who had been gone nine months. I wasn't quick enough for the shock. All I felt was anger. I felt like he had pushed me away. My emotions blared inside while outside I heard myself telling him of all the cities my job had taken me to.

He listened but didn't comment. I looked in his eyes. There was no one there. Completely empty. I felt as if I was talking to a dead man.

Finally, I said: "I'm glad you're back."

He nodded. I walked away.

Yes, I knew I had fallen asleep. But I had waited so long to see him, not knowing if I would ever see him again, and now here he was—I didn't want to be taught right then. A door inside me closed. I struggled to keep it open. But it had closed tight.

"IS THE NEED FOR ATTENTION ORGANIC?" I ASKED HIM THAT FOLLOWING Wednesday at the group meeting.

"What do you mean by 'organic'?" He looked at me curiously as though I was a strange animal in a zoo. Of course, he knew what I meant. He was forcing me to go deeper, to admit it outright.

"When I don't get the attention I expect, I get hurt," I answered. "Of course the personality wants attention, but is it something deeper than this? Does the body have a need for attention?"

He nodded now as if he had at last understood. Then he looked at his assistant, Becky, a very thin dark-haired young woman who had a good understanding of the Work and was completely devoted to him. She had been leading the group in his absence. She began to answer. I interrupted—

"With all due respect, Lord Pentland, I have waited so long for you to return, I'd like to hear your answer."

Lord Pentland smiled wanly, as one would at a child. Anger flashed up in me. He had me sitting in flames. He stared at me a while and then nodded and answered:

"After a time in the Work, one may have a supply of nervous energy," he observed. "If we identify, this higher energy becomes mixed with that of the lower centers and we get hurt. In fact, we get hurt more readily. The ascending octave is deflected or aborts. But having this energy is a sign that we are nearing self-transformation."

He looked to Becky. "You see, there was a lot behind that apparently innocent question—'Is the need for attention organic'?"

Another person was about to speak, but he suddenly turned back to me. "There comes a moment out of the blue—when there is a stop. The whole situation, everyone, surfaces then and each finds himself in a role. The role, of course, doesn't matter. For there is no ambition, no trying to get ahead, or to be superior. All that is left behind. Then the drama can actually begin."

The following Sunday at Armonk I reported to the form and color group as usual. It was headed by Mr. Freemantle, a diffident, soft-spoken English mathematician who had studied with Ouspensky in England and America in the thirties and forties. Someone came by and asked if I could be spared for the day. Mr. Freemantle answered, "Why yes, of course, you can borrow him. But what is it you need him for?" He feigned a look of puzzlement. "You see, basically, he can't do anything."

Lord Pentland came by, took me aside and said, "You've been practicing self-remembering a while, perhaps it's time you experimented. Hmmm?"

I nodded, but I had no idea what he meant.

"You've seen, I'm sure, there is this coming to and leaving sensation. So in order to stay awake longer you need to create something to help you remember."

I nodded.

"Can you think of anything?"

He observed me for a few moments while I vainly tried to think of something—then he walked away. I felt like I had failed. But he turned and came back to me. He was limping badly. He must have somehow hurt himself. He came very close to me and whispered, "Pretend you are an old man with a limp."

So the whole morning I limped about. People asked how it had happened, made way for me, and so forth. Instead of using it as a reminder to self-remember, I soon was marveling that I was able to pull it off and how mechanical everyone else was. At lunch, Lord Pentland answered a number of questions then suddenly stopped—"All these questions seem to be along the same lines," he reflected. "Has anyone tried anything different? For example, acted otherwise…put themself out on a limb, so to speak?"

I felt trapped. I knew he wanted me to speak, but I saw then what an ass I'd been. I couldn't summon the courage to talk. The fear of revealing myself was too great.

At the next Wednesday meeting he talked about obedience. "The Work is so subtle," he said, "we can't invent our own challenges and sacrifices. We need someone to tell us where to put the next peg in the board. It must not be too high. If we extend ourselves, it must be something within our reach. There are so many things which can be given but we can't just half do them. We must be obedient. Otherwise, we'll always find ourselves sitting between two stools."

Intellectually, I understood what he meant. But a group of "I"s was in resistance, in rebellion. Deep down, there was this persistent idea that he didn't love me, didn't care. As stupid and mechanical as I had observed that this was, it persisted. Therefore, I reasoned, I must not be seeing it on a deep enough level. But how to enter that level? I began to see that my wanting to see more deeply was a hindrance in itself inasmuch as the wanting came from my desire to be rid myself of these "I"s—and not to see them. This was quite a subtle point for me that had eluded me for many years.

I began to see, too, that the impressions and data that I had taken in through self-observation while, quite useful at the outset, had crystallized into a body of "knowledge" that became in itself an impediment to seeing. I had bought myself off in a way. I knew so much about these "I"s, their little gestures and games and pricklinesses, that the mechanical and unconscious feeling had formed that I didn't have any more to see—that I, as it were, had seen it.

I could talk at great length, and often did to those I would seduce or bully into listening to how these "I"s represented simply a transference from the physical to the spiritual father. I was of course mixing the teaching in with the concepts and language of ordinary mind-based psychology.

The stark fact was not so intellectually high blown. My emotional dwarfs were angry as hell. I was to have a relationship with Lord Pentland on their terms, and no other. They wanted a "personal relationship." But the more personal I tried to make it, the more Lord Pentland held the mirror up.

Another image came. It was after a meeting and Lord Pentland and Becky were talking in the hallway after a meeting. I was passing them by, in quite a self-conscious state, when he stopped me. He began speaking but then, in mid-sentence, suddenly turned to Becky.

"See?" he said like a doctor with a patient under an anesthesia. "Just a little attention, and he goes right to sleep."

I felt like a germ in a petri dish.

My observing all this with a totally notable lack of "results" once drove me to go to see Lord Pentland at his office. I had spoken about "this insistence I have to have a closer relationship with you."

It was humiliating to say this but I was desperate. Unexpectedly, he was quite kind. He nodded warmly and said, "Yes, Pat, this is very good what you have come to."

Emboldened, I continued. "I don't really know what the word 'relationship' means," I said. "But I don't feel we have a relationship. What I want to know is— is it necessary to have one for me to go forward in the Work?"

He hadn't answered directly. Instead, he traced my life for me. He pointed out all that had happened to me after I had joined he Work. "You married a fine woman," Lord Pentland said, "raised a family, held a job, and have been very successful in life."

"Yes, that's true," I answered, thinking of the state I was in when we had first met.

"But I don't think," he continued, his voice soft and resonating, "that you've put in question the relationship between a teacher and a student."

He had come right to the point and so effortlessly. "No," I said. "It's been so close to me I've never been able to really see it."

"The relationship…" there was a long pause. "It has to be *voluntary.*"

I saw in that moment with him that, yes, as much as one group of "I"s was crying to have a relationship with him—another group resisted it. And both were afraid to give him any power. For that power could be used against them, and they, both groups, felt that they had already suffered so much.

Yes, I had to give up the self-will that was behind both groups of "I"s. Surrender it voluntarily. Allow myself to be hurt. Otherwise, I could not be taught. That made the next step in our relationship impossible. Relationship was dynamic, not static. Surrender meant to remember, observe, not justify and, when the moment was right, in the interval, struggle against self-will. This struggle of the non-desires and the desires produces friction which, in turn, creates the necessary alchemical heat for the spiritual substances to coat the Kesdjan body.

It was incredible how things became so clear simply by being with him. It was as though his consciousness stimulated my own.

He went on to discuss self-remembering. "There are so many levels to self-remembering," he said. "The term is very fluid, if you know what I mean." I could feel this great wave of vibration coming to me. I could see the air and the aura about him.

"Initially," he continued, "I remember from memory. Self-remembering begins then as an idea. Later, it comes of itself as a certain taste, a sensation, a quality of being. But it only becomes real when I remember with the emotional center. Do you follow?"

We sat together for a time.

"Self-remembering and self-observation," Lord Pentland said, intuiting my question, "come together at some point. We only separate them in the beginning because all I can do then is to remember myself intellectually. The idea has to grow and that takes many years."

He stopped, and looked deeply into me.

"There comes a point in the Work when it is clear that 'I' do not remember myself. 'I am' remembers. But in coming to myself, I see with what I am identified. I am not seeing from the head but with the whole of myself. I think you have seen that self-remembering has an awakening power beyond anything that you might conceive or imagine."

Again, he stopped and observed me. I felt a fear in me rising. The fear of being taken over. I didn't fight with it, give it any energy. Instead, I ignored it, held my attention at a higher level and breathed deeply.

Lord Pentland continued: "I must separate consciousness from my sensitivity, this personal feeling of 'I' that I carry with me everywhere like some old shoebox.

Otherwise I am all the time getting hurt, if you know what I mean? Then perhaps I will see that I don't come and go from consciousness. Consciousness is a unity. It exists as a whole but it has degrees. As I pass from one state of being to another I am either ascending and actualizing higher and higher levels of being awake, of being related or...well, you know, I am personalizing everything, making a drama, descending into the muck. Do you follow?"

I had felt exposed, ridiculous. Even more so because on his desk was a lavender bag tied with a chartreuse ribbon. It was filled with hand-made chocolates. I knew he liked candy and had brought it as a gift. The bag was gaudy but I had been in a rush and didn't think it mattered. It was only when I'd entered his office, all rather plain and muted, that I saw what I was doing. The bag screamed in my hand. He had acknowledged it but hadn't taken it. The moment froze me to death. I had finally set it on the edge of his desk and sat down. At one point alluding to the question of relationship he had mentioned, "The Truth, you know, has no personal emotion in it." He didn't have to look at the bag.

Lord Pentland looked at his watch. "Well, Pat, we've been together upwards of two-and-a-half hours," he remarked. "I'm afraid I can't spare you any more time. I still have three group meetings to attend tonight."

He had given himself entirely to the Work. He practically had no time for himself. He had sacrificed, voluntarily, his personal life in order to give the Work to others. He seemed so immense, so noble, such a warrior. And yet he was misunderstood by many people. His mission was not only to enlarge the Work, but to preserve it, to protect it from popularization and the resulting distortion. To some people he seemed too severe, too austere, while to others these same qualities were what made him a remarkable man in the true Gurdjieffian sense of the word.

We got on the elevator together. I felt such deep respect for him for all that he had given me. I was going to say something. The elevator door shut. He stared at the buttons on the panel, as if he wasn't sure which one to press. It seemed as if he had gone completely to sleep. He fumbled around to such an extent that I almost told him, "Push lobby."

Finally, he pushed a button, smiling as if it were a great triumph. In an instant all my so-called deep feelings of respect evaporated.

I thought we would go our separate ways once we were outside, but he invited me to have dinner with him. We passed by a popular film for which people were lined up for blocks. "Becoming more like ants everyday, aren't we?" he said with a wry smile.

We had dinner at a Chinese restaurant on Third Avenue. He had ordered a dish called "The Buddha's Delight." He had spoken to me quite offhandedly, telling of having tea with Shunryu Suzuki Roshi and him having spilt his cup. "A lot of people I know don't think very much of him and neither did I for a time, but I think he is a great man," he said.

He said it in a way that suggested that he, Lord Pentland, was also a "great man."

True or not, I found his saying it absolutely distasteful.

The fact that a number of the vegetables of The Buddha's Delight were success-fully avoiding his determined effort to snare them with his chop sticks made my stomach almost turn.

Then he confided to me that having been in the Work such a very long time that…he looked at me imploringly, as if to ask if I could be trusted.

I watched myself, the robot, nodding. I made no judgment but there was an or-ganic revulsion at both myself and him.

"Aren't you getting a bit tired of the Work?" he asked. "I mean it was good in its day, perhaps, but now that Gurdjieff is gone—what's really the point, you know?"

I made no reply.

He ended the tussle between his chop sticks and his vegetables by putting his sticks down and, his large frame bending toward me, saying in a low heretical voice, as if not to be repeated to anyone—"God knows I'm tired of it."

OVER A LATE NIGHT DINNER WITH BARBARA, I TOLD HER WHAT HAD HAP-PENED with my father on his deathbed and later asking for a sign and seeing the three rainbows. She said nothing, but I felt her dismissal, even anger. The events I described, like many I had in Ireland, were too removed from her experience. She had yet to experience the shift from the physical to the subtle and symbolic worlds, the mythological and archetypal. So it all seemed a little fantastic. Just a lot of imagination.

"But he was in a coma!" she finally told me.

"The last thing to go was his hearing. That's what the nurse said."

"That doesn't prove he heard you."

"He was aware of me. His head moved in my direction. And a tear came from his eye."

"It doesn't prove it."

"No," I said. "But I could feel it."

Barbara remained skeptical. The candlelight was flickering. She was as beau-tiful as ever. The long swan-like neck, the Modigliani face, the sense of reserve and proportion. But there was a fear, too. She had once told me of looking out the window into the fog and "there being nothing" and that deep-down that was what she felt about the world—that there was nothing beyond the physical plane. Only the void.

"Babe, there are worlds and worlds below and above us. Even inside us. Remember what Lord Pentland said when I returned from Ireland? That he was interested in this 'peculiar Irish streak of knowing you are going on an adventure before you go.'"

She sat listening, not wanting to argue.

"He told me, 'Many are called and few are chosen.'"

"But he said, too, that he didn't mean that in 'any pious way.'"

"Right. That's right."

I refilled her glass with chardonnay, mine with Bordeaux. I knew what she was saying: don't let it go to your head.

"Look," I pleaded, "there's nothing special to this. At times of great danger or death of a loved one, some strong emotional shock—it can happen. The mind just stops. You're there. There's only consciousness. No mind filters. No self-pity. No fear."

"Didn't Lord Pentland once tell you—'You're very perceptive but you have too much imagination?'"

"Yeah." Why did we always get stopped here?

"Well…?"

"That was a long time ago."

"Not that long ago."

The space between us was like a stone. She in her chair, me in mine, both eating without speaking. Deep down, I felt this sense of futility. Why had she married me? Why couldn't we communicate about what mattered most to me? I wanted to tell her about a book I'd read, Henry Corbin's *Creative Imagination*.

"Look," I finally said, putting my knife and fork down, "there are different types of imagination. Most are just exalted or diminished dreams. Creative imagination is different. It sees and makes connections. It doesn't create in terms of fabricating. It creates the bridge between 'worlds', between the physical, psychic and spiritual."

Barbara went on silently eating, listening and not listening, pretending she wasn't there. We'd been 'here' so many times before. Why was it always the same?

"Barbara—why don't you say something?"

"You're shouting."

"You're goddamn right I'm shouting! You're ignoring me…Okay, so I don't say it just the way you'd like to hear it. And I shout. I'm sorry. But the point is I'm trying to communicate with you, tell you how I feel, what I experience. You always shut down. Why is that?"

She nodded her head but said nothing. She took the plates away and from the kitchen asked—"Do you want dessert? I've made a cherry pie."

"Okay, sure." Cherry and rhubarb were my favorites. She was a great cook. She was always experimenting, taking chances. But, I thought, it stopped at the kitchen door. I got up and went to the kitchen.

"Babe," I said softly, "can you imagine seeing three rainbows, one right after the other?"

She was cutting the pie. She looked up. But said nothing. She put wedges of the pie on plates.

"You know, I'd begun to doubt, too," I said.

She nodded and handed me a plate and we returned to the table. I poured myself another glass of Bordeaux. I had to talk to her.

"The rainbow, it's a symbol. It was a covenant between God and Noah."

She didn't reply.

Was it all association? What had happened—my Father's death, his will where he talked about "looking for the rainbow," the three rainbows I'd seen from the airplane—it was me who was seeing the connections, the hidden meanings. Was it real? Or was I projecting all this? Had my experience been imagination? Had the synchronicity, the "magic causality," been just another form of sleep?

I watched as the shadows danced on the walls like old ghosts. Outside a car roared down the street, its wheels screeching as it came to a sudden turn. The silverware gleamed on the white tablecloth. The moment hung in space. What was projection? It was when you forced yourself on the moment rather than letting it "speak" to you.

Barbara's face looked longer, withdrawn. As if she was there yet not there. Fear had put her asleep. Blanked her out. Her defense was to pretend she didn't exist, I didn't exist, that this wasn't happening...

"You don't fucking believe me, do you!" I shouted.

I was holding the fork between the thumb and forefinger, pointing it at her. She went on eating. Hiding. Being invisible. I looked down at the fork in my hand. I had gripped it so hard it had bent at the neck.

"Pat!" she cried.

"I'm sorry. I'll buy you a new one, huh?"

"That's not the point."

She cleared the dishes. I poured two Armagnacs, the cut crystal flashing in the candle light. Why the hell did she always resist looking at the world a little differently! I downed the Armagnac and poured another.

"What are you doing out there?" I called, exasperated.

"I'm coming, all right!"

A lot of barking. Sounded like that paranoid policeman's German shepherd. It must have spied a cat or some night creature. A lot of chasing, nails digging into the pavement, trying to grip on a sharp turn. I turned and looked out the side window. Our neighbor's house was dark. Tom and Mary were probably at a church bingo game. Barbara finally returned to the table.

"Remember Mary telling us she thought we were into black magic because we burned candles at dinner?"

"Yes, that was funny."

"Too much church, huh? Heavy on the good and evil."

"Well, don't you see Stanley that way?"

I had to think about that. "Yeah, you're probably right. It's hard to see someone when you're in a war with him." I'd finished the pie and went to the kitchen to cut another piece. Barbara was finishing hers. When I returned she said:

"You were brought up with a heavy dose of black-and-white thinking. Your mother can't accept any blame. She always takes the 'white side'."

"She can't help it. She doesn't see herself at all. Her father quite literally put the fear of God into her. But she's really noble and brave. Look at the way she acted at the funeral and her insisting on living down there all alone."

"She's always been very protective of her relationship with you," Barbara said softly, not looking up.

"Yes. But good-hearted."

"To some people."

"Well…the problem is you can't tell her anything."

"She's never accepted her part in what happened with your sister."

"No. Not at all."

"She's so self-righteous."

"Her dark side, all those negative 'I's—they just take her over."

"Your sister got all the dark side."

"Yeah, I got all the light side. She had a total belief in me. And she bought me everything. Raised me like a rich man's son."

"Like a king."

"Yeah, like a king…" I'd never thought of it that way, but it was true.

"Pat, don't lean back in the chair like that. Okay?" Her voice was sharp, controlled.

"I like to sit this way."

"Yes, but it ruins the legs. They all squeak now. You ruined all your mother's chairs that way."

"C'mon."

"She told me. Why will you never do anything you're told?"

"Jesus, save me." I sat up, reluctantly. "Women!"

"Are you going to talk to Lord Pentland about what happened with your father?"

"I don't know. I wrote him a letter in Florida telling him about my Father and what happened," I said. "Of course, your letter to him about Sarah…"

"Yes, it was really hard to write. I thought he would talk to me about it, but all I got was a reprimand. Sometimes it seems like the women teachers have more empathy when it comes to understanding how a woman feels."

"You don't think he understands women?"

"Well, he's very male. You think he still has something to work out with women?"

I shrugged. "Most men seem to."

"Do you understand women?"

"To the anima." I raised my glass of Armagnac. "Ever mysterious. She shows me what I am and am not."

Barbara toasted. And we blew out the candles, cleared the table, and went to bed.

The next day I sent Lord Pentland another letter, this time enclosing a photo of *The Petitioner* which I had retitled *The End of a Time*. At the following meeting, Lord Pentland gave no indication he had received my letters. Maybe he thought I should come to him directly. I wanted to, but I hesitated. I still remembered his "Pure nonsense!" reply to my telling him about the "sound." Perhaps he had been testing me? Or maybe thought that I had come to it too soon. I knew if I talked to him about my Father's death and if he played games or denied what I had experienced then I might even leave the Work. So I said nothing.

At the next meeting Lord Pentland announced that the group would divide up into study groups to meet separately outside and sometime in the Spring give a report. Barbara and I were assigned to the group studying the Food Diagram. At the end of the meeting he walked out, apparently forgetting his jacket. I noticed several letters sticking out from the inside coat pocket. Those were my letters. I knew it. He wanted me to bring him his jacket. He was giving me an excuse to see him. But why the hell didn't he just talk to me! Why couldn't he drop "the teacher." I stood frozen in anger staring at those letters. Okay, he was the teacher—he wanted me to come to him. I had set it up the other way by writing the letters. I was doing the manipulating. But not intentionally. Or was I? Okay, I would get the damn jacket! It was too late. Someone else took it to him.

The following week the lecture series at the Foundation began. The room was packed. Lord Pentland came down the aisle but acted as though he had forgotten something. He left the room. When he returned, he mounted the platform hesitantly, nearly tripping on the antique Persian rug that covered its surface. He had seemed uncertain as to which of the two chairs on the platform he should take. Beside one of the chairs was a small table with two glasses of ice water. He finally took that chair, almost knocking over one of the glasses. He shifted about in his seat, apparently unable to find a comfortable position. He inspected his dark suit for lint and several times brushed each arm. He smiled, self-conscious and somewhat embarrassed, like a man who has misplaced his door key. Finally, he searched the audience of some three hundred Work people horseshoed around the platform, his long neck furtively craning forward, trying to locate a certain face. When Dr. Welch mounted the platform, he nodded and sat back.

Dr. Welch was a broad, solid-looking man, tanned and square-jawed, ruggedly handsome, with thick, straight silver hair and glasses. A mid-Westerner turned New Yorker, he had the bearing and assurance of a tank commander, one who is used to power. And when he spoke his deep baritone voice and strong analytical mind only increased this feeling of command which he emanated. A trustee of the Foundation, he was the American doctor Gurdjieff had asked for in his final days. Of Gurdjieff's death Dr. Welch had said, "He died like a king." He, along with Lord Pentland and a handful of other teachers, led the Tuesday evening lectures and discussions.

Tonight was the first in the series of Fall lectures and apparently it had been agreed that Lord Pentland was to speak first, for several times Dr. Welch had glanced at him, but Lord Pentland had taken no notice. Finally, Dr. Welch had uncrossed his arms, cleared his throat and began exploring the theme, "The Idea and Experience of Aim." Characteristically, Dr. Welch considered each of the significant terms of the theme and then began probing it with a long series of questions elucidating various aspects of the question—"In essence does the idea and experience differ? How do I come to having a sincere aim? Does this aim change or does it remain the same? How do I stay awake to my aim? How does aim influence me? Who is it that has aim?" He went on in this manner for ten minutes or so and then checked his watch. He quickly and artfully wrapped up his talk then crossed his legs and took a glass of water from the table. He sat back and waited for Lord Pentland to begin.

But Lord Pentland seemed to be dreaming. Several times Dr. Welch glanced at him but his look was not returned. Lord Pentland, who always listened attentively, had appeared preoccupied during Dr. Welch's exposition and several times still seemed to be searching the audience for that face. When Dr. Welch stopped, he was caught unprepared. I had never seen Lord Pentland like this. I hadn't seen him since the summer recess in June. Was his age catching up with him? The heart attack? Perhaps his pacemaker wasn't working properly? I could hardly look. The impression was too painful: my teacher asleep! Lord Pentland sat there like some dunce.

And when he began to speak, it was even worse. He began by examining the question of aim from the ordinary viewpoint, but then switched abruptly to the Work's standpoint, then back again, mixing up ordinary aim with conscious aim, floundering, hesitating, making jerky body movements. Several times Dr. Welch looked at the odd figure beside him with some concern. This was not the Lord Pentland he knew. The sense of oddity spread through the big room. People moved uneasily in their chairs, coughed. The more he spoke, the more uncomfortable everyone became, the thought staring us in the face: Lord Pentland was asleep. This was the man Gurdjieff had referred to as his "St. Paul" and had appointed to head up the Work in America. He had been President of The Gurdjieff Foundation since the early 1950's, had selected this building for purchase, opened other centers around the country; and for most people in the room, certainly the young people, he was the living embodiment of the Work. And now lurching around up there on the platform was this bad joke, this poor sad mechanical man. Lord Pentland rattled on, the idiocy increasing. The big hall grew deathly silent. Dr. Welch's brow knitted. He folded his arms and stared into the Persian rug. No one looked at the platform. It was as though the enormity of the living unmistakable fact had stopped everyone's mind.

It was then, just when that moment reached its height, that Lord Pentland suddenly stopped speaking. He was in mid-sentence. For a split second he looked into his hands cupped in his lap and then he looked up. Some change had taken place. Slowly, without expression, looking from left to right, he took the measure of the audience. There was a smile then. Small though it was, it radiated throughout the large hall, changing its solidity, lifting the vibration. He again looked through the faces in the room. It was if he were taking our temperature. Then he sighed and swallowed, and with his head halfcocked turned with an inquisitive expression to Dr. Welch. The two "old dogs" exchanged a secret smile. *Lord Pentland had been acting a role!*

He had talked about aim as a man would who had no aim. His words did not match his being. He demonstrated the lying and distraction, the broken octaves, that go on all the time. And he showed, too, how culpable we all are. And the teaching he gave did not come cheaply. For he had opened himself to one terrible massive impression—that of three hundred people united in a single heavy thought—*Lord Pentland was senile.* To register the force of that. To absorb the friction. Not to identify. Voluntarily, to have taken on that degree of conscious labor and intentional suffering, and submit to it all in public. Well, when he spoke now it was in another manner and tempo altogether and *this* was an entirely different "Lord Pentland."

"I daresay," stated Lord Pentland, his body perfectly erect and relaxed, his voice barely above a whisper but filling the hall, "that these impressions have probably been a distraction. They've put us into our heads. Unless, that is, we have really been listening. For the aim is aimless...it is, and can only be, in this very moment. The impressions we receive capture us, if we say 'I' to them. And then, of course, we have a whole host of 'aims'...The mind needs to be quiet for the attention to come into the body. This will change the quality of our energy, bring us to presence. We listen from there, expand from there. All else is to be asleep, aimless. Do you follow...?"

Discussion was now to begin. But the shock he had delivered was so full. There were only a few perfunctory questions, mostly by new people, and the evening ended. Lord Pentland and Dr. Welch stood. They dismounted and strode down the aisle. Lord Pentland was in the lobby talking to some of the older people as I came out. I thought of waiting to speak with him about the letters I'd written to him, but I passed on out the door.

LORD PENTLAND HANDED ME A SQUARE WHITE ENVELOPE MADE OF STURDY and expensive paper—"It's one of the original invitations," he said.

I open the envelope. There is a white card, inscribed in calligraphy. My name is on it and that of someone named 'Charles Fort'.

"But I don't want to leave," I cry.

"I'm afraid you'll have to." Lord Pentland is sitting next to the window in a large Queen Ann chair. He gestures broadly with his hands. "You see, there's nothing to be done."

"But I—"

"I'm afraid it's not a question of what you or I want, if you see what I mean?"

"You mean...you mean—it's fate?" I ask.

He nods slowly, impassively.

Earlier, Dick Brower, a group leader and business associate of Lord Pentland's and a business colleague, had taken me to hear a psychologist and storyteller turned karma yogi and then to a Hindu swami with many psychic powers. I hadn't been impressed. Dick then had taken me to a brownstone. We had climbed several flights to a third floor apartment. It was familiar to me but I couldn't say why. He opened the door and there was Lord Pentland sitting by the window...

I reread the invitation. I want to cry. I feel such love for Lord Pentland, for all that he and the Work have done for me. I don't want to leave him. He is my teacher. But I realize there is nothing to be done. It isn't my decision.

A sense of responsibility comes—of my having to go on, and to make the best of it.

It is then I realize that I am in a dream, that all this is happening on another plane entirely. I have to remember the name, so I keep repeating it to myself—"Charles Fort, Charles Fort!"

I'd awakened with the name of "Charles Fort" on my lips. At first I had no idea who he was, but as the day went on I thought he might be a writer. I went to a local bookstore. The clerk told me I would find his books under science fiction. I hated science fiction. The only such book I had ever read that I liked was Arthur C. Clarke's *Childhood's End*. Stanley, of all people, had recommended it. I found Fort and pulled out a book. My heart sank at seeing the title—*Book of the Damned*. Was I going to hell? My hands were shaking, but I soon gathered that the "damned" weren't people but absurd facts (like frogs falling from the sky) that science scoffed at, since it had no explanation for why such things happened. Fort was long dead. How did all this relate to me? I couldn't see it. But it planted the idea in me that perhaps at sometime I would leave the Work.

I'd had this dream about the time that Barbara and I had been accepted into the Foundation. This was nearly three-and-a-half years after we had attended preparatory meetings at the Gallery. Was I really meant to leave the Work? I didn't want to leave. It was my life. But something had changed between Lord Pentland and me. I knew I'd come to a major crossroad. If he was my teacher, then I had to submit to him, be obedient, not willful. Intellectually I understood that. I didn't resist it. Yet there was this impasse between us, something unspoken that needed to be said, before I could make such a commitment. But it was too deep. I couldn't put words to it. And he wasn't waiting. Or so it seemed.

I spoke in a meeting about an exercise he had given us.

"It's time you quit working in a formatory way," Lord Pentland declared. "The ego can't give the exercise. You must sit first, connect the centers and then foresee, using the instinctive or emotional center, exactly when and where you will be present."

At another meeting: "There is a danger of discovering a knowledge too soon, when one isn't adequately prepared, when one has no sound basis, no real being, with which to support this new knowledge...when one, let us say, is opened to knowledge 'prematurely.'" Though Lord Pentland didn't say this directly to me, the words fit.

At another—"The trouble with the work is that it works. The results make people prematurely independent," observed Lord Pentland. Again an answer to someone else, but to me as well.

Then came a Tuesday night lecture whose theme was "The Nature of the Formatory Mind and the Need for an Exact Language." Lord Pentland sat alone on the small platform. The large hall, as usual, was completely filled. He was wearing a dark sportcoat with a white business shirt open at the neck; since his heart attack he had a pacemaker and seldom wore a tie. He hitched up the creases of his trousers, cupped his hands in his lap and seemed to totally empty out. It was as though he had collapsed his personality like an umbrella and laid it aside. Then, having slowly regarded the audience, he began to speak. His voice was modulated, rarely emphasizing a word, making no effort to project himself, entertain or captivate. And yet within a few words he had the whole room in his hands.

He began by noting that "we tend to act on our impulses because we are afraid our formatory mind will destroy the impulse with its reason. The formatory mind isn't the real mind at all but one that is forever formulating opinions, attitudes, conclusions, forever talking and imagining. It lives by rote and feeds off the energies of the other centers. The formatory mind has no energy of its own. It is a kind of parasite."

He paused, letting that sink in, and then when everyone's attention was ready, he resumed—

"Mr. Gurdjieff," he declared, "likened the formatory mind to that of 'a secretary'. If she would limit herself to her job, all would be fine. But she insists on intercepting all incoming communications and labeling and confusing everything."

Close to the platform, sitting on a pillow, I noticed Isabel looking like she wanted to speak. She had been in the Work perhaps twenty years. She had stopped growing somehow. She only heard what she wanted to hear. She had a hard shell around her. Rather fearless and strong-willed, she was used to getting her own way. An artist, she always fashioned herself with a dramatic look. Her skin was pale and perfect, her eyes dark, luminous and her short black hair was close cropped and curled in tight ringlets. It was a style out of the 1920's. Somehow, she was always a little out of synch.

I could see Lord Pentland's use of the word "secretary" had caught her. As soon as the lecture was opened up to questions, she immediately asked:

"Lord Pentland—couldn't we use some metaphor other than 'secretary' for the formatory mind?"

He took a moment before answering. I felt as if he was sounding out the depth of her question. It had seemed so innocent but, in fact, it was loaded. Feminism had had its effect on the Work. Some women questioned Gurdjieff's ideas as being too masculine.

Finally, he responded: "The real trouble is not the metaphor 'secretary,' but that the emperor is *all* clothes." Having thus shifted the discussion from the formatory mind to the subject of personality, Lord Pentland went on to make many interesting distinctions between personality and false personality. But I could see by Isabel's face and posture that she was having none of it.

"Thank you," Isabel replied, "but could you answer my question on a more practical level? Specifically, Lord Pentland, what I am asking is this—could some other word be used for the formatory mind than 'secretary'?"

"Computer." Lord Pentland spat the word out quickly, and turned away. Everyone laughed.

Others asked questions. All on other aspects of the topic. It was as if she had not spoken. But I felt she had raised an interesting point. For as Gurdjieff was conscious, then his language was exact. If he had used the word "secretary" to describe the formatory mind, it must be exact and have many levels of meaning. I felt he had meant that the formatory mind was passive, not active in a real way. And therefore it had no energy of its own, no life of its own. But as he had been born and raised in an Armenian and Greek society that was heavily masculine, one that in many ways denigrated the female, was there a possibility that he might not be entirely objective on this point?

Near the meeting's end, Mrs. Dooling asked a question concerning the exact use of language. Her question didn't mention the word "secretary," but it was clear it was that to which she was referring. She was an older teacher in the Work, a generation after Lord Pentland's. She had sharp chiseled features, more handsome than beautiful, and striking blue eyes. She was not a woman easily "cowed."

Lord Pentland spoke at some length but his answer didn't meet the question. Mrs. Dooling sat stone-faced and unsatisfied. Alongside her sat two other teachers of that generation, Mrs. Flinsch and Mrs. Pierce. I sensed they were unsatisfied as well. Finally Mrs. Pierce, her eyesight fading and her body a bit bent, spoke up, her words ringing out in the big hall—"What we are asking Lord Pentland is about the use of the word 'secretary'. It is a word that has many associations that may not be altogether exact."

The question hung in space, the room exploding in stillness. Lord Pentland seemed visibly upset. In all these years I had never seen him once publicly challenged by an older teacher.

He clasped his hands together and stared into them for a great while. The room was charged with electricity. Finally, he turned toward the two women teachers and threw up his left hand, as if waving them off, his manner as emphatic as his voice—

"I daresay I believe I can speak for fifty percent or more of the people here when I say I think we have said enough about this particular subject. It is time to move on."

He turned away abruptly, looking to the opposite side of the room. A few more perfunctory questions and the evening ended. I didn't understand: if this was a lecture and discussion, how could any serious question be put out of bounds? It bothered me all week. At the next group meeting I brought up Isabel's question and told him I felt that he had not answered it—

"I'm sorry, but I found myself with 'the other' fifty percent in the room," I said.

It was the first time I had ever openly challenged him. I was looking for clarification. But it was still a criticism.

He acknowledged what I said, pondered a moment and then answered, his voice very soft: "We must see where questions come from, whether they come from the higher or lower parts of our centers. We need to learn to recognize that. We have to see the source of the question. And also keep in view the context in which the question is being asked." He paused and addressed everyone. "The unity of the group comes first in any meeting. Some subjects are very delicate and the different levels of maturity within a group make communication about them next to impossible."

I didn't disagree with him, but I wasn't satisfied.

I recalled what Erich Neumann, a disciple of Jung's, had discussed in his book, *Psyche and Amour*. He maintained that men, so mental to begin with, had to come into their feelings to become whole. It was just the reverse for women. They were centered in their feelings. A woman's path, then, was to develop the mind.

"I'm sorry, Lord Pentland, but I have to persist. Your answer isn't meeting my question."

"Persistence is a sign of identification," he shot back. His eyes moved around the room and came back to mine. "You know, we are not alone. We are surrounded by many energies, by many powerful thought forms. We have to watch that they don't take us over." He paused and added. "I don't mean to intimidate you but— 'As you sow, so shall you reap'."

It was a warning. That couldn't be mistaken. He had put the subject off limits. He had never done that before. What was it about gender and the formatory mind? He had said several times over the years that in regards to the Work, "The women were a good twenty years ahead of the men." He had never explained what he meant by that. I supposed it was that women were more in touch with their feelings, were less conceptual, intellectual; perhaps had less false personality. Yet I recalled his saying, too, that in Ouspensky's book *In Search of The Miraculous,* when the question of aim is spoken of it was Madame Ouspensky who had said she wanted to be "master of myself." Originally, Ouspensky had written "mistress of myself," for that was how his wife put it. However, in reviewing the manuscript, Ouspensky had changed it, so, as Lord Pentland said, "It would be objective." Did that mean that real I, or its orientation, was masculine? The female principle is often associated with the earth and moon. The masculine is normally associated with the planetary world and the sun. In the Gurdjieff teaching, man is divided into five centers: the thinking, emotional, moving, instinctive and sexual (though there is also a higher thinking and higher emotional center which we normally don't hear and feel). Each center is spread throughout the entire body but has a specific area of gravity; for the thinking "center," the location is the brain; the emotional, the solar plexus; the moving and instinctive, the spinal cord. And each is composed of two parts: affirmative and negative, a "yes" and a "no." There isn't any mention of the centers having either male or female orientation. But it is clear that Gurdjieff sees the essence of man as being active; that of the female as being passive. He speaks of the unawakened mind as being "half-passive." The passive is the formatory. It is spoken of as the mechanical part of the thinking center, that which registers impressions; Gurdjieff had likened it to a "secretary," Ouspensky to a "card index." If it directly registered impressions, if it were actively-passive, it would function properly; helping further refine energy to make the connection to the higher emotional and thinking centers. Instead, the formatory mind takes itself for the authority in all matters. It weighs, labels and judges all impressions, internal and external, by means of memory. In this wrong functioning it is highly dualistic, immediately dividing everything into two parts. Then it compares and contrasts, running out long strings of association, taking things to extremes. It is a fount of cliches and ready-made opinion. Among its many peculiarities, it always looks for the opposite. If "black" is being discussed, it brings up "white." Staying on the surface in this way, it avoids penetrating deeply into a subject. All this it calls "thinking." I felt there was a lot to discuss here but the door had been shut. I felt, too, since my Father's death, and even before, a growing interest in the feminine principle, the anima. It was slowly becoming a prevalent thought form in society certainly, but I also sensed in myself a new movement to contact a more subtle region. I kept going around and around about this. Was this real? Or was I being taken in by a thought form? Was I developing another "I"?

Meanwhile, our study group began discussing the Food Diagram. Gurdjieff had taught that the body takes in three foods: physical food, air and impressions. These are processed through the factory of the body, the coarser becoming finer, up to the degree of being-Exioëhary, or sperm. The conscious processing of these foods is integral to the creation of the Kesdjan body. As with the gospel study group, this group soon got bogged down in words and definitions. And, as before, I decided to make my own experiment.

Instead of going out to lunch with my friends in the office, I began eating alone at the YMCA cafeteria. First, I would relax the face and come to a sensation of the body sitting in a chair, breathing and directing my attention to the places of gravity. Only then would I eat the food with the aim of doing so consciously. There were so many impressions…The muscles of the arm as I reached for a bottle of soda. The weight of the bottle as I brought it to my lips. The taste and volume of food in my mouth and the movement down through the throat and into the stomach. And, time and again, the instinctual center rumbled. It wanted to eat. Period. But to involve another center, I had to eat slowly. Gurdjieff had spoken of "the struggle between the non-desires and the desires." I had always seen it in a more elaborate context.

I spoke about this in the group meeting. For the first time in many meetings, Lord Pentland seemed pleased.

"You may have to drink a soda a hundred times before you connect with a finer energy," he said. "If you want to see something, do more of it. Seeing only with the head doesn't give any result, of course. The other centers have to be involved."

He looked to Becky to see if she had anything to add. She did not. I opened my mouth to say something but before I could utter the words, Lord Pentland spoke— as it were, right into my open mouth.

"We can't remember ourselves. We can only make ourselves available. We can only be ready so that when the shock comes and the forces separate, we are there for it. Then we are remembered."

He glanced around the room. "Many of us probably think of real will as having a master, a deputy steward, within us. The notion of a chain of command. But real will comes from having our centers in the right order. From out of this totality will appear then another will—God's Will."

He swallowed in that slow, unnerving way. But I had done as he suggested. I was aligned differently and so I met the impression rightly and it had an entirely different effect.

"Did you notice the change in tension?" His voice was very low. But I heard it without straining.

"Yes. There is a different quality to it," I answered.

"The tension is ordinarily in personality. When we are not in personality, we become aware of a different tension. One that is no longer mechanical. Do you follow?"

I made no outer response.

"You might try sensing the spine at the same time you are eating," he said.

"Of course, it could be too much at this point." He paused. "I think not."

Later, at the close of the meeting, Lord Pentland stood up to leave, but then sat back down. He bent forward toward the group, as if he were going to confide a secret to us:

"You know, we have been speaking here about service and breath and the creation of a second body, one that will survive the death of the natural body. In earlier days, I daresay, one would normally have to perform menial labor for twenty years or more before it was felt they were mature enough. But the tempo of the times has changed so dramatically. There is not all that much time left. We are in a decisive interval and energies must be consciously assimilated or, I'm afraid, we are in for a long descending octave."

I began to wonder if the question of ascent and descent of man could be seen in terms of God and Lucifer. The Angel of Light, Lucifer couldn't stomach bowing to God's creation, this pitiful clay idiot, Man. Refusing, he fell; no longer able to support that level of vibration. An egotistical act, a sin, perhaps, but it wasn't evil. Only later when Lucifer as a serpent tempts Eve and Adam, when he actively and willfully opposes God's creation, does he become Satan. Testing, provoking and tempting souls like Job's, his intention is to deflect and corrupt them, to enlist them in his service. Satan's role is primal. As such, no soul discerns his presence until it matures in its travel along the inner archetypal path. Known as *Iblis* in Sufism, he is seen by some sects as the tragic lover, eternally separated from his Beloved, stationed at the gate, protecting his Beloved from the impure. His essence is said to be imagination, both that which allows the conceiving and experiencing of the Beloved and also that which obscures and defends it with a net of illusions. This most imaginative of all archetypes may become very concrete in the days to come. In his *Answer to Job,* Jung reveals a lot about the function of Satan, believing that in the order of things, just as God took the shape and form of Jesus, overshadowing his human side, so Satan will one day take flesh on earth.

However that may be, what Jung strongly counsels is that all the archetypes are within each of us. They are not exterior. We only project them out onto the world when we have not psychologically differentiated them in ourselves. They are ordering principles primarily. Only secondarily are they reflected as energies. We experience them as moods and predilections, but at a higher level of discrimination we see them as "I"s. When a person comes to his magnetic center, when his desire for consciousness breaks through, then the real game begins. As in *The Art of Asha,* the forces of Ahura Mazda, the Creator, contend with those of Ahriman, the Destroyer.

Carrying this line of thought to another level, I began to see how deep and creative had been Gurdjieff's understanding. What he called the "Messengers from Above" had always manifested the side of Ahura Mazda. But Gurdjieff maintained there were two ends to a stick. If he took the good end, that only left the bad end for his students. So, with sublime crazy wisdom, outwardly he took the side of Ahriman, the path of blame, stepping on corns, provoking, tempting and ridiculing the imaginary "I." Perhaps it was the increasing gravity of the situation on Earth, the enormity of the deviation from traditional values, that had Gurdjieff take the role not of a saint or sage, but the most dangerous of all roles—Beelzebub.

Gurdjieff maintained that man was part of organic life, the mechanical functioning of which transmitted needed radiations to the moon to aid in its development, the creating of an atmosphere. But this function no longer needed to be fulfilled. The moon, an unborn planet, was warming. Its degree of development made this transmission no longer necessary. On this level mankind, like the animal and vegetable kingdoms, had outlived its usefulness to Nature. (Which was why, perhaps, we were seeing so many animal and plant species becoming extinct.) Unlike animals and plants, man had possibility. Man was a self-developing organism, the new seed. Through conscious labors and intentional suffering, man might transform himself to a higher level of being and objectivity. Not all could achieve a new level of being, that was law. But those who did would be the seed of a new life whose sole purpose was not the pursuit of power and riches but of consciousness. If conditions on earth made this impossible, then man might one day have the vision and will to leave all earthly identifications behind and seek a new home on the moon or some other planet.

In any case—the situation was stark. Man's mechanical role as a part of organic life had been fulfilled. Man was free now either to choose to voluntarily work to awaken and ascend in consciousness—thus making himself capable of fulfilling the role destined for him on the level of the Sun. Or, the experiment called "Man" would end. As in Aldous Huxley's *Ape and Essence,* he would lose his essence and become subhuman, descending to the level of the bestial and inevitably blow himself to kingdom come.

There are some people who step into our lives so suddenly, so unexpectedly, so intimately, that from the outset there is the recognition that the supposedly chance meeting is beyond the ordinary or accidental.

So it had been with Jane, a wealthy Englishwoman married and in her mid-fifties, whom I had first met the year before in Washington, D.C., only a few month's after my Father's death. I had given a speech at a hotel that was hosting a foodservice convention. Afterward, waiting for a cab a squat, burly, coal-black cabby threw open his back door and told me—"Get in!"

As it was an order, not a request, I at first resisted. I looked into the backseat and could see a figure, though whether it was man or woman I couldn't make out. For a split-second I had the impression that this was not a cab but a horse-drawn carriage. Drawing closer, I now saw in the backseat a woman's form. For a moment I had an odd sense that she was a queen in her carriage, the ape-like cabbie her footman. I opened the door. My first image was of light brown shoes, the tips having an intricate Grecian maze design. I was reminded of the legend of the Minotaur.

"Hello there!" a very cultivated English voice rang out. "Please get in."

I smiled and sat down beside her. She was dressed in beige wool slacks and a short mink jacket. She had intelligent, fearless dark eyes.

"Tell me," the woman asked, "is this how they do it in the States?"

"I guess when the cabs are in short supply they double you up. They don't give you a choice."

"No choice," she teased. "Really now? Well, hello there. My name is Jane."

It seemed even then that this was no chance meeting. For many months I'd been sailing along on a great gust of good fortune, the magazine having won a major journalism award, and now I'd been invited to give the keynote speech at a foodservice conference. I had decided to do as Lord Pentland did in the group meetings—not immediately speak. I wondered what the effect would be. And so when I mounted the podium in the ballroom, I just stood there. Everyone hushed. Still, I remained silent. The audience became very still. It was as though my mind and theirs had been joined in the very same spatial moment of time. I felt flooded with the power of their attention. As the moment grew in the silence I felt their expectation turning to insistence, a thin edge of violence underneath. I felt naked. My body quivered with energy. My mind rang with commands to speak. I felt every breath. The moment kept opening. I felt paralyzed. I breathed deeply, summoning all my strength and resolve, and watched as slowly, deliberately, my neck and head began to move millimeter-by-millimeter, traveling in an arc from right to left, taking in each section of the audience. The movement seemed to galvanize the audience's attention, increasing its vibration.

The normal feeling of "I," of being in the physical body, wasn't there any more. There was only this strong overwhelming impression of movement…movement in a still field of consciousness. I was just nearing the end of turning my head when the impression of consciousness became so singular and awesome that it shot me straight out of the body. That is, my center of gravity was no longer in the body.

At some point I found my consciousness back in the body and my vocal chords moving. I'd begun the speech on automatic pilot, the moving part of the intellectual center taking over. There'd been this gap, this blank, where I'd been disconnected completely from the subject-object world. Not in the sense of having become lost in a thought or emotion, but more like a sequence of missing frames in a film. I had realized this only when I returned to find "Patterson" giving a speech. The separation between this awareness and "Patterson" was such that for a time, like the audience I perceived in front of the podium, this person "Patterson" was only another object in the field of my awareness. This was no identification, no personal relationship, no psychology.

I was to catch a plane back to New York that evening. After the speech, I'd planned to go back to the National Gallery of Art. I wanted to see those paintings of women at the Freer. I'd had the intuition something would happen to me there. At breakfast an unusual looking young girl had caught my eye in the hotel coffee shop. She was dressed in gypsy garb and seemed a bit crazed. Girding her waist was a thick black belt with a large golden belt buckle. It was emblazoned with the head of a Greek goddess, probably Aphrodite, which stood out from the buckle like the prow on old ships. I had immediately sensed she was "a sign." The anima in some new way was about to enter my life. I'd been to the National Gallery the day before and had been taken with Robert Cole's *Voyage of Life* and a haunting depiction of Christ on the cross, one that was both harshly realistic and yet ecstatic and mystical, a blending of brutality, beauty and faith, by a sixteenth century German painter I had never heard of before, Matthias Grunewald. I had felt that my life was about to take some new turn.

Later, I had gone to the Freer Gallery and been captivated by a room full of Thomas Dewing's portraits of women. Very simple, turn-of-the-century studies of women reading, knitting, writing letters, playing the piano, preparing a meal—they were all engaged in very ordinary activities. They were easy to pass by. It was almost as if they weren't there. There was nothing exaggerated; the viewpoint was neither horrific nor idealized. The colors were quiet, harmonious. They spoke to me in some uncanny way I couldn't put in words. I kept going around the room, looking from painting to painting, wondering what it was that I was seeing. Then in the coffee shop seeing the crazed gypsy with the Aphrodite belt buckle the feeling of expectancy became even stronger. But nothing had happened.

Then having given the speech, experimented and struggled against my fears, the premonition I'd had manifested. I'd glided out of the hotel lobby on a stream of energy and this cabby had ordered—"Get in!"

As it turned out, the woman I'd gotten in the cab with was going to the National Gallery as well. We talked breezily all the way. She had been around the world several times. Her husband manufactured glassware and had factories in South Africa and Australia, as well as England. There had been a feeling of instant camaraderie, but I didn't want to impose myself on her and so once in the gallery I said goodbye and went on. But the feeling kept coming: I really wanted to get to know this woman—I had never met anyone like her before. There was a sense, too, that she had some message for me.

I tried to find her but it was no use. The Gallery was an enormous labyrinth of rooms. At one point, I found myself back at the rotunda next to the fountain. In its center stood a black Mercury with a caduceus. The thought came to visualize her and let my intuition guide me. It was all I had to go on. So, feeling the fool, I wandered through the immense rooms of the Old Masters following this dim feeling, not at all sure that I wasn't imagining the whole thing. Finally, I came to the entrance of a room showing the German masters. I suddenly had this strong feeling: *I would find her here standing before Grunewald's Christ.*

I entered the room. My body electrified. There she was. And she was looking at Grunewald's Christ. As I approached her, she turned ever so slightly, her lips showing a small smile. There was no surprise. It was rather more like she had been expecting me. Saying nothing, she took my arm, guiding me closer to the painting. I felt as though I had put myself—or had been put—into her hands. We stood some minutes before the strange and harsh mystical painting of the abased body of the crucified Christ. Then she began to talk about the painting, of how Grunewald had unified the polar opposites of the material and spiritual, how he had painted every wound on Christ's tortured body with this enormous quality of clarity and empathy. She pointed out how he used space to evoke the eternal. It was all stated simply and factually without false ardor and pontification. It was obvious she had a special understanding of painting. The breadth of her knowledge and vision was astonishing. I realized I'd barely seen the painting. I felt like the modern young fool in the company of Sophia, the ancient Gnostic goddess of wisdom.

We went round the gallery together then, visiting painters she admired like Corot and Caravaggio. She mentioned that Whistler was also a favorite and so we went to the Freer Gallery to see what she said was his famous *Peacock Room*. It was an elaborate and opulent interior, its large gentle green walls sumptuously painted with golden peacocks in full plumage. "He had an interesting combination of sensitivity and boldness, don't you think?" Jane remarked. "Whistler wasn't afraid to be himself."

I told her of the paintings I had seen the day before at the Freer. I wanted to see them with her, to see if she could intuit Dewing's women. By contrast with Whistler's *Peacock Room*, the gallery showing Dewing's paintings was rather plain. The difference was—I recognized it now—the paintings conveyed such a sense of spatial silence that it was palpable.

"Such quietness," Jane said. "Such a magnificent natural quietness."

And right then it came to me. These women existed in themselves. They weren't seen in projection but simply as expressions of the eternal.

"This is the feminine, isn't it?"

Jane smiled knowingly. "Yes," she said softly.

It was as if I was seeing with her eyes. She had the power to transfer the image she saw directly to me. I had lived my whole life in the masculine world. Now, through Jane, I felt I was entering the feminine. Here was a woman, I thought, who might teach me about the feminine in the way Lord Pentland had taught me the masculine.

"He painted women...as they really are, didn't he?" I said.

"Yes, William. It's marvelous, isn't it? A man with the depth to paint women as human beings."

We went from painting to painting, arm in arm, Dewing's vision of women revealing aspect after aspect of the ordinary seen in an extraordinary light. At one point, Jane murmured: "Men so rarely see women. Picasso, for example, said that women to him were either 'goddesses or doormats.' So you see, as great as his genius was, Picasso never really understood women."

"You mean he only saw them as identified with his role as a male?"

"Yes, that's right. Well said," she answered with an encouraging nudge. "You see, William, the dear man remained chained to his gender. He never explored the world beyond."

I thought of the tortured DeKooning nudes, Kokoschka's witches, Munch's vampires. Dewing's women were "outside" the drama, in their roles but in themselves as well. They were like silent pools of water, the surfaces smooth, serene, reflective. The ordinary was so extraordinary. How often did I pass it by?

We went then to the Rogues Bar in a nearby hotel. There was time enough for one drink. I felt very close to Jane. It was as if she were a long-lost elder sister. We talked of our lives. I told her about Barbara, the kids, my job. Speaking of her husband, she said he had been a pilot in the Battle of Britain. "He's a real warrior," she said.

"What's it like to live with a warrior?"

"He can be charming and a good provider," she admitted. "But the truth is poor Trevor is more at home in the company of men."

We spoke about "men" and "women" a bit and then I told her the Paddy and Molly joke I'd heard in Ireland. We both roared.

"I like your laughter," she said. "Don't lose it. You have an exceptional sensitivity if I may say so"—she gave a feline smile—"for a man."

She was flying back to London that evening. I wanted her to stay over, but she said she was cursed with an idiotic sense of duty and loyalty.

"Sacrifice is never a pretty word," she said, "and its effect is often disastrous. It more often means denying the right to something rather than foregoing the second bite of the cherry. Wouldn't it be nice if we first experienced all the things we have loyally sacrificed the right to enjoy!"

The words swam in my head. I could only nod and smile. She caught my look and her eyes smiled.

"Well, stranger, I must be going. It has been a meeting I will cherish forever. Do you understand that, William?"

"Yes," I said. "For me also."

We walked to the door and as we did she mentioned she was jealous of my being a writer, for she wanted to write as well but never really had. "I need to starve before I utilize my talent, William. I am completely indolent, you see. And the fact that I can unashamedly admit it means, of course, I have no conscience about it."

"Well, why don't you begin by writing to me?"

"Really?"

"Yes, just write and tell me what you see and feel. You have an amazing degree of perception, if I may say so for a woman." We both chuckled. "So just put it in letters. The stories will come later."

And so two strangers came to exchange addresses.

"I DROVE MY CAR UP THE STEEP, NARROW WINDING GRADIENT OF MOORLAND county in torrential summer rain that slushed the car windshield into opaqueness so that it was difficult to see even with the wipers working full pelt," wrote Jane. "Then, just as I reached the top, the rain stopped suddenly and in a burst of bright sunshine, the whole vista of open country shown green and glistening in panoramic view far below and for miles around. It was breathtaking and I stopped the car and wrote down quickly, before it eluded me, the thought that had been niggling my mind as I drove through the rain.

> *Who Are You, Stranger?*
> *Who are you, stranger?*
> *Who smiles an open heart?*
> *Who, in blinding flash, of rare perception*
> *Seems to pierce the labyrinth of my soul.*
> *Impenetrable sensitivity.*
> *Inviolate.*
> *Pure, untouched Spirit,*
> *Essence of me.*
> *Tread warily, Stranger.*
> *This is holy ground.*
> *Breathe softly your prayer to enter.*
> *Where commingling spirits create*
> *Greenness, which to be, Is.*
> *Not you, nor me*
> *Not us, nor they*
> *But One.*
> *Now who are you, Stranger?*
> *Ah yes, you gave a name—*
> *I did the same—*
> *But names are not for those*
> *who glimpse*
> *Eternity.*
> *So, gentle knight*
> *of sensibility,*
> *approach with care.*
> *There are no shapes*
> *Nor space dimensions*
> *In such Purity.*

I sat rereading a recent letter and poem of Jane's. We'd been exchanging letters for over a year and though they sometimes were a bit florid, even banal, the degree of intelligence and sensitivity of the best parts was startling. I was interested in corresponding with her, but concerned at the feelings our meeting called up in her. A fire had been lit and her letters kept throwing more and more passion upon it. I had a tiger by the tail and didn't know what to do. I didn't want to repeat what had happened with Sarah. I thought Jane's feelings would cool or diffuse with time (after all she was a grandmother with three grown children) and our communication would be a yearly Christmas card, perhaps a note once in a while. But, no, the letters grew longer and came more frequently. Her imagination was getting the better of her. She and Trevor lived on an estate of a few hundred acres just west of Halifax, about one hundred and sixty miles north of London. She had invited me to visit her, but I had easily been able to demur because of the time and money involved. And now here on my desk, lying beside a stack of her letters was the invitation from the Norwegian fish industry to visit Norway for a week. The invitation was ordinary enough and yet I felt a familiar predestined quality, one that I had felt before going to Mexico and Ireland. And again, interestingly enough, Stanley was all for my going. Again, I thought of refusing, but I didn't have the energy.

Within a matter of weeks I was in Norway, visiting the enchanting lakeside home of the composer of *Peer Gynt* as well as coastal fish canneries and fleets not far from the Arctic Circle, and soon thereafter stood in a customs line at London's Gatwick Airport. Jane was waiting for me behind the barrier. She waved a salute and smiled. My stomach still turned at the strange half-faced smile. She looked a little nervous. But she cut a handsome figure in the crowd. She was dressed in a bright green blouse with black jacket, skirt and high black boots.

"Hello, Jane."

"Hello, stranger," she said in that sparkling English accent. She winked and I gave her a little hug. "It's so good to see you, William. So good."

"Yes, but I'm surprised at being here." I was a little disconcerted at her effusion.

"You didn't want to come?" she asked. She seemed hurt.

"Oh, no. I just...I don't know."

"Well, you're here. That's all that's important. Now would you like to go to the Tate first?" she inquired. "It has a positively smashing Blake exhibition."

"Wonderful. Let's go."

We collected the bags and took a cab to London. It was a misty day with a pearl grey sky hovering overhead. Jane sat close beside me, pointing out landmarks. At one point she began speaking of telepathy. She had alluded to this in several of her letters, but I had never responded.

"Do you ever feel, William, that sometimes *I'm there with you?* I know it's silly, Trevor is forever saying such talk 'sticks in his gullet.' But all the same for some people, you know, it is quite true. Telepathy's like a radio communication, but only a few people are still and open enough to hear."

"No, I can't say as I have." I didn't want her to know what I experienced.

"Hmmmn, it's so real to me. I'm surprised..."

After we had paid the driver and were getting out of the cab, the driver made some snide comment to Jane. She hissed at him and he laughed rudely.

"What was that about?" I asked.

"Never mind, William."

Again in the Tate the ticket taker, an old ruddy faced man, made some remark as we passed by. I took it they thought I was her lover.

"People have absolutely no manners today, William. Just ignore them," said

Jane as she took my arm and led me into the cavernous gallery, filled with people and quite dark, except for the lighting of Blake's works.

We spent a good hour at the Tate. Her knowledge of Blake, I found, was as great as it was of Grunewald and Whistler. She had an amazing eye for what held an image together, for points of tension and resolution. As we went from one engraving to another, I got the sense that she was able to "enter" the image immediately, project her feelings into it, feel it in herself, and then go beyond that to the source of the artist's inspiration. In this way it all "lived" for her.

The exhibition filled the whole gallery and contained virtually all of Blake's works, but Jane particularly seemed to want me to see Blake's illustrations for *The Book of Job*. Blake had done twenty-two line engravings. Each was a powerful vision, taut with the energy of the opposites, depicting the evolution of God's agreeing to have Satan test Job's sincerity. For some time, we stood silently looking at the small black and white engravings. Finally Jane murmured:

"These could be seen as Blake's search for God. Do you think he found Him, William?"

I shrugged, but her question put the images into a context for me. Now Blake's engravings began to speak in a quite different way. Jane pulled me closer to one engraving. It showed a powerful, muscular Satan, the moon haloing his head, standing atop Job smiting him with boils while his wife kneels at his feet, grieving and helpless. In the background the sun descends below the Earth.

"Blake's Job, you see, was a man of outer righteousness. He feared God and eschewed evil in his ordinary dealings but had never been put to the test," said Jane. "My sense, William, is that it's not only a test, but what we see here is an initiation as well."

"Initiation?"

"God has withdrawn his protection to give Job a chance to see the dark side— his and God's."

"You think God has a dark side?"

Jane looked at me. Her look was serious. "Would that surprise you, William?"

"Well, what about God and the Devil?" I asked. "How does Blake see them?"

Jane paused and scanned the engravings. "I would say God and the Devil are one whole for Blake. They are bound together. They can't really be separated, except by abstraction. That, of course, makes it all false. Blake, you know, delights in energy." Jane gave a little grin and pulled me so close to her I could smell her perfume. "He was strong and sure enough of himself to create…create his own mythology. He didn't live by the rules of others, you see. He was man enough to make his own."

We walked on and were about to leave when Jane stopped and pulled me back to a drawing I had passed by. It was a small pencil portrait, the bust of a man, his large almond-shaped eyes challenging, staring directly into the viewer's. The face was full, spherical, strongly shaped; the eyebrows arched, the eyes heavy lidded and intelligent, the lips pursed. But it was Blake's peculiar rendering of the forehead that pitched the face into another dimension.

"See the egg-shaped spheres that compose the forehead," said Jane softly.

"Yes," I said, "it's like his head contains worlds upon worlds."

"Exactly."

I felt something strange working in me.

"What is it?" Jane asked.

"This...I don't feel this is an ordinary man."

"Yes...I know what you mean. Who do you suppose it is?"

"I don't know but I feel like...he's asked a question. A very big question. And now he's waiting for the answer."

The face before me was curiously familiar. Yet I had no recollection of ever seeing it before. Blake had entitled the drawing, *He Who Taught Me How To Paint In My Dreams*. Blake had drawn it in 1820, the same year he had completed *The Ghost of a Flea* (which was hung right beside it).

"I didn't want you to miss this," Jane said. She pressed her bosom against my arm, the sweet scent of her perfume filling my nostrils. "Know who it is?" she asked, smiling cryptically.

"No. But I feel...No, I don't know."

"William—this is Blake's devil."

I got a chill the way she said it. I saw what she meant. But I would never have seen it myself.

"Imagination was everything for Blake. He hated reasoning. Hated all the mental chains that bind a man's energy. Have you read his *Jerusalem?*"

"No. I've never read Blake at all. Or Job either."

She looked into my eyes, that crooked smile, Janus-like, fixed to half her face, and quoted: *"Reasonings like vast serpents/ Infold around my limbs, bruising my minute/articulations."* I felt in her this enormous power, this strong will. She was a woman used to getting what she wanted. I had never felt this so sharply. She let the moment linger. "Well," she mused at last, breathing deeply, "I suppose we better be going, if we're not to miss the train."

On the train ride north we sat in our own compartment, sipping brandy from a small silver flask Jane had produced from her purse. The greyness of the late afternoon was rather solemn and quiet, restful, but I felt none of it. There was an apprehension building in me. I had again gotten myself into something. But now with a very powerful woman who knew exactly what she wanted. Or was I imagining?

Jane opened a pack of Gauloise and offered me one.

"Smoke, William?"

"No. I smoked a pipe at one time but gave it up."

"Well, I still 'sin' as you can see." She laughed and handed me a large box of wooden matches. On its cover was a swan. My heart stopped. Like the rose of my trip to Ireland, the swan had become a symbol for me. Whenever it appeared, something happened.

"Anything wrong?" asked Jane. "The matches...they're very popular over here, William."

I struck a wooden match and lit her cigarette.

"Tell me," I asked after a bit, "have you told Trevor I was coming?"

Jane grinned. "Oh, he wouldn't care. Too busy with his boats and glass factory." She blew a long trail of smoke and looked out the window on the opposite side.

So she hadn't told him. And obviously didn't plan to. I was going to be sleeping at her house. What if he came home? I had just assumed she would have told him I'd be staying there.

We got off at Halifax and took a cab to Trevor's house near Bolington. She said he lived there during the week as it was close to the glass factory. The house was plain, thickly built. Inside, the floors were bare. The room was furnished with only the essentials. The house had the feeling of a barracks. Jane read my thoughts.

"He likes it this way. He's very military. Why do you know, William, I'm married to a hero? He was an RAF ace. He had seven kills the first year. Why he had earned a Distinguished Flying Cross before the war even began!"

"Let's get going, huh?"

We went back to the garage. Jane's Triumph sports car had a dead battery. So we took Trevor's silver Rolls Royce. Jane drove. It was twilight when we headed off into the countryside. She said their estate was a half hour or so away.

"Jane, why didn't you tell Trevor I was coming?"

She turned from the wheel. Her face had an amused, whimsical look. The one eyebrow was raised. "I suppose," she answered, "I was waiting for him to open one of your letters."

"What?"

"Don't be so serious. You never know what's in the boot, William."

"The boot?"

"Oh, forgive me. I forget I'm with an American chap. Why 'boot' means the trunk of the car."

We drove on a bit. It was pitch black now. We were into the thick of the country and the road was narrow and winding. Jane knew it by heart. She raced the car over the gravely road, its tires kicking up a trail of dust and stone.

"Jane, what if your husband comes home and finds me?"

"William, don't worry, why I'll show you where Trevor keeps his shotguns," Jane chuckled.

"But—"

"What are you expecting us to do, William?" she asked sweetly, feigning innocence.

"Jane, don't be cute."

"Are you afraid, William?" She inhaled her cigarette and blew a long draft of smoke. "Afraid of my warrior-husband?"

She was baiting me. "Jane, this is ridiculous."

I felt trapped. How could I have not have foreseen this? We drove on into the night, the road rising now as we climbed into the hills. The moon was just coming over the horizon, big and yellow. A full moon, of course.

"Jane, why are you doing this?"

"I thought you Gurdjieff people were warriors. No?"

This Jane I had never seen before. "You are really some bitch—do you know that!"

"A well-bred bitch," she answered softly in her cultured English accent, that face again giving me its awful crooked smile.

"Stop the car."

"What?"

"Stop the goddamn car!"

Jane pulled off at the next bend and turned off the motor. We overlooked a small village below and a dark womb of a valley stretching out to hills on the horizon. Jane offered me a Gauloise. She struck a wooden match herself. For a brief instant the car was illuminated. There was a look on her face I didn't like. What was I going to do? I put the window down. The night air was cool and filled with the mindless chatter of crickets. A jackrabbit bounded across the road and up the ridge. Out on the horizon an airliner's lights flashed on and off. New York seemed as if it was in another dimension of time. I felt like a fly caught in a web. Jane had set all this up. I felt like I was living out this dream of hers. *Who are you, Stranger?* Yes, who are you, Jane? This was not the soft, nurturing female I'd known those afternoons at the National Gallery and then the Tate. It was not the kind, sensitive, slightly confused "Jane" of her letters. Beside me was a cunning, strong-willed, manipulative woman. One who knew what she wanted, not afraid of it, and who knew how to get it. I felt like a boy. I was no match for her. I thought of having her drive me back to Halifax and taking the train to London. I could do that. But I wanted to see Rosslyn Chapel. And, yes, a part of me was curious. I wanted to see what this was all about. If I stayed, I was going to have to be present as much and as often as I could. That was the secret I had that she didn't know about.

"All right. I'll stay the night," I declared. "But tomorrow I want to go to Rosslyn Chapel."

"Where's that?"

"Near Edinburgh."

"That's a long drive, William…but, well, yes, of course, if that's what you'd like. Anything you like we can do. Of course."

"All right," I said closing the window. "Let's go."

"Sure?"

"Start the car."

"Oh, I'm so glad, William! So glad."

WE DROVE SILENTLY THROUGH THE NIGHT, GREAT GREY CLOUDS PASSING across the dark skies like galloping horsemen, this strange powerful woman at the wheel. I closed my eyes and sank back into the leather seat. I pretended to be asleep. How had I gotten myself into this? I went over her letters in my mind. It had been such an outpouring of thoughts and feelings, such a gusher of emotion. She could be keenly perceptive but there was so much imagination and drivel as well. I felt like I was "a last straw" and she was clutching me with all her might. Her fantasy and will were so strong. Could she have somehow "acted" upon me to bring me here? It seemed preposterous. But all the same here I was.

I closed my eyes. I thought of Lord Pentland. I had gone to see him just before leaving. He had moved to a new office on Madison and 69th Street. It was smaller but had that same spare, monastic feeling as his office in the RCA building where we'd first met—

"We're almost there, William." I heard Jane call out. "Wait till you see it!"

I kept my eyes closed, pretending to be asleep. I could see the canvas hanging in the foyer of Lord Pentland's new office. It was the image, set against a cobalt blue background, of a large goddess-like figure, reminiscent of some of Picasso's women, playing a flute. Her eyes were fixed intently on something or someone in the distance. The impression was of her using the vibrations of the flute and her attention to affect the object of her gaze. The painting was entitled *Angel.* Helen, from the old Gallery group, had painted it—

"William, it's a big stone house," Jane exclaimed. "Why it has six bedrooms, with wonderfully high ceilings. It was once a carriage house but we've made it over. Why it costs poor Trevor, the silly goat, some two thousand pounds a year to heat."

I ignored her and focused instead on Lord Pentland's office.

I saw him again as he stepped into the foyer and greeted me. He gave me that same blank "dead man" look—it still singed me—and gestured me into his office. He regarded me a few moments and then inquired:

"Have you seen Sarah?"

"No, not since she left the Work. I understand she's moved upstate."

"It's too bad she got things wrong," Lord Pentland said. "She had some very high experiences. She's not an idiot, you know?"

I nodded. I wondered what he was getting at.

"Obstinate…but not an idiot."

"Yes, I really liked her a great deal."

"She mixed personality and essence. As most of us do, you understand?"

I smiled.

"She couldn't tell what was real…what to trust in herself. So few people leave in the right way, if you know what I mean?"

Sarah had just walked out, disappeared. And Lord Pentland had spent a great deal of time with her, helping her to adjust and reorder her life. It was all there for her, but she was afraid to take the next step.

Lord Pentland and I sat in silence regarding one another. The whole room expanded. I was vibrating. He looked vacant, as if he wasn't there. Each time I saw this something in me reacted. It gave me a queasy feeling.

"The real Work," said Lord Pentland after a time, "lies somewhere between personality and essence. When one is too much in one or the other…well, then, we become emotional."

I couldn't control my chin. It was shaking with the energy. I understood that he was talking about me as well as Sarah.

"We can use our negativity as a reminding factor."

Yes, the negativity had overwhelmed Sarah, as it had me.

"We become that to which we say 'I' and so, instead of working with it, we justify our shit and act from it."

It was so odd hearing him swear. And he pronounced the word so plainly that its impact was even greater.

"It's important, too, that we don't mistake our sensitivity for consciousness. Mr. Gurdjieff frequently referred to this confusion. A person can be quite sensitive and not at all conscious. We need to separate consciousness from sensitivity."

"So if we are hearing a subtle sound," I asked, "then—"

"There are many levels of sensitivity and substance, so many worlds," Lord Pentland broke in. "And, equally, so many levels upon which to become identified. The Work can only get harder, the demand greater. The fact that a subtle vibration is heard could be called a 'gift,' to use a metaphor"—he smiled.

I immediately pictured that meeting long ago when I first spoke to him about what I had mistakenly characterized as the sound-below- sound.

"But, as I say," continued Lord Pentland, "it is consciousness that is to be emphasized. When we self-remember at the point of incoming impressions, then the impressions do not feed our associations but fall directly on centers, and provide a 'food' whose vitality can be processed to finer and finer degrees—"

"Yes. Ahh, well, I see…" I stopped, recognizing then that *the whole spectrum of impressions is always there.* "It doesn't leave us. We leave it. Fall asleep to it."

"Yes," Lord Pentland nodded. "That's right."

"But this triad," I continued, "of consciousness, sensitive energy and impressions…well, the more subtle the impression, the more sensitive the energy needed to perceive it, and the finer the separation and the more subtle the lure of identification."

"This biplicity of consciousness and sensitivity is very strong," said Lord Pentland. "You can experience it…oh, I don't know…in the attraction between male and female. It is very powerful and hypnotic, if you know what I mean?"

We spoke a bit more and then I told him of my upcoming trip to Norway and how I planned to visit Scotland. Lord Pentland's ancestral grounds were in the Pentland Hills near Edinburgh. It was at Rosslyn that his family had a chapel and a castle. I was hoping he might tell me to go there. But he made no mention of it. Instead, all I got was that look from the dead. It was as if he had disappeared—

This reverie was broken by Jane calling like an excited schoolgirl, "William! William, we're here!"

I opened my eyes and sat up in the seat. Up ahead on a rise of land with not a house in sight stood a broad and sturdy two-story, white stone house with a high pitched roof and several large chimneys. It had the feel of a fortress, albeit a disguised one, for it was thickly covered with vines and climbing pink roses and surrounded with flower beds and manicured hedges. Two tall white pillars stood sentry at the front door which was garlanded by a circular sweep of large pink roses. I carried in the bags. Inside, the house had the look and feel of a small museum full of antiques, paintings and oriental rugs. I put the bags down and Jane quickly made a small fire in the den and brought in a tray of hot chocolate. I had brought a small self-portrait for her as a gift. I had told her about it at the Tate. I didn't want to leave it with her. But what excuse could I make?

We sat on the couch, me at the end and her in the middle, warming ourselves with the hot chocolate. She pointed out a painting on the far wall. It was a relative of hers, she said. It dated from the sixteenth century. The walls were covered with paintings of Trevor's and her ancestors. I realized now my out.

I unwrapped the self-portrait and held it up for her to see. She took it at once and brought it closer. For some time she studied it, the fire cracking behind her, and the room perfectly still.

"Not bad, William," she said softly. "Not bad at all."

I went to take the painting from her but she propped it up on the coffee table. "I'm so glad that you would honor me in this way."

"Well, Jane, I don't know, do you really think it fits in here?"

She grinned and laughed to herself.

"I'm happy you've seen it," I said. "I'll take it back with me. You know, I'll send you something else."

"Would you like to know what I see, William?" asked Jane, disregarding my comments. "The face shows an interesting mixture of sensitivity and strength, but a sadness, as well. And when the three combine in a certain way...perhaps...a certain measure of brutality."

She smiled knowingly and brought the portrait into her lap. "You know, William, the mouth—I hope you won't mind me saying this...?"

"No, go ahead."

"Well, it's really rather like Trevor's. Remarkable."

"That's interesting. I think its best now if I take it back with me."

"No, no! I wouldn't dream of it," she cried. "Why...I'll tell you what. I'll keep it in my closet and only bring it out for peeks."

"Jane—"

"Or...or perhaps...perhaps I'll put 'him' under the bed. That's it!"

I pictured Trevor bounding into her bed one early morning, spending his lust, only to look down over the side of the bed and see 'him' staring up. It was obvious she wasn't going to return the portrait. At least not now. I pretended indifference. "Whatever you like," I said.

Shortly after, Jane took me upstairs. Her room was just off the staircase. She led me down the corridor to the opposite end of the house.

"Trevor's room," she said matter of factly.

I looked in. The smell of boot polish and leather filled my nostrils. It had a Spartan feel. Spare, well organized, no nonsense. A narrow uncomfortable cot. Heavy dark brown leather furniture. Small fireplace. The walls paneled in dark wood. Beamed ceiling. Sailing and flying trophies, swords and firearms, decorations and certificates everywhere. This was the room of a warrior.

"Well," said Jane with a sly smile, "there is another room."

She opened the door of the adjoining room. It was bright and cheery, painted snowy white and filled with dolls and cute figurines.

"The children's room," said Jane, one side of her mouth in a smirk.

"Fine." I put down my bags.

"Good night."

"Good night."

I locked the door. I couldn't get into bed fast enough. I buried myself in the pillows. Who was this crazy woman? She was taunting me. Challenging me. I was exhausted, angry. I fell asleep instantly. The next morning came immediately. I could hear Jane bustling around in the kitchen. The thought of another day with her seared the mind. But I had to be alert. I pushed myself out of bed. From the window I could see acres and acres of lush green fields, a flock of sheep grazing, some workmen repairing a fence. The sky above was a luminescent blue-white. It was as if "yesterday" had never happened.

I sat on the floor, crossed my legs in a half lotus and closed my eyes. I relaxed the face, breathed deeply and steadily, getting a general feeling of the body. Then I shifted the pelvis forward, felt the two sitzbones in the buttocks, straightened and lengthened the spine from the sacrum upward, raising the sternum, dropping the shoulders, slowly bringing the chin down to the sternum, moving the neck back and placing the neck on top of the spinal column, then raising the chin, bringing the head out of the shoulders— and simply breathing. After a bit, I focused the attention on the breath, and slowly came down into the abdomen, experiencing the general sensation of the body. Focusing in this way, the clutter of the mind gradually dissolved and dispersed. The sensation included more and more of the body, the pores of the skin opening and tissues and cells being lubricated. In time, and of themselves, the breath, sensation and attention balanced and blended. Keeping a whole body sensation, I focused my attention between the shoulder blades and inhaled, the whole body slowly taking on a magnetic quality. Then I placed the attention on the tip of the nose, the right hand, right foot, and so forth, maintaining a sensation of the whole while focusing on the parts and centers, circulating the energy, experiencing its expansion, and finally "rolling the ball" down the middle column. It was like a great tonic...

"Will-i-am. Cock-a-doodle-doo. Oh, Will-i-am."

All right. I was collected now. I was ready. I dressed and went downstairs. Jane was in the kitchen. She gave me a big "Good morning" and slipped the morning paper under my arm, as though "William" was the master of the house and "Jane" its mistress.

"I'm so sorry for the contretemps of the other day," she said. "You must have had a very long and tedious trip. Let's have breakfast and go to your Rosslyn right after, hmmmn?"

"Good," I said, trying to be agreeable.

She led me into the dining room and sat me at the head of the table.

"The king's chair," she said softly, her head bowing slightly.

"Very good."

The dining room was a little jewel of mirrors and antiques and silver tea sets, all polished and gleaming. Though it wasn't anything like it, I was reminded of Whistler's *Peacock Room* in the National Gallery. It was so lavish and bold, though not at all masculine.

At the end of breakfast Jane said, "William, let's go by way of the Lake District, shall we? I think you'll like that."

"Fine."

"I am truly sorry." She looked at me imploringly and patted my hand. There was a sweetness to her, an understanding and softness that I found absolutely delightful. It was the "Jane" I first met. Intelligent, charming, witty. Soft and fluid. Perhaps I was wrong. So, she didn't tell Trevor I was coming—what of it? Did I tell Barbara everything? And the swan matchbooks, they were common here. Why make so much over things?

We packed up the Rolls, Jane insisting I drive. She slid a tape into the tape deck and suddenly the car was filled with the haunting quality of Faure's *Requiem*. It was a perfect day for a drive. As we pulled out onto the main road, I noticed the license plate of the car ahead. It read: CYNG.

"Hmmnn…" murmured Jane. "The spell of the swan."

"I guess so."

"Tell me, William, how did this swan business start?"

"Well, it was a few years ago," I said. "I was driving down to Florida with Barbara and the kids to visit my parents. We stopped in Middleton Gardens, just south of Charleston."

"Yes, I've been there. How did you find Middleton Gardens?"

"Serene and beautiful, of course, but there is a great sadness there also for what happened during the Civil War and a time and quality of soul that is lost forever…. Well, anyway, I was crossing a small bridge over a pond when this black swan sees me and paddles rapidly toward me, squawking furiously."

"Really? Why do you suppose she would do that? Swans are usually very peaceful. They'll fight to protect their nest and brood or what they consider their territory. If they attack otherwise, it's generally birds of the same color." Jane paused and smiled, saying: "Tell me, William, are you 'black' at heart?"

"Oh," I answered, affecting a British accent, "Don't you know? I'm known as 'Black William.'"

"A real lady-killer. Is that it?"

I thought of Sarah. Lord Pentland once told her I was "her friend in death." I had put her through a psychic death. I hadn't meant to. But, all the same, I had triggered it.

"Perhaps it was the color of my clothes," I continued. "All I know is that swan attacked. I came down from the bridge and it actually came up out of the water, squawking and wings fluttering. It chased me as far as it could."

"Chased you? On land?"

"It couldn't go very fast or far. But it was angry. When it gave up and returned to the water, I came back. Then it lunged out of the water again. This was repeated several more times until I slipped and the swan actually pecked me on the calf. I know this sounds a bit strange."

"Not at all," said Jane, thinking something over. "Tell me, do you know much about the black swan, William?"

"I knew nothing about it back then. But I looked it up in the encyclopedia when I got home. The black swan was only a conjecture until it was first sighted in 1687—"

"In Australia."

"Yeah. How'd you know?"

"Swans have always fascinated me. They're shrouded in mystery and anomaly. Such incredible beauty. Yet very fierce. They're usually so quiet, so contained within themselves. And of course they are amphibious. I love their long snake-like necks. And the eyes of the mute swan give this black masking effect. It's as if they are attending a masqued ball. Swans have a strange, enigmatic quality, don't you think?"

"Yeah, it's like they carry or guard some secret."

"Yes, but now as you were saying, William…just how did the swan become a symbol for you?"

"It's too long to explain but after that every time an image of a swan appeared I'd meet someone special or something unusual would happen. It's like a leitmotif in an opera."

Jane sat for a bit and then lit up a Gauloise. "Have you ever heard of the Swan Knight?" she asked.

"No. But I know the swan, like the peacock, is considered a sacred bird."

"Yes, that's right. Well, the Swan Knight is Lohengrin who sat at King Arthur's round table. He was one of the knights of the Holy Grail. Wagner's opera *Lohengrin* is about the Swan Knight."

"What about the black swan?"

Jane glanced at me, her face holding that peculiar smile. "I don't know that you'd want to hear that, William."

"Thomas Mann wrote a book called *The Black Swan.*"

"Yes, well, as you might imagine, it's usually considered a symbol of evil. But then if you have Blake's vision, you don't separate the two, do you?" Jane looked off in the distance and took a long inhalation of smoke. "Of course, your being Irish you should know about swans."

"How so?"

"Swans have always been a symbol of death, of travel to 'the other world.' I believe your Irish fairy people, the Tuatha De Danaan, held the swan in high esteem." Jane arched an eyebrow knowingly.

My whole body electrified. Yes, I really was on another adventure!

We got to the ferry just as it was pulling out. We parked at the dock to await the next one. The place seemed to have special memories for her. I prodded and finally she told me this was where she and Trevor had honeymooned during the war. They had stayed at an inn in Windermere. He had invited some men friends from the reception to come along. They had entertained themselves in the bar while the bride and groom were upstairs. The marriage consummated, she said, Trevor excused himself and went down to the bar to join his chums.

"He's really happier with men," Jane said. "He finds women strange ducks. He likes it neat and known, like in golf or shooting. He's not fond of ambiguity or subtlety...but, of course, most men aren't."

The sky had turned overcast and the wind made the lake water choppy. She talked a great deal now but her manner was detached, as if she were reporting on the life events of a stranger.

"Certain people just don't fit together. And how is it that they so often end up in each other's arms? Well, we've both managed to muddle through, you know. I suppose it's our tradition of duty and all that rot. But of course I really rather admire him. I always have. It's just that we should be friends and nothing more."

"So why did you get married? What was it?"

Jane looked away, mildly startled. She ran a finger over the dash as if she was drawing a figure in sand.

"Odd. But...well, you see, I don't actually know. Now isn't that silly. Well—do you know why you married Barbara?"

I thought a moment. "I was taken with her. Completely captivated."

"I know, I know! You see, I was 'taken' with Trevor as well. It wasn't that I was swept off my feet, goodness knows. But the war was going on and here...here was this handsome hero who was in all the papers and, poor chap, who had gotten it in his head to get married. And, well...it wasn't, you understand, so much that I said 'Yes,' but it was that I simply couldn't say 'No.' How strange that I simply couldn't find any reason to say 'No.'"

"So it had a fated quality?"

"Yes, I suppose that's it. Forgive me, William, but do you know what Queen Victoria advised a young princess, about to marry a boring German prince, to do on their wedding night? Said the Queen to the Princess: 'Just lie back, dear, close your eyes, and think of merry old England!'"

We both laughed heartily. It had been raining outside and the windows were steamed. Jane wiped them with her hankie. The ferry was now in sight and in its wake trailed a flock of hungry sea gulls. The dense covering of soulless sky had lifted a bit and the lake waters had settled into a slow pulsating roll. We both looked off toward the incoming ferry. I could feel her suffering and sorrow. The heavy iron gangplank crashed down on the dock and I drove the Rolls onto the ferry. We both stayed in the car, neither of us speaking, each alone in our thoughts. As the ferry pulled into shore Jane smiled and said she recalled a manor house, Belmont Manor, that might have lodging. We disembarked and she had to feel our way along as she tried to remember the way.

"It must have been a long time since you've been here," I said as we drove up the gritty gravel of the manor's driveway.

"Yes, quite a long time, William." There was a tone in her voice that expressed her feelings far more than the words.

I was hesitant to ask but I did. "During the war?"

"Yes, our honeymoon."

Good god! I thought. She had planned all this. I felt like a fly with a spider.

"We don't have to stay here," she said softly.

Fortunately, Belmont Manor was full.

"There's another down the road by Newby Bridge," she said.

"Okay."

"I don't think you're going to like the name, William."

"Don't tell me."

Jane laughed.

Up ahead on the left side of the road—I saw it. The Swan Hotel. Jane cocked her head and rolled her eyes. I parked the Rolls by the river. By the far bank, I noticed several white swans floating silently in the dusky shadow world of twilight.

"Mute swans," said Jane.

"What else?"

Like in Ireland, I felt as if I was a character inside a story that had already been written. I was awake to the story, to its symbology and nuances, but had no idea of its meaning. I felt myself conscious on one level, mechanical on another. It was as though I had awakened inside a dream.

And this fated quality—was it a seeing deeply into the event? Or was this "fate" itself a part of the hypnotism of the event? If I identified with this fated feeling then, of course, the event would be self-fulfilling. But if I willfully acted against it—wasn't that feeding it as well? Was I being led into a deeper recognition of the feminine? Or was I being deceived? I couldn't know. The only recourse was to remember myself.

THE NEXT MORNING WE'D LEFT THE SWAN HOTEL EARLY, HOPING TO MAKE it to Rosslyn Chapel before night. The sweep of scenery had been magnificent. Long undulating mountain ranges, worn smooth with age, kept us company as we motored along the backroads. We had driven for hours and finally, tired and hungry, came down into a little hillside village, spied an old tea shop, and taken our chances. The windows were covered so there was no seeing in. I pushed the big door open. A short staircase led to the cellar. I didn't like the place but the immediate feeling was that we were meant to come here.

The old woman, gnarled and unkempt, her vacant indifferent eyes off in a space all her own, had brought fresh baked biscuits, a plate of cheese and a kettle of steaming tea. As we ate Jane told me of her early life in England. Her parents were quite religious and had drummed the Bible into her. They had become missionaries to South Africa and had all their teeth pulled before sailing off as there would be no dentists out in the bush.

"It's the genesis of this notion of duty and loyalty that hangs on me," she said. "Quite mindless. But what is there to do?"

"Did you ever read *All and Everything?*"

"Oh yes, William. Why, good God, it cost me a whole twenty-five dollars American."

"How did it strike you?"

"Would you like another copy for your birthday?"

Lord Pentland had told me it was time I brought some others into the Work. I had thought of Jane.

"I mean," Jane continued adamantly, "I am not about to fall down and worship Mr. G. just because he happened to be himself."

Upon leaving the tea shop, we signed the guestbook. I signed, "John MacFad-yean," the name of my uncle on the Patterson side, and Jane signed, "Katie Floyd."

"Who's that?"

Jane gave me a secret smile. "Oh an interesting South African witch, William." She paused and added, "No one you'd like really."

AND SO THERE WE WERE ON THE ROAD TO LORD PENTLAND'S ROSSLYN Chapel, the elegiac quality of Faure's *Requiem* in our ears, two pilgrims from Newby Bridge, a Swan Queen and her reluctant knight. Hours passed. It was nearing twilight as we approached the village of Roslin (for some reason it's name spelled differently). I could feel my heart beating. We were entering Lord Pentland's ancestral home. The small Scottish village was laid out in a cross design with its fifteenth century chapel at the top. We drove off the paved road onto a narrow dirt road.

The *Requiem* had long ago ended and I had turned on the radio. Now, as the silver Rolls clamored over the dirt road, Simon and Garfunkel began singing, appropriately enough, *Bridge Over Troubled Water.* I wondered if we had taken the wrong road when suddenly there looming before us, like a great stone ship in the sky, stood Rosslyn Chapel. Its beauty and strength, the incredible sense of silence and being it emanated, gave it the same quality of presence I had once felt upon seeing Michelangelo's *David.* It was so real I could taste every stone. Beiges and creams, burnt ochres, light oranges and roses, the muted colorings of stone spoke of great age.

At the gate a small balding man with bushy eyebrows was just locking the gate. His name, he said in a wonderful light Scottish accent, was John Taylor. He, like his father before him, was the chapel's curator. "Rosslyn," he told us, a wonderful twinkle in his eye, "has been my love."

He let us in for a quick walk around the grounds on the promise we'd return the next day to see the interior. We walked along the gravel lane leading to the chapel.

Such a deep stillness. I felt as though it had been there forever. In the now fading light it shimmered before my eyes like a rare jewel. But beyond that impression I felt something else which I could not directly name. Jane went on around the side and I stepped back to take in the whole vision. I let the impression wash over me like a wave.

The architecture was richly ornamental with conical and crocketed pinnacles, flying buttresses and a bestiary of gargoyles and an assembly of saints—the masons must have had a fine time of it. The stone carving had been done with a kind of lyrical, mad abandon that revealed a great vigor. There was a sense of humor here, as well. I felt a certain perspective, a beauty and a worldliness—a laughter in stone one could say—that I had never seen before. Yet there was no sentimentality, no fawning idealism, hope or fantasy here but more the hard rock recognition of the foolishness and ignorance with which men spend their days on earth. The chapel was like a mirror on man.

I looked about the grounds. The chapel, I discovered, was set atop a hill with fine views of the Pentland Hills and the surrounding countryside as well as the river Esk below. Nearby, hidden by trees, was Rosslyn Castle, built around 1304. The chapel was begun later in 1446 by William St. Clair (or, more commonly, Sinclair), the Prince of Orkney, one of the northernmost Scottish isles. I stood gazing at the vast expanse around me, feeling its long history. It gave me a deeper feeling for Lord Pentland and what he represented. I felt, too, I had been brought here. That I was meant to come here. I remembered Lord Pentland saying once that a person's work might take him to many places. I had been to Ephesus, the Teotihuacan pyramids, Ireland and the Aran Isles and now, finally, Rosslyn.

It was getting dark and so we left, hoping to find a room at the village's only inn, but it was full. So Jane and I drove into Edinburgh and took a room there. She was expecting I'd want her. When I showed no interest she became silently furious. There was no real connection between us, but she wouldn't, or couldn't, see it. At breakfast the next morning conversation was difficult. We drove the ten miles or so south to Rosslyn Chapel but, strangely, she was in no mood for it.

IT WAS A BRILLIANT BLUE DAY THAT MADE A PERFECT BACKDROP FOR THE CHAPEL. The experience of yesterday had been so immense that taking it in like that again didn't seem possible. Its beauty and presence were not such a surprise and yet Rosslyn Chapel still lived for me. As I walked about the exterior, the open-mouthed monkey gargoyles carved above the side entrances reminded me of the open-mouth of the feathered serpent carvings of the Teotihuacan pyramids. The mouth of the monkey mind and the mouth of the divine mind. The mouth: it was such a good image and symbol for the maintenance and transformation of life at whatever level. A long line of like thought followed. But it was getting late and I still hadn't seen the interior.

Pushing the large side door open and entering the chapel was like coming upon another world, even another cosmos. The vibration, the stillness, was so smooth, so fine. It was all like one grand carving which gave vivid testimony to the human drama. Above me was a vaulted ceiling, a long skein of roses and star shapes, symbols of love and consciousness. On the walls below was carved The Story of Man: the seven deadly sins, the seven virtues, the Dance of Death, Adam's fall, the sacrifice of Isaac, the birth of Jesus, and other Christian allegories—all interwoven in the midst of entangling botanical designs of Great Nature.

A CARVED PILLAR SOME EIGHT FEET HIGH NEAR THE CRYPT AT THE SOUTHEAST corner of the chapel immediately took my attention from the moment I saw it. All of the other pillars were uniformly and plainly carved. This pillar didn't fit. It was totally unlike the others which were just simple swirls of line like the draping in a robe. This pillar, so unusual and unexpected—a maverick pillar, so to say—was a shock, a discontinuity. Instead of plainness this pillar delighted and surprised with a rich embroidery of carving. At the pillar's base were four vines, heavy with leaves, which spiraled around the column. Intertwined among the vines at the base were eight dragons sucking the vines' energy.

The curator, John Taylor, came by. We talked awhile. He was an old soul with an innate kindness and intelligence. Sensing my interest, he told me the story of this strange pillar.

"Legend has it," he said, "that when Prince William, the builder of the chapel, gave the master mason a model for carving this special pillar, its great beauty and complexity caused the master mason to say he first wanted to see the original design. It existed in Rome or somewhere. Well, wouldn't you know, while the master mason was away the apprentice dreamed that he, and not the good master, was to carve the pillar. And so while the master was away, the apprentice did just that. Well now, he not only finished the pillar but his life as well." Mr. Taylor pointed to two heads at the west end of the chapel, each in an opposite corner. One was the master mason's, the other was the apprentice's. "Do you see any difference between them?" asked Mr. Taylor.

"Well, the apprentice has a gash on his forehead."

"Yes, 'a recognition' you might say from the master mason. You see, despite the pillar's great beauty, upon his return the master mason—in a rage either from jealousy or the breaking of tradition—struck and killed the apprentice with his mallet."

"All this symbolism here of good and evil," I said, "and there was an actual death here as well."

"Oh yes. Rosslyn Chapel had to be consecrated not once, but twice. And originally the pillar was to be called The Prince's Pillar. But now it is known as The Apprentice Pillar. So you can see a lot has taken place here."

"What about the dragons at the base of the pillar?" I asked. "In Scandinavian mythology, the dragons or serpents are at the base of the Yggdrasil Tree, the tree of Life, which unites the three worlds, Heaven, Earth and Hell. They suck all the life from the roots of the Tree. Is that what's happening here?"

"Yes, as you see, there's no fruit on the vines. The dragons have eaten the energy," said Mr. Taylor. He paused and then smiled. "There's something more to The Apprentice Pillar that I might tell you. People are a queer lot, you know. There are some, would you believe, that think the Holy Grail is buried here. Either inside the Apprentice Pillar or below it. But its been X-rayed and there's nothing there. All the same, the pillar seems to attract a lot of speculation and strange behavior. Why a few years back, a woman took off every stitch of clothes and handcuffed herself to the pillar. Very odd, people are."

Shortly after, we said goodbye. Rosslyn Chapel was empty and I sat in a pew thinking of swans, the Swan Knight and the Holy Grail. My journey here seemed to be all of a piece. The feeling came that Lord Pentland was going to die. Or that perhaps we would be separated in some way. I opened a prayer book and looked at the page. It was Jesus' farewell to his apostles; telling them that where he is going, they cannot follow and that they should love one another, for where love is there Jesus is as well. I felt as though Lord Pentland was speaking to me. It was as though I sensed he was leaving me in some way.

Jane came into the chapel with a basket of food. She had shopped in the village so we could picnic. Mr. Taylor told us of a path that would take us down the hill to the river. Soon, then, we were eating bread and cheeses and drinking red wine under the shade of a tree on the slope of a hill overlooking the River Esk. It was a bright, warm day with a lovely breeze. I was still feeling everything that went on in the chapel. Jane seemed still to be in an odd place. She began making fun of the chapel, remembering some of the carving and exclaiming, "My, now, wasn't that charming! How original." She went on mocking the chapel and, by association, my feelings for it and Lord Pentland. I didn't react. When she calmed down I told her what I had felt in the chapel and how I thought Lord Pentland was going to die.

"Well, William, It might not be such a bad thing, horrible as that might sound. You've been under his sway a long time." She paused to see how that was taken, adding: "Tell me—do you think you're a warrior?"

I thought a moment. "No, I'm a seeker."

"Yes, but comes the time the seeker has sought enough, no? Then he must become a warrior."

"You mean—have the will to live what he has been taught?"

"Is that what makes you so hard, William?"

"What do you mean?"

"You're afraid you are too soft, too sensitive, to be a warrior, and that makes you very hard on yourself. And, of course, others. You expect a great deal, you know."

Afterwards, we went to Mr. Taylor's house just down from the chapel which formerly had been an inn. He wasn't home. I left a note and we drove to Loch Lomond, the place of which my grandfather sang. It was quite serene and beautiful. Jane wanted to stay there in a cabin by the lake, but I insisted we drive on to Ayr, which was closer to the airport. We spent an uneventful night there and the following morning drove to the airport, Jane again playing the mournful *Requiem.*

"You know, William, "she mused at the departure gate, "the only problem between us…is your Mr. G."

"Why do you say that?"

"He has taught you that you should have no time for 'wasteful' relationships, to despise idiots and that life is a fool's paradise. Darling William, please open your mind, I beg you. We must all walk at our own pace, if we are not to burn out the candle too soon. Pity my poor weaknesses, pray for me certainly, but why despise me?"

"I've never said I despise you."

"But you find me—how do you put it—'not spiritual'!"

I felt her lack of fulfillment, her deep longing to have a relationship with a man. But I was not that man.

Jane shook her head in dismay. "To my dying day, I will never forget that you find me 'not spiritual.'"

"Jane, look, it just isn't anything you are interested in, is it?"

"You thought you were going to bring me into the circle of Mr. G's ideas, didn't you? And then when I refused that invitation, you have no more use for me—"

The moment stood between us like a wall. I steeled myself. I had to be cold, ruthless. Otherwise what had long ago ended was sure to flash up again, only on a much lower octave.

"Why you…you are actually going to reject me! Aren't you?"

"Yes," I answered and kissed her on the cheek, and boarded the plane. ⨎

THEATRE OF POWER

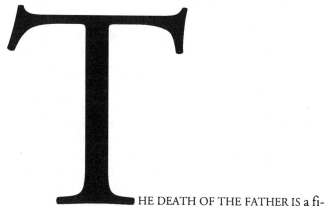

HE DEATH OF THE FATHER IS a finality for the son. It is also a release. The father is gone, never to return, and now the son is his own father. Or has the chance to be for he must have the strength to step out into life and create his life anew. He can stay his father's son and repeat old patterns or dig down in himself and follow a new trail. But old life or new, the son has been changed forever. Though I couldn't put words to it, that was what I felt.

My life outwardly went on as before, inside I felt both a death and this chance for new beginning. The job, the city and, in some ways, even the Work seemed for me like a play that had run its course. Yet within this deadness there was a certain softness. A softness, too subtle and fleeting to describe, but which I came to call an aspect of the "feminine."

My first intimation of it had been with Dewing's paintings of women. Of course, I had experienced it much earlier with Barbara and Sarah, Vali and Jane. But the first recognition, close to the surface, came with Dewing's women. Now I noticed a change in my paintings as well. The colors were darker, more muted, and I was painting much more quickly.

I'd done two canvases since my Father died. One was a large canvas, a strong woman, with a bewildered man seated behind her, riding a horse bareback in the desert. She is bare-breasted and holding the reins. In the distance behind them is a large pyramid. The second and smaller painting was a night scene of an inlet. It leads out into the dark ocean where far out above the horizon hangs a full moon, yellow-ish and vibrating, in the black of night. I noticed, too, that my editorials were focusing on women's subservient role in foodservice.

I was tired, too, of the continual battle with Stanley and was trying to meet him on new ground. I looked for places we could cooperate and tried more to externally consider his feelings and reactions. I began to enjoy some of his milder jokes and ap-preciate his wit and unvarnished insights into how, as he would say, "life really worked." In certain moments I even found myself feeling some of his suffering. In an odd way, I found myself liking parts of him, different "I"s, and I had to admit that he was certainly more interesting than Spencer and the rest of the company's top management whose one and only abiding interest was what Stanley once called, assuming a Nietzsche-like countenance, "the will to profit."

I began to see my relationship with Lord Pentland in a new way as well. These idiot feelings of complaint and rejection and bitterness and complaint—the obser-vations of them began to form an image so sharp and immediate I could no longer dismiss it. I'd seen, of course, this particular "self-portrait" before. But the light had been too dim. I hadn't lived long enough with the painting. It had hung in my mind's gallery but, instead of just living with it and letting it ooze into my being, I had put it into words. And having cleverly cut off the feelings and questioning, I had taken on the aspect of one-centered-understanding that comes so easily. Yes, this formatory mind—it was an expert at the inner game of Three Card Monte.

Now I felt this big rotten knot inside me. It was all there: the neurotic need, the demand, the projection. All these years with Lord Pentland. Not once had I been able to truly admit that I had only been acting out a compensation. Yes, all the strands of that rope led back to that hidden father wound, a wound that I had sealed in the blood of anger that day in my youth when I had vowed I would never again let the Father hurt me. I had spent so many years wrestling with it, trying to accept it, understand it. I had painted it in my imagination over and over again, but it had never dissolved, never lost its power over me. It was the unconscious mosaic of my life. My original wound. Like the medieval story of *Sir Gawain and The Green Knight,* it was a wound I hid, even from myself. My chief feature—it was all encrust-ed around and tied to that deep psychic feeling of father loss. The son with the invisible father. The psychic orphan. And I could sense that this knot was somehow beginning to unravel.

At my group's first meeting of the New Year, Lord Pentland had announced that the study groups would begin to make their reports to the main group. It had been a rather strange experience seeing the groups sitting where Lord Pentland nor-mally sat talking of the Work ideas on the Ray of Creation, Time, Different "I"s and Real I. And each group had failed rather miserably. Either they had not sufficiently studied the material and their presentation was shoddy, or, worse, they fell victim to vanity and self-love, a pretension and pride. The Work ideas, whose origin Ouspensky referred to as "the conscious circle of humanity," came from real power and intelligence. One handled them with care. And to speak of these ideas in public, and especially in front of a man like Lord Pentland, could be an onerous and withering task.

Our study group was to make the next presentation. There had been four of us, but one, an acting coach, dropped out. That left Barbara, Diane, who ran the office of the Foundation, and myself. We had met regularly since Lord Pentland had assigned the themes. Our theme was the Food Diagram. I felt it, along with the enneagram, was the key to Gurdjieff's teaching, for in it were the laws which showed how the three foods of man—physical, air and impressions—were processed in the body to produce specific substances of a finer and finer density and vibration. And how, too, the conscious receiving and assimilation of these three foods transformed their potency and potentiality to develop man's Kesdjan Body. Over the months I had made a number of experiments with the foods, fasting, eating different foods, seeing where I took in impressions, their effect and so forth. I felt ready.

But the week before our group's presentation was crazy with emotion. Stanley and I had a wicked blowout. It set the stage for all that was to follow between us.

Following my Father's death, I had less and less stomach for fighting Stanley. I felt that perhaps I had been too hard with him. We talked. Without my asking, he promised me a good-sized raise if I would, as he put it, "cooperate." What that meant was my making sales pitches to advertisers and their ad agencies with him. I'd always resisted this (unless it was one of the annual major client "dog 'n pony shows") because it weakened the separation between sales and editorial. It gave advertisers more leverage to pressure for editorial mention of their products.

"All the editors from our competition do it, Bill, and still manage to maintain editorial integrity," Stanley told me. "We can and we will. I'll back you up."

I had believed him. I had wanted to believe him. I simply went to sleep. I forgot who he was and what he represented in my world.

So I had made the sales presentations. Stanley spoke of my new "maturity." Beneath all the effusive statements I could hear the cloying laugh in his voice. I had made a mistake. A snake is a snake. The pressure from the advertisers came as predicted and Stanley of course not only didn't stand by me but argued their side. I refused to give in and reminded him that I had "cooperated" and I expected to get the raise he had promised.

I was in my office going over my notes for presentation on the Food Diagram when Stanley asked to see me in his office. He closed the door and informed me I would only get a token raise, if any.

"There's nothing I can do, Bill. My hands are tied," he said. His mouth showed that little mincing smile. "You've been your 'new person' only a short time. Let's see how things work out."

I didn't protest. I knew it was useless. But right then and there I cut him away from me. I would now only talk to him when necessary. Otherwise I would ignore him. The meeting had put me in an inner rage. I had identified immediately, gone completely to sleep—why did I always expect Stanley to be different? It was a naive hope. I had to accept him as he was. That same week Sarah had called. We hadn't seen each other in a long time. Her voice brought my body alive. It ached for her. I couldn't chance seeing her. At least not now. I was too weak. I put her off. That afternoon I'd come down with a heavy cold that with the days only went deeper. The morning of the presentation it was no better. The cold had dried up but my chest was still congested, my nose stopped up, and voice raspy. But it was too late to cancel. The day matched my mood. It was dull, gray, damp and gloomy. Driving into Manhattan from Ossining, Barbara and I were heavy with apprehension. Today would be a demonstration of whatever level of knowledge and being we had come to individually and as a group.

There had been a lot of kills on the highway. We passed a flattened ground squirrel, a skunk and a newly killed fox with a magnificent bushy tail. We were about a half hour early so we went to the Excell for tea. It was nearly empty. The waitress taking our orders was very bubbly and smiling. As she went to the kitchen, I noticed the boss angrily motioning to her. Apparently she wasn't doing the place settings as he wanted. I couldn't hear his words but I saw their effect. As she withered, sucked dry of energy, he became more alive and animated. When she brought our tea, her face was clouded and dark, her shoulders bunched and turned in. He had eaten her alive.

I sat amazed watching this psychic cannibalism. I had always thought that one class of beings eats another; that all forms of life, gross and subtle, were engaged in a kind of perpetual eating or, as Gurdjieff called it, "reciprocal maintenance." The different classes (the vertebrates, invertebrates, man and angels) are separated by what they eat, what air they breathe and in what medium they live. It had never occurred to me that within classes of beings the strong *psychically* feed on the weak. The waitress had been "food" for the boss.

The cross street on which the Foundation was located was lined with stacks of two-by-fours, plywood and pipes. As we neared the Foundation, a former three-story carriage house, the ground shook from an underground explosion. This was obviously going to be an interesting day. The presentation was to be given in a third floor meeting room called the Crow's Nest. Everyone was just taking their seats as we arrived. The seats had been ringed in a horseshoe around the three facing seats. My heart pounded, my breath coming in short pants through my mouth. I sat down in the middle seat with Barbara and Diane on either side. The plan was for me to open the presentation and then conclude it after the two women spoke. The energy in the room was tremendous. I'd never felt anything like it. Everyone sitting perfectly still, remembering themselves, waiting for us to begin. Lord Pentland sat behind and to one side of the group. I looked toward him for permission to speak. But he gave no sign.

I realized he was right: I wasn't ready. I was listening to my fear. It was fear that was urging me to begin, not intelligence. I relaxed my face and breathed down into the body, circulating the energy. I could sense myself coming to, the cells in the body changing, being magnetized with attention. I rested the mind in the sound beyond sound. A special quality of balancing of softness and tension, a readiness appeared—that which comes when attention no longer feeds personality but feeds upon it. The boundaries of the body expanded and I could feel an inner urging from Lord Pentland to begin. I looked toward him just to be sure. Imperceptibly, his head moved.

"When Lord Pentland first formed the study groups," I said, my voice rumbling and rasping but somehow clear, "he cautioned us that we might deceive ourselves into believing our understanding is more than a mere intellectual grasp of the topic—which today is the Food Diagram. So we'd like to admit at the outset that, in fact, we don't know what we are talking about. One of Gurdjieff's maxims at the Study House at the Prieuré was *Those who do not have critical minds have no place in the Work*. We ask then that you listen with a critical ear."

Barbara spoke next. Her voice was even, proportioned. She used not a word too many. She spoke about the Sacred Triamazikamno, or Law of Three; one of the two fundamental laws of the universe. She recounted how Gurdjieff had said that one of the most central of the ideas of objective knowledge is the idea of the unity of everything, of unity in diversity. These forces are the Holy-Affirming, Holy-Denying and Holy-Reconciling; or active, passive, and neutralizing. These forces correspond to the three Hindu gunas known as rajas, tamas and sattva. The Indian Samkaya system, however, had lost the recognition that these forces are changing levels of vibration, one force passing into another. And so Samkaya had fixed the forces. Active was always active, passive always passive, and so forth. This was an example of how knowledge can become distorted with heropass, with time.

When the unity of the Absolute divides itself into these three forces, the first manifestation of being-vibration is created. It is under three orders of laws; the three orders corresponding to the three forces. Successive degrees of manifestation, from fine to subtle to gross, are created as these three primary forces descend through the scale of the Ray of Creation. The lower on the Ray that a being exists, the more materially dense and less vivifying and potent its vibration, its intelligence. (Note: intelligence should not be confused with intellect.)

Because the order of laws through which manifestation projects and functions multiplies with where it is on the Ray, the lower the level the less free, less conscious, more mechanical. True evolution for a human being, then, would be to ascend to higher and higher levels of vibration, passing from identification with oneself as an indivisible entity to the stark recognition that, indeed, one is composed of many "I"s. Working with this, voluntarily living in the "fire" of one's life, striving to consciously labor and intentionally suffer to create and elaborate certain substances in accordance with the necessary shocks, one gradually evolves to greater and greater degrees of freedom and intelligence (and responsibility as well) until one reaches real I.

Whatever the frequency of vibrations in the scale of the Ray of Creation, the affirming, denying and reconciling forces manifest in all events. For no event can happen without the presence of pushing, resisting and reconciling forces. And, most important, though we are generally aware of active and passive forces, we are "third force blind." Formatory thinking is a product of split-mind that operates on too gross and heavy a level. At the higher levels of intelligence, those closer to unity, we become aware of this Holy-Reconciling force. In awakening to this third force, seekers become aware of the Sacred Triamazikamno at work and so are able to do because they are aware of and acting from wholeness and not an "I." Rightly balanced and connected, the higher being bodies can be coated, or fed. When right crystallization takes place at higher levels of vibration, an equivalent freedom, intelligence and consciousness is experienced—a human being lives in a higher world. The person may be in this world but their real I is not of it.

It was so beautiful to hear Barbara speak. There was such economy and grace.

Diane spoke next. Her subject was the Sacred Heptaparaparshinokh, or Law of Seven, the second fundamental law of the universe. The universe is made up of vibrations, extending from the finest of pure energy down to the coarsest, most dense matter. Our Ray of Creation (for there are infinite rays) descends from the Absolute down to our sun, and from the sun to the earth, and the earth to the moon. While modern science takes these vibrations to be continuous, in fact, they are always fluctuating, rising and falling, growing weaker or stronger. The vibrations do not develop uniformly. They are discontinuous. That is, the vibrations moving in octaves throughout the Ray of Creation are subject to periodic retardations, or intervals. With the musical octave of Do-Re-Mi-Fa-Sol-La-Si, for example, the smallest intervals of vibration occur between the notes Mi-Fa and Si-Do. This is precisely where retardation of the vibration of the Ray of Creation occurs. A shock, or new energy, is necessary in the intervals or the original impulse of the vibration would either be aborted or deflected from its original direction, often turning into its opposite. Nothing in the universe is static. Everything is in motion, either ascending with increasing energy, or descending with decreasing energy.

There are two types of octaves, ascending and descending. Ascending octaves are evolutionary in that they are returning to the Absolute. Descending octaves are creative in that they create something; that is, they move successively from the invisible to the visible plane of existence. By an octave receiving conscious shocks at the necessary places (between Mi-Fa and Si-Do) it can continue to move in a straight line. In man's transformation the first conscious shock is given by self-remembering. Then, by not identifying, we allow the octave to refine and elaborate its processing so that we come to the point of second conscious shock whose sudden upsurge demands even greater knowledge and being. We see the Law of Octaves at work in the Food Diagram in the air, physical food and impressions octaves.

And with that Diane glanced at me, a sly look in her eye, and went on to speak about the relationship of these foods to the Food Diagram.

I felt the body burning in anger.

We had agreed beforehand that Diane was supposed to speak only about the Law of Seven. Had she unconsciously "drifted" into my part of the presentation? Or had she done so deliberately? Had Lord Pentland asked her to give me a shock?

I couldn't know.

The energy continued to boil in my stomach. I was on the verge of being seized by this "I." But I was seeing it. The head was still clear. I was still separate from the organic reaction. I knew at once that if I let my thought mix with that energy, if I identified, I'd blow up. I had to maintain the separation. Choose and will a higher influence. Simply watch, empty out, offer no resistance. Favor, as Gurdjieff said, "the non-desires over the desires."

Slowly, of itself, I noted that the chaos of fiery energy balanced out, reorientated itself, became interior…

Diane is saying that the ingestion of the three foods, physical food, air and impressions, evolves from coarser to finer and finer substances. Each of the three foods enters the human body as the note Do and—with the help of active substances within the body and the introduction of the other foods—each food evolves to a finer substance (with the exception of impressions which require the shock of self-remembering to evolve further than its initial Do).

When the three foods are regulated and properly digested, a fine alchemical energy builds up in the body, which is the foundation of an individual's transformation to a higher level of vibration and consciousness.

She stops and glances at me.

I slowly regard everyone in the group. I do not look at Lord Pentland. There is a certain fear, apprehension, of his giving me a shock of some sort. A massive stillness comes up in the room. It is like everything and everyone is in high relief.

I begin to speak, my voice coming from deep in the abdomen. I go into the actual Food Diagram itself, moving through the process of digestion of air, physical food and impressions, showing how each of these octaves evolves within the "processing factory" that is the body. I speak, for example, of how physical food enters the human factory as Do 768 and meeting the active substance carbon refines itself to Re 192. This in turn evolves to Mi 96 and so forth onto Si 12, or being-Exioëhary.

This is dangerous, this recitation of numbers, the processing of energy along the scale of vibration. One inattentive moment, one slip, one wrong number in relating the various numbers and substances within the process—and the mind might freeze, the connection with memory blur. And I'd just be sitting there like some yokel.

This cloud of thought moves in on me. I push it away, keep my attention on what I am speaking about. At the same time, I keep the attention supple so it does not to fix and localize.

Lord Pentland makes a quick hand movement—I realize I just made a mistake with the recitation of numbering.

Immediately—not inner considering, not going into the head—I correct myself and go on, speaking about Fa 96, and realizing I hadn't planned to speak about this. But it was too late to stop.

I explain how Fa 96 is that substance in the body we call vitality or health or animal magnetism. It is what gives our bodies an "atmosphere" If we are identified with a negative emotion, if we have put our feeling of "I" in it, or a continual state of worry, then the body may make very little of the substance Fa 96. If Fa 96 is interfered with, then the next note and level of refining in the physical food process, Sol 48, may be interfered with. Sol 48 is the substance the mind uses for concentrating, thinking or making any effort of attention. So with a loss of vitality we will likely lose a power of mind.

The next note and refinement of energy in the process is La 24. It is the energy with which the emotional center works. If the previous notes have been affected, then the body will make very little La 24. Hence, a low state of emotion, a feeling of boredom, malaise and possible depression. Such interference in the processing will cause the last note and substance in the physical food octave, Si 12, or being-Exioëhary, not to "sound" strongly enough. The result is loss of potency, force, and too little substance available to saturate the cells of the body and prepare for transformation.

However, if the shock of self-remembering is given, and if the process is not distorted with identification which serves only to deplete and discolor energy, then the necessary energy will be available to coat and crystallize the Kesdjan body. As the physical food octave is processed so, too, must the air and impressions octaves be similarly elaborated without distortion for the octaves to fully develop. If this is done again and again over a sufficient period of time and with the necessary intensity and knowledge, then transformation becomes lawful. The demand has been met, the payment made and now a new level of being is crystallized.

"As was noted in the beginning," I say, "I would like to restate that none of us really knows what he or she is talking about so, hopefully, you have listened with 'a critical ear.' Are there any questions?"

I end with that, and experience an incredible surge of energy flooding the body. I feel expanded in space. I hadn't once looked directly at Lord Pentland. Now I do so. He appears not to notice. He gives me no attention…

Several questions came from the group. We handled them easily. Finally, there were no more questions and Lord Pentland closed the presentation. We all smiled at one another. It was as though we had rafted a dangerous stretch of white water and had somehow gotten through it. We hadn't capsized, hadn't identified. We'd covered the material. And taken some big chances.

Then Lord Pentland gave a summation:

"What we have heard today is the basis of real psychology, real science," he said. "It is ancient knowledge and shows, if we study it, the processes and shocks involved that lead to our coming to real I." He paused, allowing time for that to register. "Perhaps we were all surprised that a thing supposedly as dry as the Food Diagram could be spoken about with such emotion." Lord Pentland stopped, looked about the group, and then added, "A good lawyer learns to have his intellectual center function in the face of great emotion."

And with that Lord Pentland stood up and strode out of the Crow's Nest.

We'd worked so long and hard—and that was it? That was all he had to say? I couldn't believe it. That was it! Something raged in me that I could barely contain. I left the room quickly.

As I came down from the Crow's Nest, I saw him standing talking to Becky at the second floor landing. I thought he might say something, give some little nod of approval. But there was only that empty-eyed look—as if I wasn't there. Didn't exist.

It was like a torch to a stack of hay. I burst into flames inside while I bit down all outer reaction.

The strange thing was that I was seeing all this. I knew his action was deliberate. That he was teaching me. I was to see how identified I'd suddenly become. But "I" didn't want to be taught right then. "I" just wanted a little human response. We'd knocked one out of the park, and all he could do was fish-eye me! "I" was in total, magnificent reaction.

I passed him on the landing. Ignored him completely. I think he smiled even as I went by. I continued down the stairwell, not once looking back. I saw that "I" had its ears erect, waiting to hear his call to come back. But no call came.

Outside, I got the car and pulled it up alongside the Foundation. It was a dreary gray day, lifeless and cold. I sat in the car, the motor running, ten thousand thoughts running through my head. Beneath me, the ground suddenly shook. The muffled sound of a dynamite explosion. They were tunneling for the subway. Lying on the sidewalk was a dead pigeon. It must have just died as it hadn't been there earlier.

The door of the Foundation kept opening. One by one, members of the group came out. My chess player friend came over to the car. I rolled down the window. He told me "You guys really did a good job."

I forced a smile and thanked him, nodded, and rolled the window back up. I remembered him telling me that after his group had given its presentation, he'd flown out of town on business. Alone in a sterile motel room thousands of miles from New York, the recurring images of his self-love on full and glorious display before Lord Pentland and the group had him moaning his head off and beating the walls.

The Foundation door continued to open and close.

Where the hell was Barbara?

Finally, I turned off the motor. I felt like I was alone inside a bubble looking out at a world I couldn't touch.

The car jerked as more tremors and muffled explosions sounded beneath me.

What the hell was keeping her!

I sat staring out the windshield. Nothing to see but two portable toilets and stacks of pilings and pipe to be used in building the subway. Nothing but crap, and this mangy dead pigeon on the sidewalk, probably diseased. The car got cold. I turned on the motor and heater.

The door opened again. There she was—smiling.

"Where were you?" she asked, alive with energy, her eyes shining.

"I was here."

"He sent me to look for you but I couldn't find you. He talked to us about his days with Ouspensky. It was wonderful, Pat."

"Yeah. I bet it was."

"He talked about how he had learned the Food Diagram from Mr. Ouspensky, since there were no books then. He said Ouspensky would illustrate his talks with drawings he would make on the spot. The circles he made were perfect. He said Ouspensky combined movement and emotion with intellect. All his movements were so graceful, so beautiful, he said. They just flowed from one movement to another and—" Barbara stopped. "Honey! Why did you leave?"

I stepped on the gas and pulled away from the Foundation just as another chthonic blast sounded.

"Pat! What's wrong? What happened? You look so strange."

THE TENSION BETWEEN STANLEY AND ME MOUNTED, I NEVER WENT NEAR him now unless I had to. I only talked to him when it was necessary. I was polite, to the point, nothing more. I treated him like a ghost. Gave him the "silent treatment."

I was forcing matters. And I knew it. But I had had enough of Stanley. Enough of the lies, the games and schemes. Enough of the vulgarity. Enough of how he "sold" ads. Stanley was an ace trickster. Craymere, another salesman on the staff, had told me how if Stanley couldn't hook a reluctant advertiser through the commonly accepted sales techniques of flattery, sports tickets, vacations, or whores, he'd invite the prospect to a "backgammon dinner." There were all sorts of kickbacks to advertisers, Craymere said, but this was what he called, "Pure Stanley," not without a grudging respect.

Over after-dinner cigars and brandy, Craymere told me, Stanley would open his attache case and produce a small, expensively tooled backgammon set.

"Just for fun," Stanley would say and then mutter, "A dime a point?"

And of course Stanley, a consummate player, always lost and lost big.

And, always, he insisted at game's end that he and the client had been playing for not a dime a point—but ten dollars a point.

And Stanley would count onto the tablecloth three new one hundred dollar bills.

If the client protested, Stanley would give that little snorting hyena laugh and tell him—"Don't be silly! You won it fair and square."

Once the client took the money, he became Stanley's "fish." Backgammon dinners became part of the sales call and, somehow, it was now much easier to buy ad space from Stanley.

I knew what was going on. And I knew Spencer knew. Enough people had told him. But he wouldn't stop it. Stanley had something on Spencer. Or had been useful to him. That, or maybe Stanley "acted" on Spencer in some way. In any case, Spencer wasn't about to fire Stanley. Too many heads had already rolled trying to get Stanley axed.

So what was I doing now, not speaking to him? What was I asking for? I didn't care. I'd had enough.

Sarah knew Stanley better than anyone. She was working now for an engineering company up the Hudson River. She sounded wonderful when I called. We arranged to meet the next day for lunch at a roadhouse near the Palisades. I got tied up in traffic and arrived late. There was a blonde at the bar drinking a Bloody Mary with her back to the door. I mistook her for Sarah. She had the same sculpted bright red fingernails, the long sensitive fingers. I saw Sarah then at the end of a long row of booths. I smiled and sat down. It had been two or three years since we'd last seen one another. She seemed tentative, troubled. We had a few Bloody Marys, just talked casually, and there again finally was the old "Sarah." I noticed she kept looking over my shoulder. I looked around. The blonde was eating her lunch at the bar. It was a square bar and several salesmen had sat down adjacent to her. They were talking, joshing, giving off an impression. She took it all in. Very contained. Aware of them. All of her movements—the way she lifted her drink, bit into her sandwich, moved her shoulders—were clear and precise. The salesmen were in their heads talking. She talked, too, but not in words.

"She knows exactly what she's doing, doesn't she?" said Sarah.

"Yeah. Look at those guys. They don't know what to make of it."

"They know," said Sarah. "They just don't want to admit it to themselves."

"What's that?"

Sarah paused, then lit a Marlboro and inhaled deeply." Why do you pretend not to know all the time?" she asked.

I looked back at the blonde. One of the men was talking to her now. Then he made his move. He came over to her side of the bar. But she had made her move a long time ago. She was like a spider who had spun its web and then simply waited.

"She's quite a huntress, isn't she?"

Sarah nodded. Her mouth smiled. Her eyes were frozen. "She reminds me of myself," said Sarah.

I looked back at the bar. The guy was talking his head off, in love with himself, going wild with the blonde's attention. Yes, she knew exactly what she was doing.

"You see yourself like that?" I asked.

"A side of me. Or in Work terms—an 'I.' It really hurts to see it. I don't know why I come around you. This always happens."

"What's that?"

Sarah took a long drag. Her eyes were so direct. "I see something I don't want to see."

"You told me that in Mexico."

"I did? Good God!"

"Well, I don't like looking back either."

"But you look back all the time. Don't you know that?" Sarah arched an eyebrow. "It's hard for you to let things go."

"Why do you think?"

"I don't know. Maybe…maybe you believe in things too much." Sarah stared at me, the sadness in her voice still echoing in her face.

The waitress came. Sarah ordered a cheeseburger. I ordered a spinach salad and a half carafe of red wine.

"Still a vegetarian, Mr. Patterson?"

"Yeah, I guess."

"You mean Barbara's one so you're one, too."

"You might say that. She's a fanatic about it now. I wanted to write a piece about it, so I suggested we become vegetarians for three months. She refused, at first. You know, she's been to both French and Chinese cooking schools. She has all these cookbooks and not one for vegetarian cooking. But the idea soaked in and so one night I came home and there's my first vegetarian meal."

"What happened after three months?"

"Well, I felt a lot better. I did. But I'd have probably gone back to meat. But for Barbara that was it. So, in one sense, you're right. I have some meat now and then. But, actually, I do feel better."

Sarah exhaled a long draft of smoke. She sat back and glared.

"Sorry," she said at last. "Your wife always brings out the claws in me. But nothing personal. You understand? Just my 'mother' in me doing her thing." Sarah sighed. "Well…now what's this about Stanley and you?"

"Have you been seeing Lord Pentland?"

"Yes. I'm not ready to go back to group meetings yet. John and I have lunch together sometimes, the poor man."

"John?" I chuckled. "You and *John?*"

"I have this way of making gods out of people. I need not to do that anymore."

"Yes, the gods play through us. And we can recognize that. But if we make others into gods, not seeing the goddess in ourselves, then…well, we go to 'Africa.'"

Sarah nodded but she hadn't listened. "Sometimes he, you know, gets psoriasis on his hands." She must have heard herself for she added in another tone: "Very human of old John, considering all the responsibility he has."

"Yes. Some people criticize him for being too doctrinaire. But that comes out of this belief in democracy and education being the answer to all of man's ills. Just be free enough, know enough, and everything will be fine."

"It won't?" Sarah grinned, prodding me on.

"It overlooks the fundamental thing: man himself. The unconscious assumption of those ideas is that man is a unity. That he's awake. Give democracy and education to false personality and imaginary 'I' and what do you have? Just a more sophisticated, deluded ego."

"So the answer is for us to wake up to who we're not, no?"

"Right. That's the only real and lasting hope. Gurdjieff says that we have fulfilled Nature's use for us—the moon has been fed enough. It will one day have an atmosphere, become a living planet. We fulfilled that task mechanically. Now there's a greater task but a new demand. The demand is that our action be conscious."

"Otherwise?"

"What galaxy do you next want to meet in?"

"That's why the Work ideas have to be kept pure?"

"Right. It's what Pentland understands. People say he's too severe, too uncompromising. But they just don't see the scale of things, the seriousness and, yes, in another sense entirely: *The terror of the situation.*"

"But if it's that bad and people are still asleep, then don't we have to take a chance and put the Work ideas out there and hope for the best?"

"A lot of Work ideas have already entered popular culture. But they're sterile. People can't go deeply enough into them without being in the Work. You only mix the sacred with the profane at your peril. It can only lead to black magic because the ideas are understood and put in use by what? The ego. You know, there's the theory that the *Upanishads* were once esoteric, given only to the few. When that teaching was made public, it polluted the atmosphere. Look at so much of India. Almost totally tamasic, full of inertia, superstition, sleep. The ideas were taken on the level of the ego. They made things even worse. And look at what we have in this country already—corporations using spiritual practices and techniques for what? To make a buck. We're becoming the new Atlantis in its last days."

"Well, William, I see you're still in fine form."

"Ahh, let's have some more wine. Toast Dionysus."

The waitress came with the cheeseburger and spinach salad. I ordered a bottle of Mouton Cadet red.

"Enjoy," said Sarah, biting into her cheeseburger.

"You, too," I answered and we both laughed.

I told her then what had happened with Stanley. How I had made the sales presentations and how he had reneged on the raise and that I was giving him the "silent treatment."

"So you made a pact with the devil? How unlike him not to keep his side of the bargain."

"Well, I didn't see it quite that way."

"You better watch yourself, William. Stanley's dangerous."

"Yeah. Mary, one of our saleswomen just called to warn me—'He's out to get you,' she told me."

"Anyway he can, no?"

"What did she mean by that?"

"Exactly what she said, William."

"She says he's selling against *Food.*"

"What?" Sarah frowned. "That doesn't make sense."

"I agree. You know Spencer made him a vice president and a group publisher over all three of the company's food industry books? Mary says he's damning *Food* and playing up the other two books. Crazy, huh? I can't believe it. Why would he do that?"

"I don't know, but remember, Stanley doesn't play by rules. You remember that symbol in his office?"

I had forgotten. It was the year after we'd come back from Mexico. Everything I did was turning to gold. Stanley was hating it.

"The poor man had lost his grip on you. You took all his weapons. First, his magazine, then me, your guilt—he couldn't push your guilt button. You had escaped. You were robbing him of his power. He had to resort to black magic."

I remembered the story. During Christmas, Stanley went to Haiti. Stanley had told us how he had trekked up into the hills to see some voodoo witch doctor. The witch doctor had built this big campfire and put two candles in Stanley's hands. He lit the candles from the fire. Then he had pissed on the fire until it was extinguished. There they were alone in the forest together, the strange animal sounds all around, and the only light that of the two candles. Stanley had told the witch doctor of his problem. Stanley wouldn't say what it was or what the witch doctor had done but now he carried three stones in his pocket.

Sarah had understood at once what or who Stanley's "problem" was. I thought it might be Spencer. Or one of Stanley's enemies in the industry. But it was me, Sarah said. "You've gotten too big for him. He's lost control over you. He wants it back," Sarah said. We went into Stanley's office one evening after everyone had gone home. There on his bulletin board was a piece of paper with a strange symbol on it. I knew the symbol had to do with those stones. I acted instinctively. I took it down and traced over it on another piece of paper, making small inexactitudes, so that it wasn't the identical symbol. Then I pinned the copy up on the board and took the original into my office and burned it in a waste paper basket. Sarah had watched all this without saying a word. "What are you doing?" Sarah asked. "Taking the power from it," I answered. I was operating from a knowledge I didn't know I had. "Good God, you're right!" Sarah exclaimed.

The waitress came with coffee for Sarah, herbal tea for me. We looked at each other with that good feeling. It was just like the old days. I felt I had known Sarah for many lifetimes. She could be self-destructive, erratic, but there was something very wise, very ancient about her.

Our eyes met. An energy began to flow. Our faces changing, bodies expanding...

"Mexico. It seems so far away. A thousand years back," I say. "And yet it's here right now, isn't it."

"Could you take the responsibility?"

She says *responsibility* as both a reproach and a challenge. She never understood: I can only take responsibility for my own actions, not hers. Yes, the body wanted her. And I would like to have shared that energy and vibration again. But I couldn't take the chance on her getting lost in it again.

"No," I tell her. "I guess not."

Just then—flames shoot out of the ashtray! We both freeze, our eyes locked together.

"The gods, I guess. They've spoken," Sarah says...

The shock frightened and contracted me. I examined the ashtray. There was a pack of matches in it. Her cigarette had set them on fire. For most people that was enough of an explanation.

"You know, William, I've always wanted to tell you this. And I guess this is a good time. You probably don't know what a confusion it is for a woman to be touched by anyone other than her husband. I didn't want all that suffering. But just before we went to Mexico I had a breast exam and was told I had cancer. I decided then I was going to do what I really wanted to do."

"But what happened? You were all right?"

Sarah gave an ironic grin. "A false alarm. I was rechecked when I returned. Everything was fine. Wouldn't you know it?"

So each of us gave the other a new life down there. There had been all that death around us. I remembered standing with Sarah in front of the open mouths of the feathered serpents, walking arm in arm down The Street of the Dead, then climbing the Pyramid of the Sun and her exclaiming, "Look! You can see forever!"

"Well, that was a long time ago," Sarah said. "Tell me, how's things with the Work?"

I told her what had happened with the Food Diagram and Lord Pentland.

"He's not going to give an inch, you know," Sarah said. "You're going to have to knuckle under."

"I know, I know. But—"

"William, there are no 'buts' in the Work. You're going to have to submit your will to his. Don't you see?"

"Sarah, the Work has given me a lot. I know that. But I feel...well, that there's something more. I feel something, you know, is calling me."

"Maybe, the moon, huh?" Sarah joked, arching an eyebrow.

"The moon," I said. "It's a mystic symbol. A sign of the feminine."

"But in the Work—"

"Yeah, I know. The moon represents mechanical life. We feed the moon. We have to escape from the moon. But we also have to create a 'moon' in us."

Sarah lit up another cigarette. There was a certain masculine quality that came out when she smoked. She wasn't the least sentimental then.

"Well, enough of the 'moon,'" she said. "Let's get back to Stanley. You know, if you don't feed him, you're going to see his animal. You know that?"

"Yeah, I guess."

"Hmm, it might sound strange, William. Okay, you know what I think? Stanley's a vampire. He hires people he can feed off. Stanley lives off other people's energy."

Vampire—the word startled me. I'd been groping for years to "name" Stanley. There was always this sense that I knew who he was, but I could never bring the word up.

Sarah smiled and took a sip of wine. She cocked her head, fluttered her eyes, waiting for me to say something. Suddenly, it all began to make sense to me.

"You know," I said. "In the Food Diagram there's a substance called Fa 96. It's a person's magnetic force, the atmosphere around them."

"She has a lot of it, no?" Sarah's eyes shot behind me to the bar.

I turned. The blonde was walking away with the salesman. She was nodding and smiling, her arm in his, and he was still talking. It was like a three-dimensional chess set and he was playing only on the first level.

"Well, what were you saying, Mr. Patterson?"

"Now I understand the saying that "A man chases a woman until she catches him.""

"I believe we were talking about Fa 96?"

"Oh yeah," I said. "Well, sick people, dull, habitually depressed people, very negative people, evil people—they suck the juice right out of us."

"You know now why he wanted to hire a person with 'a halo'?"

"Yeah. Weird." I finished my wine.

Sarah looked at me a long time. It seemed as if she was weighing whether to tell me something or not. Finally she said:

"You know that time you got sick?"

"You mean when I got delirious after I came back from Ireland. Yeah, that was weird. I felt something alien enter me, and I knew I was going to get sick. How do you know?"

"Well, I might as well fess up—that was me."

"Really!" I remembered thinking that at the time, but then dismissing it. It seemed absurd.

"I was down near Greenville, North Carolina, where I was born. I'd just completed a free-lance assignment and was on my way to the airport. Suddenly, this feeling came to me that I was going to see a gypsy. And there she was just around the next bend, standing outside a little roadside hut."

"A gypsy?"

"She told fortunes, you know. I stopped. I felt like I knew her. She gave me one of those toothless, funny grins, and led me inside to her bedroom. It was really ornate and gaudy. She sat me down on her bed and told me to put a twenty dollar bill in each hand. She told me to hold my hands up in front of me. Then she asked what I wanted. I told her. Do you know what I told her?"

"That you wanted me?"

"Yes."

Sarah lit up another Marlboro and took a deep drag and exhaled. It was as if she was coughing up her guts. "I told her all about us and all that had happened. I was crying and near hysterical. There was all this anger in me that I could give you everything and that you could...could just walk away like that. You don't know how that hurt me. It wasn't a little wound. It went right to the quick." Her voice trailed off.

I could feel the great sadness and the rage in Sarah even now. I hadn't treated her well. She had given me her power and once I had it, I had walked away. I hadn't valued what had happened between us. I thought it would always happen and with everyone.

"I was sitting on the bed with these two twenties in my fists thinking how crazy this all was. The gypsy woman told me to close my eyes. I was to visualize what I wanted and to pray for it aloud, three times. Well, just in the middle of the third time, my face wet with tears—she snatched the money out of my hands. And pop! I felt something go out of me and I knew it was going straight into you."

Sarah looked to see how I was taking things.

"It's okay," I told her.

"Well, a day later I am sitting stuck in my car on the Major Deegan Expressway. There's been an accident, and there's this huge line of cars. The car ahead of me had four men in it. All hunters. They had a big stag tied down on their roof. The head was facing me. It had a huge rack of antlers and its eyes were open, those soft, dark mournful eyes, and from its mouth trickled this little line of dried blood. I don't know how long I sat there looking at this stag but suddenly I realized the stag was you! That I was going to kill you, if I didn't take back that wish. But I knew, too, if I took it back, someone was going to have to die. And if it wasn't going to be you— then it would be me."

She had put the energy out there. It had to go some place. Someone had to make the payment.

"And so I died, William."

"Yes, I know."

"And now, as you see, I'm alive again. Not the old 'Sarah' but a new 'Sarah.'"

"Yes," I said.

We walked out into the parking lot. She was driving a new black jeep with giant tires. It sat high off the ground. I helped her get in and closed the door. She started up the motor. She rolled down the window and smiled. That beautiful smile. She looked back to the roadhouse...

"Funny," Sarah muses, "how I always see something when I'm with you."

"Me, too."

"It was very special what we had, William."

"Yes, very special."

The great silence and space of that moment roars between us.

"No blame," she says, smiling.

"No blame, Sarah."

"To be able to say that and mean it—do you know what I've had to live through? What I've had to pay?" This is the "Sarah" who had suffered and remembered.

I shake my head. Tears well up in my eyes. Like a tree falling, everything we had lived through together, good times and bad, suddenly is there.

"You know," Sarah says at last with that familiar little grin and chuckle, "I actually do believe you care."

"Of course I do. Why could you never believe that?"

"Lord Pentland said you were 'my catalyst, my friend in death.'"

I smile, choking back the feelings.

"Me, and Charlie Brown, huh?"

Sarah laughs and gives a little cock of the head and a half wave.

"Goodbye, William," she calls and guns the black jeep out of the parking lot.

LORD PENTLAND STRODE INTO THE CROW'S NEST AND TOOK HIS SEAT IN front of the group. There was something different about him. It was the same long, erect, crane-like, broad-shouldered body. The same face: impassive, direct dark eyes, black bushy eyebrows, large elfin ears, lobeless, almost pointed at the top.

It had been many years since we first met. He had not changed outwardly, not aged at all. The only observable difference was that, following his heart attack of a few years ago, he now wore no tie and his collar was open. Otherwise Lord Pentland was the same. But there was something different with him. I could feel it. It took over the whole room. Everyone stilled immediately. It was a certain density of force, a concentration of will and power that comes together when a line of action is to be taken. He held a yellow pad of legal-sized paper. He took us in as usual one-by-one. It was as if he set and stabilized the energy in each of us and the room. But instead of waiting for questions, he tore off the top sheet from the tablet, placed the blank tablet by his feet, and read to us:

Man is asleep. He does not know himself. He has no control over himself. The sole aim of the Work is to wake a man from his dreams and imagination, from his negative emotions and formatory thinking, so that he might become an independent Individual with objective reason having a permanent I.

Man, as he is, can bear little responsibility for his actions. And, particularly so, in these meetings where we come together to experience what prevents us from remembering ourselves. As such, in this room, no one is held responsible. We leave responsibility, so to say, 'at the door.'

At the same time, we must understand when we go too far. For we must remember, that all of us here, are only human. So we must listen to ourselves when we speak as well as when we remain silent.

We must ask ourselves why we are provocative or resistant or whatever the attitude is that shows itself. In this way we awaken to ourselves and true responsibility.

I knew immediately who he was talking to. At the last meeting I had been sitting in the back row. A young blonde-haired woman, an over-effusive TV soap opera actress, had asked a rather plaintive question about not being able to observe herself. Lord Pentland had answered but he made something entirely different out of her question. I had seen him do this many times but, in this instance, I felt his answer missed the point. Could that be true?

At the end of his answer, apparently as an afterthought, he had asked—

"Tell me—what do you keep in your 'ice box'?"

"Ice box?" the actress exclaimed.

"You know…"Lord Pentland replied dryly.

The actress swept back her long mane of blonde hair, and shifted uncomfortably in her chair. She looked at him quizzically. "No," she said.

Lord Pentland stared at her. "Fridge," he said softly.

"Fridge?" The actresses' eyes were wide as quarters. It was as if the shock of the word's obvious associations had stripped her naked.

The whole room exploded in silence.

An energy in me rumbled. It didn't seem fair. I was angered. Should I say something? For a second I hesitated. Then a voice shot out of me: "You've twisted her words. You made her question into something she hadn't asked at all. You manipulated her words."

It was as if my words had risen up and slapped him hard across the face. I had struck him with the full force of my attention.

We faced one another squarely.

It was just Lord Pentland and me. Alone. No one else in the room.

I was there, not leaking, not imagining, focused in the sensation. I'd slapped him with all my might. His face showed nothing. But I could sense in him a certain immobility, a stoppage of breath, and his making an enormous effort not to react.

"I don't trust you, or the Work hierarchy," I added pointedly.

Lord Pentland nodded in agreement.

Many moments passed. Then he replied in a measured voice, laying his words carefully, like stones along a new-made path—"We must ask our own questions. Is there anything to be gained by hitching onto someone else's question? I think not."

With that he ended the meeting.

I realized I had crossed a line. I had taken a chance on myself. I had said what I really felt. I didn't trust him. All that he had done for me and I still didn't trust him. I wanted to. I knew I needed to. And this, strange as it was, was my way of telling him.

My world changed now, and quickly. Where it was headed, I had no idea. But a new energy had been released. Everything began to shift. Like a river that had broken its banks, there was no stopping it. No space or time to look back. There was only action. Event and action. Action and event.

I had been attending a weekly painting class given by Paul Reynard, a short, solidly built Frenchman with a large stoic head and strong features, who had met Gurdjieff in his youth and later studied with Madame de Salzmann (who had worked closely with Gurdjieff since 1915 and, since his death in 1949, had been the leader of the worldwide Work). Lord Pentland had brought Reynard from Paris to be the head of all the movements teachers in America. He was a group leader as well and considered by many to be Lord Pentland's heir apparent. I respected his seriousness, sincerity and commitment, and also his knowledge of the teaching and the movements, or sacred dances.

His wife, José, a slender, sensitive woman, rather shy and diffident, had a wonderful inner silence and strength. She took in everything, but said little. I had worked with her shelling peas one day in the kitchen at Armonk. She knew a great deal about the body and how to do manual work without tension. She had never attended the painting class, however, and so I was surprised when she greeted me at the door.

"Welcome," she said in a demure French accent, "...to the Theatre of Power."

I smiled and shoved my suitcase in a corner, took off my tie and jacket and put on a smock. Right after the class I had to fly to Chicago for a food convention.

Reynard said the day's exercise was to paint a picture with a partner. Each person was to make only one stroke at a time. José chose me as her partner. She motioned me to an easel holding a large poster-size sheet of paper.

"Our theatre," she said.

Everyone else got quickly to work. We stood side by side in front of the empty sheet of paper. It was corny, but that was how my life suddenly seemed. A big blank. A void.

"You first," she whispered.

"Oh, no. You be first," I said.

"But you...you are the man."

"But isn't it true," I whispered, "that we are both masculine and feminine?"

Her mouth pursed. She smiled and looked at the floor. It was more of an answer perhaps than she had expected. I was taking chances. I felt a kind of danger. But a delicious danger.

"Okay," I whispered. "I'll be first." I mixed some sap green with white and put my brush to the paper as if to make a large sweeping line—but I made only a dab in the right hand corner. It was not what she had expected.

"So small," she murmured. "Delicate."

I could feel the energy releasing inside; a surprise and warmth. I had taken the "feminine" part. Would she play the man...?

José chooses a brush and mixes a bit of white with Prussian Blue. She goes to the easel and, without hesitation, makes a thicker mark. It's just a hair larger than mine but at the opposite corner of the paper. My body vibrates. She has accepted the wordless invitation and we both now step together into the "Theatre of Power." Thus begins our silent dance, each movement, each gesture and look, each stroke of the brush, taking us deeper and deeper into the inaccessible.

I let the feminine in me paint. As we move along, I notice her strokes become bolder and bolder. She realizes I meant her to lead the way, to take the reins of the horse. My strokes are only accents, or counterpoints, to hers. The change from rigid gender pattern delights us both and we glow with energy.

After a time, out of the tangle of lines and markings, the mixing of our energies, we both sense an image on the paper waiting to be born. Saying nothing, not looking at one another, our eyes only on the creation before us—we begin to bring it forth, to strengthen or weaken the notes of the image's energy and form.

Behind us I suddenly sense another energy...

I turned. Reynard stuck his head between us to see what we were up to. A former student of Leger, he took in the painting, then cleared his throat, and moved on. He said nothing. He didn't have to. The incredible silence and feeling were gone. We tried to light the flame again, but such flames aren't lit by effort. We could never step back into the image. It remained outside us, an object. The class soon ended. José and I smiled at one another knowingly. She had in fact introduced me to The Theatre of Power. The question was—what was the name of this play I was in?

I caught a cab to La Guardia and just made the plane. But then we sat on the tarmac. An electrical problem. The plane was two hours late getting into Chicago and when it landed my luggage had been lost. I caught a cab to the Drake Hotel, but they claimed I'd never made a reservation and so it went. I finally ended up at the Continental Plaza and simply collapsed into bed. When I awoke the next morning, I reached for the book on the night table that I had brought with me, the *Bhagavad Gita*. Using it like the *I Ching*, I asked who was the God of this adventure and opened the book at random.

I am Shiva, Destroyer of Worlds it read. It was the same phrase Oppenheimer had quoted after the first atomic bomb blast. I lay in bed, staring at the words: *I am Shiva, Destroyer of Worlds.* I got that weird feeling, familiar now, that I am embarked upon another "adventure" and this is the calling card of the presiding deity.

I put the book down and looked about the room. The room was an expensive piece of nothing. Dressed up like a modern Spanish bordello. Red flocked wall paper, shiny green bedspread, prints of life in a bull ring, the matador making brilliant passes with his red cape. The last print showing the goring of the fallen matador. I was "reading" and I didn't like the message. I'd always felt Stanley's animal was the bull. He kept a small glass bull on his desk.

My mouth was pasty. The air was stale. The air conditioning wouldn't work. And the windows were screwed shut. I awoke wheezing and felt as if little men with rubber hammers had beaten me all night. Since my luggage had been lost, I had to wear yesterday's clothes. I felt groggy, but I dressed and took a cab to McCormick Place where the big food show was being held.

McCormick Place looked like a massive airplane hangar. On two floors were nearly a thousand booths with banners and signs, staffed with sales people and actors, models and magicians giving product demos, hawking the latest in man-made foods, microwaves, big stoves and ovens for volume cooking, refrigeration equipment, dishwashers, cutlery, costumes, management and motivation courses, computerized inventory and portion control systems and gadgets of all types. The top floor, covered with a plush red carpet, was for the money guys in the industry, the big name food and equipment companies. Here the aisles were wide and the exhibitors took up plenty of space, building glitzy or pseudo-refined two story booths with hideaways for private dealing and plenty of freebies. On the bottom floor, packed together like ants in an anthill, were all the no names or second-rate companies who'd clawed their way into existence or were fighting to stay there, to hold their tiny market share. It was something to see, perhaps once.

Every year, like a tribal gathering, the whole food industry met in Chicago, the slaughter house city, to hype, sell and introduce products of man-made devitalized frozen foods, colored and jelled and reduced to minimal protein; make contacts, swap war stories, hold press conferences and hospitality suites, give breakfasts, luncheons and dinners at expensive eateries and generally carouse and schmooze on the company tab. The food show at McCormick was the crown jewel, the big draw.

But the capper to the festivities was the Gold Cup Awards Dinner. It was the final gala event at which all the industry notables gathered in a mammoth hotel ballroom for a $100-a-plate, five-course meal, complete with champagne and wines. Companies bought whole tables and their executives, many in black tie or wearing company jackets and ties, arrived in stretch limos with clients in tow.

Following the meal, everyone prepared for the "big event." Don Diego cigars would come out, the lights would dim and each of the editors-in-chief of the competing industry magazines would be announced over the loud speaker—And now... *William Patterson, Editor-in-Chief of Food Magazine!* A giant spotlight would arc through the darkened ballroom to the appropriate table and seat and the illuminated editor would arise to accept a rousing ballroom ovation. Editors waved and publishers beamed and the advertisers and industry hierarchy clapped. When the last of the editors had been so anointed, the Gold Cup Awards presentation commenced with awards being given to those restaurant operators and foodservice directors who, in judgment of the assembled editors, had managed the year's best foodservice operations.

I went to McCormick Place to put in the expected "editorial appearance," we editors being regarded by some as the royalty of the industry; by others as necessary pawns in the game. I walked the red carpet, making the obligatory booth stops, showed my *Food* face, left my business card, and an hour later caught a cab back to the Continental Plaza. Something odd was happening inside me. It felt like little goldfish were swimming up and down my spine. I was having hot flashes. The body was generating loads of electricity. Too much. I felt like a rag doll coming loose at the ends. My breathing was strained. I fell into bed and closed my eyes. I was going to get sick or delirious.

I awakened. I'd had a healing dream. And now I felt wonderful. My breathing had returned to normal. The goldfish were gone. Just a sensation now. I leapt out of bed. I had an editorial presentation to make. Stanley and I were scheduled to make a pitch to a major ad agency that controlled five big food accounts. I got to the agency late but, fortunately, another magazine was still giving its presentation.

Stanley was in the reception area. Ever since Spencer had made him a vice president, Stanley was trying to look the part of a senior executive. He was smoking Dunhills now and had affected his English gentleman's look, mustache, manners and an expensive, three-piece, gray herring bone suit. He leaned over and whispered:

"Bill, where have you been? You're late!"

"Overslept."

"Jesus Christ! This is an important presentation."

"You nervous?"

"No. Of course not. Why? Do I look nervous?"

I picked up *Restaurant Business* and thumbed through it. Stanley was nervous all right. The flattery and fawning, the procuring and trickery hadn't worked here. The agency was serious. I looked over at Stanley who was busy primping.

"Welll, hellooo!" Stanley shouted, producing a big smile and laugh, and springing out of his seat to greet an agency vice president.

We were led down a long, softly-lit corridor lined with agency awards and ad campaigns into a large, expensively-appointed conference room overlooking the Chicago skyline. The long mahogany table was chair-to-chair with slick and savvy looking account and media people. Stanley was all showbiz, working the room quickly, sincere handshakes, the big adulatory greeting, the little personal remembrance. He was good at it, but always overplayed it. He took up a position then at the head of the table, standing, his hands holding the back of a chair, his head bowed, leaning towards the group. He paused for effect and then lifted his head, grinned and with great seriousness of tone told a screwball joke about editors. Polite laughter. Stanley started to tell another, but the agency head broke him off:

"Stanley, there's a big dinner tonight. Let's get on with it, if you don't mind."

"More statistics and less shtick, eh?" said Stanley, giving a choked hyena laugh.

Real laughter this time and with that Stanley flicked open his brief case, heaped a pile of reports on the conference table, and launched into a super serious intro of circulation, audience profile and readership scores of the company's three food industry magazines. He didn't say much about *Food* but ended by giving me an elaborate introduction, so elaborate it couldn't be true. I ran through a slide presentation, giving the rationale behind the editorial focus, showing how it played out in terms of stories and illustrations and ended with the awards we had won.

"*Food* has won four major journalism awards," I stated, "including what is regarded as the Pulitzer prize of business press journalism—the Neal Award for the best business publication of the year. We have nine competitors. Not one has ever won that award in their entire existence. And how many awards have our nine competitors won in the seven years *Food* has existed?" I slowly searched the faces in the room. Letting the moment build before I said: "All together they have won…just one award. That in itself says more than all the statistics and glittering generalities you'll hear today. That speaks to the quality of editorial environment you'll be placing your clients' ads in. Those ads will be read because *Food* is read. We're read by foodservice directors because *Food* has the courage to report on foodservices' real problems and possibilities."

Stanley stood for the wrap-up. His smile was so big his eyes looked like slits. He began, using his deepest, most sincere sounding voice:

"Well, William is proud of his awards. But what are awards after all? What do they really mean to readers? Do the readers care? A lot of very good fiction, for example, prize-winning fiction, is never read…" and he went on in this way, pointing out *Food's* shortcoming and playing up the strong points of the company's other two food magazines.

I sat stunned. Suddenly, I realized what I had heard from our sales people was true—Stanley was selling against my magazine. But why? It hit me then: if he could pull ad space out of *Food* and put it into our other two magazines, the resulting loss in ad revenue for *Food* would bring Spencer running. He'd be open to redesigning and repositioning *Food*. That would give Stanley the opening he needed to manipulate himself back into power again. It was a clever sacrifice. Stanley should have been a chess player. At the end of his wrap-up, I stood up and one-by-one refuted each of the points he had made against *Food*. Stanley sat with his chin buried in his throat. The ad agency executives looked bewildered. I was angry as hell.

Before the Golden Cup dinner I went to an industry party at the Bastille restaurant. I was still seething. I spied Josephine talking to Stanley in a corner. My relationship with Josephine had a short tumultuous history, all centered around the magazine. Her fiance was an ad exec for some very large food manufacturers. Josephine was a dietitian. In order to keep the fiance happy, Spencer had hired Josephine as a consultant on *Food*. Josephine, a freckly, high-spirited red head with leopard green eyes, didn't know a damn about journalism, but power and intrigue were second nature. She battled regularly with Stanley. They were like two cats hissing and clawing. Failing to become the magazine's publisher, Josephine maneuvered herself into becoming its editorial director. I was instantly in her cross-hairs. I let her do the magazine's food section, but kept her out of the editorial. One day she called me into her office, those large green eyes hard with rage. She closed the door and locked it. She was all venom, screaming, cursing—"Now Bill! You bastard! I'm the editorial director of this magazine and I will decide what we run and don't run…" That failing, Josephine went for the eyes, trying to stare me down. For a good twenty minutes we went eyeball-to-eyeball. She was quite an animal, all hate and poison pouring from that beautiful freckled face. Her emanations would have blown me out of the room if I hadn't emptied out, become passive. She reminded me of the evil witch in the fairy tales.

"Josephine's one nasty, powerful bitch, huh?" Sarah had said. "Well, William, a few scratch marks but I think you've won your wings."

Fortunately, just after the first issue Josephine's fiance was fired and Spencer paid her to leave. I hadn't seen her in years. Nor did I want to. There was something maleficent about her. She was wearing a hideous fox scarf with two fox heads hanging at either side of her bosom. Josephine spotted me and came over to the bar.

"Hello there, Bill! How you been? Here, pet my friends," Josephine told me in her nasal twangy Southern accent. She held up the two fox heads. "C'mon now, honey! They won't bite you."

A little voice told me not to pet them. Josephine insisted.

"What's a matter? Big old you afraid?" cackled Josephine.

To get rid of her, I finally petted the heads. As soon as I did I knew I shouldn't have. I felt contaminated in a certain way. The image of the Old Maid cards with the Big Bad Wolf came up. The fox was another symbol for the wolf. I could feel I was stepping back into that world again.

Two long-legged dietitians came up to the bar. They weren't going to the Golden Cup Dinner. They were going to Chez Paul and invited me to come. I decided to skip the Golden Cup. I could just see Stanley sitting there at the table with an empty chair in a spotlight. Let him explain that one. I would go back and tell Spencer what had happened with the presentation. He had to make a choice: either Stanley goes or I go. The odds were against me. But I'd had enough.

At Chez Paul the two dietitians began talking about soup bases and portion control and asking my opinion. I was feeling like I had made a mistake. One suggested that maybe I should go to the dinner. It wasn't too late. I went to the men's room. Craymere was there. He was drunk, wobbling about, trying to find his balance, looking in the mirror and trying to comb his hair. He was a damn good space salesman but Stanley, sensing a rival, had fired him. Craymere had no respect for Stanley. Like Abel and Cain, they'd gotten into it from the start. Stanley was always spreading stories about him. It had finally come down to Spencer choosing between them. Nobody wanted Stanley except Spencer. Out on the street, Craymere had run through a series of jobs, started drinking heavily, gotten divorced and, from what I heard, had run up a big debt. A smooth talking, good-looking guy, great with the ladies, Craymere was smart but didn't always act smart. Something was eating on him.

One evening it came out. He told me that his old man had run off after he was born. Craymere had never seen him until a few years ago when he was taking a whore into some broken down hotel on the Bowery and he saw this bum who looked just like him. He knew it was his father. He talked to the guy and finally got him to admit who he was. That was the first and last time he saw his father, as he died shortly thereafter. "My old man was a bum," Craymere told me. "A no good drunken son-of-a-bitch. That was my father. But, you know, Billy...I still loved him." I hadn't seen Craymere since that dinner in Houston a couple years ago. Here he was, still dressed sharp in a dark blue pin stripe but looking like ten winters had gone by.

"Cray," I said, steadying him against the sink, "how you doing?"

Craymere looked at me in the mirror. His eyes were washed out. He looked like a ghost.

"Billy! Billy! what the hell you doin' here? You're supposed to be at the dinner," he said into the mirror.

"Yeah, I know."

Craymere turned around, his brow furrowed, his voice flat—"You been fired?"

"Nah. I've just had enough of you-know-who."

Craymere stared at me. He ran my words through his head a few times. The effort seemed to sober him up a bit. He rubbed his eyes and whispered, "You ain't going? Really? Not going?"

I walked over to the urinal and pulled down my zipper. "That's right," I declared. There was a fizzing sound as the hot urine hit the ice chips at the bottom of the waist-high porcelain urinal.

"Jesus! Stanley's gonna shit in his pants."

"Yeah." Pissing on the ice chips felt great. I took a deep breath.

Craymere stumbled back against the black wall of the men's room. The comb dropped from his hand onto the white tile floor. He shook his head and looked at me. His voice was very sad. "Sure you want to do this, Billy?"

"Yeah." I zipped up, hit the handle and a film of water ran down the smooth walls of the urinal. Craymere stepped toward me as if he was walking on slippery rocks. "You know what you're gettin' into, huh?" Craymere made an ugly face. He spat into the urinal and wiped his mouth on his sleeve. "You're not gonna win. You know that, don't you, Billy?"

"We'll see." I reached down and got his comb for him.

Craymere gave me a jab in the arm. "God bless, Billy. God bless."

I finished dinner with the dietitians and walked back to the Continental. The Theatre of Power, the lost luggage, the lost reservation. It was funny how things ran together. How little things added up. We just didn't usually notice them, or give them any importance. Gurdjieff had called them "noticeable coincidences."

I thought I might feel guilty about not going to the dinner. But, no, not even any fear. I felt great. It was still early but I went to bed. I had to be ready for whatever was going to happen. There was no putting the chickens back in the coop. It was all out on the table.

The next day a salesman on one of our other food books spotted me at a booth at McCormick Place. He hurried over like he had just found me in a jungle. A suck up—he always played the percentages—he could hardly contain himself:

"Where were you?" he shouted.

"I wasn't there," I said.

He stopped cold. He'd expected an excuse. For a moment he didn't know what to say. It was just the two of us standing on a red carpet with all these people streaming around us. "Yeah," he said finally. "No kidding. What'd you have? The d.t.'s or something?"

I took him in. He froze and shrank. "No," I said simply.

A strange look came over his face. I was not lying to him. I didn't show any guilt. It made no sense. What was I trying to pull? He couldn't figure it out. Like a hand grenade, the moment exploded in his face. "Christ!" he shouted and ran off.

A few minutes later I saw him with Stanley. He was making these jerky body movements, talking a mile a minute. Stanley spotted me. His face contorted. He looked away. He didn't want to see me. Not now. "Revenge," he once told me, "is best taken on a cold stomach."

That evening at our company's hospitality suite Stanley saw me and gave a big, sniggering grin. I felt my revulsion for this man and for everything he stood for. We were in the arena now, face-to-face. All these years of combat were coming down to a single, deciding test of wills. The clarity of the moment shot through me...

STANLEY COMES STRAIGHT FOR ME, HIS EXPRESSION LIKE THAT OF A SAD BUT stern father who has to explain the facts of life to a wayward son.

"William, I'd like to see you..." he snapped. "Some time tonight?"

I remember his telling me early on that if I was ever in a confrontation, not to postpone it. Go right into it. Don't give your opponent time to plan. Use the energy of the moment, its uncertainty, to your advantage by meeting it head-on.

"What about right now?" I say.

Stanley stares at me, startled. He hadn't expected this. "Okay, okay. In there then."

He points to the bedroom. I don't react but instead motion him to go first. That's another surprise for him. He shrugs and pushes through the crowd. He stands by the door and gestures me inside, a big, splashy smile pasted on his face. But his eyes are cold and seething with contempt.

He closes and locks the door and stands before it blocking my exit. I can't escape. He puts his Scotch down on the dresser. He puts it there very carefully and then looks up, the two of us meeting face to face. I say nothing. I wait. He says nothing, waiting as well. My chin is quivering but the breath is slow and even, traveling the length of the body. Finally, he takes a deep breath and glowers, his words hitting me like daggers.

"Okay, tell me—where were you, William?"

Every word, every inch of the moment comes straight into me.

"I wasn't there."

The space crackles with energy. His little black rat eyes narrow. His chest puffs up.

"I know you weren't there." He bites each word and spits it at me.

"That's right."

"Where were you?"

He is pushing on my guilt as hard as he can. He wants an answer. Any answer. But there are no words in me.

"Where were you?" he repeats.

A funny look comes onto his face. A wolf in a gray herring bone suit. I am seeing his animal. I take a deep breath—"I wasn't there."

A huge gaping chasm opens between us. It is just me and this ugly animal.

"William," my name trembles in his mouth. "I'm going to ask you one more time. Do you understand?"

I make no reply but continue to take him in, continue to sense and see.

"And you better tell me," he warns.

Stanley's rat eyes nail me with animal fury. He is acting on me now with all his will, all his hatred. I can feel my body, filled with space and sensation, my mind cool but on a knife edge. His every movement, no matter how faint, is registered.

"Where were you last night," he screams, his hands clutched into fists. "You fucked up that whole dinner. You made me a laughing stock! *Now where the fuck were you!?*"

For a second the shock freezes me, disconnects me. I don't feel anything below the knees. And the knees are all space. The thought spreads over me: If I don't lie to him, I'll be out on the street. Like Craymere. After all, all he wants is a lie. Just a little lie. He doesn't care what kind of lie. He just wants me to save myself. Lie.

These two "I"s inside me debate. The one, very rational, mature-sounding. The arguments are so reasonable, sensible. So what if I lie—so what? But then, just at the

last instant, a feeling comes of total disgust—disgust for what stood before me, disgust with that whole way of life. And inside that feeling a silent voice declares: *I-am-
not-going-to-lie-to-him.*

I tell him: *"No excuse."*

"What!" he screams and sags, a look of horror, bewilderment, frozen to his face.
He looks pitiful, wounded, alone.

"No excuse!" I repeat, the words showing no mercy, plunging the sword still
deeper into his heart.

And something falls away and I know right then: *I have broken free of him.*

He can't stand my sight. He wheels 'round in a fury, knocking over the glass on
the bureau, the glass breaking, the drink and ice cubes spilling onto the grey carpet.
He turns the doorknob, forgetting he locked the door. "Christ!" he yells, unlocks it
and storms out.

"BUT WHY? WHY DIDN'T YOU GO TO THE DINNER?"

That was Barbara's question. I'd told her what happened while she had made dinner, our two boys, John and Matthew, running around her legs and zipping toy cars over
the floor. Now the kids were fed and in bed. We were alone in the kitchen. She by the
sink washing vegetables, me standing by the back door drinking a vodka and tonic.

"I'm not lying anymore," I said.

Barbara turned off the water and looked over her shoulder at me.

"Not lying?"

"Not lying about the way I feel."

She began dicing tofu for the stir fry in the wok. She looked so beautiful, so natural. I loved just looking at her, being with her, taking walks together after we put
the kids to bed. There was a silence and sensitivity to her that I loved. But I was never able to explain myself to her, explain what I saw and how I felt.

"So what are you going to do?" she asked.

Her voice was neutral, but I could feel her thoughts. She was frightened. What
were we going to do if I was fired?

She oiled the wok and put in the vegetables, their soft skins hissing as they
touched the hot metal. Then she put in the diced tofu and began to stir with a long
wooden spoon. I opened a bottle of chardonnay for Barbara and poured a glass. I
made myself another drink and stirred, the spoon clinking against the glass, its force
swirling around the ice and tonic water.

"You think I should apologize, huh?"

She stopped stirring. Her face looked drawn. The fear, the uncertainty, was eating her. She shrugged her shoulders.

"What do you want to do?"

I felt an anger in me. An anger that was scared. I always felt what she was feeling.
It came right into me. I could never protect myself from her. And I always reacted.

Went to sleep. I walked around the kitchen, letting out a gust of breath. I shook my head and sat down at the breakfast table.

"I don't know, Barb. I don't know."

"Spencer likes you. You said you thought you had a chance to be a vice president. You'll be giving that up."

"Yeah. But, baby"—I blew another gust of air—"these people, they bore me. Do you understand? They have nothing to say. They're dead. All they're interested in is money. Power and money. That's what they worship."

She scooped the stir fry veggies out of the wok and onto stoneware plates. I didn't like white wine so I opened up a bottle of merlot for myself and carried it and the chardonnay out onto the back porch. It had been a hot day, too hot for late May, but now in the twilight all was cooling. A wonderful breeze was coming in through the screens. I brought out the silver candle holders that had been Grandpa Scott's, and lit the long amber candles. Then I poured the wine and offered a toast:

"When all things are lived through to the end, there is no sadness, no regret, no false springtime, for each moment lived pushes out a newer, wider horizon and there is no escape—save living."

Barbara smiled. She had heard me make that toast so often.

"About time for a new one, isn't it?" she suggested softly.

"Well let me make another. An old Celtic prayer: 'May the roads rise with us, and the wind always be at our backs, and may we always walk in the palm of the Lord.'"

"I've heard that one, too," she said.

Next door in the dusky light the Donnellys were digging and planting their garden. On the other side Mr. Guiseppi was watering. In the distance a fire siren sounded. Barbara was eating even more slowly than usual.

"Look, Barb. If you want me to apologize, I will. But I don't think it will do any good."

"Why not?"

"I already told you. I feel like there's, you know, a big movement going on. Big wheels are turning. I'm at the interval in the octave. All this has to happen. I'm being moved on now."

I wished I could talk to her about what I really felt and saw. But the least abstraction and she closed down.

"Look, I've learned all I was supposed to learn from Stanley. He's been my 'black' teacher. People only think of teachers as 'white'—but there are 'black' teachers as well. Seeing how he operated, battling with him all these years, it really put my feet on the ground. I was such an idealist and didn't know it. I'm not dreaming anymore. I'm free of him."

"So you really think you're leaving the magazine?"

I sat back and took a sip of wine and looked out at the backyard. We had planted a garden out by the garage and I noticed some of the tomato plants had been trampled.

"I don't know. It depends."

"If you apologize—"

"Look—I'll apologize, okay?"

"Pat, you're shouting."

"Okay, I'm sorry. I'll apologize if you want me to. But it won't do any good. Don't you see? What has to happen is now going to happen."

She continued eating.

"Babe, don't you understand? I keep feeling like we are all in some play together that's already been written—me, you, Stanley, Spencer. It's weird. I don't know whether it's true or not. But I keep feeling it..."

We ate in a heavy silence. It was almost dark.

What was it with Barbara? Why couldn't she open up to another way of looking at things? It was true what the Work said. We could never give each other our understanding. Anyway, here we were now out on the cliff edge. Out in space. The old life behind us, the new yet to come. Chicago was the crossroads. I could have lied. It was the shock, the interval. Lying would have meant a descent. Another recurrence. I had faced my dragon. Inside and out. Now I was under a higher influence. Now the course of events would unfold differently and each of us would play our parts.

"You think it's all fated?" Barbara asked. Her voice was stronger.

"Yeah. I feel like that. But who knows? That's the only thing, you know, that I keep coming back to. The fact—*I don't know.* I've got to learn to live with that. With the not knowing."

"I love you," Barbara said softly, raising her glass. She was smiling.

I raised mine to hers.

"But I know..." she said, "I know you don't believe that."

That was true. I could feel some part of me did not believe it. What was it in me that couldn't fully accept her love? Anyone's love? In the soft quiet light of the candles she looked a thousand years wise.

"You're right, babe," I said. "I'm afraid to love, really to love."

Tears streaming from her eyes, Barbara admitted, "Me too."

Like breathing, there was always this opening and closing to each other. It was so painful to be open when the other person was closed.

There was something else, too. When I was full of life, energy, goodwill, I thought I was most myself for that was how I saw myself. But it was nothing but more identification. This "light I" was so much more difficult to see that all the dark ones because he was just that—"light." When I felt most "myself"—that should be the reminder to remember and observe my "angel of light."

Barbara got up to clear the table.

"What's for dessert? Rhubarb pie?"

"It's too early for rhubarb."

"Yeah, but I can wish, huh? Say, did anything happen while I was gone?"

She was going to say "no," but then she looked out to the garden. "There was something strange. Just before you came home there were two cats really fighting. At first they were right here by the porch. One was black and the other was orange.

The orange cat was getting the worst of it. All the hair was gone on his neck. It was just bare flesh, hanging down. You could see the bare flesh. It was horrible."

"Strange. Cats…don't usually fight like that."

"But these two were really into it. I took a broom after them. They ran into the garden and it started all over. The hissing, the arched backs. Then the black cat pounced and I had to run out again."

"Sounds like a fight to the death."

"Yes," Barbara said carrying the plates into the kitchen. "It was awful."

"And odd, too."

"What do you mean?"

"Cats don't usually fight to the death. They run away."

"Yes, that's true."

The screen door slammed shut. The street lights had gone on. I could see them between the two houses in back of us. The whole backyard and garage were lit in soft moonlight. I knew those cats fighting meant something. The oddity flowed into a perception. There was an instantaneous reading. I had entered another "Theatre of Power"; the first had only been practice. This was to be a fight to the end between us. There was no avoiding it. I had always thought that I had to beat Stanley. That one's "dragon" had to be killed in some way. Now I realized that you don't beat your dragon, that in reality, St. George doesn't really kill the dragon. He fights, yes, but he "wins" only in his not losing, in not mechanically lying, identifying, going into negative emotion, not making it personal between himself and his dragon. For knights are knights, and dragons are dragons. That's one's lot in life. The function to be fulfilled. The question is—and can only be—is one awake?

For other people, I realized, what had happened in Chicago would seem ordinary. An ego battle with the boss. Nothing special. It could be experienced and interpreted on that level. But there were many other levels besides the obvious one-dimensional static world. For just as in the Ray of Creation, there were worlds within worlds, octaves within octaves. Everything was connected and existed in dimension, low to high. Events and people could be experienced, for example, symbolically. Or mythologically. Or at the archetypal level. Or that which the Cabalists called the *En-Sof*, the ground of all Being. The Bible speaks of it in terms of powers and principalities. It's not experienced because we become too mired in the heavy material level of rigid subject and object. To open to higher worlds of experience, we have to come to a serious wish to wake up, to be conscious and real. Acting on the wish is like putting a stake in the ground. It gives one's world an orientation, a direction and weight. It is only then that concepts like "up" and "down," "good" and "evil," "sin" and "redemption" become more than words, fanciful abstractions. Life, as Gurdjieff said, is only real when I am; and on a lesser level, when there is the sincere wish to wake up. For only then can personality be made passive and essence, feeding on it, begin to grow. It is only from that moment, as Ouspensky says, that "Time is counted." For otherwise, one's life is all false personality, imaginary "I," not authentic. It has no real body. It is absurd and meaningless. It was from this level that I understood that what was transpiring between Stanley and me was, as Sarah had said, "An ancient unfinished combat."

"DON'T YOU KNOW, BILL, THEY'RE *FRIENDS?*"

Isabel, the office manager, stared at me in disbelief.

I was on my way to see Spencer when Isabel had motioned me into her office.

"Bill, what are you doing? I heard what happened in Chicago."

"Well, it's come to a boil. It's either Stanley or me. Spencer has to choose."

She got up from her desk and closed the door. "Bill, my God! This is crazy. You can't win. Don't you know that?"

"Well, I know the chances aren't too good."

The word "friends" had exploded inside me like a grenade. A thousand images flashed through my mind instantly being resorted and reframed. A whimsical smile came to Isabel's mouth as she watched all the pieces falling into a new place. I suddenly saw what I had refused to see. I'd never questioned.

"I don't believe it!" I exclaimed, shaking my head. "Je-sus!"

"Get out of this, Bill. Apologize, make some excuse."

"No. No," I said.

Any equivocation with Stanley only tied you to him and all that he represented. I had fought him all these years. This was the finale. Whether I would win or not wasn't the question—rather, it was simply to fight as well as I could. Fight and not identify. That was the trick.

I stepped off the elevator leading to the executive offices. It was as if I had entered a special cosmos. Everything spoke one word: money. Everything thought out. Cerebral. Nothing left to chance. No ornamentation. Big heavy English leather chairs. Massive Paul Jenkins' paintings oozing spectrums of color, perfectly controlled. Two smaller Mondrians. The walls paneled in dark wood. Vibrant grey carpeting, very cushy, like walking on pillows. Soft, indirect lighting. Muted colors. Everything contained, understated, meticulous. Everyone speaking softly, moving quietly, as if in church. It reminded me of the bank at Margate.

I couldn't let myself be influenced, react, be intimidated. I gathered my attention, focused on the vibration. I walked slowly up to the long polished teak desk. The receptionist looked up. Young, sleek, thin lips. I said nothing. She waited. I said nothing. A small frown. I waited. Just as she was about to speak, I said:

"Spencer."

"Who shall I—"

"Mr. Patterson."

It was enough. I steadied myself. And in a few moments I was outside Spencer's corner office.

"Mr. Spencer will be with you in a few minutes," said his bosomy new secretary, young and easily impressed. I had to smile. Spencer always played it large in every-thing he did. Every one of his secretaries had been big busted.

The door finally opened. There stood Spencer, meaty, tanned and solid, in shirt sleeves and red suspenders. I remembered the magician in him "stealing" my watch that first time I met him.

"Why hello, Bill. Good to see you," he called out like I was a long lost buddy, as he motioned me inside. In another tone he told Julia: "No calls."

"Well," he said, moving behind his desk and not mincing words, "tell me about Chicago."

"Stanley hasn't talked to you?" I took a seat by his desk.

Spencer paused. He liked to play his cards close to the vest. He smiled. He liked the fact that I'd tried to qualify the situation first.

"I'd like to hear your side," he said.

"Good," I said. I'd talked with Spencer a few hundred times. And almost every time he showed me a "new look." He was a master at playing the power game. Now the learning was over. I was on my own.

"Well, Ted, what Stanley says about me not being at the dinner...I want you to know it's all true."

Spencer came forward in his chair. The dark flat eyes fixed me. He wasn't ex-pecting that. He nodded, and waited.

"But did he tell you why I didn't go?"

"He said you refused to tell him, Bill." Spencer's voice was cryptic.

"Him—not you," I said.

Spencer liked that. He was big on loyalty. He flipped open his cigar box and clipped a Don Diego. He struck a wooden match, lit the fat cigar, and blew a big puff of smoke.

"Well, let's have it," he snapped, the anger in him just below the surface. From his point of view, I had humiliated him and the magazine by not showing up. That might cost dollars. Spencer didn't fuck around when it came to dollars.

"Ted, you won't believe this—I didn't believe this—so I want you to check it out with our sales people and the ad agency. Stanley is selling *against* the magazine!"

Spencer's jowls shook. "What!"

I ran him through everything that had happened. No interpretations. No specula-tions. Just facts. Just like he had taught me. I'd lost a lot of battles in here, but all the time I was learning. Spencer seemed to shrink in his chair. It was like I was force-feeding him with something he didn't want to eat. I had him on the ropes. I went for the kill.

"Ted, the first year we started the magazine—how many ads did we get?"

He went blank. I didn't want to rub his face in it.

"Well," I said, "you've got sixty-four magazines under your control, so I wouldn't expect you to know. But the answer is 437 pages..." I took a deep breath. The energy was roaring. I had to keep it balanced. I breathed down into my feet. "Last year—guess what we did?" I didn't wait for an answer. "A big 457 pages."

I let that sink in. I was talking numbers. Numbers were all that mattered to him. For years I'd talked editorial quality, editorial strategy. He couldn't have cared less. I only got his ear when I talked numbers. Numbers were bottom line material. "Look, Ted, let's get down and dirty, huh? Our best year in six years was what? Only 481 pages. So from first year to best year that's an increase of only forty-four pages!"

"All the books were down last year," said Spencer, deflecting and countering.

"Yeah. But 'down' from what? A fat 600-plus pages. They're almost as big as telephone books. Right?"

"Only a couple of books sell that kind of space."

"Yeah. True. But those are our two main competitors."

"Our profits have been up every year."

"Of course, but only because we raise page rates 10% every year."

Spencer jerked in his seat. I was touching close to home. Spencer scratched his ear and stubbed the Diego out in the ashtray. He came forward over his desk, forearms spread out, looking me square in the face. Behind the mask was a big lion. I had to be careful. I couldn't push him too far.

"Well—what is it you want me to do?"

"Ted—"

There was a loud knock at the door. It opened. There was Stanley.

"You wanted to see me?" Stanley said, startled to see me.

"Yeah. But not now," declared Spencer, waving him away like a fly. Stanley frowned and went out, shutting the door slowly. Spencer shook his head. "Still have to train her."

"Great boobs," I said.

"Yeah." Spencer hit the intercom on his phone. "Julia, no calls, no visits. Huh? What's that? Right. Yes, I understand."

Spencer eyed me a moment and relit his Don Diego and gesturing in Julia's direction said: "Train 'em then you lose 'em, huh?"

"Not if you treat them right, Ted."

Spencer paused. "Right, Bill." I was scoring and he knew it. But he held the cards. And he knew that too. He put on his suit jacket and slicked back the silver hair. "Okay, what's your solution?" Spencer asked.

"Fire Stanley. He's no publisher, Ted. You know that. I know that. The whole industry knows that."

Spencer's eyes pinned me. That wasn't the solution he wanted to hear.

"Or if that's not possible," I said, "then move him onto another book."

He just took it in. Made no response. But the wheels were turning. He'd heard that before. But never from me.

"Ted, get a real publisher on *Food*. Someone who knows how to sell, someone people will respect. In a year's time, I promise you we'll be up at least fifty pages in space."

Spencer's eyes narrowed.

"And do one more thing—stop treating the book like a "cash cow." Let's sink the profits back into it, not into supporting other books. We need a research guy, someone to crunch and analyze the numbers so we can back-up our stories with industry numbers. The ad agencies are hungry for numbers. They need to impress clients with their market knowledge. They need a good statistical base for their ideas which they neither have the money or expertise to get. They expect the magazines to do it for them. So in that great tradition of 'one hand washes another,' they're placing the bulk of their clients' money, buying ads, in those magazines that do them the most good."

I could feel the atmosphere in the room suddenly thicken. I'd gone too far. Spencer stood up and walked to the window, keeping his back to me. Finally, he turned his head, his eyes blazing—"Cash cow! Where the hell did you get that idea?"

Spencer was "old school." He was into wooing clients with dinners and presents, not selling them with facts, research. I'd told the emperor he had no clothes. I'd taken a chance. I had to go all the way.

"Let's not bullshit each other, Ted. I know what the book's doing. We grossed $1.5 million last year. It costs us nine dollars a name to print and mail twelve issues. That's $450K a year. Toss in another $200K for salaries. Figure another $100K for overhead, promotion, so forth. That means before taxes we're doing $750K..."

Spencer's head jerked, his jowls shook. He looked like I'd just pulled his pants down. "Where'd you get those numbers!" he barked, coming toward me.

"Am I off?"

"Where'd you get 'em?" He was standing right by my chair.

"What I've learned...I've learned from you."

That stopped him. Turning it back on him, that was the only way. Spencer chomped down hard on his Diego and swung around behind his desk. He sat down. Poured himself a glass of water from a silver pitcher. Took a big belt of it like it was Scotch.

"Bill, I hear what you say. I'll get back to you on this, okay?"

"Soon?" I wanted to pin him down. I didn't want to hang for weeks while he maneuvered.

"Soon," was all Spencer said.

A week went by. No call from Spencer. On Sunday I checked the employment section of *The Times*. Maybe there was an editor's job open. A big black bordered ad jumped out at me. "Editor-in-Chief, Business Publication." I read the copy. The words like a punch square in the gut. I fell back a step. The ad! It was...for my job. *I was getting the ax!"*

I showed the ad to Barbara.

"There are a lot of business magazines," she said. "And there's no company name. Only a box number. How do you know it's for *Food?*"

"I know it," I told her.

That Monday, by luck, I found an ad in my desk drawer that I had run the year before when the magazine had a position open. I compared the ad's box number with the new ad. They matched. I called Spencer. I couldn't get by Julia. It was apparent he's given specific instructions. I continued calling. Spencer wasn't returning my calls. I had to get to him. But how? I've been going on a feeling, an intuition, since "The Theatre of Power." How real was it? How could I trust it?

At the group meeting I sat up front facing Lord Pentland. He opened the meeting speaking about essence and personality—our essence being what we are, what we are born with, as opposed to our personality which is what we acquire.

"How does essence manifest?" I asked.

He looked at me from all that space.

"For example," I said, "can essence manifest as a strong feeling that we go with, even though we're not sure where it's taking us?"

"What's your question?" He wanted me to lay it all out.

So I took the leap. I told him about not attending the Golden Cup dinner. "I expected I'd feel guilty," I said. "But instead I feel more free, like I've broken through something."

Lord Pentland nodded. A very slow movement of his head up and down, his eyes not leaving mine. A tremendous energy hit me. He spoke very slowly, evenly. "Every act has its consequences," he said. "It isn't often that we can know all the consequences. But nothing can be all gain."

The space opened up and I felt my chest enlarging, my breath moving with his breath.

"My grandfather once posted a letter," he continued, "asking a woman to marry him. As soon as he dropped it in the mail box, he wondered what he had done..."

His face was changing. It's a face I feel I know but have never seen before.

"In any case," he added, "...you are going to suffer."

"Yes," I said.

He gazed at me a moment, weighing me, and then said as if he were pointing out the grain pattern on a piece of wood—"You are very righteous. A lot of people have had to put up with that."

"Yes. I know."

The whole group laughed. Including me. I knew it was true. All that this "I" had put him and the group through. And it was funny somehow.

Later in the meeting a woman told a long-winded story full of self-pity and complaint without ever quite getting to her question. Lord Pentland listened. He let her go on; but finally, no end in sight, he sighed and asked—

"Do you ever feel I am eating you?" he mused.

The woman stopped, perplexed.

"You have no idea..." he said softly, "how much you are eating me."

THE WHEEL WAS TURNING FASTER. I COULD FEEL IT. I HAD TO GET TO SPENCER. I couldn't just sit back and let things take their course. But how? He hadn't returned my calls. Julia, the secretary, gave one excuse after another. Her voice had that forced quality, will against beliefs. She hadn't learned to lie yet. But what was I going to say to Spencer—when and if I got to him? If I was going to be fired, I wanted a big severance. Money was his god. He wasn't just going to give it to me. I'd have to take it, force it out of him. I had to really "see" Spencer. I'd never paid too much attention to him. Now I sat in my office behind a closed door pondering, thinking back through all the meetings, presentations, hospitality suites, conjuring up everything I knew about him, trying to see who he was.

The recurring image I got was of him taking my watch that first day I had met him. I'd seen him do that trick and others for years. Spencer was a magician. He knew how to deflect people's attention and make them see and believe things that weren't there. And he was a master of the "people game." He had a radar-like instinct for knowing just where a person was, what would persuade, motivate them, put fear into them. He played people like musical instruments. But what was it that he saw about people that gave him that power?

Suddenly it struck me what Spencer saw: *it wasn't who I am but who I think I am.* Spencer played off everyone's "I"-image. That dream, that belief system—that was what he manipulated. Now my question about him reformed itself: who did Spencer think he was? I remembered Sarah once saying, "He runs the place like a feudal kingdom."

An insight flashed: Spencer needed to be seen as a white knight, a good guy. That was the image of himself he was always projecting, always feeding. He'd always told me not to believe my press clippings. But he saved everything that was ever written about him and regularly mailed copies to his business friends. He had this great, insatiable need for people to think he was somebody special. Now if I could make him think that I had the power to change that image, to make others see him as a black knight, a bad guy, then…but somehow I had to get in to see him!

A little later Alice, the managing editor, came into my office. She was holding a chocolate fudge birthday cake. There were seven lit candles. The white icing read: *Happy Anniversary, Food!*

"I thought you could use some cheering up," she said.

I leapt out of my chair and hugged her.

I had told her about the ad for my job. And she had told me Stanley had asked her to take my job, but she refused. "He gave you the chance to stick the knife in, Alice, but you didn't. I'm really proud of you." She'd grown a lot in the job and as a person and I'd come to regard her as a loyal friend. And she had brought me more than a gift. This cake was the "Trojan horse" I needed to get to Spencer.

I wrote Spencer a quick note, saying it was the magazine's birthday and thanking him for everything he had done. I told him, too, that I needed to see him and it would only take a few minutes. I called the mail boy and sent the cake up to Spencer.

I just knew it was a perfect door opener. The nature of power is to isolate. And so the big boys always vie to show each other they're in touch with the troops, that the troops still love them. I knew Spencer would carry that birthday cake right into the chairman's office, offering him a piece and, of course, telling him the story of "the troops on *Food*" that sent it to him.

Within ten minutes, my phone rang. It was Spencer, his voice ebullient, apologizing and telling me, "Of course, you can see me, Bill. Come right up," adding with a big hearty laugh that the chairman had been in his office when the cake arrived.

"Did you give him a piece?" I asked.

"Oh yeah," chortled Spencer. "Gave him one for his secretary, too."

Good God! It had worked. I put down the receiver and stared out at the red brick apartment house across the street. That old lady was there in her pink bra by the tiny sink washing dishes just as she always did.

I had this weird, familiar feeling: all this was happening as it was meant to happen. That I wasn't doing it. My only choice was whether I'd go over the cliffs with my eyes open or shut. Did I want to be awake or asleep? What was going to happen was fixed, destined. The only question was: At what level would the event, the drama, be enacted? It could be played out mechanically or consciously.

I was the deciding factor. If my wish was to be, if I made that my sole aim, if I remembered myself—then the quality of the event would change. I remembered an old Stoic dictum: *Events you can't control; your attitudes you can.*

"Hello, Bill!" called out Spencer when I entered his office. "Golly, that cake!"

"You deserve it, Ted. You've always stood behind *Food,* and we appreciate it."

Julia, in a tight black sweater, poked her head round the door.

"Mr. Spencer, remember you have an important appointment."

The son-of-a-bitch. I realized I had to act quickly. No small talk.

"Ted, just two minutes. I have some 'information' you have to know."

Those flat black eyes stared at me, trying to catch the drift.

"Okay, shoot. Julia, buzz me in five minutes."

Julia, bewildered, closed the door. Ted pointed to the small couch by the window. I sat down. He sat down beside me.

"Nice, huh?" he said, looking back to the door.

"Yeah, great smile," I said.

"No, I mean your tie." Spencer reached over and felt it.

Spencer, the old magician. He always used diversion, confusion techniques. But I wasn't buying it. I went straight for the jugular, hoping the directness and force of my statement would catch him off guard.

"Ted, I saw the ad in Sunday's paper."

He dropped my tie, frowned. "There are plenty of ads," Spencer declared. "How do you know it's ours?"

So the bastard did know about the ad. He had agreed to it.

"Ted, *I know*, okay? Now I understand you may not want to do this but you have to do it. So no hard feelings."

Spencer nodded. No emotion. He was lying low, not giving any signals.

"So let's strike a deal…let's not hurt the magazine." I looked at him. He knew what I meant.

He snorted, nodded again, got up and went to his desk and opened the cigar box. I let him close it before I said, "I'll have one, Ted, if you don't mind."

Spencer looked at me curiously. "Didn't know you smoked, Bill."

"I don't. But today is special, huh?"

"Yeah, I guess so." Spencer smiled. It was a real smile. He clipped two Don Diegos and handed me one and struck a wooden match. He lit mine. Then his. Freud would have loved this. I took a deep puff. I put an elbow up on the back of the couch. I wanted to take over the space. Make it mine. Let him know I felt no fear.

"Ted, I'm not here to save my job."

"The differences between you and Stanley—they're not reconcilable?"

By God! Spencer had reconsidered. He always liked a grandstand play like I was making. But, then he might be buying time. He didn't have an editor lined up and didn't want me to walk out. I was in a good position only by virtue of this sudden blitz attack. If I gave him time to regroup his forces, I'd lose my advantage. I had to keep up the pressure and force him to make a move.

"It's over," I told him.

"You don't want to stay?"

"Stanley and I haven't spoken in six months."

"But that's—"

"Ted, not unless you get rid of Stanley. Which I know you won't or you can't." I tapped the cigar ash into the big glass ashtray on the coffee table.

"You've paid a lot to keep Stanley," I said. "A lot of heads have rolled…"

Spencer blew a big cloud of smoke, his eyes on mine, trying to catch what I'm really saying, where this is leading.

"You have your reasons. They don't concern me, or anyone else. Now—"

"But, Bill, why not keep the job and wait till you find a new one?"

Spencer was trying to buy time, make things look good. He didn't like surprises. I had to keep attacking. Keep him with the fear of having a magazine with no editor and worse—of having an editor who's out on the street, who knows a lot of things, and a lot of people.

A buzzer sounded. Spencer yanked up the receiver on the coffee table. "No calls. I'll tell you when." He turned to me. He shook his head like he gets the drift now.

"Bill, I didn't know about the ad." He made it sound very sincere." I really didn't…"

"How could you not know?!" I heard my hurt and anger, the sense of betrayal. That in some ways Spencer had been like a father to me.

"I could tell you but it would be a long story." He took a deep breath. "Bill," Spencer said, smiling, patting my knee, "I owe you one."

I waited.

"You did a good job for me and I owe you one."

I nodded and smiled. He still hasn't committed. It's still a lot of words.

"Don't worry," he told me. "I'll take care of you."

"What do you mean 'I'll take care of you'?"

He stopped. The eyes fixed me. "I'll work things out with you. You won't have to go through Stanley."

What a clever old dog. He's still avoiding negotiating, still buying time.

"Ted, this is it: I want nine month's severance. I've trained Alice. She can fill my slot. I'll work with her. There'll be a smooth transition." And I reiterated, "The magazine won't get hurt. You've got my word on it."

Spencer swallowed. We were talking money now. He leaned back and sucked on his cigar, pretending to think over the severance. "Okay," he said, sitting up. "Don't worry. We'll work everything out when I get back from this trip."

"When will that be?" I had to pin him down.

"Next Wednesday." He was irritated.

"Nine months, Ted?"

"You're only entitled to nine weeks and three weeks vacation."

What a fox. He had the whole thing already worked out. I wasn't going to argue with him in words. I wanted him to feel my seriousness.

"Bill, we'll do right by you. Trust me." That sincere tone again.

"I do."

"When do you want to leave?"

"End of the month."

"Okay. We'll work it out."

I WAS LEAVING. WAS IT REALLY HAPPENING? I WENT TO AN OLD HAUNT FOR lunch and ordered a hot roast beef sandwich and a half carafe of wine. I thought of pyramids. Of Markum Hanrahan and Sonny Lacey and Casey. Of Vali and Soren. Jane. Of Stanley and Spencer. Sarah. I thought of my Father. This part of my life, it was all over now. Finished. Years ago I remember seeing a street magician in Central Park at the entrance to the zoo. He had pulled a rabbit out of a hat. "Imagine," he said, "the first time you saw this. It was poetry. Now it's cliche." He did a few more tricks. Then he held up an egg. "Now you see it," he said. He flicked his hand the opposite direction. "Now you don't." And he walked away.

I felt this sense that I was going to die again. Some acrobats fly from trapeze to trapeze. It seemed like I always had to go into the net before I could grab the next bar. Yes, I would die again but I didn't want to die in New York. I kept having this sense that I should go to San Francisco. There was Work out there. Lord Pentland visited there a good deal.

I called Lord Pentland at his office. He answered. It was just like that day I had first called. I could see him right away. In no time at all there I was in his office. I waited for him in the foyer. I noticed that the painting of the angel with the flute had been removed. In its place were photos of a biplane scouting arid terrain. The painting being gone gave me an odd feeling. I recalled the meetings in the basement of that townhouse. The magic of those years.

"Hello, Pat," came a soft, low voice, just above a whisper. "Please come in, won't you?"

There at the door to his office stood the tall, reed-like figure, the warrior and teacher I had known for so many years. The face was alert, impersonal, perfectly contained. He didn't look a day older.

I followed him into his office. He took a seat behind his desk. I sat in front. There was an antique Persian carpet hung on the wall. Several on the floor. Small photos of his family, his wife, Lucy, and his daughter, Mary. One of a man I took to be his father, a nice-looking man with a mustache, clever eyes and a studied smile. It was late afternoon. Through the window at Lord Pentland's back that suitably framed him, I saw the shadows had begun to fall into sharp geometric shapes. In contrast, the atmosphere in his office was soft, almost dreamlike, the lights having not yet been turned on. We sat in silence for a few moments. It was very restful. The thought came to me: *You are leaving your teacher.*

I told him what had happened with Spencer.

"There's this feeling I have that I should leave New York now and go to San Francisco and join the Work there," I said. I shrugged my shoulders.

He made no response. I was going to have to go deeper.

"My question is this: from the Work's point of view—should I go to San Francisco, or not?"

The room seemed to darken at that moment. The light was all behind him, casting him in shadows, blurring his features.

"The Work," said Lord Pentland, "has its point of view…but let me talk from yours."

I nodded.

"The Work is established now in San Francisco, and strong enough to continue after the death of people who have been actually taught by Mr. Gurdjieff." Lord Pentland paused. I could feel his energy coming into me. "But wherever you go," he said, very matter of factly, "you'll still have to face me."

I knew what he was saying, and it was true. I should stay. I was willing to stay. I was going to tell him that, but he added in a stronger voice:

"Living out West is less stressful than here. Much better for families out West."

I nodded.

"But that doesn't mean of course that it is better for the Work."

Yes, I would stay.

"There are people who find the stress of city life makes them negative and, well, perhaps a less stressful place would allow them to relax more and open up."

So I should go?

"Everyone who has ever been somebody in this world seems to have spent a stint of time in San Francisco. People like Robert Louis Stevenson and Mark Twain, for example."

I was crying inside. I really was going to leave.

"In the future I may go back to live in Scotland," he said, "but I expect always to come back to San Francisco because, after all, New York can take care of itself…whereas San Francisco, you might say, has been all mine."

So he was allowing me to leave.

We sat in silence. The room had gotten much darker, the light outside much softer. He looked like a Chinese lohan. A living statue.

"I would like to leave you with this," he said, after some time. "The 'sound' heard in silence is a support for our awareness. There are four supports. The center of gravity below the abdomen. The spine. The mind. And this vibration. Do you follow?"

"Yes," I answered.

"May I offer you some chocolate," he said, passing me a box of shell-shaped candy.

I didn't feel like any candy. I was going to refuse but he said, his voice very kind, "Go ahead, Pat. Take one."

I went back to the office. Alice was wearing a baseball cap with two silver wings on the sides. I smiled. It was the symbol of Mercury of the Romans, of Hermes of the Greeks. Hermes, the messenger of the gods, the god of commerce, god of writers and travelers, the god who leads souls to the underworld. Like Gurdjieff's sly man, if there was a sly god, it had to be Hermes. Alice, God bless her, gave it to me as a going-away present.

"WILLIAM, TELL ME, WOULD YOU LIKE TO RECONSIDER?"

Stanley's face was hard, but his voice was soft and contained.

I felt we'd played all the cards already. The "game" was over. If I stayed, it'd only be a matter of time until the next confrontation. I was getting a big severance only because I had surprised them. Next time they'd have all the cards.

"No," I said, smiling, "I think it's best if I leave."

"All right, then," said Stanley and he began to read the terms of my severance agreement.

He jerked me around for a while, obviously relishing the moment. I felt the body's sensation, breathed into it. Created a strong atmosphere.

"Well, William," Stanley said finally, "we're giving you a six-month severance. And that, I might add, is a first. The company has never given one this large."

That was a lie. "Thank you," I said.

"You've been a real pain in the ass," he exclaimed, his measured "executive voice" getting away from him. Then in another tone, surprisingly tender, "But, William, you always had...well, a certain elegance."

"Thanks, Stanley." The intelligence and sensitivity of this "Stanley Ravin" was the one Sarah always tried to show me.

"You know, you made all the right moves. I was proud of you in a way. But you never could've won. I think you knew that."

I nodded. I might have replied but did not.

"You had to play for a stalemate, and that's the hardest thing to do."

I nodded. That was true.

Stanley rose and reached across his desk and we shook hands.

"Well, William..." said Stanley with a smile that might even have been sincere, "you got your stalemate."

LORD HAVE MERCY

CALIFORNIA! IT WAS A WARM, sunny mid-August morning when we headed west. We had eaten a quick breakfast, and with the neighbors and their kids waving and calling their goodbyes and throwing kisses, we slowly backed the two cars out of the driveway, Barbara and Matthew were in the Rabbit and John and me and Thea the cat in the Hornet. We headed down the highway to the Tappan Zee Bridge at Tarrytown, pulled off the road for a last check of the tires and car carriers, and then crossed the Hudson River and headed west to California. I'd been wearing the Hermes-winged baseball cap Alice had given me for good luck. I gave it to John.

We had rented our house and, after a giant moving sale in which we'd sold most of our belongings, we'd packed up all that remained into the backseats and trunks of the Rabbit and my parent's old Hornet. Both cars were packed full to the roof with clothes, household goods, nineteen boxes of books and an antique English gateleg dining table, the only piece of furniture we had kept. Each car also had a car carrier on the roof that was loaded down with stuff. In the attic we had stored what we couldn't get into the cars: all my paintings, an easel, paints, frames and canvases, twenty-one additional boxes of books, an eight-man tent, backpacks, old letters, scrapbooks, high school and college year books and an antique pew. Both cars had been tuned up and given a new set of shocks but still, under all the weight they bore, the cars rode low to the ground.

We drove hard and made it to Pittsburgh before nightfall.

Barbara was still concerned about moving. Crown Zellerbach, a forestry company based in San Francisco, had voiced interest in hiring me. My first reaction was to turn down the job. Then I remembered Gurdjieff's phrase about "riding on the back of a devil." Crown couldn't commit until September. From the way the interviews went I felt I had the job, especially if I moved out there. New York had played itself out. A new shock was needed.

The next morning we visited my Grandfather Scott's old house in Wilkinsburg. I took a last look around, going down into the limestone cellar where my uncle had shown me how to box, and then we headed out again. We drove south down to Wheeling, West Virginia, and on into the Cincinnati area where we bought some art pottery. And then across the flatlands of Kansas and on to Colorado and the edge of the Rockies where we went up to Boulder to see an old friend still connected with Trungpa. He wanted us to stay and see Rinpoche, but I had long ago realized we weren't Buddhists. We awoke to find our car had been broken into and all the pottery stolen. On the way to Albuquerque, the kids started going crazy, having been in the car so long. Then the cars started acting up. First the Rabbit's electrical system went out. Then the Hornet needed new brakes. We had to wait overnight for the cars to be fixed.

I'd bought two new books before I left. I didn't know why I bought either of them. The first an oddly impersonal book entitled *A Moment of True Feeling*, by Peter Hanke, a young Austrian writer I'd never heard of; and the second, *The Crest Jewel of Discrimination*, by Shankara, a Hindu monk of the ninth century who I'd never heard of either. It had literally fallen off a book shelf into my hands. Though I tried, I was too tired and frazzled to read either.

I called the head of public relations at Crown Zellerbach to let him know I'd be in San Francisco soon. He told he was sorry but there had been a cutback and employment was frozen. I felt like I'd just been sucker-punched. All the wind went right out of me.

What was I doing leaving New York? It wasn't rational. It made no sense. I was going on intuition. The whole trip I had felt as if we were pushing against this giant hand, its palm pressed flat against our faces, holding us back. What did that hand symbolize? Fear? A warning? I had no clue. Uprooting my family, cutting all ties, driving three thousand miles to a city I didn't know—was I crazy! I had no answers. I had to trust what I felt. I worked to relax the body, keep the mind from dreaming. I wasn't going to get sucked into guilt.

I pushed the Hornet at top speed through the long flat stretches of empty desert. The most I could get out of it was sixty miles an hour. Barbara, with the kids in the Rabbit, who had never driven more than fifty miles a day, was now doing five hundred and better as we scrambled to get to San Francisco. The sunlight was blinding and scenery parched and morbid. From time to time, lying in wait on the shoulders of the black tar road, I'd see these ominous black snakes. But as we'd pass the snakes would transform themselves into harmless shreds of truck tires. The road itself seemed endless. The springs in the front seat of the Hornet had broken in Boulder and ever since, every bump was a jolt and a kind of searing question—*what the hell was I doing to myself and my family?*

Finally we came out of the desert and over the mountains and down into L.A. where we stayed with Barbara's parents for a few days. They were glad to see us but worried that I wouldn't find work. We took 101 north to San Francisco. The thoughts kept hounding me: Why had I left New York? What was I doing? I could feel the body contracting in fear, anxiety. I worked with it, sensing the body, keeping the mind on the moment. Finally, it let go.

Just outside San Jose, I looked out on the horizon. The sky was full of big hot air balloons. One had a big rainbow design. It was a sign, I felt. My Father and Hermes were guiding me. My spirits picked up. We got into San Francisco, ate a horrible breakfast at a fast-food eatery and headed across the Golden Gate Bridge. We chugged up the grade like the little train that thought it could. We approached the tunnel into Marin County. It was painted the colors of the rainbow. Another sign. "What you crying about, Poppy?" asked John. "Oh, seeing the rainbow," I answered. "Oh," he said, not understanding. We drove out to Muir Woods and its groves of towering redwoods. Then on to Stinson Beach where we dived into the Pacific and danced around in bare feet in the incoming tide. The great sweep of open space, the natural coastline, Mt. Tamalpais looming beyond the steep cliffs, the monumental unspoiled beauty—the images were a food. It was another world. No, I wasn't crazy. It was September 16. Our journey from the Atlantic to the Pacific Ocean had taken nearly four weeks. It felt like four centuries.

We rented an apartment looking out onto San Francisco Bay and, off in the distance, a large yellow building that we later learned was San Quentin. We weren't to go to the meetings until we had seen Lord Pentland. So we began attending the Work days on Sundays. There were good, serious people in the San Francisco Work, but no one with the unquestionable stature and presence of Lord Pentland. I had taken it all for granted. I'd given up my place in the Work, the weekly group meetings and meditations and Sunday work days with Lord Pentland. What had I done! How could I have left? But I had known all this. Coming here, exiling myself in a way—there was no suitable defense. Now the suffering really began.

Lord Pentland arrived in early November. I drove to the San Francisco foundation to see him. It was a large white stucco mansion, of Spanish design, with gates and a horseshoe driveway, a towering elm tree in the front yard and a large wooden front door. I knocked. It was mid-morning and the house felt empty. No one answered. I remembered that first meeting. Was this another game?

Presently, I heard footsteps. The big door creaked open and there stood Lord Pentland. He looked as though he didn't recognize me, but then he motioned me inside. I felt like a stranger. He shook my hand. We sat in the dark wood paneled study. We were alone except for a napping cat on the radiator. Lord Pentland's brow furrowed—"What are you doing here?" he asked in a surprised tone.

I had called him again and again right up to the day before I left and he hadn't had time to talk to me. I finally understood that he wanted me to make my own decision. Close to tears, I said: "I know now that you are my teacher. I've made a terrible mistake. I've been stupid. It's all been self-love and vanity. I see that now and I'm ready to go back to New York."

"Well, you've come this far and you've seen quite a bit. Perhaps you should stay, at least for a while."

I was willing to do whatever he told me. I nodded.

"Do you have a job yet?" he inquired.

"I've started writing a book. I'd like to finish that first."

"What's it about?"

"The death of my Father."

That seemed to shock him. He didn't pursue it. "What group leaders have you met?" he asked.

I told him.

"Choose one," he told me.

"I can't."

"Of course, not," he agreed quickly. "But choose one anyway."

"I can't," I said. I didn't want a new teacher. I just wanted to go back to New York. So he chose one. The cat yawned. Lord Pentland and I laughed.

I felt like I had been readmitted to the Work.

We had spent three weeks in a Mill Valley motel while we looked for a place to rent. To save money, we bought secondhand mattresses and a couch, and sat on orange crates around the antique gateleg table, eating day-old bread and plenty of spaghetti and shopping garage sales and church thrift shops. But no matter how we tried to cut expenses, we were spending a minimum of twelve hundred dollars a month. We couldn't go much beyond June without my working. I was determined to finish the book. I was writing six days a week. Just before New Year's, I finished the first draft. I sat at the typewriter crying and, all the while, I was watching the tears pour out. The body, the emotional center, was crying; but what watched was calm, observant, without judgment. It was an odd feeling. A sense of "disloyalty"—but to what?

At the annual birthday celebration for Gurdjieff, I carried trays of shot glasses filled with Armagnac for the traditional toast. One glass was left. I raised it for the toast and drank. Instead of alcohol, I drank air. The shot glass was empty. On the wall I noticed a saying of Gurdjieff's about not sitting in one place too long. This sense came that my time in the Work was coming to an end. I remembered talking to Jack Casey in New York before I left. He'd told me, "Your energy isn't here any more. You have to find where it has gone." I'd talked to him about the Work. Casey had said, "You can only know what you are leaving, know the value of that—you can't know where you're going."

The first draft of the book completed, I set out to find a job. Nothing but dead ends. I was discovering a bitter lesson: kings don't hire former kings. That is, having been the editor of a magazine, no editor wanted me. No one hires his replacement. Months went by. Just a few interviews. I was willing to take even an entry level job. But no takers. "San Francisco," I began to recognize, was an illusion. Talk about the great cities of America, New York-Chicago-Houston-Los Angeles, and San Francisco is always mentioned. But there were only six hundred and thirty-four thousand people in San Francisco. Include the entire Bay Area and the population is only about a million-and-a-half. In New York City there were eleven million people. Our company, in one building, published sixty-four magazines. Here, in the whole Bay area, there were no more than fifty magazines. And here the people who had jobs dug in for life. In New York there was constant motion, action. All the balls up in the air. Everything and everyone in play.

If New York was all becoming in a spiritual sense, then San Francisco was all being. One the animus, the other the anima. So I'd come to the anima city, which despite its great beauty, seemed more and more like a mausoleum, a living death. I wanted to go back, but Barbara wouldn't budge. We fought and screamed. No use. The money was going, I couldn't get a job and I couldn't convince her to leave. One evening I came into the living room to find the kids playing with the toy soldiers and cowboys I had played with as a child. The Doctor. Billy The Kid. The Snake Man. The James Brothers. Scarface. And all the soldiers and sailors. Each was made of lead and elaborately detailed. They were collectors' items. And here were the kids smashing them against one another, screaming and roaring, and all these little familiar heads without bodies strewn over the rug. It was like my childhood, my history, was being torn from me, and Barbara just sat on the couch knitting, not noticing.

I was dying out here! And I couldn't make her understand. I began to realize what had happened in New York. I couldn't put it into words. I had felt that I was going to die again. I was afraid to die in New York. For it meant I would die into the Work. The Work would be my life. And I saw now: I didn't have enough trust for that. That was why, the deep reason why, I had kept insisting on having a relationship with Lord Pentland. Some part of me knew I would have to die into the Work, be reborn in the Work, and to do that I had to trust him. Of course I was completely tangled up in my own father projection. Nothing he could have done would have helped. I was living in my own dream and I was going to have to see it flush on. It happened so fast back in New York. The Food Diagram. The actress's ice box and fridge. The no-show at the Golden Cup Dinner. I wasn't clear enough then to put it into words. I remembered Lord Pentland telling me: *You'll have to face me wherever you go.* He knew. He had given me the freedom to choose. And what had I done? I had escaped, exiled myself. Coming here, I had finessed the question.

Bought time. But I was still going to die. But now out here. All alone. I couldn't avoid "my appointment in Samara."

PSYCHOLOGICAL VOID. I RECOGNIZED ITS TASTE. IT WAS THE SAME SPACE I was in after *In New York* failed. It was like a fog bank hanging in a forest. Wherever I turned, whatever I did, there it was. Day after day at home, walking the deck, going for a paper, checking the mail, sitting around—I could feel that same space. There was no avoiding it. Nothing, nothing to do but watch. I was standing on the deck, lost in self-pity, looking across the bay at the shadows San Quentin made in the late afternoon sun, when a thought struck: *He can do nothing until he knows what he can do.*

Yes, yes, I saw it now. What I could do was to wish, wish to remember myself. And so I wished. And I was renewed. But the wish was so small. All the space began to eat me.

When we had first arrived in California, the vast raw physical space had been like a deep freeing breath. The years in the confining cement canyons of Manhattan had been so contracting. But now this same space became endless. I felt lost in it. Like I was nothing. I had exiled myself. I was alone, totally alone. The space was withering. Doubts like birds pecked at me. *How could I have left Lord Pentland! New York! The magazine!*

For days I would eat on myself. Great swings of emotion, depression, anger. At the dinner table some inane topic would come up. I'd argue for it. Then, only a few seconds later, I'd argue the opposite, just as violently. And all the time there was this sense I—whoever that was—didn't really care.

I was a battleground. Great emotional tempests. "I"s screaming, blaming, fighting to the death. And there in between dark spaces, in between the alteration between here and not-here, would be "this" to which I could give no name. At one point, I felt the dark spaces began to get blacker, deeper. I was living a life of darkness, secrecy, and withering loneliness. All these "I"s, and no axis, no center, no controlling I. I felt like I was literally "cracking up." The "I"s, a circus carousel of strange creatures, came and went like I was a swinging door. And I couldn't stop it. I couldn't do anything. I was helpless, vulnerable. There was only "this" that was seeing it all. But what was "this" that was watching it all? It was no I at all. It was so still, dispassionate, seemingly without will or desire. I could have driven straight into a wall and "this" having no power, no will, to stop it.

There was no way of knowing once I was gripped by an "I", taken under the sea, whether "this" would still remain. All the years of self-remembering had been just a prelude, a practice. Now it just came. I'd suddenly wake up to being awake. The three dimensions and the fourth, that of being awake in the invisible stillness of time, were alive in me. And I'd realize what a flat, soulless, psychological world I'd been in.

But there wasn't the energy, the will and clarity, to stay there. I would notice the body was tired or that the mind-thought had become heavier. On some level identification would take place. It happened so quickly I wasn't aware of it. Then the space would dwarf me. I felt like I, this feeling of I that persisted, was going to be rubbed out, erased. I would leak energy. I could hardly keep awake. I'd find myself being bored. Feel irritation, anger. I remembered Lord Pentland once saying, "We do not realize the scale involved in our negativity. When we are negative we should remember our mother."

And so it went, but slowly, the seizure passed. The body felt raw, fragile, porous. I had no atmosphere around me. I felt there was this hole in me, that my centers had been torn. And I was still leaking energy. It had a familiar feel. This must have been what happened after I lost *In New York*. Only then, not only did I not know, I had no knowledge of how to stop the leaking. I worked now, whenever I was able, to sense the parts of the body, the limbs and organs, front and back, directing my attention, breathing into each part, feeling the whole, changing the tempo of the blood, healing the body, softening the mind and, soon, I came back into balance again and my strength returned.

THE MONEY WAS GOING FAST. WE WERE DOWN TO OUR LAST FEW THOUSAND dollars and still no job. I kept making calls, sending out resumes. Nothing. Only a mailbox full of bills and junk mail. It was like I didn't exist. I began to paint, setting up an easel on the deck. The yellow building across the bay kept attracting my eye. In Ossining I came home every night to Sing-Sing. Here, I looked out at San Quentin. The view here was better. Had I replaced one prison for another? The paintings were all dark, predatory. I couldn't taste any colors but it felt good to have a brush in my hand.

Finally, I got an interview with Potlatch, a major timber company. I hit it off with the director of public relations. More interviews with department heads. I was going to be hired. All that remained was just a look-see interview with George M. Cheek, the senior vice president of the company. Before sending me up to Cheek's office, the director of public relations warned me about Cheek. "He's an ex-newspaperman and an intellectual. He's read just about everything. He tears people apart if he finds any discrepancies. So be sure you can back up anything you say."

The top floor of the Embarcadero Center building looked out on all of San Francisco and especially the pyramid-shaped TransAmerica Building. I was ushered into Cheek's office. Greeting me was a muscular, balding man, quite visceral, with hard challenging eyes and a solid no-nonsense handshake. The initial talk was genial, he kidded a bit, then told me a little about the company. The president, he said, was a devout Catholic who had a "mystical feeling for the land." That seemed at odds with what I had read about Potlatch. I simply nodded without comment. Then Cheek ceremoniously took an expensive briar pipe from a rack behind his desk, carefully filled it with custom tobacco, lit up, and puffed away.

Then the grilling began, the main question being why I had left such a good job. The implication was that perhaps I had trouble with alcohol, drugs, some vice. He went through my resume job by job. His questions were rapid-fire. They hit like punches. Jab, jab, then the right cross. I felt like I was in the ring. I was in the ring with a madman. I was having to fight him just as I had fought Stanley and Spencer, and, in some ways, Lord Pentland. I learned every time but I hated it. Why was I always having to fight?

I answered each question but gave no more information than was asked. I kept circling, bobbing and weaving, keeping my guard up, my answers short and direct, giving him nothing to hit. Still puffing away, he tried my personal life next. He already knew all the answers. He was looking for any telltale twitches, excesses, a reluctance or evasion.

"You married?" he asked in a tone that questioned my sexuality.

"Yes," I said, "and I have two sons." And so it went, cat and mouse. I knew the game. He didn't like that. I could feel his insecurity, his need for control. The questions became more blunt, brutal even. He wanted to know about my wife, how we had met. He learned she had graduated from Berkeley. He paused. I could see him toying with the idea of her being a radical.

"Do you hunt or fish?" he asked casually.

"Camp," I tell him.

Cheek's eyes glinted. "What do you do when you camp?"

"What do I do?"

"Yes—what do you do?"

"Oh, I see, well I...I hike."

"Ever read London's *How to Light a Fire?*"

"No."

"No? And you say you're a writer, a camper?" Cheek feigned surprise. "Well," he said after a bit, "what about sports? Did you play any sports in college?"

"I got a college football scholarship."

"Oh, yeah. And—?"

"Well, in high school I played guard and was fast and medium-sized, but by college standards I was small and slow."

"Let's see where did you go?" Cheek shuffled papers on his desk looking for my resume.

"Bowling Green State University," I told him.

"I was Michigan State," he said taking a big draw from his pipe. "I was a collegiate boxer. I won the light heavy intercollegiate championship."

"Oh, really? My Uncle was a professional boxer. A middleweight," I told him trying to warm things up.

"Oh, yeah? Who'd he fight?" Cheek challenged.

"One-eyed Harry Greb for one. He was Dempsey's sparring partner. One of them."

Cheek put down his pipe and lit a cigarette, and leaned back in his big leather swivel chair, trying to look casual. "You know much about boxing?" he inquired.

"A little. I wanted to fight Golden Gloves as a kid."

"Yeah? Why not?"

"Skin's too soft. Cuts too easy."

"Yeah," said Cheek. "Well, who do you think is the best fighter of all time?" Cheek's voice was less forceful.

"Sugar Ray and Muhammed Ali."

"Robinson wasn't so good." Cheek came forward in his chair, his chin out. "Joey Maxim beat him."

"Yeah, but Ray was ahead. Maxim only won because Ray couldn't come out for the thirteenth. He had heat prostration."

"The fourteenth!" snapped Cheek, glaring at me, daring me to disagree.

If I backed down, he'd rip up the particular "I" that had surfaced in me. I studied him a moment. "I really do seem to remember it being the thirteenth."

"No, no," Cheek said.

He put out the cigarette and reached back and selected an expensive Meerschaum from his pipe rack, filled it and jammed it into his mouth, flicking the lighter violently, drawing the light into the white bowl, puffing in short spurts, exhaling, then pointing the stem of the pipe at me. "The fourteenth."

"Well, maybe you're right." I said, as a more reasonable "I" struggled to the top of the pack. Perhaps we should look it up in the record book. I'll buy you a drink, if you're right." I forced a smile and a laugh. "What kind of English did you major in?" Cheek demanded.

"What kind? Oh, I see what you mean. Creative writing."

"What was that like?"

That was twenty-five years ago. I couldn't remember. "Really good," I told him, adding, "we'd read a novel and then write another chapter after the ending."

"How could you do that?" Cheek was frowning.

"Well, you know, endings and beginnings are arbitrary."

"What! That's impossible."

"Maybe, but it shows how well you've understood what you've read."

"Take O. Henry. All his stories have trick endings. How would you add to that?"

"You'd have to add another trick, I suppose. Maybe a counter trick. I don't know, I agree, it's hard to do."

"Impossible."

"I remember Eliot writing in his *Four Quartets,* 'In my ends are my beginnings.' So maybe life is circular. In that case it wouldn't matter where you began or ended."

Cheek snorted. I thought he was an intellectual, that he'd enjoy mixing it up, countering with his own point of view. But my cocky "I" had fallen in love with itself. I hadn't been listening.

"What books have you read recently?" asked Cheek.

I hesitated. In my mind's eye was the picture of the cover of *The Crest Jewel of Discrimination* which I'd finally begun reading. Tell him that and I'm dead in the water. And I needed this job. I remembered about the president being Catholic.

"Simon Called Peter."

"What else?"

"I'm reading a novel, *A Moment of True Feeling*. By Peter Hanke."

"Yeah—what's that about?"

"I'm just getting into it, but I think Hanke's pointing out that most of the feeling we have isn't real feeling at all. It's all conditioned, mechanical."

Cheek didn't want to go down that road. "Anything else?" he asked. "Sartre, maybe?"

Sartre was a communist. Cheek was clever. "No, I'm more interested in Heidegger."

"Heidegger?"

"Yes."

"Yeah, what about the best sellers?"

"Never read them." I had answered too quickly.

"And why not?"

"Too commercial, too mental." The words were out of my mouth before I could stop them. I was identified with books. How stupid!

Cheek took a long puff. Stared into the ceiling. I looked outside. There was the cement pyramid of the TransAmerica Building. Finally, exasperated, Cheek barked: "Well—what do you read then?"

"Jung," I said.

"Why?"

Why! Why the fuck was I reading Jung? An angry, rebel "I" was talking me out of this job. Did I really want to be a flack? I paused, lowered my voice, tried to speak what I felt. "His concepts of the anima and animus, archetypes and synchronicity—they're grids. You can see reality through them. Like scaffolding on an invisible building."

George M. Cheek, senior vice president, stared at me, his eyes like a hunter's who had unexpectedly happened upon a strange duck. The game was over. Cheek thought he had me pegged. Probably a closet environmentalist or a New Age intellectual. Certainly not a Republican or a capitalist. He knew I wasn't one of them. No company wants a maverick. "Yes, we want wild ducks," my boss at IBM had told me long ago, "but wild ducks who fly in formation."

"I HAD TO FIGHT HIM, HAD TO SHOW OFF. THIS BIG GODDAMN MOUTH—I couldn't keep it shut. And I had the job—it was only a look-see interview!"

Barbara sat at the table, nodding, looking down at her plate, saying nothing.

The impulse flashed. I picked up my plate and smashed it on the floor. The jagged shards shot and scattered like dice over the linoleum.

A week or so later I smashed a wine glass on the table, gashing the palm of my hand. It needed stitches. Giant mood swings came. I would sit on the couch for hours not saying a word, then rant and rave about some injustice. "Patterson" came into full bloom. He saw Barbara as the Ice Princess. Remote. Unobtainable. Silent. Invisible. That was her way of avoiding life.

She was the focal point of my love, my anger. I loved her. She was so noble, pure, without greed or pretension, always tolerant, giving, self-sacrificing, with a strong sense of the spiritual. And loyal, yes. A big word, especially in light of my actions. She was so open to ballet, music, opera and yet so closed when it came to any real thinking or questioning. So many times I'd tried to communicate with her. Not really. She was too afraid. She just went blank. Many were the nights I'd put her literally to sleep at the dinner table. She'd had the power to break out of her parent's materialism, their atheism, but the upbringing had left its mark. Her parent's were good people, solid citizens but, scarred by the Depression, the fear, the lack of love in their families, they in turn had insisted on a flat, economic, cause and effect view of the world that was without dimension. Unwittingly, Barbara picked up some of that. She could never see it was all conditioning, false personality. And what one doesn't own up to, the other has to work with. My Mother had spoiled me, I didn't want to work with anyone's baggage. I took it as an affront and bitched. I could eat it for a while but sooner or later it came out. Anytime I raised my voice Barbara would become silent, retreat, be there but not be there, like one of those animals that when in danger pretends it is not alive. I would talk louder and more extensively, trying to make her understand. Of course, that only made it worse. Her father had put a lot of fear into her. When the family would go on motor trips, she told me, he would hang a thick leather belt over the car seat as a warning against acting up.

What were we doing together was what I didn't understand. I was captivated by her beauty and bearing, her sense of proportion Her silence seemed to hold great mysteries. But I was unable to plumb them. She didn't think much of my writing, insisted one evening that I wasn't a writer. "But I make my living writing," I told her. "Strangers pay me to write. I must be a writer." She made no reply. "Well," I said, "who is a writer?" "Tolstoy," she answered. "Tolstoy! I never said I wrote on that level." She had high standards but I didn't realize how high they were. My Mother flooded me with compliments, Barbara hardly any. She was very Nordic. This was good for me, I knew, but tough as a perpetual diet.

Yes, she loved me, she would say. We had so many beautiful moments together. But I wondered what she meant by the word. Her mother had kept the pressure on her about getting married. In my darker moments I wondered if she had just succumbed finally and I was all that was available. She seemed to have no interest in what was strongest in me, my imagination and daring, my creativity, my seeking. "Why did you marry me?" I would ask. "Why did you do this? You have no real interest in me. You never want to read anything I write. My ideas put you to sleep. What are we doing together?" It all seemed so futile. A snake was coiled around her throat. A snake of fear. A thousand times my St. George had pulled that viper from her neck and killed it. She would see it. There'd be a fusing of souls. But then, in a day or so, the serpent again coiled itself around her. The fear blocked her from seeing herself. She seemed afraid of any self-criticism, any admission of being wrong. And so there never seemed to be any real suffering, real questioning.

For myself, I felt I had worked through (at least for a time) the masculine side of my nature, the Father side. Now I was trying to communicate with the feminine, the female part of me, the Mother. My Mother was one expression of the feminine, Barbara another. They constituted the two poles of my feminine. I could see my Mother now so vividly, standing before me, starving for love, a bottomless pit; all the time pleading, crying for attention, for recognition, and always rejecting it. "It" was never pure enough. I saw her coming toward me, and me holding my school books in front of me like a shield, and her wanting me to kiss that face, that horrible, self-pitying open wound. I didn't want to kiss it. But she made me kiss her. I wiped it off on my sleeve and spat and hurried to school; leaving her standing there on the porch, her face red and covered with tears. And me, feeling guilty I'd hurt her, and crying inside angry at myself, and all the time hating that devouring stupid mother.

Yes. And I saw Barbara now coming close to me, and feeling that same fear, fear of the Mother. The fear of being devoured. Both of us afraid. Her of the masculine; me of the feminine. The two of us caught in a "relationship." Stick figures in a pretty house of cards. And yes, in a strange way, it was Sarah who had saved us. She who had loved fearlessly, passionately; she, who had given everything. She, the bad girl, the mistress, the adulteress, the home-breaker. She, that whole group of "I"s. And, yes, it was she whom I rejected. I had killed her. Killed love as I always killed love. I wanted love yes but not to be possessed by love. I loved with a love that was afraid to love. Only the innocent, the solar hero, the lunar heroine, is capable of love. I was a coward. I faced the ancient human illusion now full face—the illusion that "I"s could ever love anything but themselves. The ego, by its nature, cannot love.

Sarah had put a question to me—choose between us. It had never been a question for me. I had never thought of the consequences of my relationship with her, where it might lead. I'd never considered leaving Barbara until Sarah put the question. It was a question that nearly killed me, sent me to Ireland, to "the other world," to that little girl in the car, facing the devil, chancing everything. I was no rapist, that I knew. But why then had it happened? The question had drained me and, like "Anne Boleyn," the woman I had met earlier on the Spanish part of the trip, I had no atmosphere. My 'skin' raw, exposed to everyone's vibration. Perhaps I had picked up the little girl's fear and, it mixing with my anger and frustration at Barbara, had turned around and projected itself on that little girl. That was as close as I had come to an explanation. But it was so psychological, so modern. Perhaps a devil had entered me, an auric force. Whatever, it was only the training I had received in the Work which had brought me through. That, and grace.

Yes, and this whole thing with my Father, with Lord Pentland. The lack of relationship, the lack of love and genuine feeling, the ambivalence. The incredible blind selfishness. Was it that what I couldn't understand at a higher plane of existence I was to live and understand on this plane? Did my life on the physical plane mirror what I'd become too dense to see on a higher plane? Or, to put it another way, was I living through the confusion of a higher plane on a lower plane?

As above, so below—was the opposite of this teaching true? That is, *So below, as above?* It was not in reality, of course, but only in terms of misunderstanding, of vibration contracting and descending to the psychological level? Had I refused and rebelled in some way on a higher plane? Had I projected then what, in fact, was my own rejection? Had I taken a vow that I would never let myself be hurt again? If so didn't it follow that all of this—what I called my life—had already happened in another dimension of time?

And if that were true then these physical lives of ours weren't about the idea that so consumes us all—that of changing our life, changing ourselves. No, the idea and purpose was to come to know what I could do. And the answer was that, in fact, "I" could do nothing. We were all asleep to ourselves, our lives. Each of us had one task: to watch our movie. Watch or sleep: the choice was ours. That was our free will.

Not long after this, I was given a graphic representation of just where I was. I opened the *San Francisco Chronicle*—and there facing me was an eerie, three column, black-and-white photograph of death. The image was that of hundreds of dead swans, huddled together in a cloudy winter darkness, their once graceful bodies now frozen rock hard. No sign of life. Only the vast macabre outline of countless swan bodies, frozen silent, buried beneath mounds of snow, their long necks and heads turned tailward. The headline read:

Swans' Icy Graveyard

> On a lake in Hokkaido Island, to the north of Japan, the great whooper swans of Siberia usually wait out the winter, serenely gliding through the mist after their annual migration to escape the intense northern cold. But in a cruel deception of nature, danger lurks in Hokkaido, too…

> If the climate of the island turns savage, as it frequently can, both land and lakes freeze over, cutting the swans off from the water weeds, roots and grasses which form their diet. As the temperatures drop, the birds which have found water swim frantically backwards and forwards, striving to keep a channel open. Their effort flags and the ice takes over.

> For all their grace in the water, they are clumsy in their attempts to take to the air. The swans can take off only by a tremendous act of strength. They stretch forward with their upper bodies out of the water, necks craned, and finally, by massive beating of their wings, lumber aloft like overloaded seaplanes.

Already weak from cold and hunger, they cannot muster the strength. So, as the cold creeps over Hokkaido and the thickening ice separates them from their sustenance, they huddle together for warmth. It is not enough. A cold night kills, to produce in the morning a haunting tableau of death.

It felt like I was reading about myself. I showed the story to Barbara. She didn't see any connection. That wasn't the way she saw life, she told me. She was happy here. She didn't want to return to New York. Originally, she had not wanted to come to California. That had been my idea. I had uprooted her and the boys, sold off our belongings and left behind the first home that we owned. Now she had settled in after a difficult transition and found she preferred life in Northern California, where she had graduated from college. I had brought her home. She felt good here. John was in school. In her mind, leaving made no sense.

I was alone. Alone in all this space. And the space was killing me.

There was still no job. Not even any prospects. Money was running out. What were we going to do? I walked the deck. I painted. I waited.

HEY, MY FRIEND, HOW 'BOUT GETTING OFF YOUR BUTT AND GOING FISHING?"

The voice on the phone was that of Geoff Hinden, a jovial carpenter I had met out here in the Work. He had bought an old tug boat and invited me to go fishing with him and Phil, a friend of his from the Work. We fished the Bay from morning to afternoon. Everyone's bucket was full of fish except mine. I couldn't even catch a fucking fish! The water had turned choppy and it had gotten chilly, the sun disappearing behind a bank of morose grey clouds. Geoff started up the engine to return to the marina.

Just then a big wind came up. The grey Stetson I was wearing was yanked from my head and sent sailing into the wake of the boat. It was my Uncle's hat. I wasn't losing it! I tore off my shoes and leapt overboard, swimming out and grabbing the soaking hat. But I couldn't get back to the boat. The current was too strong. Geoff shut off the engine. I still couldn't catch up with the boat. He started up the engine and circled back. Geoff and Phil were laughing and so was I. Geoff brought the tug as close as he could, cut the engine, dropped anchor and tossed the life preserver to me. It sailed through the air like a giant frisbee, landing just five feet or so in front of me. I swam fast but couldn't reach it. The current was too swift. Nothing stayed still, the current carrying both the preserver and the boat far away from me. He started the engine again and came 'round again and dropped anchor. More throws. But I couldn't reach it.

Winds were blowing. The bay was choppy. The water kept slapping my face. A storm was coming up. I was tiring now. My strength was going. I was breathing hard, starting to wheeze. My clothes were heavy, kept pulling me down. I was having to fight to stay above water. My vision became panoramic. The whole scene—me in the water, the boat, the surrounding land, the sky above—opened up as if a curtain had suddenly been pulled back. A huge gaping silence. Nobody laughing now. The recognition struck: *I might drown.*

"Damn!" I shouted to myself. "This is stupid! Drowning trying to save my Uncle's hat!"

Phil, who had been watching the whole time, suggested—"Throw it behind him."

On Geoff's next throw, the preserver sailed over my head. Now nature worked for me. The current brought the preserver right to me.

On the way back to the marina, I saw Phil examining the water logged hat, looking at me strangely. It was just a hat. Why would anyone risk his life for it?

"It was my Uncle's." I told him. "I loved him. I wasn't going to lose it."

"Oh," said Phil, like he understood. But he didn't, couldn't.

We climbed the ladder up to the wheel house and broke open a few beers. "I've just about lost everything coming out here," I told them, feeling both angry and embarrassed. "I wasn't about to lose that, too."

We drank the beers and watched the night falling in the distance around Mt. Tamalpais.

When he dropped me off, Geoff opened up the back of his old station wagon and took out a four-foot leopard shark. Ugly and slimy as sin. He carried it into our apartment.

"What are you doin'?"

"Look what your husband caught!" he told my wife.

"I'm not cleaning it," said Barbara, backing well away from the long, slithery, spotted shark.

"Okay," I said. "I'll do it."

"You know how?" Barbara asked. She knew I didn't know "how."

"No," I said. "But I'll learn."

I took hold of the tail and carried the dead shark, water still dripping from its jaws, into the kitchen. "How do you clean this mother?" I asked Geoff.

"You slit open the belly. Then reach in and pull out the intestines," said Geoff, a big smile on his face.

"I'm not watching," said Barbara who went into the living room.

I took a big knife from a drawer. The only thing I had ever cut was a steak. I slit open the shark's stomach. Then I put my hand inside. It went in up to the wrist. I got hold of the shark's guts. Sticky and runny. A gelatinous, oozy mass. An untouchable. A strange silence came up. I stood with my hand buried in its slurpy belly, gripping the shark's guts. Suddenly, I felt the power of its nature. I felt it passing into me, moving through the skin into the tissues and cells. The feeling was ancient, primordial. And I knew with a certainty that went beyond the mind: *my luck was going to change.*

And, as in the days of old, I went to my lady and offered her my good fortune.

She screamed and I chased her around the apartment, whooping and hollering, threatening to give her a "facial", all the while Geoff laughing and breaking open some ice cold beers.

Now a new time started very quickly.

I painted two canvases with a bright palette. The first was a small painting I called *Constantine's Death*. I had named it so because I believed that the Roman general Constantine of history had only converted from paganism to Christianity as a political strategy, not through revelation or faith. The painting showed Constantine, a modern-day Christian, as a large-headed, bald man, very much in his head, apprehensive. His eyes peered out from a pair of horn rim glasses. Dressed in a blue business suit, he wore shoes but had forgotten to put on socks. He sat in a deep, large womb-like red chair. In his right hand he held a single red rose. A large potted dracaena cane plant, which had outgrown its pot, hovered over him. Behind him was a window, its shade drawn, the light outside a strong yellow. The window pane looked like a cross. On the floor by his side sat a corpulent earthy female, completely nude. Her hand was placed atop his left hand, as if to restrain or protect him. Behind Constantine's chair stood an older woman, his mother, reaching toward him, trying to hold him back. By the open door stood a weird-looking, thin bald man, the Angel of Death, greeting *That* which had just knocked. That represented the unknown or, in this case, Hermes, guide of souls to the Underworld. This was a moment then when one was between two worlds. The old one in which one had lived and the new to which one was going. Like the Charles Fort dream I had much earlier with its "original invitation" to leave the Work, the choice wasn't between whether to stay or go. To go was one's fate. The only choice was the wish to remember oneself, or not. One either redirected the attention to a global sensation of the body, separating the sensation from feeling, or stayed asleep.

Dying in my doubt, I had been given a new life. I felt a new surge of energy and confidence and only then realized how down I'd been. I was riding on this feeling when leafing through a weekly newspaper, I noticed an item that I'd been seeing for months and vaguely wondering about:

> Rare-Born Mystic, 90-Year-Old Sunyata Will
> Speak Aboard S.S. Vallejo, Gate 5 Road, Sausalito,
> Tues., 7:30 P.M. Donation.

Rare-born mystic—I had no idea what that meant, but I did know that the S.S. Vallejo was Alan Watts' old houseboat. I felt as if I had a connection with Watts. His *The Book on the Taboo Against Knowing Who You Are* was the first spiritual book I'd ever read. And it was at a lecture of his in New York that I had first meditated. I'd read many of his books and was impressed with his erudition and the ease of his writing style. Whoever this "Sunyata" character turned out to be...well, at least I would see Watts' houseboat.

Fittingly enough, on April Fools' Day I found myself on a dirt road standing in front of the S. S. Vallejo, a listing old boat, its hull sunk in a sea of mud on Richardson Bay. The Ark a few millennia after the flood. It was low tide. The dark and starlit sky overhead seemed immense. The air had a heavy smell of brine. I tramped up the gangplank. The water gently lapping against the sides of the resting hull, a few old alley cats dozed on deck in between an assortment of potted flowers and plants. I left my shoes with some twelve or fifteen other pairs by the big potted jade plant at the entrance to the main cabin. I almost bashed my head on the low ceiling. The room was filled with flickering candles and the heavy scent of incense. A motley tribe of characters, some sitting on cushions, some in chairs, all faced a cot in the corner. In the distance came the forlorn call of fog horns, the squawking of sea gulls. I felt as if I had happened upon a seance.

Presently, the most unlikely and bizarre figure I'd ever seen padded quickly between the chairs. Dressed in a maroon turban, orange kurta and black Chinese slippers, he sat down on the edge of Watts' bed. Was this a man? A woman? Was he androgynous? I couldn't be sure. He had large, heavily veined farmer hands, quite expressive, and twinkling blue eyes, one of which wandered a bit. He seemed like a dopey old coot. A Holy Fool, rather shy and ill at ease. He had none of the presence and power of a Lord Pentland. In fact, if anything, he seemed a bit daft. Vacant.

A bearded nervous man from the Alan Watts Society introduced him. Sunya Bhai, he said, took peasant birth, being born on a farm in Denmark in 1890. He had very little "headucation," as he liked to call it. "The mind never developed enough to cause any trouble," Sunya said. Sunya loved to be alone for, as he explained, "I am never more myself than when I am alone."

Taken for a simpleton, Sunya had worked in England as a gardener raising carnations at Dartington Hall where he met Tagore, the poet, who recognized him and asked that the Danish gardener, "Come to India to teach Silence."

There on a short holiday, Sunya, or Alfred Sorensen or Brother Alfred as he was then known, found an intuition among the people not generally experienced in the West and so decided to settle there, wandering about and finally building a one-room stone hut at Kesar Devi, a hill at the top of Kalimat, which itself was high above the hill station of Almora. Each morning Alfred awoke to look out on Ananda Devi, the third largest peak of the Himalayas surrounded by a twenty-three mile range of snow-capped mountains.

Introduced to Ramana Maharshi by the author Paul Brunton, this simple Dane was seen by Ramana as a rare-born mystic, an enlightened being who was born so, and who sitting in Ramana Maharshi's presence was telepathically given the one realization he yet needed—Ramana telling Brother Alfred, "We are always aware Sunyata." And so, several years later, Alfred Julius Emmanuel Sorensen took the name "Sunyata"—whose meaning is full, solid emptiness—and returned to his hut to, as he was fond of saying, "do nothing and be nothing and enjoy nothing."

Over the years, word of this rare-born mystic spread and he was visited by and became close friends with Ananda Mai, Yashoda Mai, Krishna Prem and Sri Anirvan, Lama Govinda, Evans Wentz, the Jawaharal Nehru family, and the Chilean diplomat, writer and mystic, Miguel Serrano; who in one of his books, *The Serpent's*

Paradise, recounted how he came to the culmination of his search to know his true Self in meeting Sunya, whom he called "The Brother of Silence."

Much later, members of the Alan Watts Society, visiting the holy places of India and taking darshan from many of its spiritual masters, accidentally discovered Sunya. Directed to Sunya Bhai's stone hut by Professor Pant, a local guide, who told them that here abided one "who actually lived the sayings of the Great Sages," the group was instantly charmed and delighted with Sunya's emptiness and simplicity. They wanted him to come to America, but Sunya insisted he had "Nothing to teach, nothing to sell." After persistent efforts, the group finally convinced Sunya a year later to come for a short visit. Sunya was delighted with the openness of the people he met, "the Yankee guys and girlies," as he called them, and said California was where "The new race of silent, intuitive people was being born."

The bearded man, much more contained now, said in a beautiful and heartfelt voice, "Congratulations on your good luck in being here."

Everyone now looked to the enigmatic figure on the cot who did nothing but sit for a while and who gave off a feeling that seemed to me neither rare nor exceptional but, if anything, a rather incredible ordinariness.

Finally, when he did begin to speak, he spoke with no special authority and often seemed to be finding his way along, not having himself a hint of what he might say next. His voice was quite pleasing, though, being soft and whispery and vibrating on a lot of levels. His voice had a lot of water in it. He spoke without pretension and, at times, his large hands came off his knees fluttering like birds in flight as he made a point. As he spoke, and this mainly of his early life on the family farm in Denmark, his one eye wandered a bit which gave the disconcerting feeling that he was looking in two directions at the same time. Near the end he mentioned of what he called "the living Silence," but he spoke so softly and with so little force that it was hard to hear all of what he was saying.

When he stopped speaking, I had a strange impression of silence in that there were something like two silences in the room. The one was a strained or embarrassed surface silence, and the other without any such personal quality and existing at a much deeper and inclusive, if fainter, level.

Finally, amid a coughing and rustling about, someone asked: "What's the meaning of Genesis?"

"It refers to the fall of the ego," said Sunya. "God told Adam and Eve not to eat from the Tree of Knowledge but of course He knew that would be the first thing they'd do. It was due."

"Due?"

"It had to be."

"What?"

"Otherwise there'd be no play."

There was a long silence. He gazed at me a moment. I was sitting in the back. He asked that I sit closer. There were many pillows empty in the first row. I sat in the second row.

"The witness is a very high state," he said after a bit.

"You've never said that before," someone said.

He smiled. "It's true."

"But what about good and evil then?" another asked.

"Nothing is good or bad but thinking makes it so."

He said it so simply, so clearly. All the studying and pondering I had done. And it was all in the mind. Yes, I saw that and I wanted to laugh.

"But that's Shakespeare," someone said, a hint of accusation in the voice.

The turbaned figure on the bed nodded and smiled. "The mind can make a hell of heaven or heaven of hell," he whispered.

"Well, what's the mind and ego then?"

"The mind-ridden ego, the ego-ridden mind. I see very little difference."

There was an aging blonde in a long black smock beside me with enormous breasts. She was wearing no bra and her nipples showed. "Sunya, I don't feel any sexuality coming from you," she said.

He laughed. "Mystics aren't sexual."

"Oh Sunya…" exclaimed the blonde, laughing, her two hands reaching toward him, her cleavage squeezing and ballooning up between her arms.

"Oh the little egoji thinks it is separate," he said in that whispery playful voice. "And that starts the dance. Mere ego. Mere knowledge." His hand waved it away as if it were nothing.

More questions. They were either very heady or emotional, very personal, or psychological. Lord Pentland would have pointed that out. But this Sunya seemed interested in them all, not that he answered, for either he told about his life or admitted that he didn't know. "I never had that problem," he said.

I was going to leave. Something told me to stay. I gazed at him, trying to take him in, get a feel for his vibration. He seemed totally unconcerned. It struck me: No one was there!

It was that same quality I had felt with Lord Pentland. It was as if he was dead in some way.

"States," he said "aren't real. They come and go. It's only Being that is real. *Tat Twam Asi*. Being, consciousness, grace. Not all these tantric tricks, ego fuss and shakti business." He giggled.

I could feel my heart pounding, the urging that I should ask a question. But I had no question. There was a long engulfing silence. More fog horns and the tinkling of wind chimes. Finally, I took the leap:

"I was in New York a long time. I felt I should come out here. It didn't make any sense. But I did. I've had to give up a great deal. I've gone through a lot of suffering."

"A little death now and then is salutary."

I nodded. I wasn't sure I believed him. But it sounded right. "I was asleep and wanted to wake up so I entered a spiritual discipline. I've found that as good as it was that somehow I couldn't submit or conform. Perhaps I didn't take it in the right way…The result is that I feel like I have a bigger problem now than when I started."

Yes, that is what happens, isn't it?

He didn't say that in words, but in the silence these words came through.

"Only a mature ego," he said, "can surrender itself."

As I listened to Sunya I began to sense that no one was talking. There was no "I" or ego. there seemed to be both an absence and a presence, the ambiguity of which I had no words.

"The ego gets so large that one day"—he raised his hand above his head and, like a magician, pulled an imaginary rabbit from his head—"it just happens. Poof! All gone."

He was serious. Reveling in death. This guy was very playful but very deadly.

"I have nothing to sell, nothing to teach," he said impishly. "I never had to dominate myself. I was born so."

The space seemed to open up, become endless, dynamic.

The figure on the cot, this crazy amazing exasperating old fool, murmured, "Delightful uncertainty." He looked about the room, a soft childlike smile shining on us. "Such beautiful differences," he exclaimed. And then he began to recite from Edward Arnold's poetic translation of the *Bhagavad Gita;*

> *Never the Spirit was born; the spirit shall cease to be—never.*
> *Never the time it was not; Ends and beginnings are dreams!*
> *Birthless and deathless and changeless remaineth the Spirit forever.*
> *Death has not touched it at all, dead though the form (the house)*
> *of it seems.*

And with that he got up and puckishly danced away.

Later, I tried telling Barbara about "Sunyata," but there were so many contradictions, I finally just sighed and shut-up.

"Well," she said, "I think you should go back."

"Why?"

"You look a lot more mellow."

And I realized then that I felt a lot better. That something had been lifted or taken from me. I wasn't sure if I would go back. It seemed a little dippy. But every week thereafter I'd find myself walking up the S. S. Vallejo's gangplank. I began to see Sunya every Saturday morning at the hillside home in Mill Valley in which the Alan Watts Society had rented a room for him. It had a wonderful view of the bay and Tiburon and Angel Island. We'd just sit around and talk or remain silent. Then we'd go to lunch, sometimes a movie. Nothing special, but so very special. For Sunya was empty. There were so very few "I"s there. And what was there, as Sunya would say, "was never any trouble." For him, the body-mind was *in* consciousness; not consciousness in the body-mind. Sunya abided in what is called, *Sahja Samadhi,* non-duality, effortless and completely free of any "I"-identification. He had never had a language to express this consciousness but, over the years, what he called "the

Wu language had bubbled up." Wu was taken by Sunya to mean "beyond 'yes' and 'no'." He delighted, when asked a tricky question in answering with a resounding "Wu!" While he did not have likes or dislikes, he did admit that some things he "favored" over others. He didn't put much store in things at all. For Sunya, it was only an egoji way of seeing. "Too mental," he would say.

Soon after that April Fools' Day meeting with Sunya, I had the belated recognition that "kings don't hire former kings." That is, no editor-in-chief hires his replacement. So I rewrote my resume, downplaying and deleting experience. Finally, I got a job as a field reporter at a big drop in pay with *Industry Week,* a national business magazine based in Cleveland, Ohio. The magazine needed a field reporter to cover Silicon Valley's high tech industry.

In the meantime I saw Sunya regularly and continued to attend the weekly group meetings of the Work. I knew that someday I might have to make a choice between the Work and Sunya. I was simply letting it unfold, waiting and watching.

After so many years in Lord Pentland's group, not to have him there made me realize how fortunate I had been. He did come out from New York three or four times a year, but his time was always limited. He was loved and valued in a different way out here, there being so many other teachers and influences in New York.

Though I didn't know it, Charles Fort's invitation had finally arrived in the form of the "Holy Fool." It certainly was an original invitation all right!

THE DAY OF DECISION ARRIVED NINETEEN MONTHS LATER. THE S.S. VALLEJO was sold and Sunya's weekly darshan moved to another houseboat, the Omphales. It was only available night was the same evening as my weekly Work meeting. Now I had to choose between Lord Pentland and Sunya, between the Work and Sunya's extremely laid back style of Advaita or non-dualism. And, of course, there was no choice really.

Lord Pentland had a powerful presence and intellect. He was a master teacher and a man of will and real knowledge. He was the consummate spiritual warrior and was born into a lineage of warrior chieftains. He was that rare combination of a man of the world and a man of the spirit. Like St. Paul, he had devoted his life to establishing the teaching of The Fourth Way throughout America. His wisdom and presence had opened many doors for me that otherwise might have remained closed. In the true sense of the word, I took him as my spiritual father.

Sunya was...what to say about him? He had no presence and little intellect in the usual meaning of the term. He was not a teacher, had no will and what knowledge he had, and he would never call it that, was contained in his oft mentioned message, "Be still and know that I am is God." He had taken what he called "peasant birth." He was a rather androgynous looking man who was neither a man of the world nor the spirit in that he took his stand on the groundless ground of sunyata, or what he called "full, solid emptiness." I really didn't know what to say about him other than I laughed a lot in his company, always felt good being around him, and there was this incredible sense of space and emptiness.

The teaching was a progressive path with many concentric circles of understanding and a teaching that was simple and yet rich and elegant in the subtlety and extension of its principles and axioms. The teaching of the Fourth Way which Gurdjieff had brought was, as he had told Ouspensky, "completely self-supporting and independent of other lines [Egyptian, Hebraic, Persian and Hindu] and it has been completely unknown up to the present time."[1] He had brought the teaching because, as he said, "Unless the 'wisdom' of the East and the 'energy' of the West could be harnessed and used harmoniously, the world would be destroyed."[2]

Sunya had no teaching, as such. In fact, mention the word and he would laugh. There was nothing and nobody to teach. Arnie, street-smart former New York journalist, who existed by raiding the garbage cans of the wealthy and selling the contents at weekly flea markets, gave him a large button with the words "Mr. Nobody." Thereafter, Sunya wore the button with pride and in his "typed darshans," long and repetitive letters he wrote to of course no one, he would refer to himself as "Mr. Nobody." If the Work was a progressive teaching, Sunya's was more than direct. It was nonexistent in any formal sense. Most people didn't "see" Sunya. People in the Work who knew Sunya totally dismissed him as an eccentric and harmless fool.

No, this decision required no great deliberation.

The darshan on the Omphales was my meeting of choice.

But my little mind, of course, couldn't just accept that.

Hadn't Trungpa warned about sunyata, saying that "It was a medicine that if taken too early could be a poison"? Was this too early? And if not, how could I know? I had a lot invested in the Work. Twelve years. Its authenticity was for me beyond question. And after all those years of study and discipline and inner work, Sunya's little houseboat meeting that attracted no more than a dozen people, many rather marginal at best, was not exactly what I was used to. Also, I had practically no friends outside the Work. I was unlikely to make any among the other "sunyasins," as one wag called us. Most of the people I found lost in fantasies and imagination of themselves and had no idea of working on themselves in any way. Weird as I found most of this band of renegade maverick pilgrims, I did feel comfortable among them. My heart and energy were with Sunya. I was leaving the organized Work, not the *inner work*. That I could never leave. And so, not a little doubting my sanity, I enlisted in this motley army in its Hesse-like *Journey to The East*.

Friends would ask me what my interest in Advaita was. I asked them in return what was the self, or Self, in self-remembering. I felt like I was speaking two languages. Advaita was like a manual for operations in the meta-metaphysical. The Fourth Way a manual within the physical and metaphysical. Gurdjieff began his

---

[1] P. D. Ouspensky, *In Search of the Miraculous*, p. 286.
[2] Fritz Peters, *Gurdjieff Remembered*, p. 122.

cosmology with the Creator God. Advaita began with the silence, the emptiness, before all manifestation. It regarded all manifestation as essentially unreal. Gurdjieff introduced scale of vibration linking all levels from the unmanifest to the manifest. Advaita's stance was a rigorous philosophical affirmation of unity opposing all forms or superimpositions of duality and, as a consequence, anything smacking of progression. Sudden versus gradual, or progressive, enlightenment had been and still was a serious topic of debate among non-dualists and dualists.

But Sunya never got into any philosophical discussions. Everything he said, and he often said the same thing, word for word, repeatedly (until it nearly drove you out of your mind which, in retrospect, may have been the method to this particular form of divine madness)…everything could easily be boiled down to a quote from the Bible that was a favorite with him: "Be still and know that I am is God." Sunya's interjection of the verb "is" is brilliant, of course, in that it returns the assertion from the personal to the impersonal level. But one had to be with him a long time until the power and rightness of these "tweakings" made itself felt. All I really had to go on was this feeling of incredible emptiness I got from Sunya. I had to trust my intuition, for in essence this emptiness was beyond any categories. I realized only much later why *The Crest Jewel of Discrimination* had fallen off that bookshelf back in New York. Like the "bishop sacrifice" in the chess game with Lord Pentland, I simply had to trust my intuition and act based on that trust.

Lord Pentland had always said few people had ever left the Work in the right way. Most simply found some excuse not to come and never directly faced their decision. I always took that as being cowardly, but who knows—perhaps that was the only way they could leave.

There were four reasons why people left the Work, according to Lord Pentland: "their grandmother, indigestion, money or sex." Now I saw there was a fifth reason, and it wasn't a reason at all for it was beyond all reason and was so absurd that no name could adequately describe it. What was I doing!

It was September when Sunya's darshan moved to the Omphales, an interesting name. I went to a few Work meetings but it was clear my heart had already left. As it happened, I was scheduled to be in New York in October to cover a computer systems conference for *Industry Week*. So I wrote to Lord Pentland to arrange a time to see him.

Returning to New York, I felt such nostalgia. It had been two years since Barbara and the kids and I packed up the cars and headed west. I felt like I'd been away a few centuries. I got a hotel, immediately unpacked and took the subway down to Casey's. I found him teaching a class, as usual. It was like he had never moved. I remembered him standing to the side of an easel, just making a few brush strokes, painting only with black faces and bodies appearing on the white paper, images moving to the background, coming to the foreground, entwining, turning. His brush was alive with its own life. As usual, he was just supplying the hand and Jungian synchronicity. But as I listened I realized he was talking about painting in a way I'd never heard him speak before. The principal idea was to paint not out of a desire or an idea, but from one's emptiness.

"How can we begin without taking the image apart?" Casey asked. "Usually we take it apart and then put it back together again. Could we begin in a different way? You know, just treating everything as it is, nothing standing out?"

After everybody had gone home and the studio was quiet again, we sat at the old metal lunch table and drank wine.

"Where'd you get that hat?" Casey asked. "Looks like it's out of a 1930's gangster movie."

"Yeah. It was my Uncle's." I told Casey about having to fish the hat out of the drink.

"That's a real hat," Casey exclaimed.

I told him then why I had returned and what I planned to do. He listened, puffing on his corncob. He didn't say much but his parting words to me were:

"You can't know if you're right or not—you can only know the risk of giving up what you have, and probably not even that!"

Casey gave me two framed prints of his, an alchemical king and a queen, Sol and Luna. "A gift," he said with smile and wink.

Before my meeting with Lord Pentland the following day, I went to Bloomingdale's. They were having a special Irish celebration. The store was festooned with Irish flags and shamrocks and images of elves and dwarfs and the Tuatha da Danaan, the children of the goddess Diana in their leprechaun form. Over the sound system lively, laughing Irish reels filled the large, handsome space. Videos played, too, of *Brendan's Voyage,* a modern day Irishman who set out in a small leather-skinned boat to discover the New World just as St. Brendan had done in the sixth century. I didn't know where my leaving the organized Work led, but I knew now I was on beam. After looking about I chose an expensive charcoal gray wool scarf, handmade in Ireland, as a gift for my teacher. I watched as the wrapping girl placed the scarf into a long rectangular box and wrapped it in the antique gold paper I'd chosen. Affixed to every package, I noticed, was a lowercase initial "b" for the name of the store. The "b" happened to be of a matching antique gold. I saw that if several "b"s were placed on the box the initials would look like musical notes and produce a visual vibration. The girl got a kick out of this inspiration and put the "b"s on both sides of the box. Standing back to appraise her work, she laughed and declared—

"He'll think it's a tie."

I hadn't thought of that, but I saw she was right.

I still had some time before my appointment with Lord Pentland so, on a whim, I took a taxi to Rockefeller Center. I stood on the Fifth Avenue sidewalk in front of the towering skyscrapers looking at the enormous fifteen-foot figure of Atlas who bore the weight of the world on his shoulders. Ah, yes, the Greek gods again!

Atlas the brother of Prometheus and a Titan, the race of giants who had warred against Zeus. Defeated, Atlas' punishment was to bear the weight of the world. Instead of the planet Earth, the artist had put on Atlas' shoulders an enormous armillary sphere, its axis pointing to the North Star. It showed the positions of the important circles of the celestial sphere, along with the twelve signs of the zodiac. I had never seen the connection before, but all the knowledge and power that the Greek gods represented, along with their responsibility for governing the world, seemed to me very much in the line of the Work.

I walked to the RCA building. I was surprised by the image above the doorway. How often I had come here and never noticed it. There at the entrance was a large figure of Zeus in the heavens. I noticed he was holding a compass, stretched to its maximum. Between the ends of the compass was the inscription: *Wisdom and Knowledge shall be the stability of thy times.*

Twelve years before I had first passed through this doorway. In my mind's eye I saw again my uncertain groping down the darkened hallway to see this "Lord Pentland." I watched as the tall slender figure moved quietly toward me. I saw again that incredibly silent face, the bushy eyebrows, the large elfin ears, the intelligent eyes.

Now here I am again these many years later come to say goodbye and give a token of my gratitude to the man to whom in a real sense I owe my life and the life I am about to embark upon.

I STAND BEFORE LORD PENTLAND'S DOOR FOR A MOMENT. THEN I KNOCK. and just as it was with that first knock twelve years before, again, no answer. But now I smile and try the door knob. The door opens and I go in. I sit down in the foyer. Presently, the familiar tall, erect figure comes out of the office. He motions me into his office.

"Let me welcome you back with a piece of candy," Lord Pentland says, his voice soft and pleasant. He holds out a small tin of candy.

I smile, thank him, and choose a chocolate egg. We both sit down then, he behind his desk; I on the other side. I put my attache case on the floor, laying it on its side and snapping open the top so I can open it later without delay.

"When were you last at the Foundation in San Francisco?" he asks.

"Last Sunday," I tell him.

"Was there anything special that happened that day?"

"No, I don't think so."

I remembered then that I had also gone to the Foundation briefly the Thursday after that. I wanted to pick up my movements' slippers. I had met Thelma Titus, Lord Pentland's secretary. She had sensed something and so I told her that I was going to New York to tell Lord Pentland I was leaving. She had taken me into a small room and had read me a passage from *All and Everything* on the five Obligolnian strivings that a man should make to perfect himself. It was as if she had initiated me. I was going to mention this when he asked:

"At what were you working?"

"I was working up on the roof."

"I see. Anything else?"

"It was a difficult day for me."

"Yes, and why was that?"

I look away a moment. We both know why I am here. I have to get it out, make my move, and quickly. "I wanted to leave. I don't think the Work is the right place for me. I'm an intuitive, artistic type and the Work is scientific."

He observes me from across the desk in that same way he began the meetings.

"You are negative," he says. "You should watch that."

I make no reply.

"The aim is to be able separate sensation from feeling," he says. "Tell me, do you have…pure feelings?"

"What do you mean?" I remember Hanke's book, *A Moment of True Feeling.* Is he referring to conditioned and unconditioned feelings? I have never heard Lord Pentland use this expression before.

"You know," he says casually, "one can have negative emotions, but not feelings."

"The word 'pure' bothers me, Lord Pentland. I don't know how you are using that word."

He lets my question hang there awhile. Finally, he answers—"Unmixed."

"Unmixed?"

He acts as if I am a bit of a fool. That long neck stretches, the bushy eyebrows move slightly.

"Feel-ings," he states, enunciating the word fully. "Feelings not mixed with thought."

Pure feeling? Had I ever had a pure feeling? Intuition was pure. There was only feeling at first. The words came later.

"Yes," I tell him.

He seems surprised.

"Do you have many?" he inquires laconically, a touch of sarcasm in his tone.

Are we speaking about the same thing? Maybe, maybe not. I can feel the strength of his mind. I see the logical trap he is setting: *If in leaving the Work I am acting on feeling—and if these feelings aren't pure—then how can I trust them?*

"I don't know. It's not something I count."

He seems a bit exasperated. "Well, would you say 'frequently'?"

"I would say…'Not infrequently.'"

He sighs and shakes his head.

"Becoming a real human being, that takes a great deal of time," Lord Pentland declares with certainty. He grins, giving the impression that having a pure feeling might take all of one's life, and perhaps a bit longer.

It's pointless to argue about the "purity" of feelings. I say nothing. The space becomes very heavy between us.

"Oh, yes," he remarks finally, in another tone, "thank you for the article you sent. I travel a lot to the various Work centers and am appreciative of having something to read. I am old now but a part of me is still young, still wants to know."

I had written an article on computers, pointing out that their seeming neutrality was bogus and warned of the calculative, soulless world of control and organization they were capable of creating, unless they were used consciously. I had quoted Heidegger's *The Question of Technology* and René Guénon's *The Reign of Quantity*.

"You are a serious writer," he says. "I was interested in your explanation of how computers work but, as for the rest, I'm afraid I don't quite see things the way you do."

I don't reply. I don't want to talk about computers. I have to remember why I have come. He's a sly old bird.

He waits. I stay silent. Finally, he challenges—"What's wrong with computers?"

The words shoot out of me—"They're not neutral, as some would have us believe. They order and limit human thinking. They've bastardized human language. For example, calling a machine 'intelligent.' And they're creating a machine language of their own which will likely become the common language of the world. Not only that, but in the case of—"

Lord Pentland breaks me off. "But take some yokel out on a farm pushing his plow…"

The "yokel" he means is obvious.

"A pretty sunset comes and what does the yokel do? He forgets all about plowing. Now is he any better off than a man sitting at a computer? I think not."

Did he understand what I had written? That wasn't the point at all. He intuits my thought and adds, now his tone more conciliatory: "Even if it is as you say, wouldn't you agree that the good thing about computers is that the challenge to our identity and freedom which they face us with might also provide the necessary shock and impetus to awaken, to come to being?"

"Yes, that might be said. But would you mind, Lord Pentland, if we changed the conversation back to what we were originally speaking about?"

"Not at all."

My heart pounds in my throat. This is the moment. I take a deep breath and exhale, sensing and feeling, hearing. I look at him directly and say flatly:

"The time has come when I think I should leave the Work. It's not right for me any longer."

He seems surprised.

For an instant, an emotion crosses his face. He turns to the wall. A spurt of air shoots from his mouth, he swallows hard. I killed him before he killed me. That is the thought that flashes. He turns back. The room, the atmosphere, Lord Pentland—completely different. A new world exists. Has been born. But he and I, we are now no longer in the same world. It's as if I am not there for him at all. It's as if I have been erased from his world entirely.

We sit facing one another. There is a shift. The moment stops. Finally he speaks, the words coming almost as a whisper: "You have never been closer to the Work than you are now."

But it is too late. I am leaving, have already in fact left. I only want this to end well. I am not sneaking off in the night. I want him to know exactly why I am leaving.

"Lord Pentland, I'd like to make my position clear to you." I reach down, open my attache case and take out the piece of hotel stationary. "May I read this to you? Or would you like to read it yourself?" I offer him the sheet of paper.

Again, a small register of surprise. Finally, he agrees:

"All right. But could you pull your chair closer to the desk?"

I feel suddenly as if I am in a court of law. I collect myself, focus on the vibration, and begin to read. Slowly. Deliberately.

"I question whether I belong in the Work. My nature seems to be intuitive, artistic, perhaps instinctive. When I paint and write, my inclination is to let things happen, to be painted, to be written through. I like to laugh and celebrate. I have a devotional side, a need to worship. The Work seems to me to be scientific, based on right discrimination, right suffering, right intention, leading to understanding. But I question who is it that wants to know—"

"Yes, that's right," Lord Pentland interjects. *"Scientific."*

The word zings through my body.

"Artists," he adds, "all seem to do a lot of suffering."

"Yes, that's true."

"The history of artists' lives is filled with suffering," he states, his voice rising slightly.

"Yes."

"Un-con-sci-ous suffering."

Again, a zinging. It is felt, absorbed. No reaction.

Lord Pentland peers into me, trying to gauge the effect, alert to the slightest stiffening, like that day at the bazaar.

Moments pass.

I can't risk answering, chance being deflected. I take up the paper again and begin reading. I feel as if I am reading aloud to myself. I conclude as quickly as possible—

"My heart and interest do not seem to be in the Work any longer. My gravitation is more to the teaching of Ramana Maharshi and Nisargadatta."

I deliberately do not mention Sunyata. The dissimilarity between Lord Pentland and Sunya is so great that had he heard about him, I feel he would discount him. Sunya is in the same Advaitic line as Shankara, Nisargadatta and Ramana Maharshi, and they are much more respectable intellectually.

Lord Pentland waits for me to finish.

"All this being the case," I say, "I am questioning whether the time has not arrived when it would be best for me and the Work that I should leave."

"Nisar—who?" Lord Pentland leans forward.

"Nisargadatta."

"Oh, you mean that man in Bombay?"

"Yes."

"Nisargadatta? Is he still living?" inquires Lord Pentland. "Yes, I suppose he is. Lizelle Reymond knew him."

"Really?"

"I'm afraid she much preferred Sri Anirvan."

Anirvan, a mystic Baul, was in rapport with the Work's point of view. I didn't want to bring up Sunya's close relationship to Anirvan.

"Are you going to India?" Lord Pentland asks.

"No. I have no plans to do that."

"Well, let me know if I can be of any help to you, will you?" he says, about to get up.

I nod and reach into the attache case. I take out the long rectangular box. The gold wrapping glistens. I offer it to Lord Pentland. He seems nonplussed. He makes no movement to accept it.

"I'd like to give you this," I explain, still holding the gift in my outstretched hand.

"I don't wear ties."

"It's not a tie."

I hear this pleading in my voice. I want to give him a gift. Why won't he accept it? Finally, I set the gold box down on the desk.

"Please accept it, won't you, Lord Pentland? You've done a lot for me and I appreciate it. I've watched you like a hawk all these years and I've never seen you once take unfair advantage of anyone."

He seems to like that. He softens a bit, nods, but still leaves the gift on the edge of the desk. He rises, gestures me toward the door. He offers his hand to me. Our palms and fingers touch. There is no movement. Only long silent empty space.

And then…as I had come, I left.

THAT WAS THE LAST TIME I WOULD SEE LORD PENTLAND ALIVE. SIXTEEN months afterward word of his death arrived. He died on Valentine's day, the fourteenth of February. *The New York Times* ran his obituary and photo. It described him as a "British businessman who had served as president of the Gurdjieff Foundation for thirty-one years." It went on to report that he was nearly seventy-seven years-old and, under his direction, three of Mr. Gurdjieff's books had been translated and published. He was born Henry John Sinclair in London. Upon the death of his father in December 1924, he inherited his father's title. His father had served as Governor General of the Indian state of Madras. His grandfather had been Governor General of Canada and his great-great grandfather had negotiated the U.S.-Canada border. He had graduated from Cambridge University and studied at the University of Heidelberg. In 1944 he came to the United States to serve on the wartime Combined Production and Resources Board, a cooperative effort of the United States, France and England. He became a permanent resident of the United States in the early 1950's and in 1954 founded the American British Electric Corporation, a firm specializing in marketing British engineering services to American clients. He served as president until five years before his death. Lord Pentland had also been the U.S. representative of the Hunting Group of Companies, a British concern.

The day of his funeral, Thursday, the sixteenth, was gray and overcast. It came in the wake of a departing storm. The temperature, expected to be in the fifties, was a chilly thirty-four degrees. A full moon was to appear that evening. The funeral was held at St. Vincent Ferrer Church at Lexington and 66th Street. At the front door,

Sam Shepard, the playwright, silently greeted mourners as they entered the vestibule. Inside, acting as ushers, were Rodger Lipsey, Terry Lindahl, Bob Fitzgerald, Hector Goa, David Wolk and Bill Tapley.

It was a large church with a long nave and towering vaults. Streams of people, quietly and with care, walked down the aisles. Nearly all the pews soon filled. Sitting down beside me was the TV actress I had defended. Her hair was cut short and dyed red. She did not recognize me. Sarah came down the aisle and sat about five rows ahead of me. An immense silence and space filled the church, a wordless benediction, a great and final prayer. Then the doors of the vestibule opened and a large mahogany casket appeared flanked by pall bearers: Jacob Needleman, Max Huntoon, Dick Brower, David Taylor, Steven Grant and Doug Spitz. It was carried down the aisle and placed just before the steps to the altar. Then through the doors of the vestibule came Lady Pentland, the former Lucy Babbington-Smith, who walked slowly and knowingly down the aisle. At her side was her daughter, Mary. Following behind was Mary's husband, Dr. John Rothenberg, and Paul Reynard.

After the initial ceremony by the Catholic priest, Mary Sinclair Rothenberg came to the pulpit. Tall and erect like her father, she read from the Bible and then from *Sword of the North,* a novel about Prince Henry Sinclair, a remarkable ancestor of the thirteenth century who had built Rosslyn Castle. The passage she read was of Prince Henry's death. Her voice was strong and clear and carried throughout the cavernous neo-gothic church. But when she came to the last line—"And another Sinclair chieftain is dead"—her voice escaped her, the word "dead" shooting like a fountain into the high vaulting of the church and echoing down on those in the pews.

Then Frank Sinclair, no relation, a long-time pupil of Lord Pentland's and a group leader, came to the pulpit. He read from Corinthians where it speaks of the vanity of man and then of the two bodies of man; the one, his natural body, the other, his spiritual body. "Lord Pentland," he noted at the end of the reading, "believed in the mystery of the Resurrection."

After Mr. Sinclair, William Segal, a close friend of Lord Pentland's and a senior group leader, spoke from the pulpit. "Lord Pentland," he said, "was the leader of the Gurdjieff Work in America and a man who never spared himself in his role as a guide, as a teacher and as an administrator." He drew an intimate and loving portrait of Lord Pentland, explaining that he was much more carefree than many realized. "Lord Pentland was not afraid to laugh at himself," he said, noting that just that past Saturday he had been with him at a small group. "A well-known philosopher was there who, when introduced to Lord Pentland, said: 'So you are the famous Lord Pentland!' Everyone laughed…" noted Mr. Segal, "especially Lord Pentland." He ended with the observation that, in directing the work of the Gurdjieff Foundation, Lord Pentland had taken on "impossible challenges." He then added with emphasis, "Lord Pentland was not afraid to be misunderstood."

Henri Tracol, a leader of the Work in Paris, followed Mr. Segal. To Lord Pentland's family and friends, Mr. Tracol expressed the sympathies of Madame de

Salzmann who did not attend. He did not say why. He spoke of the intensity of feeling that Lady Pentland was experiencing. Strangely, he made no mention of Lord Pentland or his accomplishments. Instead, he reminded everyone of the need for unity and to move on.

William Welch, a senior group leader, followed Mr. Tracol to the pulpit. Dr. Welch read from *All and Everything, First Series.* The passage concerned the one river forking into the two streams of man—the streams symbolizing true evolution and involution—and what it meant to be a real man, and not a man in quotation marks. His deep rich voice filling the whole of the church, Dr. Welch read about the two streams of the river of life and a man's consciously crystallizing in himself the data necessary to die and be resurrected. The organ then played a nineteenth century hymn of trial and conflict, "Once To Every Man And Nation" and everyone sang.

The ceremony ended with Paul Reynard and John Rothenberg leading the family up the aisle, followed by the Work's senior-most teachers. And then row by row the church emptied. The pall bearers carried the casket out of the church and down the steps and placed it into the back of a black hearse. Sarah came out of the church and as she passed me for a long silent moment our eyes met and our hands briefly touched, and then she walked slowly away. It would be the last time that we would see one another.

Jacob Needleman got into the front seat of the hearse and as it moved away into traffic a long caravan of cars followed. It had been prearranged that the funeral cortege would stop on the Upper West Side to await other cars. When they arrived, a large fire had broken out in one of the buildings. The resulting traffic jam delayed by a half-hour the cortege's journey to the cemetery at Valhalla in Westchester County, north of the city.

I drove to Valhalla with some friends. Lord Pentland's grave site was just above a pond on a small hillside by a tree. The site looked out upon the Hudson River and the high sheer cliffs of the Palisades. The weather had not broken, the day was still overcast. Friends and family, perhaps a hundred or so, stood by the grave. The coffin was lowered. Paul Reynard stepped forward and picked up a shovel. Beside the open grave was a mound of freshly dug dirt. With one certain motion, he sank the shovel into the dirt, turned and threw it atop the coffin. It made a little thud. A line formed and one-by-one people walked to the grave, took a handful of dirt, said a silent goodbye, and threw the dirt atop the casket. It began to drizzle but no one left. Lady Pentland, her family and the Work teachers of her generation, Dr. Welch, Mr. Segal, Mr. Foreman, Mrs. Welch, Mrs. Flinsch, Mrs. Dooling, and Mrs. Bry, along with Henri Tracol, stood under a canopy watching silently. It seemed a fitting end.

So many familiar faces came and stood before the open grave and said their last goodbye. Some I remembered well; others I knew only slightly. Among them were James Wyckoff, Henry Brown, Steven Grant, Becky Brower, Barbara Wheeler, Ted Magus, Lorraine Corfield, Kathy Minneropp, Linda Scott, John Sullivan, John Holtzman, Leon and Vicki Sterling, Freda Barry, Donna Boss, Ted Relay, and Anita Treash. I thought of how much Lord Pentland had endured and how, yes, he was not afraid to be misunderstood. He had often been criticized for being too severe, too authoritarian, for not being progressive enough, and so forth. But he had understood the Work and its need for a vehicle uncontaminated with the thought forms of the time. He had resolutely sought to guard the teachings against any and all deviation, so that it might be passed down intact. I had been among those who had misunderstood this remarkable and invincible man and the rare skill and rectitude with which he had guided the Work.

Across the way a solitary wild duck walked across the frozen pond, the cold winter having temporarily separated him from his water home below the ice. I recalled the dream of Lord Pentland's death that had come to me many years before. In the dream he had died at seventy-six years of age, and so he had. I remembered now how he had appeared to me in a vivid dream only a month before.

Lord Pentland and I are walking down San Anselmo Avenue near my home in California. We were not talking, just enjoying being with one another. I take a big cigar out of my pocket and so does he. We smoke the cigars, smiling at one other, walking together along the street. And so what was not reconciled on one plane was on another.

I recalled too, how a few months ago I had unexpectedly run into a fellow in the Work in San Francisco who had told me that he had just seen Lord Pentland and that he had grown a white beard. The fellow said that he had stopped by Lord Pentland's office on the way back from a vacation to Turkey. He and his wife had rented a car in Istanbul and driven to the fortress town of Kars, an ancient and remote village where Gurdjieff had grown up. The drive over rutted dirt mountain roads and desolate terrain had been a harrowing experience and Kars now he said was just a group of mud huts, but still they had felt something there. Later, his wife and he had gone to the city of Konya, a Naqshbandi and Melevi dervish center. They visited Jalal al-Din Rumi's tomb and other Sufi holy places. Then, seemingly by chance, they met an old man on the backstreet of a bazaar who handcrafted dervish hats. He was the only one authorized to do so. They wanted to buy a white sheik's turban but could not without permission. That was finally granted and in New York they had presented the sheik's turban to Lord Pentland. He was surprised and pleased. He placed the white turban on his head. "He looked wonderful in it," my fellow had said. "Perfect..."

It was not long before my turn came to approach Lord Pentland's grave. I did as the others had before me. I stooped and reached into the pile of dirt with both hands, taking up all I could hold. I stood and peered into the open grave and the large casket it held. I said a last goodbye to my great warrior chieftain, and then deliberately tossed the dirt onto the large casket. I stood a moment, re-establishing in the vibration, and offered a silent prayer:

Lord Have Mercy...Lord Have Mercy...Lord Jesus Christ Have Mercy.

EPILOGUE

IT WOULD BE SOME TWELVE YEARS LATER ON A COOL BUT BRIGHT AUGUST afternoon that I would visit Lord Pentland's grave at Valhalla, a small hamlet in Westchester north of New York City. I'd forgotten the name of the cemetery and no landmark seemed familiar. Stopping to ask directions at a filling station I was told there was not one cemetery but five. That was a surprise. I had to be back in the City for a talk that evening and so time was short. I smiled to myself. Lord Pentland never made it easy. "Was the person you're looking for Jewish?" I was asked. "No, he wasn't," I answered, "Well, two of the five are Jewish. Was he Catholic?" "No, not unless he converted at the last moment." "Well...probably Kensico then."

At Kensico a very warm and gracious lady gave me a map showing where he was buried. How many times a day she must do that, I thought, yet she is still alive to the moment. I drove by a small lake that I did remember and parked the turquoise van which I'd named Hermes I. A great flock of wild geese were about the lake and by its edge swam a solitary white swan. I smiled remembering the swan at Middleton Gardens. Even with the map it was a lot of trial and error before I found Lord Pentland's grave. It rested on a gently sloping hillside beneath a great oak in a lush sea of green. His tombstone was a light rose-colored granite carved with a large drawing of his design. Medieval in style, it showed two entwined dragons' bodies, one with a lamb's head and the other with a wolf's or dragon's head. Between them and higher, forming a triad, was a fish, symbol of the soul, looking as though it had just leapt out of the water. The border was a simple Celtic interlacing of lines. It was so perfect, so exactly him. In front of the gravestone begonias had been planted, red on either side of white. Through the petals I noticed words carved in the stone. I leaned down, parting the begonias... *Commit thy work to God* read the inscription. These five words had always been his message, the understanding that he embodied and lived by example. I stood and reached out toward his gravestone much as I had done that first day in his office some twenty-six years ago when he was going to give me his copy of Mr. Gurdjieff's *All and Everything*. As he taught then, he taught now. Behind a bush a few yards from his grave a lawnmower had been hidden. Presently, a workman appeared and with a silent nod started its engine and began mowing the lawn. I was going to leave but felt an inward urge to stay, and so sat down on the grass. I crossed my legs, closed my eyes and smiled to myself amid the lush green and the mechanical noise. *How right it all was.*

I began to think of all the people I had written about in *Eating The "I."* Seven years after my Father died my Mother had sold the house in Florida and moved to

California. At her insistence, she had lived in an apartment of her own until five years ago when she moved in with my family. Last year at the age of ninety-four she died. Sunyata had passed on the same year as Lord Pentland. Jane had died of stomach cancer two years before that. And a few years after I left *Food*, Spencer had finally fired Stanley who, I was told, enrolled in a seminary to study for a doctorate in religion. More shockingly, after a failed big-time business deal, Spencer had committed suicide, jumping from his seventh floor condominium in Steamboat Springs, Florida. Soren and Miriam, the last I heard, had moved to a little village in upstate New York where he grew and experimented with mushrooms while she studied for a degree in criminal law. After Lord Pentland's funeral, Sarah disappeared from sight. Now these many years later what had been lived so intensely and had meant so much at the time had a feeling of having been a *Midsummer Night's Dream*. But those moments molded the present. The people, the situations and issues of any time pass on, but the essential values they embody, if stood for and, if necessary, sacrificed for, live on.

I started up Hermes I and drove back to the City. That evening I was to give a talk at The Quest bookshop on "Exploring the Teacher-Student Relationship," which was the theme of my second book *Struggle of the Magicians*. With my wife Barbara and two friends, I was on a 10,000 mile journey around the rim of the country talking about the book and giving workshops. Though I had left the organized Work and gone on to explore another teaching, I carried the inner Work with me. The only difference was that now I "spoke" two languages, each eminently applicable in its place. The room at the bookshop was filled when I arrived. I redirected my attention, emptied out, and remembering Lord Pentland's gravestone, I began to speak.... ✗

Listed here is only a fragment of the great and growing corpus of Work material and related sources. For a complete listing of all Gurdjieff material see: *Gurdjieff: An Annotated Bibliography*, Garland Press, New York. Reference is made to only that material pertinent to the subjects considered in the present work.

All and Everything by G. I. Gurdjieff, 1950, E. P. Dutton
    The Struggle of The Magicians, 1957, Privately printed. The Stourton Press, Cape Town, South Africa
In Search of The Miraculous by P. D. Ouspensky, 1949, Harcourt Brace & World
Philokalia, 1954, Faber and Faber Ltd., London
"The Search for Lucidity" by Michel de Salzmann, 1983, Parabola, Vol. 8
The New Man by Maurice Nicoll, 1967, Penguin Books Inc.
Living Time, 1952, Stuart & Watkins, London
The Art of Asha by Edmond S. Bordeaux, 1966, Mille Meditations
Lost Christianity by Jacob Needleman, 1980, Doubleday & Co.
The Nag Hammadi Library, James M. Robinson, general editor, 1977, Harper & Row
The Gnostic Religion by Hans Jonas, 1958, Beacon Press
Reign of Quantity by René Guénon, 1945, Penguin Books Inc.
    The Multiple States of Being, 1984, Larson Publications Inc.
    Man and His Becoming, 1981, Oriental Books Reprint Corporation, New Delhi
Creative Imagination in the Sufism of Ibn Arabi by Henry Corbin, 1969, Princeton University Press
Answer to Job by C. G. Jung, 1951, World Publications
    Mysterium Conjunctionis, 1963, Princeton University Press
Serpent in Paradise by Miguel Serrano, 1972, Harper Colophon Books
    The Visits of the Queen of Sheba, 1960, Routledge & Kegan Paul Ltd., London
    C. G. Jung & Hermann Hesse: A Record of Two Friendships, 1966, Schocken Books
Being and Time by Martin Heidegger, 1962, Harper & Row
    What is Called Thinking?, 1968, Harper Colophon Books
Grunewald by Anthony Bertram, 1950, Studio Publications
The Art of William Blake by Martin Butlin,1978, Tate Gallery Publications, London
Max Beckmann—Retrospective, 1984, Saint Louis Art Museum, St. Louis, Missouri
"The Art of Other Consciousness: Painting Techniques and Mind States" by Donald L. Stacy, Journal of Altered States of Consciousness, Vol 3, 1977-78
Vali Myers. A book of drawings and paintings published in 1980. Contact: Open House, 228 Fulham Road, London SW10 9NB.
Sunyata: The Life and Sayings of a Rare-Born Mystic edited by Betty Camhi and Elliot Isenberg, 1990, North Atlantic Books
Sri Wuji, Vol 1 and Vol 3, 1984, Sunyata Society, P.O. Box 804, San Anselmo, CA 94960
Who Am I? The Sacred Quest by Jean Klein, 1988, Element Books, London, England

EXPLORE TELOS

TELOS IS THE FIRST AND ONLY INTERNATIONAL QUARTERLY
devoted to exploring self-transformation in the contemporary world
through the Fourth Way teaching of G. I. Gurdjieff.
A sixteen-page, illustrated journal established in 1992,
Telos publishes interviews, essays,
book excerpts, and film and book reviews.
It does not, and will not, carry advertising.

If you would like a complimentary copy,
please send the accompanying postcard or write:

Telos, P.O. Box 58, Fairfax, CA 94978-0058

E-mail: telos9@aol.com
Worldwide Web Site: http://members.aol.com/telos9

STRUGGLE of the MAGICIANS
EXPLORING THE TEACHER-STUDENT RELATIONSHIP

BY WILLIAM PATRICK PATTERSON

"YES, WHAT AN EXCELLENT BOOK—FULL OF things I didn't know. A real contribution to our understanding of Gurdjieff and Uspenskii."
—Colin Wilson

"FOR MANY OF US, GURDJIEFF AND USPENSKII have remained mysteriously attractive but dauntingly difficult to grasp. *Struggle of the Magicians* is a 'hard-to-put-down' exception to much of the literature available about Gurdjieff, presenting his life and work almost like a play against the panoramic backdrop of his turbulent times, from World War I and the Russian Revolution thorough World War II.

"The central focus of the book is the sacred, archetypal relationship of the Master and disciple. An intimate view is given of Gurdjieff's work with his students including many who, like the famous Uspenskii, were unwilling to pay the price. Thus revealing look at the roles of Guru and disciple in the compelling work of self-transformation makes the book special interest and value to those on any path."
—*Light of Consciousness Magazine*

$16.95 Softcover. 272 pages. 5.5 x 8.5. Notes, Bibliography and Index. Acid-free paper. ISBN: 1-879514-80-X

Struggle of the Magicians is available at all serious bookstores. Or write the publisher: Arete Communications, 773 Center Boulevard #58, Fairfax, California 94978-0058. Add $3.50 for postage within continental U.S.A. Outside, add $7.00 for surface; $14 for air mail.

Distributors. US: *Bookpeople, New Leaf, Moving Books, Samuel Weiser*, and *Baker & Taylor*. Europe: *Golden Square Books, Picadilly*, London: *Eureka Books*, Utrecht, Holland: Australia: *Banyan Tree*

EATING THE "I"

An Account of the Fourth Way–
The Way of Transformation in Ordinary Life

by William Patrick Patterson

Eating the "I" represents a genre which happens to be a personal favorite of mine: an autobiographical narrative of an individual's involvement in an interesting religious group or spiritual path. In this case it is both. The author was a member of a New York Gurdjieff group under the direction of the legendary Lord John Pentland, the British aristocrat appointed by Gurdjieff himself to head the Work in America. Pentland fulfilled this task consummately until his death in 1984, and *Eating the "I"* culminates with an account of "L.P.'s" funeral.

Besides being very well written as literature, spiritual autobiography of the highest quality ought to meet three further criteria. First, it must be completely honest, presenting the narrator's and the group's flaws and failings as candidly as it does the virtues and successes. Second, it must communicate the worldview and practices of the path adequately, and do so largely through narration rather than didacticism. Third, it should make clear what kind of impact this practice has on the living of everyday life by a real person of our time.

So far as writing and these three points are concerned, *Eating the "I"* is about as good as it gets. Patterson is an excellent writer, with a gifted novelist's ability to capture a character through a few lines of dialogue or seemingly casual notes on expression or dress. Who, after reading the accounts here, will forget Pentland's heavy, deadpan tones and the cutting insight which could be behind them?

As for honesty about himself, Patterson's work is in a class with Christopher Isherwood's devastatingly frank, and brilliant, story of his spiritual quest, *My Guru and His Disciple.* The Gurdjieff years here recounted were also, for Patterson, years of various vocational and marital crises, and of life among assorted exotic Greenwich Village types and well-living but hollow Madison Avenue yuppies. Amid incessant ups and downs he only gradually gained counterbalancing insight into himself with the help of the Work. As he does, we gain some insight too into what it's all about. We perceive how painstakingly difficult the demanded level of self-examination can be, and how in the end it can perhaps uniquely enable you truly to wake up and see yourself as you are seen by others, and by the universe.

If there is a fault, it is in the length. My feeling is that this could have been profitably cut by about a third to leave a leaner story focused more directly on experience with the Gurdjieff Work. There are many reminiscences which, though unfailingly of some human interest, seem only tangential to that story.

Writers in the Gurdjieff tradition tend to do autobiography. There are the classic accounts of life with Mr. Gurdjieff by Ouspensky, de Hartmann, Peters, and others. *Eating the "I"*—to the best of my knowledge the first entirely post-Gurdjieffian autobiography centering on life in the Work—will find an honored place in that series.

—Robert S. Ellwood
Chairman, Department of Religion
University of Southern California

Reviewed for *Syzygy*

WILLIAM PATRICK PATTERSON
BIOGRAPHY

A longtime student of John Pentland, the man Gurdjieff chose to lead the Work in America, Mr. Patterson has actively practiced the principles of the teaching for over twenty-five years. He is the founder and editor of *Telos*, the first international quarterly devoted to the Fourth Way, now in its fourth year of publication. A seasoned public speaker, Mr. Patterson regularly lectures on transformational themes, gives seminars, and conducts applied research.

For many years he worked in publishing and advertising in New York City and later in Silicon Valley and San Francisco. His work in journalism won many awards including the Jesse H. Neal Award, considered the Pulitzer Prize of business press journalism. In New York he worked for many large companies such as IBM, Harcourt Brace, J. Walter Thompson, and BBD&O, as well as founding and editing his own consumer magazine, *In New York*. He lives in a small town in Northern California with his wife and two sons.